Hockey America

Kevin Hubbard & Stan Fischler

MASTERS PRESS

A Division of Howard W. Sams & Co.

Published by Masters Press
A Division of Howard W. Sams & Company
2647 Waterfront Pkwy. E. Drive, Indianapolis, IN 46214

97 98 99 00 01   10 9 8 7 6 5 4 3 2 1

Library of Congress Cataloging-in-Publication Data Pending
Hubbard, Kevin, 1956-
        Hockey America / Kevin Hubbard & Stan Fischler.
                p.   cm.
        ISBN 1-57028-196-3
        1. Hockey--United States--History.   I. Fischler, Stan.
    II. Title.   97-47381
    GV848.4.U6H83   1997   CIP

Acknowledgments

Love and thanks to Gordon & Kitty Hubbard, Diane & Bill Bailey, Chet & Helen Hubbard, Ray Hubbard, Yvonne Seaman, Mary Prince, Ed & Sharon Tousignant, John & Kim Seaman, Bernie & Donna Seaman, and Jaclyn Leonhard McKenney.

Special thanks to Paul Robicheau, Geoffrey Day, Dennis Murphy, Mick Colageo, Woody Trenholm, Mark Fritz, Claire Neely, Sky, Esmi, John Weagle, Bob Long and Rick McHale.

For their support: Jimmy Durante, Alicia Page, Frank Grace, Rory Falkinburg, Patty Arellano, Paul Murray, Mike Kennedy, Bill Desmond, Peter Terreri, Don Poirier, Peter Porter, Fred Eliot, Doug Willis, Gerard Smith, Steve Bernstein, Frank Mauriello, Walter Thomas Kennedy III and Judy Harwood.

Thanks to Stan Fischler for his faith; Donald Clark for his vast historical knowledge; Steve Babineau for his time and efforts; Kerry Gwydir for his Long Island hockey info; Mike Donato for his extensive Massachusetts high school background; Dave Shea for his hockey insights; Leslie Kirschner for Roller Hockey and current trend consultation; Julie Piacentini for women's hockey consultation; Mike Nardello for Coast Guard Cutters research; George Michael for Flyers info; Tony Marmo for Massport Jets background; Sammy Wallace for minor-pro league info; Dick Johnson & The New England Sports Museum for valuable research tools; Thomas and Lucy Barrasso for extensive historical info; Bill Cleary for college and Olympic stories; Vic Morren for television expertise, Bob Norton for New England names and facts; Joe Bertagna for college background; Julie Andeberhan for women's hockey history; Bob Nystrom for Islanders background; David Frechtman for Manhattan and Long Island comparisons; Russ Conway for South Florida history; Bill Putnam for expansion facts; Mike Shalin for Rangers history; Herb Brooks for Olympic background and present evaluations; Benjamin Mayer for saving the data; John Halligan for minor league backgrounds; Rae Briggle, Chuck Menke, Heather Ahearn, Kris

Pleiman and all at USA Hockey who were most accommodating in providing various stats and info; and Ted Brill, JoAnn Kochar and Paulette Laakkonen at the United States Hockey Hall of Fame.

Carl Abrams, Steve Adams, Randy Allen, Virginia Aronson, Dan Bell, Rick Benej, Red Berenson, John Blue, Tony Bova, Andrea Bradley, Ted Butler, Sherry Bryant, Neil Carnes, Ann Carpenter, John Chambers, Paul Chapey, Steve Cherwonak, Peter Cooney, Dr. Edmund T. Cranch, Cleon Daskalakis, Maria Dennis, Bert Dickerson, Ted Drury, Kelly Dyer, Phil Esposito, Jill Flye, Bill Gaine, Bob Fallon, Steve Filmer, Mike Gilbert, Pat Graham, Scott Gummer, Tom Haggerty, Alice Hansen, Jim Harrington, Rich Harvey, Bob Hines, Betty Hogan, John Holcomb, Teresa Huffman, Regina Hugo, Chris Hurley, Brian Hurst, Rich Igo, Paul Kelly, Tom King, Jack Kirrane, Frank Kizska, Tom Koester, Heather Krueger, Pete Lafleur, Todd LaFleur, Mike Lambert, Rich Lapchick, Diane Lamb, David Larsen, Paul LaVenture, Mike Levine, Gerry Linehan, Dr. Gerry Linette, Donna Mabry, Nancy Marrapese, Kevin McCormack, Joe McEachern, Loftus McGuire, Jodi McKenna, Gary Meagher, Mike Meyer, Dave Moross, Jim Murray, John Murray, Chris Nilan, Mike O'Connell, Tony Ommen, John Painter, Jack Parker, Mike Patterson, Fred & Kirk Popelick, Robin Racine, Kevin Ring, Ed Ronan, Doug Ross, Husam Sahin, Derek Sanderson, Mathieu Schneider, Carrie Schuldt, Greg Scott, Bob Scuderi, Tom Sersha, Dave Silk, Jeff Sklar, Donna Sorrentino, Charlene Stanion, Art & Pat Stevens, Paul Stewart, Katie Stone, Dana Sylvia, Mary Lou Thimas, Rick Thorne, Ronn Tomassoni, Barry & Roger Wakeford, Jeff Weiss, Mark Whitkin, Vince Wladika, Christine Yanetti, Steve Zimmerman and YES, whose music has provided an unlimited supply of inspiration.

And for saving my life: EMILE ARMSTRONG and PRISCILLA AND WAYNE SHEELY.

Preface

Historically, ice hockey has been underexposed and underappreciated in the United States, struggling in the shadow of football, baseball and basketball. That is changing rapidly as we approach the millennium. Largely as a result of NHL and minor league expansion as well as increased TV coverage, hockey in the United States is gaining momentum, and stands poised to take its rightful place next to the three other major team sports. Jaded sports fans are discovering the drama and dynamism of hockey, and kids all over the country, propelled by the popularity of in-line skating, are taking to the rinks and parks in record numbers. The sport has spread from its traditional bastions — Canada, the Northeast and Upper Midwest — to the Sun Belt. The next generation's Bobby Orr or Wayne Gretzky may be finding his or her ice legs in a parking lot in Phoenix or a back alley in Tampa.

This book seeks to document the history and growth of hockey in the United States, and to pay homage to the individuals and teams who have nurtured and championed the sport. A theme throughout the text is how the Canadians brought the game south, and how Americans have caught on to it. This is outlined in a detailed chronological history, featuring the Canadian-born superstars whose talents and charisma inspired hockey devotees to build rinks and establish youth and high school programs that thrive today. Highlighted are the American-born stars who have benefited from these legacies.

Stan Fischler and I believe that at this critical juncture, it is time to revisit the past, capture the present, and assess the future of this thrilling, increasingly popular, yet still undervalued sport.

Kevin Hubbard
Cambridge, MA
November, 1997

Foreword

When Kevin Hubbard approached me about helping with this project, I had mixed feelings.

He was a first-time author with expected shortcomings as a hockey historian. With that in mind, I did as much as I could to discourage him from moving ahead.

But Hubbard believed in his idea the way Thomas Alva Edison must have had faith in his idea for an electric light. Eventually, Kevin's passion and persistence convinced me that the green light should be flashed.

I agreed to edit this raw manuscript and make all the necessary historic additions. Still I nursed some misgivings.

Would he deliver a comprehensive history? Would his enthusiasm become dissipated with time? Would we be able to successfully collaborate?

Once our publisher, Masters Press, signalled approval of the subject Hubbard proceeded to erase all my doubts.

He has covered Uncle Sam's hockey history in an all-encompassing manner, from roller hockey to Robbie Ftorek. His elan never wavered. And, pleasurably I report, our literary gears meshed as perfectly as could expect.

As a result I am proud to share co-authorship with Kevin and I am tickled to be a part of this history of hockey in the good old U.S.A.

If we missed any individual team or subject, rest assured that it only was for lack of space.

Economic limitations dictate that a book can only be so long. Certainly, we could have written this volume twice as long had the spirit and fiscal requirements allowed.

Nevertheless, as an American-born (Brooklyn) roller and ice hockey player, I am proud to present this all-inclusive look at our favorite sport development in our favorite country.

I hope you like it as much as Kevin and I enjoyed writing it.

Stan Fischler
New York, NY
August 1997

Contents

Dedication

This book is dedicated to Donald Clark, a man who has devoted much of his life to the advancement of ice hockey in the United States.

Born in North Dakota in May, 1915 and raised in Faribault, Minnesota, Don has done it all. He first developed an interest in ice hockey at age eight while watching Faribault's Shattuck School team take on teams from the Twin Cities area.

A three-sport athlete at Faribault High, Don went on to play both amateur hockey and baseball in the Gopher State. In 1947, he helped form the Minnesota Amateur Hockey Association (MAHA). In addition to serving as president and secretary-treasurer, his accomplishments with MAHA include organizing the nation's first state bantam hockey tournament in 1951.

In 1958 Don managed the first U. S. National team to ever play in the Soviet Union. 1958 also marked the year he became vice presi-

dent of the Amateur Hockey Association of the United States (AHAUS, which later became USA Hockey), a position he would hold for 20 years.

When the United States Hockey Hall of Fame in Eveleth, Minnesota opened in 1974, Don became its first president. A year later he experienced what he considers to be one of the biggest thrills of his life when he received the Lester Patrick Award for his contributions to developing youth hockey programs.

Accolades continued to come his way. In 1987 he received the U. S. Hockey Hall of Fame Heritage Award and in 1990 the Minnesota North Stars Maroosh Award.

At 82, Donald lives in Cumberland, Wisconsin with Harriet, his wife of 53 years. Regarded by many as one of the foremost United States hockey historians, Donald Clark represents everything good about American sports.

Chapter 1

Hockey's Boom Of The Nineties

Behind the Soaring National Interest in Hockey

Ice Hockey — touted by its promoters as "The World's Fastest Sport" — is in the process of graduating from a regional to a national pastime in the United States; a status that baseball, football and basketball have enjoyed for many years.

Since the 1890s ice hockey has thrived in such traditional Frost Belt hotbeds as Minnesota, Michigan and New England. But sparked by Wayne Gretzky's arrival in Los Angeles in 1988, the Ice Game and its close relatives, street hockey and roller hockey, have spread throughout California, across the Southwest and into the Deep South —

not traditional hockey areas. Sports fans across the Sun Belt are now packing arenas to take in either National Hockey League or minor league hockey — whichever is available to them.

The number of public skating rinks and skaters is growing everywhere. And where there aren't enough ice rinks, tennis courts, parking lots, cul de sacs and in-line rinks have become sites of pick-up roller hockey games.

Recognizing what "The Great One," Wayne Gretzky, had started in Southern California, the NHL set out to spread the gospel into other non-traditional hockey areas.

Expansion and relocation into markets such as San Jose, Anaheim, Phoenix, Denver, Dallas, Tampa Bay, Miami, and now Greensboro/Raleigh, North Carolina, St. Paul-Minneapolis, Nashville, Atlanta and Columbus, Ohio, has fueled interest in hockey. Cable and network television contracts have been secured and the hiring of a marketing-savvy commissioner, Gary Bettman, has galvanized the hockey explosion and given the sport the exposure it previously lacked.

In 1990 the NHL awarded former Oakland Seals owner George Gund and his brother, Gordon, an expansion franchise in the Bay Area that became the San Jose Sharks. When the Sharks stepped on to the ice to begin the 1991-92 season they became the league's first new club since 1979, when the NHL absorbed four franchises from the now-defunct World Hockey Association.

Upon purchasing the new club the Gunds immediately hired an aggressive, "cutting edge" marketing team that spent 13 months testing and researching an eye-catching logo (a shark chomping a hockey stick in half) and color scheme (teal, gray, black and white). The combination was an instant hit and the sale of products bearing the Sharks logo sold in the $100-million range during the team's first fiscal year.

Steve Babineau
Sharks' first-ever draft pick Pat Falloon.

The Sharks front office team also went to work developing a strong fan base through its community development department. Projects such as "Score With School," which reaches out to 5,000 students per year promoting sportsmanship, teamwork and goal-setting, and "San Jose Sharks and Parks," a street hockey program that teaches kids the basics of the game, have extended the club's roots deep into the community.

In 1992, NHL owners and officials voted to expand the league and add new franchises in Ottawa and Tampa Bay in 1992-93 and Florida and Anaheim in 1993-94.

The Tampa Bay Lightning and Miami-based Florida Panthers have been a smash hit in South Florida. The Lightning, who averaged just under 20,000 fans per game during their three seasons at the massive Thunderdome, often sell out their new state-of-the-art 19,500-seat Tampa Ice Palace.

The Panthers, owned by sports magnate Wayne Huizenga, became competitive immediately through the amateur and expansion drafts as well as creative free agent signings. They made the Stanley Cup finals in only their third year.

The Disney-owned Mighty Ducks of Anaheim, named after the hit movies, regularly fill Arrowhead Pond, affectionately known as "The Pond." Their two superstars, Paul Kariya and Teemu Selanne, are the perfect showcases for an organization that has made its name cultivating young audiences.

Following the Sharks' successful marketing strategy, the new clubs developed their own catchy logos and innovative color schemes. Panthers and Lightning merchandise has gone over big in Florida where even some of the high-end men's stores sell everything from hats to sweaters and windbreakers sporting the teams' logos.

The Mighty Ducks logo, which features a duck bill-shaped goalie mask over crossed hockey sticks accented by a unique color scheme of purple, jade, silver and white, has become as popular as the Sharks. In 1994, the Mighty Ducks boasted the top-selling logo in team sports, surpassing the NFL's Oakland Raiders and the NBA's Chicago Bulls.

Apart from setting the pace for a new fashion wave in pro sports and becoming a model for fan development, the Sharks' success has spawned a copycat culture; the Tallahassee Tiger Sharks of the East Coast Hockey League and the Fargo-Moorhead Ice Sharks of the United States Junior League are further examples of the Sharks' legacy.

"The Sharks have shown everybody what

Steve Babineau

The Mighty Ducks have also brought mascots and cheerleaders into the NHL.

you can do with ingenuity, creativity and style," Buffalo Sabres Vice Chairman and Counsel Robert Swados told *Financial World* magazine in 1996. "They woke everybody up."[1]

Pivotal to hockey's growth spurt has been television. Although it was slow to exploit the medium in years past, the NHL is now making the most of electronic video advances. A large TV audience is developing as both regular season and playoff games are being aired nationally on ESPN, ESPN2 and, most recently, the Fox television network.

In 1992-93 ESPN won back the NHL contract it had lost when it was outbid by SportsChannel America in 1988. During the 1992-93 and 1993-94 playoffs, games were aired on both ESPN and its network parent ABC. In 1994, ESPN and Fox inked a deal with the NHL to share a five-year contract that will run through the 1998-99 season.

ESPN's production of game telecasts has

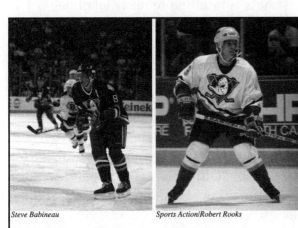
Steve Babineau   *Sports Action/Robert Rooks*

Left: Swedish-born Teemu Selanne joined the Ducks midway throught the 1995-1996 season and immediately helped to make them a contender. *Right:* After winning a national championship at U Maine, Mighty Ducks' superstar Paul Kariya has been thrilling Southern California crowds.

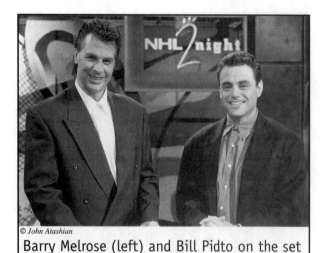

© John Atashian

Barry Melrose (left) and Bill Pidto on the set of ESPN2's "NHL 2night."

Donald Weller/Courtesy of Fox Sports

Courtesy of Fox Sports

Top: Skeletal view of puck Fox uses to produce glowing effect. *Bottom:* The "comet tail" effect of blistering slap shots is insulting to many longtime fans, but amusing the game's younger audience.

been superb, with innovations such as the goal-cam and rocker-cam. The goal-cam, a TV camera located inside the net, provides the viewer with close-up angles on replays of goals and great saves. The rocker-cam, installed on top of the goal judge booths at each end of the ice, allows the viewing audience a better angle on power plays.

"We've worked hard at enhancement and making the game easier to watch," says Vic Morren, coordinator of production and research for the network's *National Hockey Night and Fire on Ice*, "but more important than the cameras is the proper execution to make the game more appealing. A lot of the credit goes to the production crew. If you look at the way we do games — we concentrate on faces, we cut low when we see that there's a hit coming. We do everything possible to embellish the event without interfering with the game itself."

ESPN supplements its game telecasts with an informative and analytical show called *NHL 2night*, hosted by Bill Pidto and Barry Melrose. The show, which features game highlights and commentary accented by screaming rock guitar sounds, is aired six nights a week during the regular season and playoffs.

While ESPN puts hockey on the cable network with the most subscribers in the United States, Fox gives the NHL the ability to be seen in 98 percent of U.S. households. "We think it's a growth sport of the '90s," says Vince Wladika, Vice President of Media Relations for Fox Sports. "Our plans are to hopefully someday have a hockey Game of the Week, like *Hockey Night in Canada*. We're trying to create America's hockey viewing habit, and not just in New York or Boston, but in Des Moines, Austin, Santa Fe — places like that."

In order to enhance its telecasts, Fox came up with FoxTrax, a glowing-puck technology created to make it easier for hockey's new fans to follow the puck when watching a game on television. FoxTrax employs a specially modified puck with internal infrared components and a computer chip that are used to transmit data to 16 receivers around the rink. The receivers highlight the puck with a translucent blue dot which can be seen on TV, but not at the rink. The system also processes a variety of information, including the speed of slap shots. Shots exceeding 75 mph produce a red "streak" effect, similar to that of a comet tail.

"The glowing puck made people aware of the sport, especially in areas that haven't been hockey hotbeds," says Dave Maloney, Fox's studio analyst and a former defenseman for the New York Rangers. "Now, the technique must be perfected."[2]

Fox is hoping that with time FoxTrax can be used to produce additional information such as how much time the puck spends in each zone and where a team's shots on goal came from, in close or out at the blue line.

Other innovations created by Fox are FoxBox and FoxBots. FoxBox, which was initially used on Fox NFL telecasts, appears in the upper left corner of the screen and indicates the score, period and time remaining. In the future, FoxBox will be used to provide more information, such as how many goals a player has scored, how many penalty minutes a player has amassed and how many saves the goaltender has made during a game. FoxBots are the computer-generated robots that appear on the screen after a goal has been scored. Like FoxTrax, FoxBots are another effect designed to entertain and hook the younger audience.

"More kids are watching hockey on Fox than baseball and NCAA basketball," says Ed Goren, Fox Sports executive producer. "The effect may not be instantaneous, but a foundation is being built among fans who are getting interested in hockey because of FoxTrax."[3]

The proof is beginning to show in the rat-

Steve Babineau

NHL commissioner Gary Bettman has been a major force in hockey's rising popularity.

ings. Neilsen numbers for the 1996 playoffs were the highest to date and in 1997 they continued to rise. Games Two and Four of the lopsided 1997 Stanley Cup Finals between Detroit and Philadelphia each achieved a 4.38 rating (3.127-million households) on ESPN, the second highest rating ever for a hockey game in the United States, behind only Game Seven of the Rangers-Canucks final series in 1994.

NHL Commissioner Gary Bettman, a former member of the NBA braintrust that was partly responsible for basketball's popularity explosion during the 1980s, has given the league a leader with experience in marketing and television. Bettman's expertise in those areas has helped the league make some quick strides toward gaining national exposure.

Bettman's marketing team, NHL Enterprises, has been highly successful at luring such name corporate sponsors as J.C. Penney, MasterCard, Dodge and Nike to the NHL team. Another avenue utilized by Bettman, Inc. is custom publishing, which has produced such works as *A Day in the Life of the NHL*, *The Coolest Guys on Ice* and *Power Play* magazine, a collaboration between the league and the NHL Players' Association.

"Gary Bettman has surrounded himself with some very good people, including Brian Burke, Steve Solomon and Arthur Pincus," says Russ Conway, author of *Game Misconduct*, the startling account of former player-rep Alan Eagleson's wrongdoings. "He's got some good people and he's got the vision. The NBA had the vision. They had the fortune of having three marquee players come along at the same time — or a few years apart. I think Bettman saw bigger things and he didn't wear the blinders as his predecessors did. And by the same token the NHLPA's leader, Bob Goodenow, has represented his people very well. For the first time ever the NHL has a more than formidable Players' Association." Conway adds: "Both the league administrators and Players' Association have done a good job attracting new hockey areas and they all have vision — that's the key. They've picked some good owners. Take a look at the most recent ones. Huizenga has a lot of money and has been very successful. And Disney, whoever is going to quarrel with that?"

No one knows how important it is for an administration to have vision better than Conway, who for years had been advocating NHL expansion into South Florida. He almost saw it happen back in the '70s, when Miami-Hollywood Speedway owner Norm Johnson helped finance a venue called the Sportatorium. Johnson, with Conway's advice, figured that between locals, travel

tourists and "snowbirds" (semi-retirees from northern climes), hockey could draw in South Florida. Johnson, however, was unsuccessful in trying to sell the NHL on the idea and plans were scrapped. Johnson later tried to buy the Cleveland Crusaders franchise of the World Hockey Association and move it to Hollywood, Florida, but former Crusaders owner Nick Mileti had a clause in his agreement with the current owners that if the franchise were going to be moved, he would have the option of buying back the team. Mileti examined the Florida site and opted to move the club to St. Paul instead.

It wasn't until 1990 that NHL hockey was finally given the go-ahead to invade the Sunshine State. It happened during the regime of then-commissioner John Ziegler, who for years had ignored Florida. The $50-million offer from the Phil Esposito-led Tampa Bay group was irresistible. With NHL and minor-pro league franchises now thriving in Florida, hindsight suggests that the NHL missed a chance more than two decades ago to enjoy some highly successful, warm climate expansion.

The farsighted strategies of Bettman's administration not only have the league hard at work building the sport's fan-base but its potential talent pool as well. NHL Enterprises is involved in two major grass roots programs at the national level. "Nike NHL Street," a street hockey program based on San Jose's "Sharks and Parks" program and "NHL Breakout," a multi-city street and roller hockey tournament series, are bringing thousands of people of both genders and all ages into the NHL experience each summer.

The popularity growth of in-line skates has been an interesting phenomenon. It has provided a viable substitute for the lack of ice facilities in warm-weather locales. No longer do kids have to find a rink and rent ice time to play. All they need to do is throw on their in-lines, skate over to a nearby tennis court or parking lot and join a pick-up game. And if a pair of blades is unaffordable, sneakers will suffice. Both street hockey and Dek hockey have also become quite popular. Street hockey, which is played in Canada under the name "ball hockey," is the most convenient and least expensive of all forms of hockey and can be played almost anywhere. Dek Hockey, which is another form of street hockey, is played in arenas on a plastic surface.

At USA Hockey's World Hockey Summit in July 1996, NHL vice president of fan development Ken Yaffe explained a concept called "The Pyramid of Influence." The top of the pyramid — ice hockey — is the most important form of the game. Its growth is driven by the other segments — roller hockey and street hockey.

Apart from expansion, increased television exposure, a new commissioner and the advent of the in-line skate, several other factors have contributed to hockey's recent boom in the United States: The influence of Mario Lemieux and the offensively high-powered Penguins

Steve Babineau

Roller hockey's accessibility has made it convenient for youths in America's warm climate areas to play hockey.

on the Pittsburgh area; the magical playoff run of the Gretzky-led Kings during the 1992-93 postseason; the New York Rangers' curse-breaking Stanley Cup triumph in 1993-94, which drew high TV ratings; and the 1995-96 Stanley Cup finals between Florida and Colorado, significant in that both franchises are located in relatively new markets.

This boom, however, was temporarily slowed at one point by

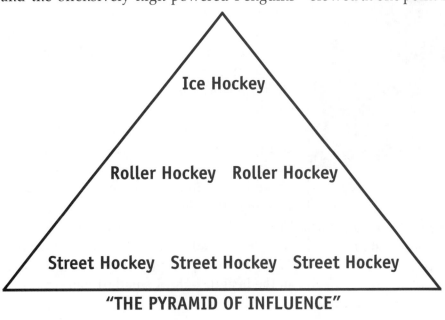

Ice Hockey

Roller Hockey   Roller Hockey

Street Hockey   Street Hockey   Street Hockey

"THE PYRAMID OF INFLUENCE"

Steve Babineau

The great Mario Lemieux, who retired after the 1996-97 season, ignited hockey interest in the The Steel City.

Steve Babineau

Czechoslovakian Jaromir Jagr's dazzling moves have thrilled many North American audiences.

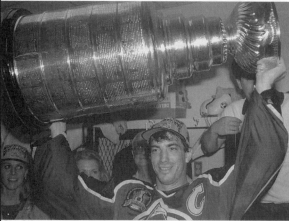

Steve Babineau

Colorado Avalanche superstar Joe Sakic proudly hoists the Stanley Cup after helping to bring Denver its first-ever pro sports championship in 1995-96.

a major bump in the road. The surge in popularity the sport was enjoying in the wake of the thrilling Rangers-Canucks final series of 1994 was temporarily stunted by an owners' lockout imposed just prior to the start of the 1994-95 season. As the season was drawing near, hockey was eyeing a major opportunity to grab the national spotlight because a mid-summer strike had forced Major League Baseball to cancel the remainder of its season and the World Series.

The gridlock between the NHL and its Players' Association went on for more than three months until the two sides finally came to terms on a new collective bargaining agreement in early January 1995. The resolution came just in time to avoid cancellation of the entire season, although many scheduled games were foregone.

Since then the NHL has slowly but surely recovered from the lockout and has managed to build back most of the momentum it had lost as a result of the dispute.

A large portion of hockey's boom is happening at the minor-pro level, where the game has never been more popular. The International Hockey League (IHL) and the American Hockey League (AHL) have each grown to 18 teams. The AHL, which is the NHL's number one developmental league, enjoyed record-breaking attendances in 1995-96 and 1996-97. And the AHL All-Star Game, which matches Canadian-born stars against players from all over the world, is now televised annually on ESPN2.

The East Coast Hockey League, which recently absorbed the now-defunct Southern League, has grown to 24 teams with new franchises in such unlikely places as Baton Rouge, Birmingham, Charlotte, Pensacola, Jacksonville, Tallahassee, New Orleans, Biloxi and Mobile. The Tallahassee Tiger Sharks average 6,000 fans per game in spite of their location in the League's third-smallest market.

"A true indicator of the growth of professional hockey in the non-traditional areas of the United States is the East Coast Hockey League," says Jackson, Mississippi native Sammy Wallace, who currently serves as director of information for the also-expanding West Coast Hockey League. "Along one corridor of Interstate 10 in the Gulf Coast region, you can see as many as 10 different hockey games within a ten-hour stretch in the road and sit in a crowd of five or six thousand rabid fans who hadn't seen a hockey puck until about two or three years ago."

There are several other relatively new circuits that are made up essentially of franchises located in non-traditional hockey markets. Two of the most notable are the West Coast Hockey League (WCHL) and the Western Professional Hockey League (WPHL). The WCHL features teams in Fresno, Bakersfield and San Diego, California; Reno, Nevada; and Anchorage and Fairbanks, Alaska. The WPHL began its first season in 1996-97 with six franchises and doubled to twelve for 1997-98. It has invaded lizard and desert country like no other hockey league with franchises in such scorching hot spots as Albuquerque, Amarillo, Waco, Austin and El Paso.

With pro hockey packing arenas from California to Florida, it's safe to say that hockey is becoming firmly established throughout the U.S. But although the Sun Belt has already been conquered, neither the NHL nor the minor pro leagues are finished yet.

The NHL recently voted to add four new franchises by the start of the 2000-2001 season. Nashville will begin play in 1998-99, Atlanta will start its first season in 1999-2000 and St. Paul and Columbus, Ohio, will commence operations in 2000-2001.

At the minor league level the AHL will add Lowell, Massachusetts, in 1998-99 and is currently considering Palm Beach, Florida, as a possible future site. The ECHL is adding

Greenville, South Carolina, and possibly Trenton, New Jersey, for '98-99. The Central Hockey League is adding St. Charles, Missouri, in '98-99 and is also eyeing Tupelo, Mississippi, as a future location. Eugene, Oregon, Colorado Springs, Sacramento, Los Angeles and The Bay Area are all being looked at by the West Coast Hockey League as future possibilities. The Western Professional Hockey League, which doubled its team total from six to twelve in only one year, will be invading Corpus Christi in 1998-99. The WPHL is also examining Lubbock, Texas; Alexandria, Louisiana; and Little Rock, Arkansas; as well as Jackson and Tupelo, Mississippi, for future expansion.

In addition to the 114 professional hockey franchises now based in the land of Stars and Stripes, there are now three American-based Junior Leagues: the Junior-A United States Hockey League (USHL), the Junior-A North American Junior League (NAJL) and the Junior-B American Frontier Hockey League (AFHL).

Although the U.S.-based Junior leagues are a notch below Canada's top Junior circuits, each of them has drawn very well. The USHL's Omaha Lancers have sold out over 200 consecutive games at the 6,124-seat Aksarben Coliseum and the Lincoln Stars played before packed houses throughout the entire 1996-97 season. Other thriving USHL clubs are Green Bay and Des Moines, which each average better than 3,000 per game. North American Junior League teams such as Compuware, Detroit, Lakeland, Indianapolis and Cleveland regularly sell out their games as well.

There are also four Junior teams located in the Pacific Northwest region of the United States. Portland, Seattle, Spokane and Tri City (Kennewick, WA) all belong to the Western Hockey League section of the Canadian Hockey League.

College hockey, which has grown only

CURRENT MAKEUP OF PROFESSIONAL HOCKEY IN NORTH AMERICA

National Hockey League (NHL)
Anaheim, Boston, Buffalo, Calgary, Carolina, Chicago, Colorado, Dallas, Detroit, Edmonton, Florida, Los Angeles, Montreal, New Jersey, NY Islanders, NY Rangers, Ottawa, Philadelphia, Phoenix, Pittsburgh, St. Louis, San Jose, Tampa Bay, Toronto, Vancouver, Washington.

American Hockey League (AHL)
Adirondack (Glens Falls, NY), Albany, Cincinnati, Fredericton (New Brunswick), Hamilton (Ontario), Hartford, Hershey (PA), Kentucky (Lexington), New Haven (CT), Philadelphia, Portland (ME), Providence (RI), Rochester (NY), Saint John (New Brunswick), Springfield (MA), St. John's (Newfoundland), Syracuse (NY), Worcester (MA).

International Hockey League (IHL)
Chicago, Cincinnati, Cleveland, Detroit, Fort Wayne (IN), Grand Rapids (MI), Houston, Indianapolis, Kansas City, Las Vegas, Long Beach (CA), Manitoba (Winnipeg), Michigan (Kalamazoo), Milwaukee, Orlando, Quebec (Quebec City), San Antonio, Utah (Salt Lake City).

East Coast Hockey League (ECHL)
Baton Rouge (LA), Birmingham (AL), Charlotte (NC), Chesapeake (Upper Marlboro, MD), Columbus (OH), Dayton (OH), Hampton Roads (VA), Huntington (WV), Jacksonville (FL), Johnstown (PA), Florence (SC), Louisiana (Lafayette), Louisville (KY), Mississippi (Biloxi), Mobile (AL), Pensacola (FL), Peoria (IL), Raleigh (NC), Richmond (VA), Roanoke (VA), South Carolina (Charleston), Tallahassee (FL), Toledo (OH), Wheeling (WV), New Orleans (LA).

Central Hockey League (CHL)
Columbus (GA), Fayetteville (NC), Fort Worth (TX), Huntsville (AL), Macon (GA), Memphis (TN), Nashville (TN), Oklahoma City (OK), Tulsa (OK), Wichita (KS).

United Hockey League (UHL, formerly Colonial Hockey League)
Binghamton (NY), Brantford (Ontario), Dayton (OH), Flint (MI), Madison (WI), Muskegon (MI), Port Huron (MI), Quad Cities (Moline & Rock Island, IL; Davenport & Bettendorf, IA), Saginaw (MI), Thunder Bay (Ontario), Winston Salem (NC).

West Coast Hockey League (WCHL)
Anchorage (AK), Bakersfield (CA), Fresno (CA), Idaho (Boise), Reno (NV), San Diego, Tacoma (WA), Tucson (AZ), Phoenix.

Western Professional Hockey League (WPHL)
Amarillo (TX), Austin (TX), Central Texas (Belton), El Paso (TX), New Mexico (Albuquerque), Waco (TX), Fort Worth (TX), Lake Charles (LA), Monroe (LA), Odessa (TX), San Angelo (TX), Shreveport (LA).

slightly due to high costs and Title IX constraints, has also managed to filter down into non-traditional spots. It's now big at such warm climate schools as the University of Arizona, Arizona State and the University of Alabama-Huntsville. The success of the Austin Ice Bats of the Western Professional Hockey League has recently led the University of Texas to consider adding ice hockey as an intercollegiate sport.

While the ice game has spread both west and south at every possible level, traditional hockey hotbeds have continued to thrive and grow. Chicago, Detroit and Philadelphia each have at least two pro teams now. Before becoming Stanley Cup Champions in 1997, the Detroit Red Wings consistently sold out the 20,000-seat Joe Louis Arena despite competing for the sports entertainment dollar with the IHL's Detroit Vipers, Compuware of the North American Junior League, the OHL Whalers of the Canadian Junior ranks and several Division I college hockey programs. This can only attest to the fact that the state of Michigan is one of the largest and most thriving hockey markets in the United States.

Everywhere you look the ice game is exploding and perhaps the most telling stats come from USA Hockey, the national governing body for the sport of ice hockey in the United States. Team participation increased seven-fold from 1969-70 to 1996-97 and total participants rose from just over 200,000 to nearly 450,000 over the past seven years.

A key demographic in the ice game's growth potential is the evolution of and growing participation in women's ice hockey. Like ice hockey and roller hockey, it's also one of the fastest growing sports in the U.S. and the world. USA Hockey reports a rise in female registration from 5,573 in 1990-91 to more than 23,000 in 1996-97. The women's game has unlimited potential partly because women's ice hockey will share the spotlight at the upcom-

Russian sensation Sergie Fedorov helped return the Stanley Cup to the Motor City in 1996-97, ending a 42-year drought.

Steve Babineau

ing 1998 Winter Olympics in Nagano, Japan, where the women's competition debuts as a medal sport. The NHL will shut down for two weeks to allow their stars to play for their various national teams. Unlike the men's basketball competition, where the United States shamefully puts a squad far superior to any other country's on the court, the men's ice hockey tournament will feature at least seven countries with squads that are well-stocked with NHL stars. It will be the ultimate showcase for hockey and a monumental event in the sport's history.

"The NHL's participation in the Olympics is not a 'Dream Team' concept," says Commissioner Bettman, "it's a 'Dream Tournament' concept. It's not about blowouts."

Team USA is confident about its chances for a medal after its September 1996 World Cup triumph. Formerly the Canada Cup, the World Cup Tournament has been dominated for years by its host nation. But in 1996 Team USA pulled out two straight thrillers in Montreal to secure Uncle Sam's first World Cup.

The World Cup victory is a testament to the vastly improved American talent pool. Because of earlier catalysts such as Bobby Orr and the "Big, Bad Bruins," and the 1980 U.S.

11

USA HOCKEY REGISTRATIONS FOR MEN & WOMEN

Year	Players	Coaches	Officials	Total	Teams
1969-70	—	—	—	—	4,255
1990-91	195,125	—	10,316	205,441	14,969
1991-92	230,201	—	11,280	241,491	16,671
1992-93	262,873	23,057	11,788	297,718	18,637
1993-94	303,611	30,985	12,418	347,014	21,150
1994-95	350,007	38,688	13,838	402,533	24,555
1995-96	368,259	45,094	16,422	429,775	26,902
1996-97	384,183	45,985	19,071	449,239	29,749

Olympic Hockey Team, a rich harvest of American talent has been produced in the nation's traditional hotbeds, Minnesota, Michigan and New England.

"Winning that World Cup really helped," says Team USA goalie Jim Carey. "It put us on — not an even level with Canada — but it certainly closed the gap. It was a big step for USA hockey and the United States."

The harvests of talent produced in traditional American hockey hotbeds over the past 25 years have not only made the U.S. more competitive at the international level, but have turned the fifty states into a prosperous breeding ground for the various professional leagues. Four of the NHL's top 12 goal-scorers in 1996-97 — including the league's leading scorer — were American. Pretty impressive considering the recent influx of European talent.

With many new pro teams attracting new fans in non-traditional areas and participation in ice and in-line hockey exploding all over the map, hockey's potential in the United States is unlimited.

Left: Tony Amonte of Hingham, MA, notched the game-winning goal for team USA against Canada in the deciding game of the 1996 World Cup. *Middle:* Michigan-born defenseman Derian Hatcher was a standout for Team USA in the World Cup. *Right:* Team USA's Gary Suter and Canada's Theo Fleury collide in World Cup competition.

Brian Babineau

Boston native Keith Tkachuk led
NHL goal-scorers in 1996-97.

1. *1997 NHL All-Star Game* magazine, NHL Publishing, New York, 1997, Sharks, Inc., by Paul Freeman, p. 23.
2. *1997 NHL All-Star Game* magazine, NHL Publishing, New York, 1997, Crazy Like a Fox, by Jim Baker, p. 88.
3. Ibid., p. 88.

TOP 12 NHL GOAL-SCORERS, 1996-97

Player	Place of Birth	Goals
KEITH TKACHUK	MELROSE, MA	52
Teemu Selanne	Helsinki, Finland	51
Mario Lemieux	Montreal, Quebec	50
JOHN LECLAIR	ST. ALBANS, VT	50
Ziggy Palffy	Skalica, Czech.	48
Brendan Shanahan	Mimico, Ontario	47
Jaromir Jagr	Kladno, Czech.	47
Peter Bondra	Luck, USSR	46
Paul Kariya	Vancouver, BC	44
BRETT HULL	CHICAGO, IL	42
TONY AMONTE	HINGHAM, MA	41
Mats Sundin	Bromma, Sweden	41

Chapter 2

Beginnings

From Hockey's Birth in the
19th Century to World War I

For more than a century, hockey historians found that precisely tracing the sport's origin is not only a difficult task but a virtual impossibility. Therefore we can only try to deduce for ourselves from the records, claims and accounts which are available to us, when, where, and by whom the first ice hockey was played.

Ice hockey is traceable to games played on fields as far back as nearly 2500 years ago. In 478 BC, a Greek soldier, Hemostocoles, built a wall in Athens which contained a sculptured scene portraying two athletes in a faceoff-like stance holding sticks similar to those later used in field hockey.

Perhaps native Americans were the first to play hockey-like games. The Indians of Canada invented the field game lacrosse, which is known by legislative act as Canada's national sport.

The Algonquins who inhabited the shores of the St. Lawrence River played an ice game similar to lacrosse called "baggataway," played without skates and with an unlimited number of participants. These matches were witnessed by French explorers who visited the St. Lawrence River area and northern areas of the United States in the 1700s.

According to the *Dictionary of Language of Micmac Indians*, published in 1888, the Micmacs of Eastern Canada played an ice game call "oochamkunutk," which was played with a bat or stick. Another ice game played by the Micmacs was "alchamadijik," which was referred to in *Legends of the Micmacs*, issued in 1894.

Early hockey-like games that came from across the Atlantic include the field game hurley from Ireland, field hockey from England, and the ice games English bandy and Kolven from Holland. Hurley is a ground game that is still popular in Ireland. It was originally played by an unlimited number of players representing one parish against another. A flat field hockey-like stick and a large ball were used. Hurley was brought to Canada by Irish immigrants, who came to work on the Shubenacadie Canal near Dartmouth, Nova Scotia, in 1831. Some believe that oochamkunutk is hurley on ice.

Field hockey was played in 1870 in England, as well as Egypt and India. Although the rules for field hockey played a major role in the early evolution of ice hockey in Canada, most students of the game doubt that field hockey was the forerunner of ice hockey because each started at about the same time. Despite its overwhelming popularity as primarily a women's sport in North America, field hockey didn't arrive in America until 1901, when Miss Constance Applebee of England arrived at Harvard Summer School and organized a game with a group of students and teachers.

Bandy was the first hockey-like game played by the English, who began playing it as far back as the late 18th century. It is still played today in Russia, Sweden, Norway, Finland and the United States (Minnesota). Many of the stars of the early Soviet hockey teams had been bandy players. It is played on a large sheet of ice with short sticks, a ball and large goals.

The Dutch, long known for their ice skating ability, have played the game of Kolven since the 1600s. It is played with a golf-like stick, a ball, and posts stuck in the ice for goals. Evidence of this game can be seen in 17th century Dutch paintings. Emigrants from Holland who settled in New York City played the game in their new locale.

The lone hockey-like game played on both sides of the Atlantic was shinny. It was played on the frozen ponds of North America and Northern Europe — Scotland in particular. A block of wood or a ball served as a puck and a couple of large rocks or chunks of wood were used to mark-off the goals. For the faceoff players had to "shinny on their own side," which meant they had to take it right-handed.

Ever since the advent of organized ice hockey, the name shinny has been used to describe unorganized or sandlot (if you will) hockey. There is an ongoing debate among hockey historians as to whether or not some of the "first hockey ever played" claims were actually ice hockey or instead, one of the hockey-like games like shinny.

A committee appointed by the Canadian Amateur Hockey Association concluded that the first hockey was played in Halifax, Nova Scotia, in 1855, by the Royal Canadian Rifles, an Imperial Army Unit stationed at Kingston.

Some believe the game they were playing was probably shinny.

An English historian once claimed that the Royal Family created the game in the early 1850s, on a lake behind Windsor Castle. But most likely the British royalty was playing either shinny or a bandy-like game instead.

Apart from shinny, the precursor to ice hockey in the United States was ice polo, a purely American creation that was derived from the indoor sport of roller polo.

Ice polo was played on outdoor ice by the early to mid-1880s in New England, Minnesota and Michigan's Upper Peninsula. It was most likely played first at the St. Paul's School in Concord, New Hampshire, in the early 1880s. In 1883, a four-team ice polo league was formed in St. Paul, Minnesota. The formation of this league led to the organization of ice polo tournaments held annually in conjunction with the famous St. Paul Winter Carnival. By the turn of the century, ice hockey had replaced ice polo in the U.S.

The first organized indoor ice hockey game supposedly took place in Canada on March 3, 1875. Montreal's Victoria Skating Rink was the site of the game which was organized by James Creighton, an ice hurley player from Halifax. After a local exhibition of ice lacrosse drew little, if any public interest, Creighton proposed ice hockey instead and ordered sticks to be shipped from Halifax to Montreal for the event.

The game was played with nine-man sides on a surface that measured 80 feet by 204 feet. The contest ended in a 2-1 victory for Creighton's team — and, believe or not — the game included a fight! "Shins and heads were battered, benches smashed, and the lady spectators fled in confusion,"[1] reported a wire dispatch of Kingston's Daily British Whig from Montreal. A terrible scene indeed, but there is a silver lining: We may not know when outdoor ice hockey began but we do know

that fighting in hockey is at least as old as its first indoor game.

What we can determine, despite our inability to pinpoint where and by whom the first outdoor game was played, is that ice hockey is primarily a Canadian creation.

What we can also assume is that since humans have inhabited the earth, they have invented, along with other recreational forms of entertainment and amusement, games which have required, or better yet served, to fulfill man's need for exercise. Where there have been meadows, fields, parks and backyards, games have been played. The same is true for ice, whether it be frozen ponds, lakes, rivers, or even puddles.

In the years following that first indoor game, Canadians began to shape and hone the new sport to their liking. In 1876, the object being struck with sticks was referred to as a "puck" for the first time, and 1877 saw the first publicized set of ice hockey rules, all seven of which were taken directly from field hockey. Further ideas and rule decisions were adapted and made respectively by McGill University students W.F. Robertson and R.F. Smith in 1879.

Ice hockey's popularity grew rapidly in Canada where it soon became the sport of choice — a preference that has stuck to this day. NHL forward Brendan Shanahan summed up his country's partiality for hockey in 1996 when he stated: "Lacrosse is our national sport, but hockey is our beloved national sport."

By 1883 there were three teams in Montreal and one in Quebec City. Ice hockey's first-ever championship series was featured at the 1883 Montreal Winter Carnival with the McGill University team taking top honors. Tournament rules called for seven men to a side and two 30-minute periods with a ten minute intermission.

The annual carnival continued to feature the novel sport and served as a showcase for innovations as well as a testing ground for rule revisions. By 1886, stick width was limited to three inches and pucks achieved their standard specs: one inch thick by three inches in diameter and made of vulcanized rubber. These new standards for the tools of the game were later brought to the States by Charles E. Courtney, a master at the St. Paul's School.

One of the first amateur leagues in Canada was the Ontario Hockey Association founded in Toronto in 1890. It was divided into three groups: junior, intermediate and senior. The OHA was responsible for producing some of the game's greatest players in those early days.

In 1892 Lord Stanley of Preston, the sixth Governor General of Canada and an avid fan of the game, sent his aide Captain Charles Colvill to England to purchase a trophy to be awarded annually to the amateur champions of Canada. For a mere 50 pounds, Colvill bought what has become the oldest and most prestigious trophy in North American sports.

Governor Stanley's initiative was symbolic of the level of popularity the game had already achieved throughout the dominion of Canada. The coveted trophy soon became known as — appropriately enough — the Stanley Cup. To this day it is considered the ultimate goal in professional hockey.

It wasn't only men who chose to partake of this thrilling ice game; the year 1890 also marked the time when the first organized and recorded all-female ice hockey game took place in Ottawa, Ontario. Later, women would compete

regularly in "Bakers Leagues" which were organized in most of Canada's major cities.

Ice hockey continued to spread across Canada during the early to mid-1890s, when it was just beginning to filter into the United States.

Scholars of the game have struggled to locate hockey's American roots, which have become a prime subject for debate. The transition from ice polo to ice hockey has clouded hockey's beginnings below the 49th parallel, leaving Uncle Sam without a definitive hockey birth certificate.

In the summer of 1894, a group of American and Canadian tennis players competed in a tournament held at Niagara Falls, New York. While attending an off-court social occasion, some Americans and Canadians got around to comparing notes about winter sports. Both were surprised to find they were playing similar but different games on ice. Upon learning that the Americans were playing ice polo instead of ice hockey, the Canadians invited their North American counterparts to visit Canada

Clark Collection

Duluth (MN) Ice Polo Club, 1892-93 season.

the next winter to play exhibition games of both sports against their border buddies.

George Wright, founder of Wright & Ditson, a manufacturer and distributor of athletic equipment, organized a series of doubleheaders featuring both sports to be played in Montreal, Ottawa, Kingston and Toronto. Each night the teams played two periods each of polo and hockey, the former being played with five men to a side, the latter with seven. The Maple Leafs swept all four of the hockey games with the Yanks winning two and tying two of the polo matches. Capacity crowds witnessed America's discovery of a better ice game.

Alexander Meikeljohn, a Brown graduate who made the trip, described the Americans' consensus: "It was pretty well agreed among us, as a result of the trip, that the Canadian game was better than ours. Having learned the rudiments of play, we brought back with us the flat skates and pucks and sticks and proceeded to forget old habits and take on new ones. The AP man, on our return, raised money for the building of the old St. Nicholas Ice Rink in New York."[2]

The St. Nicholas Rink, which opened in 1895 to become the home of the famous St. Nicholas Hockey Club, was not Manhattan's first. The Ice Palace, believed by most to be the first indoor rink in the United States, opened December 14, 1894. Located on Lexington Avenue and 101st Street, the Ice Palace soon became the home of the old New York Hockey Club, which in 1895 brought organized hockey to the big city. According to hockey historian Donald Clark, there may have been an earlier rink built in San Francisco in connection with the Northern California Fair, but attempts to trace it have failed.

In 1896 Yale became the first Ivy League school to make the transition from ice polo to ice hockey. Malcolm Chace, a Brown to Yale transfer and Arthur E. Foote, both of whom accompanied Meikeljohn & Company to Canada, were instrumental in bringing the new ice game to New Haven.

Others believe that hockey was first brought to the States by Montrealer M.C. Shearer, a student at Johns Hopkins University in Baltimore. Shearer organized a team of fellow students and set up a game with a team from Quebec. The Quebec team may have been the first Canadian club to play south of the border.

The North Avenue Rink in Baltimore opened on December 26, 1894, approximately two weeks after the Ice Palace. The premiere was christened with an ice hockey game between the Baltimore Athletic Club and Johns Hopkins University. What also could have been the first organized ice hockey game in the United States ended in a 2-2 tie.

At about the same time the game was also being played in Minneapolis; Hallock, Minnesota; at the St. Paul's School; and possibly in Montclair, New Jersey, although it is possible that ice hockey was played at an earlier date somewhere else in the United States.

According to the United States Hockey Hall of Fame, the first game of organized ice hockey in Minnesota was played between two Minneapolis teams in January of 1895.

There are reports that shortly thereafter, the University of Minnesota played a short series against the Minneapolis Hockey Club, most likely either one of the two aforementioned Minneapolis teams or a combination of both. The matches served as warmups for their upcoming game with the Winnipeg Victorias, one of Canada's finest. Newspaper reports follow:

Minnesota Ariel, February 16, 1895, page 5:

The University of Minnesota hockey team will play a game for the championship of Minneapolis against the Minneapolis Hockey Club at their rink, at the corner of Fourth Avenue and Eleventh Street South.

The game is preparatory to the game to be played Monday afternoon by Winnipeg and the University of Minnesota. Winnipeg is champion of the world.* Winnipeg has returned from a rough trip through eastern Canada and has defeated without too much trouble Montreal, Toronto, Victoria, Ottawa, Quebec, and the Limestones.

The University started practice two or three weeks ago and played against a Minneapolis team, being defeated 4-1. A week and one half ago they defeated the same team 6-4. Tonight they play the tie off for the championship. Dr. H.A. Parkyn has been coaching the boys every afternoon.

He has a couple of stars in Willis Walker and Russel. Walker plays point and Russel coverpoint, with Van Campen in goal. Parkyn and Albert are center forwards. Dr. Parkyn's long experience with the Victoria team of Toronto, one of the best, makes him a fine player. Thompsen and Head, the other two forwards are old ice polo players and skate fast and pass well. Van Campen, quarterback on last year's football team, plays goal well. Many tickets have been sold for tonight's and also Monday's game. Tickets are 25 cents, ladies come free.

The excitement of these games is intense, and surpasses that at a football game.

* This statement is false: Winnipeg did not win the Stanley Cup until 1896.

St. Paul Pioneer Press February, 19, 1895, page 6:

The first international hockey game between Winnipeg and the University of Minnesota was played yesterday, and won by the visitors 11-3. The day was perfect and 300 spectators occupied the grandstand, coeds of the University being well represented. Features of the game was the team play of the Canadians, and individual play of

Parkyn, Walker, and Head for the University. Hockey promises to become as popular a sport at the University as football, baseball, and rowing.

Malcolm K. Gordon, former hockey coach and faculty member at St. Paul's Prep School, claimed that the game had been played at his school since the 1880s. This cannot be proven, but what is documented is that in 1895 Gordon took his St. Paul's team to New York City for a game against the alumni. His varsity squad lost to the grads 3-1, but began a tradition that continued for decades. The St. Paul's varsity traveled to the Big Apple to take on a prep school opponent at Madison Square Garden.

In 1896, the annual St. Paul Winter Carnival was the stage for what may have been the first international ice hockey tournament held in America. Tourney entries included teams from Winnipeg, Minneapolis, and two squads from St. Paul — St. Paul One & St. Paul Two.

In first round action of the single elimination format, Winnipeg trounced St. Paul One 13-2, while Minneapolis defeated St. Paul Two by the score of 4-1. In the final, Winnipeg continued its dominance by downing Minneapolis 7-2.

"The games were attended by large crowds. The Winnipeg team received a silver stein for winning the carnival championship while the Minneapolis team members were given sticks,"[3] reported the *St. Paul Globe* in its January 26 edition.

The overwhelming success enjoyed by the Winnipeg team came as no surprise to the Americans. After all, the Canadians had many more years of hockey experience than their counterparts south of the border.

That same year, youth hockey programs were organized in the St. Paul area and before long other areas followed suit. These programs collectively became the breeding ground for an abundance of hockey talent developed in Minnesota.

Although the sport was played in Hallock, Minnesota in the mid-1890s, it wasn't until the turn of century that ice hockey spread to other communities in the state's northwestern corner such as Warroad, Roseau, Thief River Falls, Crookston and Baudette. By 1902 it made its way to the Iron Range where it became a religion in the town of Eveleth, a future perennial state high school champion.

In November 1896, the first U.S. amateur hockey league was formed. Officially it was named the American Amateur Hockey League. Members of the AAHL in its inaugural season included the St. Nicholas Hockey Club; New York Athletic Club; Crescent Athletic Club; and the Skating Club of Brooklyn, which played its home games at the recently opened Brooklyn Ice Palace on Atlantic Avenue near Bedford Avenue, near downtown Brooklyn.

The St. Nicholas Hockey Club was organized by another Gordon (no relation to Malcolm) — Kenneth Gordon of West Orange, New Jersey. Gordon coached the St. Nick's until later giving way to Anton "Pop" Von

Bernuth, a former standout hockey player at Columbia. Von Bernuth had the good fortune of guiding the team through the entire Hobey Baker era, when it enjoyed its greatest success. This included the championship seasons of 1911-12 and 1913-14.

Later additions to the league were the New York Hockey Club; New York Wanderers; New York Irish-American Club in 1913; Boston Athletic Association in 1915; Harvard Club in 1916; and lastly the Boston Arena Club. At some point, although a date is not known, the Crescent Athletic Club became the Crescent-Hamilton Club.

The New York Athletic Club dominated the first two seasons of the Manhattan-based AAHL by winning back-to-back championships. Their reign ended in 1899 when the Brooklyn Skating Club won the title.

The rosters of these AAHL teams were dominated by Canadian-born players, with only a few Americans on the squads. But if you wanted to see some good hockey, you could find it in America's largest city.

The second amateur league organized in the United States was the Baltimore Hockey League, which premiered in January of 1897.

It comprised four teams: Maryland Athletic Club; Northampton Athletic Club; University of Maryland; and Johns Hopkins University. These clubs played each other twice for a total of six matches each from early February to late March at Baltimore's North Avenue Rink. The League winner earned the honor of being presented the Northampton Cup, which was donated by Maryland hockey promoter Mr. J.S. Filon.

At the same time both the AAHL and the BHL got rolling, ice hockey at the collegiate level was organized at some of the top institutions in the east. Yale and Johns Hopkins were among the

Clark Collection

The first St. Nicholas Hockey Club, 1896.

AAHL CHAMPIONS

1896-97	NYAC	1907-08	NY Crescent AC
1897-98	NYAC	1908-09	NYAC
1898-99	Brooklyn SC	1909-10	NYAC
1899-00	NY Crescent AC	1910-11	NY Crescent AC
1900-01	NY Crescent AC	1911-12	NY Crescent AC
1901-02	NY Crescent AC	1912-13	NYHC (Hockey Club of New York)
1902-03	NY Crescent AC	1913-14	St. Nicholas HC
1903-04	NY Wanderers HC	1914-15	St. Nicholas HC
1904-05	NY Crescent AC	1915-16	Boston AA
1905-06	NY Crescent AC	1916-17	Boston AA
1906-07	St. Nicholas HC	1917-18	World War I

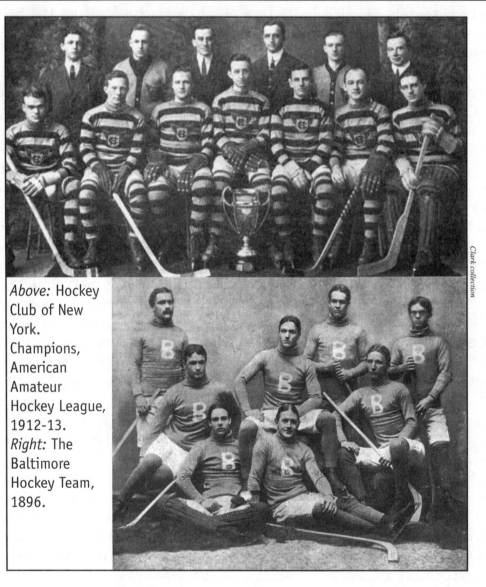

Clark collection

Above: Hockey Club of New York. Champions, American Amateur Hockey League, 1912-13. *Right:* The Baltimore Hockey Team, 1896.

first schools to play the sport.

On February 14, 1896, another U.S. hockey first took place at the North Avenue Rink in Baltimore: Yale defeated Johns Hopkins 2-1, in the first-ever game between two American colleges.

The Yale ice hockey program was organized in late 1895. The Elis' landmark victory over Johns Hopkins in 1896 was the only recorded game of that season for the Bulldogs. On January 23, 1897, the two schools faced-off in a rematch with Yale posting a 2-0 shutout.

Other Ivy League schools soon followed Yale's lead and formed ice hockey teams. Columbia was next, followed by Harvard, Brown and later Princeton, Cornell, and Dartmouth.

Yale played two more games during the winter of 1897, losing 3-0 to Queens College (Canada) and downing Columbia 7-2. They played five games in 1898; losing to Brown twice, and winning two and tying one against Columbia.

While there have been claims that Brown played the first college hockey in the United States, that is not correct. Brown and Harvard were playing ice polo until late 1897-early 1898. Harvard formed a hockey team in late '97, but it wasn't until 1898 that the Harvard Ice Polo Association, founded by Frederick Elliot and J.W. Dunlop, changed the word "polo" to "hockey" in its name.

Brown was Harvard's big rival at ice polo during those early years. The rivalry carried over to hockey as the two schools played their first official game in 1898 at Boston's Franklin Field in Dorchester where the Bears blanked the Crimson by the score of 6-0.

Later that same season Brown traveled to Brooklyn to participate in a tournament for an intercollegiate cup offered by a Mr. Ireland of the Skating Club of Brooklyn. Yale and Columbia were the other competitors. Brown won the cup by going undefeated. Yale took second place.

Not surprisingly, uniforms and equipment in those early days were primitive. This excerpt from *Collier's Weekly* aptly describes what the Brown squad had to work with in its first season of ice hockey:

The first uniforms worn that year — 1898 — were makeshift at best. The Brown players wore baseball trousers and turtleneck sweaters, of the sort then in collegiate vogue. Over heavy stockings they wore the leg guards adopted from ice polo. The goalie's pads were no different from the others. Heavy wool or leather gloves were worn. The players bought their own skates, usually of the clamp variety. You would attach the skates to ordinary shoes, either with a little lever to make them take hold or with a key that screwed them on. They cost about six dollars. The hockey sticks lasted a man all season and cost between sixty cents and a dollar.[4]

The following season of 1899 saw Harvard and Brown meet again. This time the crowd was treated to a much closer match with Brown prevailing by a score of 2-1. Brown continued its hockey program until 1906, playing their home games on natural ice at Roger Williams Park. After the 1905-06 season the sport was dropped and not resumed until 1926.

Harvard played its first game with Yale on February 26, 1900, at the St. Nicholas Rink in New York. Yale edged the Crimson 5-4, and another rivalry began. These early contests between eastern schools established new rivalries that lent excitement and intensity to America's first collegiate hockey league.

The Intercollegiate Hockey League was formed during the winter of 1900 consisting of schools that would later form the Ivy League. The league soon became a breeding ground for the St. Nick's as well as other amateur organizations. In its inaugural season it was a five-team league with Yale, Columbia,

Harvard, Princeton and Brown entering competition. Cornell and Dartmouth would join later.

Although Princeton became a charter member of the League when it opened in 1900, it wasn't until February of 1904 that ice hockey was recognized as an official sport and admitted to the University Athletic Association. In early years the team practiced on dance floors or on the ice at Stony Brook. Aside from league play, they competed against amateur teams from the AAHL as well as college and high school teams from the Northeast.

The Tigers' first competitive team was the 1902-03 edition. The season ended in disappointment, however, as the club was headed for a post-season playoff with Harvard until the faculty disbanded the team for "loafing."[5] Later that year a young man from Wissahickon, PA, near Philadelphia, who would eventually bring Princeton great success in hockey and football, enrolled at the St. Paul's School. The lad's name was Hobart Amory Hare Baker.

Princeton won hockey championships in 1907 and 1910 with the '09-10 squad suffering only one loss all season — that coming, interestingly enough — at the hands of Baker and his St. Paul's team. In the fall of 1910 Hobey entered Princeton. It was during his era that the university enjoyed its greatest stretch, winning three consecutive Intercollegiate Hockey League titles from 1912 to 1914, and national titles in '12 and '14.

At the time there was no freshman hockey at Princeton so Baker could only practice during the 1910-11 season. He skated with the varsity in New York and on lakes and ponds in the area. He wanted to join St. Nick's to keep in game shape but was not permitted to do so because of school regulations.

The following season, with Baker playing the position of rover, the Tigers took the league title and the national championship.

In his junior year, 1912-13, Princeton won the league title but lost two out of three to Harvard (which was not a member of the league that season) for tops in the nation.

Stan Fischler collection

Hobey Baker.

The sensational Princeton team of 1913-14 featured six seniors (including Baker) and one junior. They recaptured the national championship, while losing only three games, one of which is regarded as one of the greatest collegiate games ever played.

On Saturday, January 24, 1914, Baker's Princeton team took on a tough Harvard squad coached by Crimson legend Ralph Winsor at the Boston Arena before a sellout crowd of over 6,000 fans. Tickets were scalped and bets were placed with Princeton favored by 10-7 odds. At the end of regulation the score was tied at one goal apiece, setting the stage for sudden death overtime. After 23 minutes of overtime and an average weight loss of four and one half pounds per player, Harvard's Leverett Saltonstall lofted a 25-footer past Tiger goalie Frank Winants, ending the longest American college game to date.

In the days of seven-man hockey and no forward passing, Hobey Baker typified the position of "rover," the offensive player permitted to roam all over the ice. Since Princeton didn't have a home rink in those early years, most of their games were played away in cities before large crowds. Whenever Baker gathered a rebound in his own end, circled the net and took off, the crowd would rise to its feet and shout, "Here he comes!"[6]

Perhaps the February 20, 1913 edition of the

Boston Journal best summed up what Hobey Baker meant to the game when it said he "is without doubt the greatest amateur hockey player ever developed in this country or in Canada."[7]

The Dartmouth College hockey program didn't get underway until just after the turn of the century, with its first team entering competition in 1905-06. Player/coach and captain Gene Brooks led the Indians squad that first season — and by example too — scoring the first goal in Dartmouth hockey history. The season was highlighted by a 4-2 victory over Williams at the Capitol Arena in Albany under gaslights on January 20, 1906.

The first Dartmouth hat trick came the following season, when on December 29, 1906 Warren Foote netted each tally in a 3-2 win over Massachusetts Institute of Technology.

Since few teams were willing to travel to "out of the way" Hanover, the Indians seldom played host. What few home games they had were played on "Alumni Oval," which was flooded for such rare occasions.

If the Intercollegiate League had awarded a Lady Byng Trophy in those days, they would have given it to the entire 1908-09 Dartmouth squad. This version of the green and white accomplished something very unique: they played the entire regular season without taking a single penalty! And, believe it or not, this remarkable show of restraint actually brought them success — some, at least — as they finished second in the league behind only Harvard.

The Indians had what could have been the first 20-goal scorer in college hockey history in Clarence "Bags" Wanamaker, who played rover. Wanamaker, along with Leon Tuck, John Dellinger, and goalie Art Donahue, led Dartmouth to 8-2-0 and 7-2-0 seasons and the program's first victory over Harvard, 4-2, in 1915.

Following graduation, Wanamaker became the school's next varsity hockey coach. His tenure lasted five seasons (including the war years), during which he posted an overall record of 21-16.

While amateur and college hockey were taking off in the States, Canadians continued to modify the sport they created. In 1900, referee Fred Waghorne introduced his new faceoff method of dropping the puck at a game in Southwestern Ontario. This innovation received favorable reviews and Waghorne was granted permission to use his new technique the next winter in a National Hockey Association game at Almonte, Ontario. It soon

EARLY COLLEGE LEADERS

1898-99	Yale	1909-10	Princeton
1899-00	Yale	1910-11	Cornell
1900-01	Yale	1911-12	Princeton
1901-02	Yale	1912-13	Harvard
1902-03	Harvard	1913-14	Princeton
1903-04	Harvard	1914-15	Princeton
1904-05	Harvard	1915-16	Harvard
1905-06	Harvard	1916-17	Harvard
1906-07	Princeton	1917-18	World War I
1907-08	Yale	1918-19	World War I
1908-09	Harvard		

became the norm and has remained so ever since.

Meanwhile, back in the States, the biggest hockey hotbed was the state of Minnesota. But while eastern colleges were enjoying the privilege of organized competition, schools in the midwest were deprived of such. The University of Minnesota attempted to organize varsity ice hockey in November of 1900 when a committee was appointed to confer with the school's Athletic Board regarding a venue for home games. The two parties vetoed the flooding of Northrop Field and, instead, voted to use Como Lake in St. Paul as the team's home ice.

No scheduled games were played until late in the season of 1903 when the University defeated Minneapolis Central High School 4-0, and the St. Paul Virginias of the Twin City league 4-3. 1903 was the last year that games of ice hockey were played on a formal basis at the University until 1920.

In 1910, efforts by the University of Minnesota were made to interest other midwestern schools in the sport and start up Big Ten Intercollegiate Conference competition. The endeavor, however, was met with failure.

In the mid-teens some fraternities at the University began taking an interest in the game. By 1915, 16 frats were competing in a league organized by professor O.S. Zelner. These contests were played on outdoor ice at Northrop Field with the playoffs being held at the Hippodrome in St. Paul. The Bros brothers, Chet and Ben, were the dominant players of that league.

The Hippodrome, along with the Curling Club of Duluth, opened in 1912 when ice hockey in "The Land of 10,000 Lakes" was just beginning to make its way from some of those frozen lakes to newly built city arenas.

To accommodate the need for organized hockey in the Gopher State just after the century's turn, the Twin City League was formed to open play in 1902-03. It was comprised of Minneapolis and St. Paul teams. All of its players came from Minnesota, mostly the Twin Cities — there were no imports.

Another region of the U.S. where ice hockey became popular by the late 1890s was the Pittsburgh area. An amateur league comprised of teams from Western Pennsylvania thrived in those days, satisfying the thirst for the ice game in and around The Steel City. Members of this league also occasionally mixed it up with such eastern schools as Yale, which traveled to Pittsburgh to do hockey battle.

By 1904 in Canada and the United States, there were at least a half dozen amateur hockey leagues in existence. Interestingly, considering how much farther advanced Canada was than the U.S. at the relatively young game, it was in the United States that the very first professional hockey league was organized.

The International Hockey League, or IHL, was based in Michigan's Upper Peninsula. In its maiden season of 1904-05, it was a four-team league with franchises in Portage Lake, MI; Calumet, MI; Sault Ste. Marie, MI (aka American Soo); and Sault Ste. Marie, Ontario (Canadian Soo). Pittsburgh joined later.

In 1902-03 there was a four-team league in Upper Michigan with teams in Houghton; Hancock; Laurium; and Sault Ste. Marie, MI. This amateur league could very well have been the forerunner to the IHL. The Portage Lakers played an independent schedule during the winter of 1903-04 before joining the IHL the following season.

In that first season (playoffs included) the Lakers lost only twice in 26 games, scoring a remarkable 273 goals and allowing only 48. Their only regular season loss came at the hands of American Soo by the score of 7-6. In the U.S. playoffs they dropped a 5-2 decision to Pittsburgh before beating them 5-1 and 7-0 for the American championship. They then traveled to the Amphidrome in Houghton where in front of crowds of over 5,000, they laid claim to the world championship by trouncing Canada's best, the Montreal Wanderers, by scores of 8-4, and 9-2.

The Lakers were put together by a man named James R. Dee, who built the team around "Doc" Gibson, their captain and leading scorer. It was Gibson who selected smooth-skating playmaker Joe Linder to join the squad. Linder, a Copper Country product out of Hancock, Michigan High School where he starred in hockey, football and baseball, was described by his contemporaries as the "first great American-born hockey player."[8]

After taking out Montreal for the world title at the end of that first season, they had earned the reputation throughout the Northern United States and Canada of being the toughest team on ice.

Upon joining the IHL, the Lakers immediately became the class of the league and ruled it during its brief history. After winning the league title in the spring of 1905, Portage Lake sent notice to the Stanley Cup Board of Governors challenging the Ottawa Silver Seven to a championship series. They were turned down. In 1906 they issued the same challenge to Montreal and were again refused.

Although it lasted only three years, the IHL produced some very good hockey. The league featured many of the game's best players at the time, most of whom were Canadian. Aside from Gibson and Linder, they included Riley Hern, Hod and Bruce Stewart and Cyclone Taylor. The league dissolved when Gibson returned to Canada to enter the medical profession and a good many of the players were lured back over the border to sign with Canadian teams.

Around the time of the IHL's final season of 1906-07, there were a couple of professional hockey leagues in Canada, but like the IHL, they did not last. The National Hockey Association (NHA), which was organized in 1908, was the first Canadian pro league to make an impact. In its inaugural season, 1909-10, its member teams were the Montreal Wanderers, Montreal Canadiens, Montreal Shamrocks, Cobalt, Renfrew, Haileybury, Ottawa, Quebec, Torontos, Tecumsehs, Ontarios, Shamrocks (Toronto), & 23rd Battalion. These clubs competed annually for the Stanley Cup until the NHA folded in 1917.

Hockey in New England's Hub city received a shot in the arm in 1910 when the Boston Arena was completed. It served as home to the Boston Athletic Association hockey team

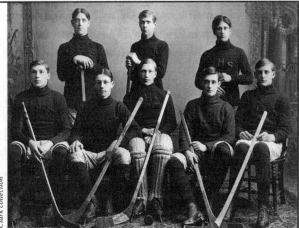

Left: The 1904 world champion Portage Lake Hockey Team. *Right:* Houghton (MI) High School Hockey Team.

The famous Boston Athletic Association (BAA) Team, U.S. champions in 1916.

attle. And for the first time ever — thanks to hockey's Royal Family — sports fans in the Great Northwest got a chance to sample the exciting new game on ice.

While 1912 marked the year that the Pacific Coast Hockey Association held its first championship playoffs, it could also be remembered as a year for rule changes. The age of seven-man hockey and no forward passing took its first steps towards extinction when the National Hockey Association changed from seven-man to six-man hockey and the pro leagues voted to allow forward passing within a 20-foot zone in front of the goal. The NHA's change to six-man hockey eliminated the position of rover and the game has been played six-on-six ever since. Forward passing within the 20-foot zone was the first step toward the allowance of forward passing in all areas of the ice, which with the exception of red line (pros only) and blue line offsides is the standard that has stuck to this day.

A couple of amateur leagues that came into existence in the mid-teens were the American Amateur Hockey Association and the National Amateur Hockey League. Neither lasted very long.

The American Amateur Hockey Association, or AAHA, was organized in 1913. Its first season was 1913-14. The member teams were Portage Lake; Calumet; Sault Ste. Marie, MI/ American Soo; Cleveland Athletic Club; Boston Athletic Association; and the Boston Arenas — all of which competed for the McNaughton Cup which went to the league's playoff champion.

The McNaughton Cup was donated by James McNaughton, president of Calumet and Hecla Copper Company, and a devoted supporter of amateur hockey. The prized trophy, which stands nearly three feet high and

which was put together by American hockey pioneer George Brown. The BAA team, which joined the American Amateur Hockey League in 1915, not only competed against the fine amateur clubs of the AAHL like the St. Nick's and the New York Wanderers, but also skated against top Canadian and college teams as well.

In 1918, the Boston Arena was lost to fire and Brown formed a corporation to construct a new Arena. When the new building was finished, Brown managed both the Arena and the BAA team, which by the early twenties had seven future Olympians on its roster.

By the end of the new century's first decade, ice hockey was becoming well established in Canada and the U.S., but only from the Atlantic Coast to middle North America. In 1910 however, the Patrick Brothers, Lester and Frank, became hockey's version of Lewis and Clark by moving west and starting up the Pacific Coast Hockey Association. The PCHA began play in 1911-12 and ran until 1923-24. It featured franchises in Victoria, Vancouver, New Westminster, Portland, Spokane and Se-

weighs 40 pounds, is handcrafted of pure silver taken from local mines. In 1923, the Upper Michigan teams pulled out of the AAHL to form their own league and the Cup went with them. It remained in the Copper Country until 1951 when it was passed on to the newly-formed Western Intercollegiate Hockey League which soon became the Western Collegiate Hockey Association.

In its inaugural season of 1913-14, the Cleveland Athletic Club, led by Duluth-born speedskater Frank "Coddy" Winters, defeated Sault Ste. Marie, Michigan in the final by the score of 4-2. A former rover turned defenseman, Winters was described by one writer as follows: "Coddy rushed the chunk of rubber up and down the ice and across the back with his old daring and recklessness and he hurdled and twisted with small ceremony although with much eclat."[9]

The Cleveland AC followed their championship season of 1913-14 by tying for the title the following year. After edging the Boston Athletic Association 4-3, and losing to the Boston Arenas 9-4, Cleveland wound up the 1914-15 campaign as co-champions, sharing honors with American Soo.

In the league's final season of existence, 1915-16, the St. Paul Athletic Club, with mostly local

AAHA CHAMPIONS	
1914	Cleveland AC
1915	Cleveland AC; American Soo (tie)
1916	St. Paul AC
1917	League dissolved because of the war

players, defeated American Soo to win the Cup. They were led by high-scoring defenseman Frank "Moose" Goheen. Goheen was a product of White Bear Lake, Minnesota, where aside from collecting ice-time, he also excelled in football and baseball. As Jacques Plante was the first to don a goalie mask, Goheen was also a pioneer of head gear in his own right by originating the wearing of helmets to protect from flying pucks and falls to the ice. He was later drafted by the Boston Bruins and offered a contract by the Toronto Maple Leafs, both of which he turned down to remain in Minnesota with the Northern States Power Company. Goheen was selected to the Hockey Hall of Fame in Toronto in 1952, and to the United States Hockey Hall of Fame in 1973.

Other key contributors to the AC's success in that championship season were Tony Conroy, Eddie Fitzgerald, Cy Weidenbroner and high-scoring center Nick Kahler. With the exception of Kahler, each of the aforementioned St. Paul stars played on the 1920 U.S. Olympic squad. After taking the AAHA title, St. Paul went on to defeat Lachine, Quebec, 7-6, in Montreal for the Ross Cup International Championship.

When the United States entered the First World War in the early spring of 1917 and peace was no longer a reality, the AAHA

Clark collection

Cleveland Elysium, opened 1908.

dissolved with it.

In 1917, the International Skating Union took control as the governing body of amateur ice hockey. In doing so it oversaw the formation of the National Amateur Hockey League which lasted for only one season. In that sole season of 1917-18, the Pittsburgh Athletic Association emerged as the NAHL's only champion.

1917 also marked the first year that hockey's biggest prize — the Stanley Cup — made its annual (but brief in those days) post-season stay in an American city. The Seattle Metropolitans of the Pacific Coast Hockey Association became the first American-based team to lay claim to hockey's most coveted silverware when they took out the defending champion Montreal Canadiens three games to one.

Just like baseball's World Series, where each game is played under the rules of the home team's league (American League uses a designated hitter whereas in the National League the pitcher must hit), the 1917 Stanley Cup Finals employed a similar compromise:

Since the PCHA still played the seven-man game and the NHA had eliminated the rover by switching to a six-man system, the series alternated the rules for each game. After dropping Game One by the count of 8-4 — despite playing by Western rules — the Mets bounced back — again, ironically, under Eastern rules and trounced the Habs 6-1, in Game Two. Seattle ran with their momentum and took the next two contests to wrap up the series in four games, thus giving Uncle Sam his first drink out of Lord Stanley's Cup.

The previous year the Portland Rosebuds had become the first American team to get their names on the Cup, but they were not the true Stanley Cup champions. After winning the 1915-16 PCHA title, the Rosebuds prematurely engraved their names on the Cup, but it was acknowledged that the winner of the annual East-West challenge between the NHA and the PCHA champions would be the Stanley Cup champs.

The Rosebuds lost their claim to the big prize when the Montreal Canadiens, behind the stellar goaltending of Georges Vezina, defeated Portland 2-1 in the fifth and deciding game of the series.

Financial problems and disagreements among club owners caused the NHA to close its doors by the fall of 1917. In November a new professional league was formed — the National Hockey League. From the time of its inception to the present it has not only featured the world's highest calibre of play but has served as a showcase for the best hockey players on the planet.

Unfortunately, the era covered in this chapter ended with some very bad news: The man acclaimed as the greatest American hockey player of his generation died in a plane crash near Toul, France.

After receiving his discharge papers on the morning of December 21, 1918, 26-year-old Hobey Baker, a member of the American Army squadron Lafayette Escadrille Flying Corps, decided to take one final flight in a favorite plane of his, the Princeton-colored orange and black Spad. Before boarding, he changed his mind and decided to test-fly a recently repaired plane to make sure it was fixed properly. When he was 500 meters above the field, the motor suddenly stopped, causing the plane to fall from the sky and crash into the French countryside — unexpectedly ending the life of one of America's greatest athletes of all time.

1. Stan and Shirley Fischler, *Great Book of Hockey* (Lincolnwood, IL: Publications, International, Limited, 1991), p. 9.
2. S. Kip Farrington, Jr., *Skates, Sticks and Men* (New York, NY: David McKay Company, Inc., 1972), p. 65.
3. *St. Paul Globe*, January 26, 1896.
4. Farrington, p. 67.
5. Ibid., p. 51.
6. John Dunn Davies, *The Legend of Hobey Baker* (Boston: Little Brown, 1966), p. xx of preface.
7. Ibid., p. 43.
8. United States Hockey Hall of Fame booklet of inductees, p. 51.
9. Ibid., p. 67.

Chapter 3

In Canada's Shadow

The American Game From the
Twenties Through the Fifties

When critics refer to "North American
Hockey," it is really the Canadian game about which they are talking. Until
recently — despite a few isolated moments of glory — the United States had
always taken a back seat to Canada when it came to hockey excellence. The
period from the end of World War I to the late 1950s is no exception.

The Great War finally came to an end on November 11, 1918. When it did, the North
American hockey scene was in dire need of regaining some of the momentum it had
lost during the conflict.

The International Skating Union continued to oversee amateur ice hockey ranks in the United States after peace was restored. Under its control the American Amateur Hockey Association resurfaced for the season of 1919-20. The St. Paul Athletic Club, which won the McNaughton Cup in 1915-16, shared the 1920 AAHA title with Canadian Soo.

That same year one of the major hockey events of the century occurred when Antwerp, Belgium, played host to the first Winter Olympic Games. Although they were considered "unofficial," the 1920 Winter Games launched an every-four-years tradition that has continued to the present.

In the ice hockey competition, the United States squad finished second only to Canada. The team featured four stars from the 1915-16 AAHA champion St. Paul Athletic Club — Moose Goheen, Tony Conroy, Eddie Fitzgerald and Cy Weidenbroner. Nick Kahler, who also starred for St. Paul during that championship season of 1915-16, was chosen but declined due to financial obligations. There were two Boston players on the team — Leon Tuck and George Geran — who later played for the NHL Boston Bruins. What raised a stirring controversy was the fact that there were four Canadians on the team — Herb Drury, Joe McCormack and Larry McCormick from the Pittsburgh AA, and Frank Synott of Boston AA. They were allowed to play but not until after a protest from the Canadian press.

In the Autumn of 1920, the International Skating Union, which had a working agreement with the Amateur Athletic Union and the Canadian Amateur Hockey Association, gave way to the United States Amateur Hockey Association (USAHA) as the governing body of amateur hockey in America. At a meeting held in Philadelphia on October 25, the ISU, with the approval of the AAU, passed a resolution to turn control of the sport over to the USAHA.

AMATEUR CHAMPIONS DURING USAHA'S RULE

USAHA GROUP I
1921	Boston AA
1922	Boston Westminster HC
1923	Boston AA
1924	Boston AA
1925	Pittsburgh Hornets

GROUP II
1921	Cleveland HC
1922	St. Paul AC
1923	St. Paul AC
1924	Pitt. Yellowjackets
1925	Pitt. Yellowjackets

GROUP III
1921	Eveleth Reds
1922	Eveleth Reds
1923	No Competition
1924	No Competition
1925	No Competition

NATIONAL CHAMPIONS
1914	Cleveland AC
1915	No Series
1916	St. Paul AC
1917	No Series
1918	Pittsburgh AA
1919	No Series
1920	Pittsburgh AA
1921	Cleveland HC
1922	Bos. Westminster HC
1923	Boston AA
1924	Pitt. Yellow Jackets
1925	Pitt. Yellow Jackets
1926	Minneapolis Rockets

CENTRAL HOCKEY LEAGUE
1926	Minneapolis Rockets

Built in 1919, the Eveleth Recreational Building still stands.

Built in 1922, the Eveleth Hippodrome has been remodeled three times.

All photos this page: Clark collection

Cleveland Hockey Club, 1923. (l to r): Harry Quesnelle, C; Austin Wilke, RW; Alfred Holman, D; Verne Turner, G.; Jimmy Cree, LW; Frank McGuire, LW; Joe Debernadi, RW; Walter Henderson, D; Frank "Coddy" Winters, D; Wilfred Talbot, G; Clarence Jamieson, D; Nelson Stewart, C.

St. Paul Athletic Club, 1922-23.

Eveleth Reds of the USAHA, 1922.

The USAHA only lasted four years, but was responsible for creating enormous growth. Many leagues were organized — and in turn — rinks were built.

Several new indoor arenas were constructed on Minnesota's Iron Range. The town of Eveleth built a recreational building as a venue for ice hockey in 1919, but since it lacked the capacity to handle the increasing crowds, the town constructed its first Hippodrome in 1921.

Upon its formation the USAHA created a league including such teams as Eveleth, Duluth, Boston AA, Boston Westminster HC, Pittsburgh Hornets, Pittsburgh Yellow Jackets, Cleveland HC, St. Paul AC, and others. The National Championship playoff, which began in 1914, was continued after World War I, and from 1921-1925 it produced the overall USAHA champion between its three divided groups. The first National Champion under the USAHA's guidance was the Cleveland Athletic Club in 1920-21.

Six-man hockey, which had become the norm in the States, was played during the 1920-21 season. Rosters in those days were relatively small. Seven to nine players were normally used per game and by the mid-twenties, 11 to 12. A team usually carried only one goalie. If he was injured either a defenseman or forward had to suit up, or a goalie in the stands — if one was present and willing — was permitted to substitute.

Quality referees were not abundant in the early days of the USAHA. At a game in Soo, Michigan, St. Paul coach Ed Fitzgerald protested a ref's call and tried to inform him that a rule to which he referred was not in the book. The ref retorted, "There ain't any rule book. Up here it's played the way I say." Then he tore the rule book in half and tossed it into the stands.

The brand of hockey played at the senior amateur level in the States from the early to mid-twenties was extremely rough. Former St. Paul forward Emy Garrett had this description: "When we started on a road trip to the other rinks it was like going to war. Visiting teams often lost and had to be escorted off the ice by police."

The level of play in the U.S. amateur ranks in those days was just below that seen in Canada's top circuit — the National Hockey League.

Another pro league that thrived north of the border at that time was the Western Canadian Hockey League. The WCHL had franchises in Edmonton, Calgary, Regina, and Saskatoon, with Victoria and Vancouver joining after the Pacific Coast Hockey Association folded in 1924. Like those who followed the NHL or the USAHA, fans in WCHL cities were treated to a high calibre of play. The Western League was laced with an abundance of fine talent — all of which was bought up by the NHL when the WCHL folded in 1926.

The first official Winter Olympic Games were hosted by the French at Chamonix in 1924. Unlike in the 1920 games, no Canadians played for the United States squad which was comprised mostly of skaters from the Boston AA team. Aside from Taffy Abel, George Geran and Herb Drury, a lot of the top skaters from the Northern Midwest stayed home such as Goheen, Conroy, Iver Anderson (goalie from Duluth), Gus Olsen (Duluth), Nobby Clark (Duluth), and Victor DesJardins (forward, Sault Ste. Marie, MI). Despite the absence of those stars, the U.S. again did itself proud by finishing in second place behind Canada.

In February of 1924 the National Hockey League finally expanded south of the 49th parallel when the Boston Bruins became the league's first American franchise. The NHL was an instant success in Beantown.

The Bruins wasted no time becoming competitive. Owner Charles Adams hired former

NHA and NHL star Art Ross to manage the new club. As architect, the hockey-savvy Ross immediately set out to make his team an instant contender. When the folding of the Western League was imminent, Ross tried to buy seven of its top players for $50,000. The move, however, was met with considerable opposition from fellow franchise owners and the league halted the deal.

After forcing Boston to cancel its near-coup, the league went ahead and bought up all of the Western players for a grand sum of $258,000 and awarded them by random draw. The Bruins not only got their $50,000 back, but also three of the players they originally bought and one more as Harry Meeking, Harry Oliver, Duke Keats and superstar defenseman Eddie Shore all headed to Boston.

Shore immediately became the heart and soul of the Bruins. It was his gritty style that formed the basis of what would become the franchise's personality — rough, tough, aggressive and hard working. This philosophy yielded a top-notch level of performance highlighted by tight defense and excellent goaltending.

In only their third season, Boston made it all the way to the Stanley Cup finals before bowing to Ottawa for the Cup. More than 29,000 applications were received by the Bruins for tickets to the final series. It was clearly evident that pro hockey was a smash hit in Boston.

Two years later, the Bruins moved into the newly-built Boston Garden and rewarded their rapidly growing fan base by winning their first Stanley Cup. Boston was led by recently-acquired goaltender Cecil "Tiny" Thompson, formerly of the Minneapolis Millers. Thompson shut out the Canadiens twice in a three-game semifinal series and held the Rangers to only one goal in two games in the finals, posting a 0.60 goals-against average through the five games.

The Bruins' Cup run was also aided by the solid defensive play of a couple of local boys. Canadian-born but Boston-bred George Owen joined The Black and Gold in 1928-29, pitching in nicely behind the Boston blue line. Owen was a hometown favorite, having played at Harvard, where he had enjoyed a fine collegiate career. Also joining the B's that championship season was Boston-born Myles J. Lane, a defenseman from Dartmouth, who became the first American collegian to enter the pro ranks.

Aside from Lane's jump from college to pro, two other major hockey breakthroughs occurred in 1928. The first was a new rule which allowed forward passing in each zone — i.e., the defensive, neutral and offensive zones. This opened up the game considerably, especially since there was no red line back then.

Clark collection

Cecil "Tiny" Thompson won four Vezina Trophies with the Boston Bruins before being traded to the Detroit Red Wings.

And on December 22, Montreal radio station CJAD helped bring hockey into a new era and into the home when it broadcast its first Canadiens game.

A year after the Bruins arrived on the scene in 1924, the NHL added two more American-based franchises, the New York Americans and Pittsburgh Pirates.

Percy Thompson, who owned the Hamilton Tigers sold the franchise to New York sportsman Bill Dwyer for $75,000. Fight promoter Tex Rickard was in the process of building Madison Square Garden. Dwyer made an arrangement with Rickard for his new club, the Americans, to play their home games in the new arena. A crowd of 17,000 turned out on opening night and big league hockey was off and running in Manhattan.

The Americans were led by former Edmonton Eskimos defensive star "Bullet" Joe Simpson, who played a big part in the Eskimos' WCHL championship in 1922-23. Although the Amerks were rarely competitive (finishing over .500 only once, 19-18-11 in 1937-38) and had to compete with the Rangers for attendance, they fared remarkably well at the gate and managed to last until 1942, when the onset of the Second World War caused their demise.

Due to its long-standing reputation as a hockey hotbed and the success of its amateur Yellow Jackets of the United States Amateur League, Pittsburgh was also awarded an NHL franchise to enter competition in 1925-26. The nickname chosen for the new club was the same as the city's National League baseball team — the Pirates. Longtime Canadiens' star Odie Cleghorn served as player-manager of a squad comprised mostly of former Yellow Jackets.

The Pirates finished the 1925-26 campaign in third place with a respectable 19-16-1 record. After dropping well below .500 the next season, they bounced back with a win-

ning record in 1927-28. But then the bottom fell out. The team won only 14 games over the next two seasons and attendance dropped off significantly. With trouble at the gate and the Great Depression underway, the Pirates were forced to move to Philadelphia where boxing champ Benny Leonard took over and changed the team's name to Quakers. The City of Brotherly Love, however, provided no remedy as box office woes continued, and, at the end of the 1930-31 season, the franchise folded.

Just as the Boston Bruins benefited from the big Western deal of 1926, so did the league. The WCHL's collapse created an overflow of top-notch talent with proven ability and helped pave the way for the addition of three more American franchises. The New York Rangers, Chicago Blackhawks and Detroit Cougars all became part of what by the beginning of the 1926-27 season had become a ten-club, two-division league.

The Rangers, New York's second NHL franchise, came to Gotham on the coattails of the

Clark collection

Ivan "Ching" Johnson played amateur hockey for Eveleth and Minneapolis before joining the New York Rangers in 1926-27.

overwhelming success achieved by the Americans at the gate. They were owned by Madison Square Garden Corporation, which hired Conn Smythe to put together a team. Smythe, a Toronto native, shrewdly assembled a talented, well-balanced squad to begin the franchise's first year of competition.

Among Smythe's recruits were defensemen Ching Johnson and Sault Ste. Marie, Michigan native Taffy Abel, who was not only the first, but for many years remained the only American-born player in the NHL. Smythe also signed goalie Lorne Chabot from the amateur Port Arthur club.

From the draw following the Western deal came forwards Bill and Bun Cook, who both played for the Soo Greyhounds of the Northern Ontario Hockey Association and then Newsy Lalonde's Saskatoon club, as well as sharp-shooting left winger Frank Boucher.

From solid defensemen to rugged forwards, Smythe signed a total of 31 players for only $32,000. Although the Rangers hadn't played a single game, they were — on paper — a powerhouse. And what did Smythe get for his troubles? He was fired before the season opener in a dispute with Garden management. Following his dismissal, Smythe returned to Toronto where he became a hockey legend by piloting the Maple Leafs to many years of glory. The Rangers' owners then hired Lester Patrick to manage and coach the pieces Smythe had put in place.

On the ice the Rangers were even more of an instant success story than the Bruins. In their first season, 1926-27, they finished an impressive 25-13-6, good for first place in the American Division. In only their second season they won the Stanley Cup — and did it with the help of an unexpected hero.

After eliminating Pittsburgh and Boston, the Rangers found themselves in the Stanley Cup finals against the Montreal Maroons, who shut them out by a score of 2-0 in Game One.

Clark collection

Nels Stuart in his first year at Cleveland before joining the Montreal Maroons to win the Stanley Cup in 1926. Stewart was the first player to score 300 goals in the NHL.

Early in the second period of Game Two, Ranger goalie Lorne Chabot was forced to leave after catching a puck in the eye off the stick of Nels Stewart. In need of a replacement, Lester Patrick asked Maroons' manager Eddie Gerard for permission to use either Ottawa's Alex Connell or minor leaguer Hughie McCormick, both of whom were goalies who happened to be in the crowd. When Gerard refused, an upset Patrick returned to the Rangers dressing room asking his club for suggestions.

Frank Boucher — half-kidding — suggested, "How about you playing goal?"[1]

Patrick, who was 44, retired, and had never played goal, pondered the idea for a moment and then courageously replied, "Okay, I'll do it."[2]

Amazingly, Patrick turned aside 18 of 19 shots over a 43-minute span to lead his team to an overtime win which tied the series at a game apiece. The Rangers went on to win the series in five games thanks to two game-winning goals by Boucher.

The next logical area for NHL expansion was the Midwest. Chicago and Detroit were chosen as the sites.

The Blackhawks treated their Windy City fans to a fine inaugural season, finishing just below the .500 mark and qualifying for the playoffs. The Hawks were a scoring machine in that first year, lighting the lamp a league-leading 115 times. They had the second and fifth leading scorers in the league in their captain, Dick Irvin (18-18-36), and former Toronto sniper Babe Dye (25-5-30). But then they were cursed.

At the end of the 1926-27 campaign, owner Fred McLaughlin fired coach Pete Muldoon. Muldoon, upset over his unfair dismissal — according to legend — placed a "curse" on McLaughlin by supposedly warning him that the Hawks would never win an NHL regular season title. This "curse" lasted 40 years. It wasn't until 1967 that Chicago would finish first overall.

Without Muldoon the Hawks suffered back-to-back cellar finishes. Despite the "Muldoon Curse" the Blackhawks enjoyed some success in the thirties. They were Cup-winners in 1933-34, and again in 1937-38.

Michigan's hunger for pro hockey was satisfied when a Detroit syndicate bought the Victoria Cougars of the Western League and moved them to the Motor City. After finishing their first season in the cellar of the American Division, the club began to rebound the next season with a new leader and a new home.

Ownership named former Toronto star Jack Adams as manager and coach and moved the team into a sparkling new arena — Olympia Stadium. With Adams at the helm the club immediately improved to the .500 mark in 1927-28. In 1930 the franchise changed its nickname from Cougars to Falcons. Three years later Chicago industrialist James Norris, who had operated the semipro Chi-

cago Shamrocks, bought both the hockey team and the arena and renamed the Falcons the Red Wings. Like their Midwestern rivals, the Blackhawks, the Wings managed to reach hockey's highest pinnacle by the mid-thirties when they won back-to-back Stanley Cups in 1935-36 and 1936-37. Their 1937-38 squad included American-born defenseman Peter Bessone, who starred in football, baseball and hockey at West Springfield, Massachusetts High School. Bessone was later a member of the 1944-45 Calder Cup Champion Cleveland Barons with Minneapolis-raised Earl Bartholome, one of the AHL's best all-around players. Peter's brother Amo was varsity hockey coach at Michigan Tech and later Michigan State.

Both Chicago and Detroit experienced considerable box office success in those early days. That early success was solidified by their Cup triumphs of the mid-thirties. The NHL was firmly-rooted in the Midwest.

While the National Hockey League was in the business of providing five of Uncle Sam's major cities the privilege of witnessing the best hockey in the world, the American amateur ranks continued to grow.

In 1925 the Eastern Amateur Hockey Association was born. Boston entries included the Boston AA and the Pere Marquette Council of the Knights of Columbus. New York, which had not enjoyed amateur hockey since the closing of the American Amateur Hockey League during World War I, entered three teams — the New York Athletic Club, the Knickerbocker Hockey Club and the once popular St. Nicks. Unfortunately, after only one full season, the EAHA was forced to shut down when the United States Amateur Hockey Association closed its doors in early 1927.

The EAHA was only one of several leagues to come into existence in the mid-twenties. One of the more prominent ones was the Central Hockey Association, which was formed in 1925. The CHA was a six-team league featuring Duluth, Minneapolis, St. Paul, Winnipeg, Hibbing-Eveleth, and American Soo. In 1925-26 the Minneapolis Rockets captured what was to be the only Central Hockey Association title, as later in 1926 the CHA went pro and became the American Hockey Association, which lasted through 1942.

The AHA kept sites in Duluth, Minneapolis, St. Paul and Winnipeg and added Chicago. In time franchises were added in the South when Tulsa, Kansas City, Omaha, St. Louis, Wichita, Dallas and Fort Worth entered the AHA fold.

In 1925 a professional league was formed on the West Coast called the California Hockey League. It featured teams mostly from Southern California and the Bay Area. Los Angeles, Hollywood, Culver City, Oakland and San Francisco were among the cities to ice teams in the CHL, which folded after the 1932-33 season.

The following year saw an explosion of new leagues in North America, many of which were American-based. Below is a list of amateur and pro leagues that came into existence in 1926:

NAME	LASTED UNTIL
Amateur:	
Copper Country League	1929
Arrowhead League	1931
American Hockey Association	1942
Metro Amateur Hockey Association	*
Pro:	
Canadian Professional Hockey league	1929
Canadian-American Hockey League	1936
Prairie Hockey League	1928
* Eventually became Metro Junior League	

COPPER COUNTRY LEAGUE CHAMPS

1927	Calumet
1928	Calumet
1929	Ironwood

Clark collection

The three Hanson Brothers, from the 1977 hit movie "Slapshot," were named after the original five Hanson Brothers who played for Augsburg College of Minneapolis in the 1920s.

Just when the amateur scene was beginning to thrive in the Land of Stars and Stripes, the organization that had built it up abruptly shut down. The United States Amateur Hockey Association closed its doors in 1927, and from 1927 to 1930 there was no controlling body for amateur hockey in America.

The lack of leadership not only affected the amateur ranks in a negative way but also proved catastrophic for the U.S. Olympic hockey program. As a result of the USAHA's demise the United States was unable to send a hockey team to the 1928 Winter Games at St. Moritz, Switzerland.

William S. Haddock of Pittsburgh, chairman of the Amateur Athletic Union Ice Hockey Committee, approached four teams regarding participation in the games — Harvard University; University Club of Boston (which featured the likes of George Owen, John Chase and Myles Lane); Eveleth Junior College; and Augsburg College of Minneapolis, led by the five Hanson Brothers. Either due to lack of funds or poor class attendance, all of the clubs but Augsburg passed on the chance. But after

Augsburg had accepted and was making plans to attend, General Douglas MacArthur, who was Chairman of the United States Olympic Committee, termed them "not representative of American hockey,"[3] and vetoed them as a choice.

As a result no U.S. team was sent to the games and a dark cloud hovered over amateur ice hockey in America.

Pro hockey was unaffected by the turmoil and continued to expand as two new leagues with franchises in both the U.S. and Canada were organized in the late twenties.

In 1928 the Pacific Coast Hockey League was formed with franchises in Seattle, Portland, Tacoma, Victoria and Vancouver. Although there has been some dispute over the question of how professional the PCHL really was, the league did bring the ice game back to some of the same cities that had previously held franchises in the old Pacific Coast Hockey Association. However, its existence was relatively short-lived. After only three seasons it closed down.

In 1929 the second league to be called the International Hockey League was organized. The new IHL iced teams in Detroit, Cleveland, Pittsburgh, Buffalo, Syracuse, Newark, Windsor, Stratford, Hamilton, London and Niagara Falls. It lasted until 1936 when it ceased operations and merged with the Canadian-American Hockey League (which had also folded) to form the American Hockey League.

While pro hockey was blooming and the amateur game was experiencing a lull, college hockey was becoming even more firmly established in the East as well as reaching out into parts of the Midwest and even the West Coast.

When the First World War came to an end, Eastern schools that previously had built up their programs, picked up where they had left off.

When ice hockey returned to Harvard in 1919 the team was without a home because the old Boston Arena had burned down in the fall of 1918. The team was forced to use any one of several outdoor rinks in Soldiers Field. In 1920 the situation was upgraded by the use of a new indoor rink in Cambridge called the Pavilion, which had an ice surface so tiny that only six men could play on a side. One of Harvard's more memorable comebacks occurred that season on Pavilion ice, when, trailing 4-1 going into the final period, the Crimson came storming back to defeat Yale 5-4.

When the new Boston Arena was erected in 1921, Harvard once again had a first-class facility on which to practice and play. The Arena continued to serve their needs until Boston Garden, the Boston Skating Club and the school's own Watson Rink were built.

The Yale ice hockey program received a boost in 1927 when a new arena opened in New Haven. The event was marked by a game between the Yale varsity and the St. Nicholas Hockey Club. The St. Nicks, with five former Yale captains, won in a hard-fought contest, 3-2.

Yale was coached by Holcombe York, a former goaltender who backstopped the Elis during the mid-teens. York's coaching career at Yale was highlighted by winning the national championship in 1922 and by sharing it in 1925, 1927, 1929, 1930, 1931 and 1935. He later co-authored a landmark text, *Hockey*, with former Yale star Dick Vaughan. S. Kip Farrington, in his historical account of early U.S. hockey, *Skates, Sticks & Men*, chose Vaughan as his first team all-star center for Yale for the period 1920-1945.

York coached Yale until 1938 when the legendary former Rangers ace John Murray Murdoch took over. Murdoch coached the Elis until 1966. During those years he guided Yale to many successful seasons. Murdoch was ex-

Clark collection

Ralph "Cooney" Weiland centered the famous "Dynamite Line" for the Boston Bruins before becoming coach at Harvard. Weiland scored 43 goals in 44 games for Boston in their 1928-29 championship season.

In 1934 the Ivy Hockey League was formed. Its member schools included Harvard, Yale, Princeton and Dartmouth. Later, when Army joined, it became the Pentagonal League. It was called the Ivy League again in 1948 when Army was replaced by Brown. Cornell became a member in 1958, and Pennsylvania joined in 1967, making it a seven-team circuit.

By the late twenties, many Eastern schools had adopted ice hockey as a varsity sport. Successful programs were established at such leading institutions as Boston University, Boston College, Northeastern, Holy Cross, Massachusetts, Williams, Springfield College (the YMCA college where basketball started), Vermont, Norwich, Middlebury, New Hampshire, Bowdoin, Bates, Providence College, Connecticut Agricultural College, Army, St. Lawrence, Union, Clarkson Tech, Colgate, Hamilton, and Rensselaer Polytechnic Institute.

College hockey was not divided into divisions in those early years. Small schools not only competed against each other but regularly against larger schools as well.

Boston University and Boston College gave ice hockey varsity status during World War I. The two large schools, both located not far from Harvard, clashed in what was BU's only game in its first season of 1917-18. The BU Terriers defeated their crosstown rivals by the score of 3-1. The following season BU's only game was a loss as BC returned the favor by the same score.

Each year BU added more games to its schedule and in 1924-25 enjoyed its first winning season (7-5-1) under rookie coach George Gann. Gann remained behind the Terriers' bench until 1928-29 when he was replaced by Wayland Vaughn, who kept the reigns until 1939-40.

Boston College's best season in those early years was 1922-23 when BC upped its schedule to 14 games and went 12-1-1 under the

tremely dedicated to the ice game and was known for his ability to get the most out of his teams. Harvard coach Cooney Weiland once said of him: "He's a great credit to hockey — especially college hockey...He teaches hockey as it should be played in college. His teams have always been sound fundamentally. They've always shown desire, hustle, and will to win, regardless of material."[4]

Most of the fresh young talent with which colleges such as Harvard and Yale built their rosters came from some of the fine preparatory schools of the East. As the ice hockey programs at these colleges became more established, prep schools such as St. Paul's, Noble & Greenough, Milton Academy and Exeter continued to be major sources of talent.

leadership of coach Fred Rocque and captain Ed Garrity. A legacy began in 1932-33 when John "Snooks" Kelley took over as coach. Throughout a long and illustrious career at the Heights, Kelley guided the Eagles to many great triumphs, including the National Championship season of 1949 before he finally retired after the 1971-72 season.

Northeastern, another Boston institution, adopted ice hockey as a varsity sport in 1929-30. The Huskies played their home games at the Boston Arena. Their first coach, H. Nelson Raymond, established a solid ice hockey program at the school during his seven-year stint. His 1931-32 team finished an impressive 6-1-0, and his 1933-34 team, which was captained by the young man who would become the Huskies' next coach — H.W. Gallagher — went 6-2-2. Gallagher took over as coach in 1936 and remained behind the bench until 1955 when James Bell took over.

Providence College's first ice hockey team took the ice in 1926-27 and went 1-7-0 under three different coaches. Dr. Landry coached the team for two games, winning the first game 6-4, at Springfield. Team captain John Graham took over for the next four games and lost them all. Clement Trihey became the team's third coach for the final two games, losing both of them. Then, due to lack of ice, the program was halted until the 1952 season.

Many Eastern and Midwestern colleges encountered lack-of-ice problems in those early years. Schools were either forced to quit, as was the case with Providence, or had to exist on a hit or miss basis due to the weather.

Another Eastern hockey power in those days was Army, which was unique in that the Cadets played their home games in an enormous rink approximately 235 feet long.

An example of a smaller Eastern school with an excellent hockey program was Williams College. Under the direction of coach "Boots" Sniveley, it produced such stellar players as

Ben Langmaid, who captained the world champion 1933 national team; Harry Watkins and Whitney Popham, who went on to star for the St. Nicks; and Bill Moseley, the only of three brothers to "escape" from Harvard. He also played for the St. Nicks as well as the Wissahickon team of the Winter Club League.

Many of the Eastern non-Ivy League colleges united in 1938 when the Central Office for Eastern Intercollegiate Athletics opened in New York City. This was the forerunner of the Eastern Collegiate Athletic Conference. Asa Bushnell, the Office's first Executive Director, immediately set out to bring the various programs under the same umbrella. One of the first steps he took was to sponsor a schedule making convention, which soon became a standard procedure of the ECAC fall membership meeting. Aside from the Ivy League, the ECAC remained the sole conference in the East until 1984 when Hockey East was created.

The college game was also spreading across parts of the Midwest. Varsity programs were established at the University of Minnesota, Michigan, Michigan State, Michigan Tech, Marquette, Wisconsin and Notre Dame, as well as many of the small colleges in Minnesota where there were almost as many schools playing ice hockey as there are today.

The fraternity and intramural teams that were organized at the University of Minnesota during the teens continued to compete against one another after World War I. By 1920 there were more than 20 such teams. Around the same time a women's league was also organized at the university. Some of the women's teams were coached by frat players. In 1920-21 a men's team was organized by a student named Beaupre Eldridge and a few games were played as a varsity sport. But it wasn't until 1921 that the Athletic Board of Control officially made ice hockey a varsity sport.

The 1921-22 team under the guidance of

coach I.D. MacDonald and captain Chet Bros defeated Wisconsin, Luther Seminary, Hamline and Michigan Mines en route to an overall record of seven wins and three losses. They challenged the University of Michigan for the Big Ten title, but the challenge was declined.

In 1923 Emil Iverson, an exhibition skater and skating instructor from Denmark, became coach of the Gophers. A strong rivalry was established with Marquette University which was coached by Iverson's brother Kay. Iverson enjoyed instant success. His first team (1923-24) went 13-1-0 and was declared National Champion. They were led by captain Frank Pond and standout goalie Fred Schade.

The following season the Gophers moved into the newly constructed Minneapolis Arena where they brought the university no less than a share of top national honors for six consecutive seasons. During those years they compiled an astonishing record of 75-10-11. The 1925-26 squad, led by captain Ed Olson, went undefeated at 12-0-4.

In the fall of 1930 Two Harbors native and former varsity captain Frank Pond became head coach of Gopher hockey. Under Pond the Gophers continued to be successful, compiling a combined record of 34-8-1 during his first three seasons. Minnesota continued to compete against such schools as Michigan, Michigan Tech, Marquette and Wisconsin, while adding Manitoba to its schedule. Marquette dropped the sport after 1932-33 as did Wisconsin after the 1934-35 season.

In 1935-36 Pond was replaced by former St. Paul Saints coach Larry Armstrong. Armstrong coached the team for 12 seasons before giving way to ex-NHLer Doc Romnes in 1947. Former Gopher star defenseman John "Maroosh" Mariucci came on to coach the team in 1952-53 and lasted until 1965-66, with the exception of '55-56 when he was on leave.

During the late 1920s and early 1930s the following small Minnesota schools were playing varsity ice hockey: Eveleth Junior College, Moorhead Teachers College, Hamline, St. Johns, St. Paul Luther, Hibbing Junior College, Gustavus Adolphus, St. Mary's, St. Cloud Teachers College, St. Thomas, Macalester, Carleton, Duluth Junior College and Augsburg, which began its program in 1927 when the Hanson Brothers arrived.

Eveleth Junior College was coached by Cliff Thompson, the legendary coach of Eveleth High School, where from 1920-58 he compiled an astounding record of 534-26-9. Thompson's record at Eveleth Junior College wasn't too shabby either. He won 171 games and lost only 28. The most telling statistic related to Thompson's coaching prowess was that 11 of

Clark collection

The 1935-36 University of Minnesota squad featured goalie Bud Wilkinson, coach Larry Armstrong and Ted Mitchell. Wilkinson later became football coach at U of Oklahoma.

Clark collection

Coached by Cliff Thompson (top left), the 1926-27 Eveleth High School team featured seven players who later turned professional.

his players went on to play in the National Hockey league.

Perhaps most surprising is the fact that good college hockey was being played in California from the late twenties until just after the United States entered the Second World War. The California Hockey League (not to be confused with the pro league which went by the same name) was launched in 1929-30 and lasted through the 1941-42 season. Some of the best college hockey in the nation was played during its existence. Loyola of California, USC, UCLA, Southwestern, Los Angeles Junior College, the University of California at Berkeley and Santa Rosa Junior College all competed for the Hoover Cup, which was awarded annually to the League's champion. Curiously, the finals were held at an outdoor rink in Yosemite Park.

The CHL's member colleges also played teams such as the Gonzaga University Club in Spokane, Washington. Most of the league's best players were from Canada and Minnesota with a few coming from the Eastern U.S. During its existence Loyola and USC were not only the dominant teams of the CHL but were among the very best teams in the nation. Each school shared national honors four times.

The coaches of the two Western powers offered a stark contrast. Loyola's leader was a great all-around athlete who starred in hockey at Notre Dame, whereas USC was coached by a man who had no hockey background whatsoever.

Loyola was coached by Tom Lieb, a native of Faribault, Minnesota, who played football for Knute Rockne in 1921 and 1922. He won two NCAA discus titles and won the bronze medal in discus at the 1924 Olympics in Paris. He also coached football at Notre Dame under Rockne and led the 1929 team to the national title while taking the place of the hospitalized Rockne — a feat for which he never received proper recognition.

Loyola, located in Los Angeles, had dreams of playing big-time college football like nearby Catholic schools St. Mary's and Santa Clara. In the fall of 1930, Lieb was coaching football at Loyola. He recruited several football players from Minnesota's Iron Range. These players turned out to be outstanding hockey players as well and thus Loyola became a strong hockey school and yearly challenged USC for the Hoover Cup. Be-

Clark collection

The 1937-38 Loyola University Team, coached by Tom Lieb (far right) was composed almost entirely of players who later turned professional.

tween 1935 and 1938 Loyola went 47-5-3, winning a share of the national title each of those four years. However, after the 1938 season Lieb was fired. He then went to Florida State where he wound up as head football coach. His firing may have been a watershed moment for the ice game in the Southwest. Many believe that if Lieb had stayed at Loyola, college hockey would have continued to this day to be part of the athletic programs in Southern California.

USC's coach was Arnold Eddy, a native Californian who never owned a pair of skates and never even saw a hockey game before becoming coach of the Trojans in 1929. He learned to skate and mastered the rules of the game and soon was the winningest hockey coach in California. His teams shared national honors in 1933, 1939, 1941 and 1942. Like Lieb's Loyola squads, most of Eddy's players were from Canada and Minnesota with a few from the Eastern U.S.

The Loyola-USC games of the 1930s were bitterly fought and attended by large crowds and rabid fans. When his coaching days were over, Eddy remained at USC and became the school's athletic director.

The California Hockey League ceased operations in 1942, shortly after the United States entered the Second World War. After the war Cal-Berkeley was the only former CHL school to ice a team but only for a few years. No varsity college hockey has been played in California since 1949.

COLLEGE CHAMPIONS from 1918 to 1947

1918 War	1935 Clarkson, Yale, St. Cloud, Loyola of California
1919 War	
1920 Harvard	1936 Minnesota, Loyola of California, Clarkson, Harvard
1921 Harvard	
1922 Yale	1937 Harvard, Loyola of California
1923 Harvard, Boston College, Dartmouth	1938 Dartmouth, Loyola of California, Gonzaga
1924 Minnesota	
1925 Minnesota, Yale, Dartmouth	1939 Dartmouth, Minnesota, USC
1926 Minnesota, Harvard	1940 Minnesota
1927 Minnesota, Michigan, Yale, Dartmouth	1941 Princeton, Bos. College, Illinois, USC
1928 Minnesota, Marquette, Harvard, Eveleth Junior College	1942 Dartmouth, Bos. College, Illinois, USC, Colorado College
1929 Minnesota, Eveleth Junior College, Yale	1943 Dartmouth, Minnesota
1930 Yale, Marquette, Harvard	1944 Dartmouth
1931 Yale, Michigan, Marquette	1945 Dartmouth, Minnesota
1932 Harvard, Minnesota, Princeton	1946 Michigan
1933 Minnesota, Harvard, USC	1947 Dartmouth, Michigan
1934 Minnesota	1948 Start of NCAA Tourney

When the stock market crashed in 1929 the United States found itself in the throes of the Great Depression. But in 1930 amateur and Olympic hockey was revived when the Amateur Athletic Union assumed control of the sport ending a five-year span without a governing body.

Beginning in 1931 the Amateur Athletic Association of the United States (AAAUS) — operated by the AAU — organized a national championship playoff as a springboard to the 1932 Olympics. The New York Crescent AC was the first winner of this tournament. It continued until 1937, when the Amateur Hockey Association of the United States (AHAUS) took control.

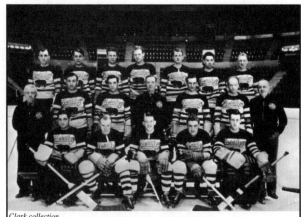

Clark collection

Hershey Bears, 1937-38 Eastern Amateur Hockey League Champions.

AAAUS NATIONAL CHAMPIONS

1931	New York Crescent AC
1932	Atlantic City Sea Gulls
1933	Atlantic City Sea Gulls
1934	Detroit White Star Oilers
1935	Chicago Baby Ruths HC
1936	No Series (Due to Extensive Olympic Tryout Program)
1937	Boston Olympics

AAU CHAMPIONS / AHA CHAMPIONS

	AAU CHAMPIONS	AHA CHAMPIONS
1938	Boston Olympics	Hershey Bears
1939	Cleveland American Legion	NY Rovers
1940	University of Minnesota	Holzbaugh Fords
1941	St. Nicholas HC	Atlantic City Sea Gulls
1942	Boston College	NY Rovers
1943	War Year	Coast Guard Cutters
1944	War Year	Coast Guard Cutters
1945	War Year	Seattle Ironmen
1946	War Year	Vancouver Canucks
1947	Hanover (NH) Indians	Boston Olympics
1948	Colgate University	Toledo Mercurys
1949	No Championship Held	Spokane Flyers
1950	No Championship Held	Spokane Flyers/Chatham Maroons
1951	No Championship Held	Toledo Mercurys

The amateur game in the 1930s was best described by St. Nick's and Crescent Athletic Club star Stewart Iglehart. Although some of Iglehart's Crescent teammates such as the Colville Brothers, Alex Shibicky, Muzz Patrick, Joe Cooper and Bert Gardiner, all opted for professional careers with the New York Rangers, Stewart preferred to remain amateur. In a 1935 edition of the Literary Digest, he explained:

"Amateur hockey has been terribly successful. It often outdraws professional hockey even in the Garden. There is more spirit in amateur play. The crowds are strongly partisan...there is more spirit to play — and the crowds go wild."[5]

His teammate Neil Colville, however, probably best expressed the practical side of why players left the less-pressured more spirited amateur ranks for the pros when he said, "Playing with the Crescents is a lot of fun but a fellow can't be broke all his life."[6]

If a player wanted to play pro hockey but wasn't good enough for the NHL, there were other options. Those options were expanded in 1931 with the Central Hockey League which began as an amateur league but changed to professional in its second season. Based in Minnesota, the CHL lasted from 1931-32 through 1934-35. In its maiden season the Central League's member teams were Minneapolis, St. Paul, Virginia, Eveleth and Hibbing. After one season Virginia dropped out making it a four-team league until Duluth came along in 1933. The League, with few exceptions, was comprised of Minnesota natives and competed favorably with the American Hockey Association as part of an interlocking schedule in 1934-35. That season St. Paul defeated St. Louis three games to none in the interleague playoffs. Crowds of 5,000-6,000 attended many of these games. Results of the interlocking scheduled games and the playoffs attest to the fact that the Central League's

level of play was on a par with that of the AHA.

Clark collection

Former Yale star Stewart Iglehart when he was starring with the New York Rovers before coming to the St. Nicks.

Having failed to place a team in the 1928 Winter Olympic Games and the first-ever world championship tournament in 1930, amateur hockey in the U.S. — thanks to the Amateur Athletic Union — was back on track and ready to return to international competition.

The second world championship ice hockey tournament was held in 1931 at Krynicka, Poland. The U.S. rebounded with a second place finish, setting the stage for its return to Olympic competition the following year.

The 1932 Olympic team was coached by Harvard legend Ralph Winsor who led a strong squad of players such as Douglas Everett, Ding Palmer and the team's captain John Chase, another Harvard man who went on to coach the Crimson in the '40s. The result was another silver medal for the Yanks — the up side of which being that whenever you can finish second in the world in any competition, you've done very well. The down side, however, was that once again the members of Uncle Sam's team were bridesmaids to their rivals from the north.

The United States next iced a team which launched an extensive European tour, the highlight of which would be the 1933 World Championship at Prague, Czechoslovakia. The team was managed by Walter Brown of

Boston who selected a squad of ten players, seven of whom were Bostonians.

Among the Beantowners chosen were ex-Notre Dame football ace Frank Holland; center Chan Hilliard of Dartmouth; left winger Sherman Forbes of Boston University; center and right winger Pete Sanford of Boston College; defenseman John Garrison of Harvard; goaltender Gerry Cosby; and Ben Langmaid, a tall, stocky defenseman from Williams who served as captain.

The three non-Boston selections were Yalemen Stewart Iglehart, Jimmy Breckenridge and Ding Palmer. Iglehart, who was also a world class polo player, was hockey's answer to a utility infielder, pitching in at defense, center and right wing during the trip.

Breckenridge was a solid right winger who was known for having a hard as well as heavy shot. And Palmer — a sniper at left wing — was considered by many, including goaltender Gerry Cosby, as the greatest hockey player Yale ever had.

On Christmas Eve of 1932 the team called the Boston Olympics — which upon its arrival in Europe was nicknamed the "Massachusetts Rangers" — set out on the four-month, seven-country trip. While visiting Great Britain, France, Germany, Italy, Switzerland, Austria and Czechoslovakia, the U.S. team compiled an amazing record of 44 wins, 3 losses and 3 ties, scoring 240 goals to their opponent's 40.

This was the third successive year that the team known as the Boston Olympics under Brown's direction had made a successful invasion of Europe. This trip, however, was unique as the team received the permission of the Amateur Athletic Union to attend the world championship tournament at Prague from February 19-26.

By mid-February, the team had concluded the partying that was characteristic earlier on the trip and was ready to get down to the business of serious hockey. After successive shutouts over Switzerland, Poland, Czechoslovakia and, again, Poland, the U.S. team found itself in the finals against the Canadian Allan Cup Champion Toronto Nationals.

The tourney's feature game was a tight, defensive, hard-fought battle. By the end of regulation the game was knotted at 1-1. The game was decided in dramatic fashion when John Garrison, the tournament's standout performer who hadn't joined the squad until the world championship had begun, scored in overtime to give the United States its first-ever world title in ice hockey. For a short period Uncle Sam stepped out of Canada's shadow, thanks to a 2-1 final-round victory over their "mentors" from the north.

Team Members	College	Hometown
Frank Holland	Notre Dame	Brookline, MA
Channing Hilliard	BU	Arlington, MA
Sherman Forbes	Boston U	Arlington, MA
Pete Sanford	BC	Melrose, MA
John Garrison	Harvard	Newton, MA
Gerald Cosby	None	Roxbury, MA
Benjamin Langmaid	Williams	Swampscott, MA
Stewart Iglehart	Yale	Westbury, NY
James Breckenridge	Yale	New York, NY
Winthrop "Ding" Palmer	Yale	Warehouse Pt., CT

RESULTS OF GAMES:

USA	7	Switzerland	0
USA	4	Poland	0
USA	6	Czechoslovakia	0
USA	4	Austria	0
USA	2	Canada	1

NATIONAL TEAM CHAMPIONS & USA FINISH

Year	Site	Champion & Runnerup	USA Finish
1930	Germany & France	Canada Germany	*
1931	Krynicka, Poland	Canada USA	2nd
1933	Prague, Czechoslovakia	USA Canada	1st
1934	Milan, Italy	Canada USA	2nd
1935	Davos, Switzerland	Canada Switzerland	*
1937	London, England	Canada Great Britain	*
1938	Prague, Czechoslovakia	Canada Great Britain	8th
1939	Switzerland	Canada United States	2nd
1947	Prague, Czechoslovakia	Czechoslovakia Sweden	5th
1949	Stockholm, Sweden	Czechoslovakia Canada	3rd
1950	London, England	Canada United States	2nd
1951	Paris, France	Canada Sweden	5th
1953	Switzerland	Sweden Germany	*
1954	Stockholm, Sweden	USSR Canada	*
1955	Germany	Canada USSR	4th
1957	Moscow, USSR	Sweden USSR	*
1958	Oslo, Norway	Canada USSR	5th

1959	Czechoslovakia	Canada	4th
		USSR	
1961	Geneva, Switzerland	Canada	7th
		Czechoslovakia	
1962	Colorado Springs, CO, USA	Sweden	3rd
		Canada	
1963	Stockholm, Sweden	USSR	8th
		Sweden	
1965	Tampere, Finland	USSR	6th
		Czechoslovakia	
1966	Ljudljana, Yugoslavia	USSR	6th
		Czechoslovakia	
1967	Vienna, Austria	USSR	5th
		Sweden	
1969	Stockholm, Sweden	USSR	6th
		Sweden	
1970	Stockholm, Sweden	USSR	* *
		Sweden	
1971	Geneva, Switzerland	USSR	6th
		Czechoslovakia	
1973	Moscow, USSR	USSR	* *
		Sweden	
1974	Helsinki, Finland	USSR	* *
		Czechoslovakia	
1975	West Germany	USSR	6th
		Czechoslovakia	
1977	Vienna, Austria	Czechoslovakia	6th
		Sweden	
1978	Prague, Czechoslovakia	USSR	6th
		Czechoslovakia	
1979	Moscow, USSR	USSR	7th
		Czechoslovakia	
1981	Gothenburg, Sweden	USSR	5th
		Sweden	
1982	Finland	USSR	8th
		Czechoslovakia	
1983	West Germany	USSR	* *
		Czechoslovakia	
1985	Prague, Czechoslovakia	Czechoslovakia	4th
		Canada	
1986	Moscow, USSR	USSR	6th
		Sweden	
1987	Vienna, Austria	Sweden	7th
		USSR	

1989	Stockholm, Sweden	USSR	6th
		Canada	
1990	Bern & Fribourg, Switz.	USSR	5th
		Sweden	
1991	Turku & Tampere, Finland	Sweden	4th
		Canada	
1992	Prague & Bratislava, Czech.	Sweden	7th
		Finland	
1993	Dortmund & Munchen, Germany	Russia	6th
		Sweden	
1995	Stockholm & Gavle, Sweden	Finland	6th
		Sweden	
1996	Vienna, Austria	Czech Republic	3rd
		Canada	
1997	Turku & Tampere, Finland	Canada	6th
		Sweden	

* U.S. did not play   * * U.S. competed in Pool "B"

The year 1933 was significant for several reasons, not the least of which was the appearance of two more leagues. One was the Eastern Amateur Hockey League, an outgrowth of the Tri-State League of the previous season. The other was the Northwestern Hockey League, a pro circuit which evolved when the Western Canadian Hockey League dropped Regina and Saskatoon and added Seattle and Portland.

In 1934 St. Louis became the sixth American city to get a National Hockey League franchise when the Ottawa Senators left the Canadian Capital for the Gateway City to become the St. Louis Eagles. The NHL's move into America's heartland was short-lived. After only one season the St. Louis franchise dissolved. Although the team — as it had for the past several seasons of its Ottawa existence — finished last, Missourians did get a brief taste of pro hockey at its highest level. The Eagles featured the first NHL player from North Dakota in "Fido" Purpur, who, while with Chicago in the Forties, was used to shadow the great Maurice "Rocket" Richard.

Stan Fischler collection

"Dog" is a term used for lousy hockey players. Here's a really good one named after a pup — Cliff "Fido" Purpur of the 1937-38 Chicago Blackhawks.

When his playing days were over, Purpur coached the University of North Dakota from 1949-56.

The 1936 U.S. Olympic Hockey Team was coached by Hamilton College coach Al Prettyman and captained by Harvard's John Garrison, the hero of the 1933 world championship. At the Winter Games at Garmisch, Germany the U.S. won the bronze, again finishing behind Canada, but this time in more ways than one. Their third place finish found them behind not only the team which was sent to represent their border rivals, but gold medal winner Great Britain, which somehow managed to ice a team made up of mostly Canadians.

Later in 1936 two leagues with teams in both the U.S. and Canada arrived on the North American hockey scene. The International Amateur League was comprised of teams from Minnesota's Iron Range and Ontario. Its members were Duluth, Eveleth, Hibbing, Virginia, Fort Frances, Fort William and Port Arthur. The other was a pro league called the International American Hockey League, with franchises in Springfield, Boston, New Haven, Providence, Philadelphia, The Bronx, Indianapolis, Hershey and Quebec.

In 1937 the Amateur Athletic Association of the United States was replaced by the Amateur Hockey Association of the United States (AHAUS) as the game's governing body. AHAUS was founded by Thomas Lockhart, who also was responsible for organizing the Eastern Amateur Hockey League in 1933. Although AHAUS eventually changed its name to USA Hockey, the organization still administers and promotes the amateur game today.

Having made their mark in international competition, Americans — with the rare exception of a Taffy Abel — had yet to make an impact on the NHL. But that would soon change thanks to Major Fred McLaughlin, the eccentric owner of the Chicago Blackhawks.

By the mid-'30s there were only a handful of American-born players in the NHL, and nine of them (including the coach) played for the same team — the Blackhawks. How competitive could this team be with so many Americans on its roster? Not good enough to finish even close to .500, but good enough to win a Stanley Cup! The story of the 1937-38 Cinderella Chicago Blackhawks is an incredible one.

Major McLaughlin had a habit of firing coaches. He had gone through ten of them over a six-year span. At the beginning of the 1937-38 season the unpredictable owner hired a referee, Bill Stewart, to coach the team. Stewart, who was also a National League baseball umpire during the summer months, was from Boston so he fit perfectly into McLaughlin's American theme.

The Hawks were led by a pair of Minnesota boys — goalie sensation Mike Karakas and speedy rookie center Carl "Cully" Dahlstrom. Karakas, one of a long line of fine hockey players to hail from Eveleth, won the Calder Trophy as the league's top rookie in 1935-36 when he posted a 1.92 goals-against average and nine shutouts in 48 games. Dahlstrom, a product of Minneapolis South High, was discovered by McLaughlin while playing for the Minneapolis Millers of the American Hockey Association and would soon become the 1937-38 Calder Trophy winner.

When the NHL's regular season came to an end in late March of 1938, the Hawks barely qualified for the postseason with a disappointing record of 14-25-9. For a first round playoff opponent the Hawks drew the Montreal Canadiens. (The two-game, total-goals format which had been used to decide the first two playoff rounds was replaced in 1937 by a best-of-three series.) The series came down to overtime of Game Three. With almost 12 minutes gone by, Paul Thompson scored to propel

The Cinderella Hawks fought off the New York Americans in the semi-finals of the 1938 Stanley Cup playoffs before ousting Toronto for the Cup.

Stan Fischler collection

the Hawks into the semi-finals and a date with the New York Americans.

With New York leading the series 1-0, the teams battled through regulation of Game Two to a scoreless tie. The surprising Hawks now had their backs to the wall and were desperately in need of another overtime hero. The teams continued their scoreless struggle for better than 13 minutes of extended play until Cully Dahlstrom gave the Hawks new life with a series-tying tally. The Hawks completed the comeback by taking Game Three and the series from the Amerks to earn a trip to the Stanley Cup finals.

Chicago's final round opponent, Toronto, had surprisingly disposed of the heavily-favored Bruins in three straight games.

Just prior to Game One in Toronto, Hawks goalie Mike Karakas was forced out of the lineup because of an injured toe. Bill Stewart wanted to use Ranger goalie Dave Kerr, who was in attendance, but Leafs manager Conn Smythe refused. Stewart and Smythe then engaged in a tiff outside the dressing room before both parties finally agreed that the replacement would be Pittsburgh's Alfie Moore, who was found at a nearby pub where he planned to listen to the game. Moore served as a more than adequate replacement for Karakas and backstopped Chicago to a 3-1 victory.

NHL president Frank Calder declared Moore ineligible for the rest of the series, leaving Stewart and the Blackhawks still looking for a viable replacement. A search went out for Paul Goodman, a backup goalie in the Hawks organization whom Stewart had never even seen, let alone seen perform. Goodman was finally found in a movie theater two and a half hours before game time and summoned to suit up. Toronto bounced the Hawks 5-1 to tie the best-of-five series at one game apiece.

The third game found Karakas back in goal with a steel-toed boot. Doc Romnes thrilled the jam-packed Chicago Stadium when he scored late in the third period to break a 1-1 tie. Once again the Hawks had the upper hand in the series.

In the second period of Game Four Johnny Gottselig set up Carl Voss for the go-ahead strike and the amazing Hawks never looked back en route to a 4-1, Cup-clinching victory. The newly-crowned champs sprinted over to the goal and carried Karakas off the ice before more than 17,000 screaming fans. Uncle Sam's impact had now been felt in hockey's premier league.

On the following page is a list of the American-born Blackhawks of 1937-38, broken into two categories — American developed and Canadian developed.

Not until the last decade of the 20th cen-

U.S. BORN & DEVELOPED

Name	Position	Born
Bill Stewart	Coach	Boston, MA
Mike Karakas	Goalie	Eveleth, MN
Carl Dahlstrom	Center	Minneapolis, MN
Virgil Johnson	Defenseman	Minneapolis, MN
Doc Romnes	Forward	White Bear Lake, MN
Vic Heyliger	Center	Concord, MA

U.S. BORN, CANADIAN DEVELOPED

Name	Position	Born
Alex Levinsky	Defenseman	Syracuse, NY
Carl Voss	Center	Chelsea, MA
Louis Trudel	Left Wing	Salem, MA
Roger Jenkins	Defenseman	Appleton, WI

tury would there be as many Americans on a Stanley Cup winner as the 1938 Cinderella Blackhawks. But from a fan interest standpoint, many more converts would soon be made in New England and Michigan thanks to Cup triumphs by Boston and Detroit.

The Boston Bruins were the next American-based franchise to experience great success. The Bruins of the late thirties-early forties were led by the legendary "Kraut Line" of Milt Schmidt, Bobby Bauer and Woody Dumart, with "Mr. Zero," Frankie Brimsek, one of several great goaltenders to hail from Eveleth, Minnesota between the pipes. Brimsek earned his flattering nickname just after he was called to the NHL by posting an incredible six shutouts in his first eight games. This version of the Black and Gold won two Stanley Cups just prior to World War II — in 1938-39 and 1940-41.

After the Bruins'1941 Stanley Cup triumph, the Detroit Red Wings were the only American-based franchise to win the Cup until the Chicago Blackhawks brought home the hardware in 1961. The Wings treated their loyal Michigan fans to an impressive five Cup victories from 1943 to 1955.

By the late '30s high school hockey was played only in most of the hockey-concentrated areas of the country. But an event of major importance occurred in 1938 when Brookline High coach and athletic director Tom Hines, who was also president of the Eastern Massachussets Hockey League, organized the Metropolitan Hockey Tournament, which was not only the first official state tournament in Massachusetts, but in the United States as well. Dr. Henry Lynch from Cambridge Rindge & Latin School, who ran the Greater Boston League, was also instrumental in arranging this landmark event. It was held at the old Boston Arena before a crowd of about 500, who witnessed four schools from the

Clark collection

Frankie Brimsek of Eveleth, MN, backstopped the Boston Bruins to two Stanley Cups just prior to World War II.

1912 Mechanic Arts High School Team, St. Paul, Minnesota.

Clark collection

eastern part of the state battle it out for the right to be called the best in the Bay State. Central Massachussets teams began competing in the late forties and in 1968 schools from the western part of the state began taking part in the competition. The entire tournament was played at Boston Arena until 1970 when the finals were played at the Boston Garden. Today the tournament is broken up into divisions and played at various sites includ-

ing five dates at Boston's FleetCenter and four dates at Boston College's Conte Forum. The top division (Div. 1-A) is comprised of eight teams. They are chosen by committee to play-off in a double-elimination format for the state championship. Both public and Catholic schools are eligible to compete. Private schools have their own tournament which encompasses all of New England.

The next state to organize a statewide high

High school hockey was also popular in New York City in the early 1900s. Pictured is the 1908 De Witt Clinton High School Team.

Clark collection

From 1970 to 1995, the old Boston Garden was the site of the Massachusetts State High School Hockey Tournament.

Steve Babineau

Chelmsford (MA) High celebrates after capturing the 1995 Division 1 championship at the Boston Garden.

Brian Babineau

school tournament was Minnesota in 1945. It was organized by schoolboy hockey pioneer Eugene Aldrich. Future University of Michigan star Wally Grant, who was a member of the famous "G" line, scored both the tying and go-ahead goals to lead Eveleth High over Thief River Falls in the championship game of that first-ever Minnesota State High School Hockey Tournament. By the early '70s the three-day, eight-team tourney drew as many as 100,000 fans. Today it is divided into two tournaments for levels A & AA. Together they draw about 130,000 people.

Roseau High took the title in 1946 under the guidance of coach Oscar Almquist, a former Eveleth High goaltender better known as the "Giant of the North." Almquist retired in 1967 after leading Roseau to four state championships and compiling an outstanding record of 404-148-51.

St. Paul Johnson, one of several dominant St. Paul schools, won in 1947 before Eveleth returned to the top of the Gopher State schoolboy ranks by winning four consecutive state championships from 1948-51.

Another dominant high school in the Land of 10,000 Lakes was International Falls, which was coached by former University of Minnesota star Larry Ross. Under Ross' tutelage, the Broncos won six state championships and an incredible 58 straight games from 1964-66. Ross, who also started the hockey program at Rainy River Community College and wrote a book entitled *Hockey For Everyone*, received the National High School Special Sports Award, awarded by the National High School Athletic Coaches Association, in 1985.

Other states to follow suit and stage state championship tournaments were New Hampshire and Maine in 1947, and Connecticut in 1948. By 1987 there were 18 states nationwide with high schools playing varsity ice hockey. Today there are 25 and the number is still growing.

As was the case with the First World War, World War II inevitably interrupted the progress of sports at the college, amateur and professional levels. The Eastern Amateur Hockey League, however, was a rare beneficiary of the War years during the 1942-43 and 1943-44 seasons thanks to the addition of a special team to its circuit — the Coast Guard Cutters.

Each player was a serviceman in the United States Coast Guard, stationed at Curtis Bay, Baltimore. Captain Clifford MacLean, a former hockey player who was stationed there at the time, was responsible for organizing the team. The Cutters were a conglomeration of NHLers, American Leaguers and amateurs. The result of this unique blend of mostly American hockey talent was a powerhouse club that dominated during the only two years of its existence, winning two National Senior Open Championships, two EAHL regular season titles, and an EAHL championship.

Other member teams of the EAHL at that time were the Boston Olympics, the New York Rovers and the Philadelphia Falcons, who featured future NHL player, coach and general manager Emile "The Cat" Francis.

Non-league opponents included teams from the New York Metropolitan League; some Canadian service teams such as the Ottawa Commandos, featuring the Colville brothers, Neil and Mac; a Navy team from Toronto, HMCS York; the Commandos who played at Uline Arena in Washington; the Hershey Bears; and the Detroit Red Wings, who were Stanley Cup champions in 1942-43.

The Cutters were coached by Mel Harwood, a former NHL referee, who while serving duty was given the not-so-flattering title of Second Class Motor Machinist. The squad was made up in large part of Minnesota players, with some coming from Massachusetts, New York, and Upper Michigan as well as Canada.

Among the more notable members of the Cutters were NHL stars John "Maroosh" Mariucci of the Chicago Blackhawks, Boston puckstopper Frankie Brimsek, Detroit center Alex Motter and defenseman Art Coulter, who captained the New York Rangers to the Stanley Cup in 1939-40.

Added to the cast were American Hockey League stars Bud Cook and Eddie Olson, both of whom played for the Cleveland Barons and came from big hockey families. Bud, who was Canadian-born, was the younger brother of NHL greats Bill and Bun Cook. Olson was one of nine brothers from a great Marquette hockey family who later went on to coach Victoria of the Western Hockey League, making him the only American up until that time to coach a Canadian pro team.

Other key players included Kenny Lundberg, a forward who played for the Boston Olympics; Joe Kucler, a winger from

Left: John "Maroosh" Mariucci led the Coast Guard Cutters to the 1943 EAHL championship. *Right:* Lieutenant Commander Clifford MacLean organized the Cutters.

Stan Fischler collection

Stan Fischler collection

Clark collection

United States Coast Guard Cutters, Eastern Amateur Hockey League champs 1942-43. Front (l to r): Cotlow; Dill; Mariucci; Lt. Commander Maclean; Murray; Nelson; Coulter, Captain; Kucler; Olson; Gilray. Middle: Brown; Dupuy; Hunter; Reilly; Webright; Corsetti; Hale; Barry; Plitt; Dunsmore. Back: Mel Harwood, Coach; C.W.O. Alvin Lane, Business Manager; Captain LeRoy Reinburg, Commandant, Coast Guard Yard; E. Zemarel, Scorekeeper; Karademoulis, Asst. Trainer; Weidner, Trainer; Captain B.C. Thron, Executive Officer, Coast Guard Yard; Lt. R.W. Beall, Asst. Manager; C.P.O. Ed Rittenhouse, Secretary-Treasurer

Eveleth, Minnesota, who was the EAHL's leading scorer in 1942-43 playing on a line with Lundberg and Olson; and goalie Hub Nelson from Minneapolis, who over a 12-year pro career in the Central League and the American Hockey Association recorded an outstanding 1.87 goals-against average. Nelson was considered by many as the best American goalie who never played in the NHL. Another top Cutters goalie was Muzz Murray.

The following players rounded out the rest of the Coast Guard Cutters squad during either or both of their two seasons of existence: Lieutenant Commander C.R. Captain MacLean; Bob Dill, a defenseman who later played for the New York Rangers; Ozzie Asmundson, a winger who played for the 1932 Rangers; Eddie Barry, a winger from Boston who played for the Boston Olympics and the Bruins after the war before becoming the head coach at U Mass; Manny Cotlow, a defenseman from Minnesota; Charlie Plitt, a winger who played minor league baseball as a pitcher; Sonny Hunter, a winger from Boston; Billy Purcell, a winger who had played for the Washington Lions of the American League; Milt Dunsmore, a center who played

in Florida; center Bobby Gilray; defenseman Gerry Dupuy; Jack Brown; Tommy Curry; John Webright; Sammy Hale; Tommy Brennan; John Chambers; and Mike Nardello, a center and defenseman for the EAHL's New York Rovers, who joined the Cutters just after graduating from St. Francis Prep in Brooklyn.

Nardello, who now serves as an off-ice official for the New Jersey Devils and an evaluator of officials for USA Hockey, remembers how awestruck he was after he received the call of duty and suddenly found himself among the likes of Mariucci and company.

"I can relate to some of these kids who are brought up today as teenagers and put alongside established NHL players who have been around for a long time," says Nardello. "Some of those guys like Mariucci, Coulter, Bud Cook, and Hub Nelson were about 10 or 11 years older than me."

When the Cutters' second season ended in late March of 1944 their team members were either sent out on assignment or reassigned to different parts of the world. When the war's end was imminent the following fall, the team was disbanded and its players left the service either to rejoin their old teams or join new ones.

EAHL CHAMPIONS

1934 Atlantic City Seagulls
1935 New York Crescents
1936 Hershey Bears
1937 Hershey Bears
1938 Hershey Bears
1939 New York Rovers
1940 Baltimore Orioles
1941 Washington Eagles
1942 New York Rovers
1943 Coast Guard Cutters
1944 Boston Olympics
1945 Boston Olympics
1946 Boston Olympics
1947 New York Rovers
1948 Baltimore Clippers

Clark collection

Boston Olympics, AHAUS National Junior champions, 1942. Front (l to r): Al Cardiff; Tom Dugan; Frank Sullivan; Hans Marsden, Asst. Coach; Fred Terrazzano; Herb Galliher, Coach; Ernie Garron; Ray McCarthy; Jerry Bauer. Back: Ben Bertini, Trainer; Herb Ralby, Manager; Norman Walker; Hector Rousseau; Ralph Warburton; Mary DesRoche; Perly Grant; Bob Wallace; Russ Priestley; Bob Hall; A. Notagiacomo, Asst. Manager; Jim Lawson, Asst. Trainer.

A college feat of significance that began during the War years was Dartmouth College's 46-game winning streak, which extended from 1942-46 under the guidance of Eddie Jeremiah, who coached the Indians from 1936-67. His best player during the streak was Dick Rondeau, who led the nation in scoring in 1941-42, and captained the 1942-43 and 1943-44 squads.

When the Second World War finally came to an end with the Allies claiming a glorious victory, it was once again time for the North American ice hockey scene to regroup and pick up the pieces and put them together again.

The first restoration project involved the reorganization of the American Hockey Association into the United States Hockey League. In its first season of 1945-46, the USHL's member teams were St. Paul, Minneapolis, Omaha, Dallas, Fort Worth, Tulsa, Kansas City, Louisville, Milwaukee, Houston and Denver. Until the League ceased operations at the end of the 1950-51 season, sports fans in each of these cites were given the opportunity to enjoy a quality brand of hockey at an affordable price.

In December of 1945 the International Hockey League organized as an outgrowth of the Windsor City Senior League. In its first year the IHL was comprised mostly of teams from in and around the Detroit-Windsor area, but before long it expanded into other areas of North America. The "I" continued to grow over the years, and, in doing so, it established the reputation it has today as one of the top professional leagues in all of hockey.

On June 10, 1947 the American Amateur Hockey Association came into existence. Its charter members were the Rochester Mustangs, St. Paul Tallys, St. Paul Koppys, Minneapolis Jerseys, Minneapolis Bermans and the White Bear Seven-ups. Through the years the league expanded into adjacent states

Clark collection

Duluth mayor George Johnson presents a key to the city to Duluth Glen Avon Pee Wee team after they captured the 1951 National Pee Wee Championship.

hockey teams, causing a controversy over which American team would be allowed to participate. The International Olympic Committee gave the nod to the AHAUS team because of its affiliation with the International Ice Hockey Federation. The IIHF had threatened to withdraw hockey from the Games if the AHAUS team was not allowed to play. The Swiss Organizing Committee had no choice but to go along with the wishes of the IIHF since it was planning to finance a great portion of the Games through ice hockey gate receipts. Without the finances, Switzerland would have been forced to abandon all of the Winter Games.

Although the AHAUS team missed out on a medal, it turned in a respectable fourth place finish. The team was coached by former National Team and Olympic star John Garrison. The squad featured such notables as forward Jack Garrity and defenseman Jack Kirrane. Garrity led Medford High School to the Massachusetts State Championship before going on to star at Boston University. Kirrane, a native of Brookline, Mass., would later help the 1960 Olympic team to a gold medal. A 16-year-old Minnesota high school star, center John Matchefts, was invited to Boston to try out for the team but was disqualified from the tryout because of state high school league rules. Matchefts did get his chance at Olympic competition in 1956, when he helped the U.S. earn a silver medal at Cortina, Italy.

In 1948 collegiate hockey got what a lot of today's college football fans, players and coaches have wanted for years — a national championship tournament. It was sponsored by the Broadmoor Hotel of Colorado Springs

and Canada before merging with the Midwest Junior League. After the merger it was composed of a combination of junior and senior teams but when the senior teams pulled out of the league it became a full-fledged junior circuit.

Another significant event occurred in 1947 when Donald Clark and Robert Ridder cofounded the Minnesota Amateur Hockey Association. While with the MAHA, Clark founded the first bantam level state tournament in the nation. The eight-team tournament, for ages 14 and under, was held at White Bear Lake in 1951. Duluth Glen Avon defeated White Bear Lake in the finals by a score of 2-1. This event was important for the advancement of youth hockey in America as it set the pace for other tournaments of its kind in other States in the Union.

The 1948 Winter Olympics were held at St. Moritz, Switzerland. Both the Amateur Athletic Union and the Amateur Hockey Association of the United States sent ice

63

president William Thayer Tutt and held at Colorado's Broadmoor Arena in cooperation with the Broadmoor Hotel.

The first-ever official NCAA Hockey Championship was won by the University of Michigan who defeated Eddie Jeremiah's Dartmouth squad in the final game 8-4. It was the first of six national championships won by the Wolverines during the coaching era of Concord, Massachusetts native Vic Heyliger.

The tournament was held at the Broadmoor Arena annually through 1957 when it was moved to various sites around the U.S. For his pioneering efforts, Thayer Tutt will always be remembered as the "Father of the NCAA Hockey Tournament."

Another important development in college hockey was the formation in 1951 of the Mid-West Collegiate Hockey League. Members included Minnesota, North Dakota, Colorado College, Denver, Michigan, Michigan State and Michigan Tech. In 1953 it was renamed the Western Intercollegiate Hockey League. It remained the WIHL until March, 1958 when the League disbanded for one year. In 1959 the seven original schools were reunited under the name Western Collegiate Hockey Association (WCHA).

COLLEGE CHAMPIONS from 1948 to 1959	
1948	Michigan
1949	Boston College
1950	Colorado College
1951	Michigan
1952	Michigan
1953	Michigan
1954	Rensselaer
1955	Michigan
1956	Michigan
1957	Colorado College
1958	Denver University
1959	North Dakota

A college hockey tradition was born in Boston on December 27, 1952 when Harvard beat Boston University, 7-4, in the final game of the first-ever Beanpot Hockey Tournament. This annual battle, decided by a round robin format, was the first tournament of its kind. Its popularity has grown over the years into one of the major local sports events in the Boston area.

The 1952 Olympic Hockey Team was coached by former Eveleth High and Eveleth Junior College star Connie Pleban, who

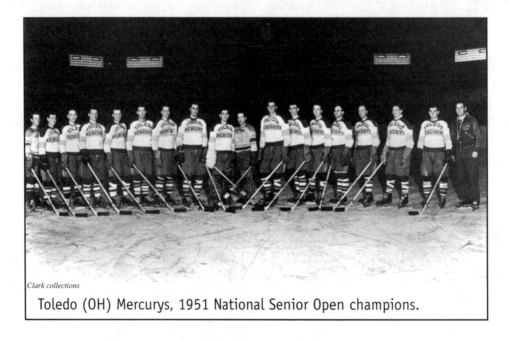

Clark collections

Toledo (OH) Mercurys, 1951 National Senior Open champions.

guided the United States to its first medal since the 1936 Games and its first silver medal since 1932. The team included Kenneth Yackel, a forward and defenseman from St. Paul, Minnesota, who became one of only two American developed players to make the NHL during the 1950s when he joined the Boston Bruins in 1958; goalie Richard Desmond from Medford, Massachusetts, a former Dartmouth star who was named as MVP of the 1950 world championship tournament held at London, England; and Boston College star Len Ceglarski, who scored the tying goal against Dartmouth in the 1949 NCAA championship game. Ceglarski went on to achieve great success as a coach at both the high school and college levels.

The 1956 Winter Olympic Games were held at Cortina, Italy in the Italian Alps. The United States sent an extremely talented squad, which featured the likes of standout goalie Willard Ikola of Eveleth, Minnesota; forwards John Matchefts and John Mayasich, both of whom also hailed from Eveleth; and Harvard scoring machine Bill Cleary.

Ikola starred at Eveleth High from 1946-50, including the undefeated teams of 1948, '49 and '50. He later went on to a very successful coaching career at Edina High (Minnesota), where from 1958-91 he compiled a tremendous 600-140-38 record. Mayasich led the University of Minnesota in scoring in all four of his years as a Golden Gopher, and in his last two seasons (1954 and 1955) he was the WIHL scoring champion.

The team lived up to its expectations by finishing ahead of Canada and bringing back the silver medal. But it wasn't the medal that was the prize, at least for Cleary, who was faced with a big decision prior to his appearance at Cortina. He was on the Montreal Canadiens' protected list and also had an offer from the Boston Bruins. Had he opted to turn pro, he would have been ineligible for Olympic competition.

"I turned down the pros and that's probably the best thing I ever did in retrospect because if I hadn't, I never would have played in two Olympic Games," explained Cleary, reflecting on what an impact his first Olympic experience had on him at such a young age.

"You could win 100 Stanley Cups and it would not come close to matching the experience — not of winning a medal — but of marching in the Olympic parade. That to me is the greatest memory I will ever have. It wasn't long after the Second World War and we didn't know much about the Russians in those days. I was just a young 21-year-old and I'm looking around...You know, I was always lucky enough just to get across the Charles River, never mind the Atlantic Ocean, and the next thing I know I'm in the middle of the majestic Alps, and there I am marching with the USA and I see all these other counties. And I got to tell you, that is the greatest experience I ever had. And there's nothing wrong with being proud of representing your country. There's nothing wrong with waving flags — I don't care what anyone says! You've got to experience it to know what I'm talking about. To me — THAT is the greatest experience. I would have missed that if I had signed as a pro. It was the best move I ever made."

What Cleary gleaned from that first Olympic experience is something that seems almost forgotten today:

"It's not whether you win a medal, it's the experience. It's meeting people from other countries. That's the purpose of the Olympics. The good will of the Olympic Games does more for world peace than all politicians will ever do."

As the 1950s were drawing to a close, a racial barrier was broken in the National Hockey League and it was one of the NHL's American-based franchises that broke it. Pro hockey's equivalent to Jackie Robinson ar-

OLYMPIC MEDALS CHAMPIONS & USA FINISH

Year	Site	Medal Winners	USA Finish
1920	Antwerp, Belgium	Canada USA Czechoslovakia	2nd
1924	Chamonix, France	Canada USA Great Britain	2nd
1928	St. Moritz, Switzerland	Canada Sweden Switzerland	*
1932	Lake Placid, NY, USA	Canada USA Germany	2nd
1936	Garmisch, Germany	Great Britain Canada USA	3rd
1948	St. Moritz, Switzerland	Canada Czechoslovakia Switzerland	4th
1952	Oslo, Norway	Canada USA Sweden	2nd
1956	Cortina, Italy	USSR USA Canada	2nd
1960	Squaw Valley, CA, USA	USA Canada USSR	1st

rived on the scene in January of 1958 when the Boston Bruins promoted left winger Willie O'Ree from their Quebec Aces farm club. O'Ree, a New Brunswick native, played in only two games for Boston that season, but was called up to the big team again in 1960-61 for a 43-game stint, during which he recorded four goals and ten assists. Although his pro career was brief, O'Ree will always be remembered as the first African-Canadian to play in the world's top league.

1. Edited by Zander Hollander, *The Complete Encyclopedia of Hockey* (Detroit: Visible Ink Press, 1993), p. 23.
2. Ibid., p. 23.
3. United States Olympic Committee.
4. S. Kip Farrington, *Skates, Sticks and Men* (New York, NY: David McKay Company, Inc., 1972), p. 46.
5. Ibid., p. 15.
6. Ibid., p. 15.

1964	Innsbruck, Austria	USSR Sweden Czechoslovakia	5th
1968	Grenoble, France	USSR Czechoslovakia Canada	6th
1972	Sapporo, Japan	USSR USA Czechoslovakia	2nd
1976	Innsbruck, Austria	USSR Czechoslovakia West Germany	4th
1980	Lake Placid, NY, USA	USA USSR Sweden	1st
1984	Sarajevo, Yugoslavia	USSR Czechoslovakia Sweden	7th
1988	Calgary, Alberta, Canada	USSR Finland Sweden	7th
1992	Albertville, France	Unified team Canada Czechoslovakia	4th
1994	Lillehammer, Norway	Sweden Canada Finland	8th
1998	Nagano, Japan		

* U.S. did not send a team

Chapter 4

Squaw Valley

*The 1960 United States Olympic Team
Wins the Gold Medal*

Having never placed higher than second in Olympic competition, American Olympic hockey leaders in November of 1959 resumed the delicate process of selecting a team for the upcoming Winter Games at Squaw Valley (California).

Subsectional tryouts were held at various sites in the East and Midwest. Those who qualified advanced to the sectionals which were held at Boston Arena under the guidance of Harry Cleverly and at Williams Arena in Minneapolis, supervised by John Mariucci. By mid-December the field of candidates was narrowed to a squad of 22

Clark collection

1960 U.S. Olympic Hockey Team. Front row (l to r): Larry Palmer, Jack Kirrane, Bill Cleary, Bob Owen, Bill Christian, Jack McCartan. Middle row: Jim Claypool (manager), Bob Cleary, Bob McVey, Rod Paavola, Roger Christian, Gene Grazia, Tommy Williams, Jack Riley (coach). Back row: John Mayasich, Paul Johnson, Weldy Olson, Dick Rodenhiser, Dick Meredith, Ben Bertini (trainer).

which began a monthlong trial held at Army's large, Olympic-size rink to determine the final 17 roster spots.

The man chosen to run the final training camp and coach the team was Army coach Jack Riley, Jr. A Boston native and former Dartmouth star, Riley was the perfect man for the job. He had ten years of experience coaching a team that played on a large ice surface (235 ft. long) and was no stranger to international competition. As a player he helped the 1948 Olympic team to a fourth place finish at St. Moritz, Switzerland. As a player-coach, he led the 1949 National Team to third place at the World Tournament in Stockholm, Sweden.

Riley was also a man who played no favorites and was intent on icing only the best possible team for the competition. This was evidenced by the fact that by month's end, two of his five cuts were Army stars Thomas Harvey and James O'Connor.

Before the team left West Point in mid-January for an exhibition tour two more roster changes were made: Malden, Massachusetts native Dick Rodenhiser replaced former University of Minnesota star Richard Burg at wing, and Burg's former Gopher teammate Jack McCartan replaced Brown's Harry Batchelder in goal.

The exhibition tour included dates with college and amateur teams until the final week, when the Americans finished with games against Czechoslovakia and Japan. In early February as the tour wound down, the team stopped in Colorado for a couple of games with Denver University. In the Mile High City the Cleary brothers, Bill and Bob, were added to the roster. Dropped from the squad were defenseman Robert Dupuis, and a man whose mark would not be made on Olympic history until some 20 years later — Herb Brooks.

Bob Cleary was added because Bill Cleary, who was highly coveted, would not join the team unless his brother was invited to play as well. "They wanted Billy but not Bobby, but Billy wouldn't come without Bobby," recalls team captain Jack Kirrane. According to Kirrane there was some dissension on the team as a result of Bob's arrival. Dissension or not, the Clearys proved to be valuable as-

sets for what was to become a team of destiny.

A final addition to the team was made at Squaw Valley just prior to the preliminary round when John Mayasich of Eveleth, Minnesota replaced Larry Alm on defense. Mayasich, who had broken every scoring record in the book as a center at the University of Minnesota, added solid defense and more offense to the team's attack. He also contributed more experience. Six players had previously been part of an Olympic team. Kirrane was a member of the 1948 club, and Mayasich, Meredith, Olson, Rodenhiser and Bill Cleary were all members of the 1956 squad which brought home the silver. Every team member except Larry Palmer had played on at least one national team.

When the preliminary competition began on February 17 the squad lined up as follows:

	Name	Age	College	Hometown
GOAL:	Jack McCartan	24	Minnesota	St. Paul, MN
	Larry Palmer	22	Army	Wakefield, MA
DEFENSE:	Jack Kirrane	29	None	Brookline, MA
	John Mayasich	26	Minnesota	Eveleth, MN
	Bob Owen	23	Harvard	St. Louis Pk., MN
	Rod Paavola	20	None	Hancock, MI
CENTER:	Bob McVey	23	Harvard	Hamden, CT
	Paul Johnson	22	None	W. St. Paul, MN
	Tommy Williams	19	None	Duluth, MN
WING:	Dick Rodenhiser	27	BC	Malden, MA
	Dick Meredith	27	Minnesota	Minneapolis, MN
	Weldy Olson	27	Mich. St.	Marquette, MI
	Bill Cleary	25	Harvard	Cambridge, MA
	Bob Cleary	23	Harvard	Cambridge, MA
	Roger Christian	24	None	Warroad, MN
	Bill Christian	21	None	Warroad, MN
	Gene Grazia	25	Mich. St.	W. Springfield, MA

The preliminary round divided the nine-team field into three separate groups of three. By way of a round robin format, the top two teams in each group advanced to the medal round. The United States drew Czechoslovakia and Australia in its group.

Uncle Sam's first opponent was the Czechs, who held a 4-3 lead after two periods of play. With 1:58 gone in the third Paul Johnson netted the tying tally from Mayasich and McVey. Then Mayasich banged home a blast from the blue line for his third goal of the game. The score not only completed a hat trick for the team's newest member, but proved to be the game-winner as the U.S. rolled to a 7-5 victory.

The team's next opponent was Australia, which was totally overmatched against the talent and experience of the newly improved U.S. squad. The Yanks advanced by routing the Aussies 12-1, as 10 players got into the scoring act. The next step was the six-team championship round robin. The other teams qualifying for the final round were Sweden, Germany, Canada, Russia and Czechoslovakia.

Despite the late additions and a fairly impressive preliminary round, the United States was considered by the experts to be a longshot to win a medal. Critics not only rated the U.S. below the defending gold medalists from Russia and Canada's world championship team, but under Czechoslovakia and Sweden as well. Riley was nonplussed. He went with McCartan in goal and used the following lines and defense pairings:

The underdog American squad's first test in the final round came on February 22, against Sweden. Riley's sextet wasted little time in responding to the challenge by jumping out to a 4-0 first period lead on goals by Roger Christian, Bob Cleary, McVey and Johnson. Jack McCartan made the early lead stand up by making 36 saves en route to a 6-3 victory for Team USA. Roger Christian added a goal in the second and another in the third to complete a hat trick. Bill Christian was the game's outstanding playmaker, recording three assists while Bill Cleary and Williams pitched in with two apiece.

Germany was next. They were regarded as the only team in the championship round that the U.S. could beat. And win they did, 9-1. The U.S. attack was led by Bill Cleary, who turned in a dazzling four-goal performance. Mayasich potted a pair and Bob Cleary, Williams and Johnson added one each. It was a relatively easy night for McCartan who turned aside 23 of the 24 shots he faced.

The next day 8500 roaring fans packed the Blyth Arena and millions tuned in their television sets to witness Uncle Sam's feisty underdogs take on the world champions from Canada.

Bob Cleary put the United States on the board at 12:47 of the first period by slamming home the rebound of a Mayasich slapper that caromed off the stick of Canadian goalie Don Head. The U.S. clinged to its slim one-goal advantage through the rest of the first period

Left Wing	**Center**	**Right Wing**
Weldy Olson	Paul Johnson	Dick Rodenhiser
Bill Christian	Tom Williams	Roger Christian
Bill Cleary	Bob McVey	Bob Cleary

Left Defense	**Right Defense**
Jack Kirrane	John Mayasich
Bob Owen	Rod Paavola

and most of the second thanks to some magnificent goaltending by McCartan, who kept Canada off the scoreboard by making one incredible stop after another. "All I could see were streaks of green Canadians,"[1] said McCartan, who made 39 saves.

With six minutes left in the second, the Yanks got some much needed insurance when Johnson stole a pass, streaked down the left side, and slapped a backhander past Head from 35 feet out.

Steve Babineau

After the Olympics, Bill Cleary became coach and then (currently) athletic director at Harvard.

The relentless Canadian attack continued into the third period but McCartan kept coming up big. Canada finally broke the shutout when Jim Connelly tapped one in at 13:38, but it was too little, too late for the favorites from north of the border.

The loss was a major setback for Canada, which had been looking to regain the gold medal it had failed to bring home from Cortina in 1956, when they finished third behind Russia and the U.S. Team Canada's captain and star defenseman Harry Sinden, in his book *Hockey Showdown*, which documented the 1972 Team Canada-Russia series, called Canada's 2-1 loss in 1960 the "most disappointing thing"[2] of his career.

With a record of three wins and no losses, and a major upset under their belts, the scrappy Americans were beginning to make believers out of people. Surprisingly, the USA-Russia game was now the marquee matchup of the tournament. Apparently Riley's skaters surprised the networks and the schedule makers as well. Bill Cleary explained how his team's unexpected success put a crimp in the best-laid plans:

"They had the Canadians-Russians game at three o'clock on Sunday," recalled Cleary. "They thought that was gonna be the feature. No one gave us a chance. Before the games started I think they had us finishing twelfth. But then — what happened — we started to win and people got excited."

After a much needed and well deserved day of rest, the United States took the ice against the mighty Soviet Union team which was looking to rebound after being tied by Sweden. Once again the scrappy USA team looked to pull off a big upset in front of another packed house and millions of TV viewers.

Bill Cleary put the Yanks up early in the first period by beating Russian goalie Nikolai Puchkov on a feed from brother Bob. The lead was short lived, however, as seconds later Vaniamin Aleksandrov beat McCartan on a screen shot to tie the score. Almost five minutes later, Mikhail Bychkov fired the puck off the crossbar and into the net to give the Russians the lead.

Midway through the second period Team USA's other brother combination went to work. Billy Christian took a pass from Roger, skated down the left side, and fired one home to knot the score at two apiece. The game remained tied until late in the final period when the Christians struck again. This time Billy converted on passes from Williams and Roger at 14:59 to put the Americans in the lead. McCartan and the solid defense in front of him kept the Russians off the board for the remaining five minutes. When the buzzer went off the crowd feverishly cheered an underdog United States squad that was now in the driver's seat to win its first-ever Olympic gold medal in hockey.

Driver's seat or not, there was no time to savor the win over the Russians. Nor was there any rest for the weary, as the final game against the Czechs was scheduled for 8 o'clock the next morning.

The United States controlled its own destiny. A win would automatically give them the gold. But a loss, coupled with a Canadian victory over the Russians, and America would have (on a goal-spread basis) had to settle for the silver.

For the first two periods the Czechs had the edge in play and took a 4-3 lead into the second intermission. It appeared as if the Yanks had suffered a letdown after their two big victories over Canada and Russia, but according to Mayasich fatigue was setting in: "I think we were just tighter. Looking at our defensive corps, there were four of us. We had two sets of defense and played every game — and that takes a lot out of you," said John. "We played on Saturday afternoon and had to get up at five in the morning on Sunday. You look at all those things and realize that everybody had at least one good period left in him."

During that final intermission Russian captain Nikolai "Solly" Sologubov, who was friendly with some of the American players, came into the locker room and suggested that the players take whiffs of oxygen to bolster

their energy level. Some did, but according to coach Riley in S. Kip Farrington's *Skates, Sticks and Men*, it was his team's burning desire to win that eventually made the difference.

The third period belonged to the Americans. Roger Christian tied the score at 5:50 on a pass from brother Billy. Less than two minutes later, Bob Cleary took a pass from Mayasich and drove home what proved to be the game-winner. Bob added another for insurance almost four minutes later and the rout was on. Roger Christian and Bill Cleary each found the back of the net within a 38-second span before Roger struck once more at 17:56 to complete a four-goal morning. It was as if they saved their best for last, outscoring the Czechs 6-0 in the final frame to secure the first-ever Olympic gold medal in ice hockey for the United States.

Later that day team captain Jack Kirrane was called up to the podium and presented with the medal. While the rest of the squad proudly observed, he gratefully accepted the shiny hardware that he and his teammates had worked so hard to attain.

That evening the team members flew back to their respective homes where, upon their arrival, they were welcomed with rousing ovations from scores of proud Americans.

When Mayasich arrived at Austin Strawbel Airport in Green Bay, he was greeted by several hundred fans. Kirrane, Rodenhiser, the Cleary brothers and trainer Ben Bertini all flew back to Boston on the same flight, which, after being delayed in Chicago, didn't arrive until eleven o'clock Monday morning. When they got off the plane they were greeted by a crowd of about 1,000. Kirrane, a fireman himself, had a truck waiting at the airport to take him back to Brookline for a tour through town before jumping into a Limo for a swing through Boston. Meanwhile, Rodenhiser spent the afternoon being chauffeured around his hometown of Malden, while the Clearys paraded through their native Cambridge.

Immediately following the triumph at Squaw Valley, Jack McCartan signed with the Rangers. The Blueshirts were suffering at the gate and in signing McCartan they saw an opportunity to remedy their box office troubles by putting a national hero in goal. General manager Muzz Patrick originally offered McCartan $500 per game but the Olympic star demanded a grand. Madison Square Garden president Ned Irish overruled Patrick and McCartan got what he wanted.

On March 6, the former University of Minnesota star made his NHL debut and defeated the Detroit Red Wings 3-1 before a packed Garden. McCartan played in four games for New York that season allowing only seven goals for an impressive 1.75 goals-against average. The St. Paul native, however, did not fare so well the following season, spending most of it in the minors before being released. In 1972-73 McCartan returned to pro hockey with Minnesota of the newly-formed World Hockey Association. McCartan appeared in only 40 games over three seasons with the Fighting Saints before retiring for good after the 1974-75 season.

Months after the gold medal victory Tommy Williams was signed by the Boston Bruins organization. Williams played for the Bruins' Kingston affiliate of the Eastern Professional Hockey League in 1960-61 before being called up to the big club the following season. After playing eight seasons in Boston, the Duluth native continued his pro career with the Minnesota North Stars, California Golden Seals and New England of the WHA before finishing with the Washington Capitals. Over his 15-year pro career (playoffs included), Williams amassed 546 points in 831 games.

The Olympic triumph at Squaw Valley — thanks to the national TV coverage — created a fair amount of excitement around America. But it had only a minimal effect in inspiring kids to learn skating and hockey. The Olympic triumph was, however, a spectacular moment in United States hockey history.

FINAL STANDINGS

	W	L	T	Pts	GF	GA
USA	5	0	0	10	29	11
Canada	4	1	0	8	31	12
Russia	2	2	1	5	24	19
Czechs	2	3	0	4	21	23
Sweden	1	3	1	3	19	21
Germany	0	5	0	0	7	45

SCORES OF ALL U.S. GAMES

Exhibition Games:

	USA	Opponents
Country Kitchens (Lewiston, ME)	7	2
Berlin (NH) Maroons	9	3
Boston University*	5	2
Harvard University*	5	1
Boston College*	2	2
Northeastern*	6	0
Philadelphia Ramblers	5	4
Green Bay Bob-Cats	5	6
Michigan Tech College	5	1
Michigan Tech College	2	5
University of Minnesota	4	4
University of Minnesota	6	2
Warroad Lakers	5	7
North Dakota University	7	2
North Dakota University	8	8
Denver University	5	7
Denver University	5	5
Czechoslovakia	4	3
Czechoslovakia	5	5
Japan	10	0

* Played one period against each opponent, outscoring them by a combined 18-5.

Preliminary Games:

Czechoslovakia	7	5
Australia	12	1

Championship Games:

Sweden	6	3
Germany	9	1
Canada	2	1
Russia	3	2
Czechoslovakia	9	4

Overall Record: 17 Wins, 4 losses, 4 ties

RESULTS OF ALL GAMES IN CHAMPIONSHIP ROUND

USA	6	Canada	12	Russia	8
Sweden	3	Germany	0	Czechoslovakia	5
USA	9	Canada	4	Russia	2
Germany	1	Czechoslovakia	0	Sweden	2
USA	2	Czechoslovakia	3	Russia	7
Canada	1	Sweden	1	Germany	1
USA	3	Canada	6	Czechoslovakia	9
Russia	2	Sweden	5	Germany	1
USA	9	Canada	8	Sweden	8
Czechoslovakia	4	Russia	5	Germany	4

SCORING SUMMARY:

	G	A	Pts
Bill Cleary	6	6	12
Roger Christian	7	2	9
Bill Christian	2	7	9
Bob Cleary	5	3	8
Paul Johnson	3	2	5
John Mayasich	2	3	5
Tom Williams	1	4	5
Bob McVey	2	2	4
Jack Kirrane	0	3	3
Weldy Olson	1	0	1
Dick Meredith	0	1	1
Totals	29	33	62

Goalie Jack McCartan allowed 11 goals in five games for a goals-per-game average of 2.2. He stopped 134 of the 145 shots he faced for a save percentage of 0.924.

Two men who also deserve a lot of credit for their efforts are manager Jim Claypool of Duluth and trainer Ben Bertini of Boston. They each earned the respect and appreciation of all involved for the remarkable jobs they did.

1. S. Kip Farrington, *Skates, Sticks and Men* (New York, NY: David McKay Company, Inc., 1972), p.103.
2. Harry Sinden and Will McDonough, Hockey Showdown, *The Canada-Russia Hockey Series* (Toronto: Doubleday Canada, 1972) p. 44.

Chapter 5

New England Catches Fire
The Impact of Bobby Orr and the Big, Bad Bruins

"It was a phenomenal thing to watch happen. You don't really realize it at the time. It's taking place, but you don't know how long it's gonna last, so you just ride the wave. And it was a tidal wave really, it just stayed. It got to a crest, and it kept cresting."
— Derek Sanderson

In the fall of 1966, an 18-year-old kid named Robert Gordon Orr arrived in Boston with a brush cut and a baby face. The Bruins had owned his rights since age 12 and hoped that someday he would come to town and resurrect what had been a failing franchise since the late 1950s.

Boston was always known as a baseball and hockey town. New England sports fans followed their beloved Red Sox year after year, through exciting summers filled with hope and joy that invariably ended in September disappointment. But when October came, it was the Bruins' turn to grab the spotlight.

During the late '50s and most of the '60s, the Boston Celtics became the pride of Boston, winning 11 championships in 13 years — a milestone likely never to be matched in professional sports. Despite this remarkable accomplishment, the Celts were still outdrawn by the cellar-dwelling Bruins. The area had a fairly rich high school and college hockey tradition, second only in the U.S. to the northern Midwest states of Minnesota, Wisconsin and Michigan. But Boston wasn't nearly the hockey town it was about to become.

The Bruins' following consisted of dedicated fans who loved the game and continued to come year after year, despite the lack of recent success by the boys who wore the black and gold. Among these followers were the Gallery Gods, a group of diehard season ticket-holders who sat in the third balcony and were known to shout their minds more than occasionally.

This was a franchise that had some great teams since its inception in 1924. The 1928-29 club that brought home Boston's first Stanley Cup included the immortal Eddie Shore, whose gutsy play became a standard for future Bruins teams. By 1958, the year the B's had last made the finals, they had appeared in the finals ten times and had won three Stanley Cups. But from 1959-66, they finished

Steve Babineau

When Bobby Orr began a rush in his own end it often resulted in a Boston score.

either last or next to last.

The Bruins were last again in the 1966-67 season, finishing with a dismal 17-43-10 record — 14 points behind fifth-place Detroit. But hope was on the horizon, as Boston fans were impressed by the dazzling play of Orr, the rookie defenseman from Parry Sound, Ontario, who wore number 4. His superb play won him Rookie of the Year honors and a second-place finish in balloting for the annual Norris Trophy, an award given to the league's best defenseman.

The 1966-67 season was the last full year of Orr's career that he didn't win the Norris, the last year the Bruins would miss the playoffs until 1997, and the last year of the NHL as a six-team league.

The NHL had been a six-team league since 1942, but would soon become a 12-team league, as six new franchises were scheduled to begin the 1967-68 season. Philadelphia, Pittsburgh, Minnesota, St. Louis, Oakland and Los Angeles were the new entries, and with this expansion came a draft that would inevitably deplete the rosters of the Original Six.

The Bruins were hurt by this draft at least as much as any other team. They lost Gary Dornhoefer and Bernie Parent to the Philadelphia Flyers. Ironically, each went on to beat Boston in the 1974 Stanley Cup finals as members of the Flyers.

However, this loss was remedied during that same off-season. On May 15, 1967, General Manager Milt Schmidt pulled off a blockbuster trade assuring the Bruins of contention in the soon-to-be-expanded NHL. The Bruins sent center Pit Martin, defenseman Gilles Marotte and goalie Jack Norris to Chicago in exchange for centers Phil Esposito and Fred Stanfield, and right wing Ken Hodge. Time proved this deal to be a heist as Schmidt parted with three players of no more than average calibre. In return he got three impact players, one of whom went on to become the greatest goal scorer of his time: Phil Esposito.

The big trade gave the Bruins insurance for what they might (and did) lose in the expansion draft. It was also the deal that helped put them over the hump, making them a legitimate contender for the Stanley Cup. In Ken Hodge, they acquired a big, hard-hitting forward who played the right side on what became the league's highest scoring line, with center Phil Esposito and rugged left winger Wayne Cashman. Fred Stanfield became a key component of the club by centering the Bruins' second line, as well as playing the left point on what was to become the league's most potent power play.

This young and promising team not only had their young superstar in Orr, but another youngster of star calibre in center Derek Sanderson, who won the Calder Trophy as Rookie of the Year for the 1967-68 season, as Orr had done the previous year. To this day, it's only the second time in NHL history that back-to-back winners of that award came from the same team. And it's ironic that the two fought in a Juniors game held at Boston Garden in the mid-'60s.

The Bruins had owned the rights to Sanderson since age 12, as they had Orr. Because of their last-place status, Boston was the perfect organization for a young player with star potential. "As a player, you look at coming to a town that was — in my time — historically in last place, which was good when you were a youngster," reflects Sanderson. "You look in the paper and you say, 'Okay, I hope the Bruins keep losing, then maybe I'll get a chance to make the team.'" It turned out, however, that he could have made any team.

Sanderson immediately gained the respect of the Gallery Gods with his highly effective combination of physical play and finesse. He was a hard working, tight-checking forward who never backed down from a scrap. At the same time, he was a smooth-skating, skillful passer and shooter, adept at winning faceoffs. He was also a fine penalty killer and very good defensively. They called him "Turk," a nickname he acquired in Ontario when he was

Steve Babineau

Derek Sanderson's superb all-around play and charismatic personality made him a big hit in Boston.

growing up. A local paper depicted him in a cartoon as a "Whirling Dervish," a Turkish performer who performs whirling dances in ecstatic devotion — so people took to calling him Turk. When Derek arrived in Boston, he immediately became a sex symbol. His good looks and cocky attitude made him a favorite of the young women of Beantown.

The Bruins were a team full of nicknames. Aside from "Turk," there was "Espo" (Phil Esposito), "Cash" (Wayne Cashman), "Cheesy" (Gerry Cheevers), "Pie" (Johnny McKenzie), "Bugsy" (Don Awrey), "Swoop" (Wayne Carleton), "Terrible Teddy" (Green), "Ace" (Garnet Bailey), "Shaky" (Mike Walton) and "The Chief" (Johnny Bucyk). Of course while Bobby Orr didn't need a nickname; a lot of hockey fans thought of him as god.

Gerry Cheevers became a Bruin in 1965, after being named American Hockey League (AHL) Goalie of the Year the previous season. He saw little action his first two seasons, but by 1967-68, he was given an equal share of the netminding chores, alternating with veteran Eddie Johnston. This tandem combined to give the Bruins the solid goaltending they needed to complement their high-powered offense. Whenever Cheevers was hit in the mask by a puck, trainer John "Frosty" Forrestal would mark the spot by drawing in stitchmarks with a black magic marker. Cheevers' mask eventually had marks painted all over it. They became his trademark.

Johnny McKenzie played right wing on the Bruins' second line. He soon became one of the most popular Bruins, because he was a scrappy little guy who always hustled. He had an uncanny ability to make good things happen when the team looked flat. It was "Pie" who often provided the spark when the B's needed a jumpstart. He would throw a hard check or steal the puck and create a scoring opportunity. This got the fans going, and suddenly the rest of the team began to jell. It made him a very important part of the team chemistry — something the Bruins had in abundance.

The Boston defensive corps enjoyed considerable depth. It was anchored by Orr, and although he was known mostly for his offensive prowess, he was exceptional in his own end as well. Then there was "Terrible Teddy" Green, who was known around the league as the toughest defenseman in the game, and Don "Bugsy" Awrey, a stocky blueliner who had a knack for blocking shots. The rest of the supporting cast on defense featured the unrelated Smith brothers, Dallas and Rick, who were rock solid in their own end; Billy Speer, who was a tenacious body-checker, and Gary Doak, a defenseman who got the job done when called upon.

Ed Westfall played right wing on the Bruins third line with Derek Sanderson and Wayne Carleton. Eddie was known for his unique ability to shadow the opposition's

Steve Babineau

Johnny "Pie" McKenzie (l), seen here with Bobby Orr, was the spark plug that ignited the Bruins when they needed a lift.

left winger. Westfall was a key to the team's mastery of the Chicago Blackhawks in the 1970 Eastern Conference Finals, as he was the main reason that Bobby Hull didn't score a goal in the series.

Ace Bailey was a solid left-winger who joined the club in the 1968-69 season. His big moment came in the '72 finals against the Rangers, when he scored the game-winner in the high-scoring series opener.

The man to whom they all looked up was their captain, veteran left winger Johnny Bucyk. They called him "Chief," a name given to him by ex-teammate Bronco Horvath because John's dark complexion reminded Horvath of some Indians he had seen. But it was a fitting nickname for him, since he had been with the club much longer than any current Bruin (since 1957), and served as the perfect leader for this unique bunch of lovable crazies.

During the summer and early autumn of 1967, New Englanders were treated to one of the greatest pennant races in baseball history. The Boston Red Sox found themselves involved in a four-way battle for the American League flag with the Minnesota Twins, Detroit Tigers and Chicago White Sox. The Cinderella Sox beat the Twins on the last day of the season, forging what became known as "The Impossible Dream."

Back in training camp, the oddsmakers had given them 100-to-one odds to win the pennant. But what the oddsmakers didn't foresee was that Carl Yastrzemski was to have one of the greatest seasons a professional athlete ever had: winning the Triple Crown (the last player to do so), and making great play after great play against the Green Monster in Fenway Park's left field. The team turned Boston upside down and, despite the fact that they lost the World Series in seven games to the St. Louis Cardinals, they became the toast of the town.

From a perspective of pure sports enthusiasm, the '67 Sox primed Boston for the emergence of the "Big, Bad Bruins." New Englanders had enjoyed a taste of the excitement a successful young team could offer, and they were ready for more. But this was only one of several factors which explained the craze that was about to rock Beantown.

Boston is a college town. Many students who are not originally from the area take a liking to the city and stay when they finish school. The young people of the late '60s were in the midst of turbulent times with the Vietnam War at its peak and the assassinations of Robert Kennedy and Martin Luther King, Jr. They were seeing their friends come home in pine boxes, and sports provided an outlet for them to escape from the harsh realities of life. In 1968, Derek Sanderson and Joe Namath opened a popular night spot in town called the Bachelor's III. It was the second of its kind; Namath had already opened one in New York. Athletes frequented the place and became popular celebrities. All the young people went there to meet somebody, and party where their sports heroes did.

When the 1967-68 season began, Bruins fans had good reason to be optimistic that Stanley Cup playoff action would soon return to the Boston Garden. Yet those chances were not any better because of expansion. The six new teams were put in their own division, the West, leaving the original six in the East. The B's did have a much better chance of having their first winning season in eight years, because 24 of their 74 scheduled regular-season games were to be against the newcomers. But in order to qualify for the playoffs, they had to — like any previous year — finish at least fourth among the same six.

The Bruins not only had a winning season (finishing 37-27-10), but made the playoffs with a third-place finish. They also established themselves as a scoring machine by collecting a league-leading 259 goals. This attack was led by newcomer Phil Esposito, who finished second in league scoring with 84 points, only three points behind his former Blackhawks teammate Stan Mikita.

The Bruins drew Montreal in the first round of the playoffs, and lost in four straight games. Getting swept was no big surprise: the Canadiens were not the matchup the B's had hoped for. It was a pairing between one team with extensive playoff experience, and another with very little. Nevertheless, it was a learning experience for Boston to take into the next season. They were young and on their way up, and it was important just to get that initial taste of playoff intensity.

In the fall of 1968, the Bruins became the team to watch in the Hub. "When Orr arrived in 1966, you could get a seat. But by '68 the Garden was sold out every night," says Jack Parker, former player and now head coach of varsity hockey at Boston University. "That was the first indication that people were jacked up about hockey."

The Bruins were off to a good start in the 1968-69 season and by late December, took over first place. Then they went on a lengthy unbeaten streak and looked like they were going to run away with the Eastern Division flag — until they were hit by a rash of injuries. By late February, the B's found themselves mired in a slump that ultimately cost them the division. Going into the last weekend of the season, they were three points behind Montreal, with only a home-and-home series against the Habs remaining. They lost in Montreal and ended up settling for second place.

Despite losing the race for first, the Bruins had taken another step toward the top by passing the Rangers to finish one spot higher in the standings than the previous year. They finished with 100 points, 16 better than the previous year, and scored a remarkable 303

goals — the first time a team had ever cracked the 300 mark. Other milestones included Phil Esposito's 126 points, which earned him the Hart Trophy as the league's most valuable player, and Bobby Orr's breaking of all scoring records for defensemen. It is important to note, however, that these numbers are all somewhat inflated, because expansion had watered down the talent level of the entire league.

The Bruins' first playoff opponent was the Toronto Maple Leafs, who had rebounded from late-season turmoil to overtake the fading Detroit Red Wings for the last playoff spot in the East. Leafs center and future Bruin Mike Walton and legendary coach Punch Imlach didn't see eye to eye, resulting in Walton's late February walk-out. The dispute was soon settled: Walton came back to help his team snag fourth place, earning them the beating of their lives at Boston Garden.

The Bruins won the first game 10-0. Sometimes it can be a bad omen for a team to win the first game by a blowout. They go into the next game feeling invincible, lose it, and then find themselves in a dogfight for the rest of the series. Not the case here though. The Big, Black Machine handed out a 7-0 whipping in Game Two, and took the next two games in Toronto to wrap up the series. This humiliating sweep meant the end of an illustrious coaching career for Punch Imlach, who was fired by club president Stafford Smythe minutes after the final game.

Meanwhile, the Montreal Canadiens were sweeping the New York Rangers, setting the stage for another Boston-Montreal showdown, this time in the East Division Finals. Everybody knew that the Eastern Finals were more competitive than the Stanley Cup Finals because of the weakness of the West. It was only Bobby Orr's third season, and the Bruins were virtually one playoff series away from the Cup.

Having been swept by the Habs the year before, the Bruins were looking for revenge. They knew they had a much better chance of beating the Canadiens, because they knew they were a much better team than they were at the same time the year before. They finished one spot higher in the standings, had another full season of experience together, and a couple of playoff series under their belts. They also knew that most of Montreal's key veterans were now a year older and maybe a tad slower.

In what was widely regarded as one of the finest playoff series of all time, experience prevailed and the Canadiens beat the B's in a hard fought six-game series. Three of the four Montreal wins came in sudden-death overtime, including the clincher, which was settled in a second OT. Had the Bruins won at least one of the OT games the story most certainly would have had a different outcome. But they went 0 for 3, and the dreaded Habs advanced for a second consecutive mismatch with the St. Louis Blues, resulting in yet another celebration on St. Catherine's Street.

The Bruins may not have won the Cup in 1968-69, but they had taken a giant leap toward hockey's Holy Grail. Their aggressive and sometimes brutal style of play had earned them the title "The Big, Bad Bruins," and the flashy, offensive-minded style of their 21-year-old defenseman was beginning to revolutionize the sport. This highly-talented, charismatic team was on the verge of taking the area by storm, and fan fever — near epidemic proportions in Boston — was beginning to spread rapidly throughout New England.

For those who weren't lucky enough to have tickets, the games could be seen on Boston's UHF station, WSBK Channel 38. A local Magnavox dealer named Chuck Sozio scored big sales on TVs with UHF. Everybody had to have one, and those who lived well outside the Boston area needed a strong antenna to pick up the signal. Steve Bernstein, a four-time U.S. champion in table hockey, recalls the struggle to get a better signal. "When I was a teenager, we lived in Worcester on the back side of a large hill. I remember being up on the roof and always trying to get this antenna higher and higher," Bernstein says. "I used extra poles and had the thing up to 40 feet with all these wires hanging down."

The TV-38 broadcasts were of good quality for the time and announcer Don Earle was a favorite of the Boston fans. "Shot, GOOOAAAL," he'd say, instead of the common phrase, "Shot, SCORE." When Earle left Boston, former radio announcer Fred Cusick took his place as TV play-by-play man, and Bob Wilson took Cusick's place on radio. Cusick and Wilson have since been inducted into the Broadcasters Hall of Fame. Theme music for the telecasts was "The Nutrocker," written by a group called Bee Bumble and the Stingers. It became the favorite tune of many a Bruins fan.

Steve Babineau

Orr skated circles around opponents who tried in vain to catch him.

As people began to anticipate the 1969-70 season, it became obvious that this fiery young gang of Canadian-born and raised skaters were destined to win the hearts of the Hub — if they hadn't already. But what no one could have foreseen was the impact they were to have, not only for fans, but as an inspiration for people — kids in particular — to pick up the sport.

People loved to watch Orr. His amazing agility was complemented by an assortment of speeds he used to deceive his opponents. He would lull them into slowing down before he kicked it back into high gear and sprung free. He was also a great passer with a blistering slap-shot. It was exciting to watch him, knowing that at any time he might dazzle with one of his beautiful end-to-end rushes, many times resulting in a goal.

When you saw it, it made you want to do it. Former Olympic star and current Harvard Athletic Director Bill Cleary said it best: "He revolutionized the game of hockey, and I think for the better too, because it's a much more offensive game with more skating. And Bobby put that in. I think because people liked that,

it gave a lot more pizazz to the sport. Bobby is really the catalyst that created the interest."

New rinks began to open and were booked into the wee hours. Skates and hockey equipment flew out of stores like pucks into nets. Ponds began to fill up with games of shinny hockey, and for convenience, fathers built little rinks in their back yards for kids to practice.

If ice wasn't accessible, children played street hockey. "You'd see kids in the street emulate the Big, Bad Bruins all the time," Cleary says.

The torch had been lit, but it was during the 1969-70 season that fan interest spread like wildfire. Thousands of kids were inspired to participate in the sport, and youth hockey programs were created all over the Boston area. This boom produced an entire generation of fine hockey players at all levels, including some of today's premier pros.

In the late '60s, there were only a handful of American-born and raised players in the NHL, and one of them played center for the Bruins. Tommy Williams, a native of Duluth, Minnesota, and a star on the 1960 gold medal winning Olympic team, had been with the B's

Steve Babineau

Far left: For years, Minnesotan Tommy Williams (pictured here with Washington) owned the distinction of being the only American in the NHL. *Left:* Michigan native Doug Roberts played for Detroit, Oakland and Boston of the NHL before finishing his career with the New England Whalers of the WHA.

since 1961, but was not destined to share in the glory to be. He left Boston during the 1969 off-season for his home state, to play for the Minnesota North Stars.

Other Americans included North Stars center Charlie Burns and Oakland Seals defenseman Doug Roberts, both from Detroit, and Montreal centers Larry Pleau and Bobby Sheehan, a couple of Boston area boys.

With the exception of these few Americans, every other player in the National Hockey League was from Canada. Canada's Junior A system was the perfect breeding ground for kids whose dream was to play in the NHL. When a Canadian boy reaches his mid-teens, he begins competing at the Junior level, where he faces the kind of competition necessary to develop his talents for a pro career. When an American boy reached his mid-teens, he didn't have such a league to join. If his high school had a team (and many didn't), joining was not the right step to take if he had pro ambitions. He had to find a league that had older guys with more advanced skills than those at the high school level, and to find a way to join despite being under-age.

When Tommy Williams, at age 15, was ready to play for Duluth Central High, his father told him no. At his dad's insistence, Tommy joined a senior league where he had a chance to compete against guys whose ages ranged from 22-35.

Thankfully high school and college programs in the United States are much better now than they were in the late '60s, and there are many more of them. For that reason, there are a lot of Americans playing in the pros today. The Boston area is one of, if not the best, breeding grounds for college and pro talent, as this chapter will explain.

Before the 1969-70 season even began, the

Steve Babineau

Bobby Sheehan of Weymouth, Mass., left the NHL in 1972-73 to score 35 goals for the WHA New York Raiders.

Bruins suffered a devastating blow to their Cup hopes. In an Ottawa exhibition game against the Blues, St. Louis left winger Wayne Maki viciously sticked all-star defenseman Ted Green in the head. Green underwent emergency brain surgery. The procedure was a success — a relief to all that his life was saved. But the Bruins lost their rugged defenseman for the entire season.

However, the team was not about to let this near tragic occurrence dampen its championship hopes. Instead, the players used it as an incentive, coming closer together, and dedicating their run for the Cup to Teddy.

The Bruins opened the regular season at home with a win over the New York Rangers, beginning an unbeaten streak that stretched to seven games until they visited Toronto's Maple Leaf Gardens, where they hadn't won in 22 regular season games. The jinx was about to be broken when, with the score tied at one in the second period, the Bruins applied the pressure, only to have Phil Esposito and Ron Murphy hit posts. The Leafs got the go-ahead goal on a slapper by Mike Walton, and never looked back en route to a 4-2 victory.

The Toronto loss began a slide for the B's, as they won only three of their next 12 games, slipping from first to third place in the East.

On December 10th, the Bruins acquired rangy left winger Wayne Carleton from Toronto, in a trade for center Jim Harrison. The trade paid immediate dividends the following night. Carleton scored both goals in a 2-1 victory that gave the Bruins a much-needed split of a home-and-home series with the Rangers. Wayne was nicknamed "Swoop" because of his long arms and legs, which enabled him to outreach opposing players. He became part of the Bruins' third line with Sanderson and Westfall.

As the holidays drew near, excitement was growing throughout the Boston area. More and more people wanted to share in the fun of rooting for a team with championship po-

tential. They had a certain enticing charm that lured new fans — women included — to follow in their pursuit of Lord Stanley's Cup.

Former Bruins player and coach, and later New York Islanders coach and general manager, Mike Milbury, grew up in the Boston suburb of Walpole. "Everybody in that era was fixated on the Bruins. They were a great team, because of Orr, but more so because of the personalities involved," he recalls. "There was always something going on, like a funny story to be told, but that wouldn't work unless they had a great team. It caught everybody, not just the hockey fan. It caught any sports fan at all. It just swept them up in its web."

Beginning in 1969, and continuing on into the mid-'70s, the holiday season in New England was instrumental in the increase in

Steve Babineau

left: Phil Esposito anxiously waits for a rebound as Guy Lafleur moves in to pursue. *right:* Espo talks to a reporter after a game.

eager participants in the sport of hockey. When parents would take their kids to shopping malls to sit on Santa's lap, a common request was a pair of ice skates. Other hopes were hockey gloves, sticks, pucks, goalie masks, pads — you name it, they wanted it. If you owned a sporting goods store, sales of hockey equipment kept you in business. And although sales reached peak levels during the Orr era, ice and street hockey supplies have continued to be big sellers throughout the New England area.

After finding their requested goodies under the Christmas tree, anxious young recipients immediately took to the streets and ponds to spend the day breaking in their new toys, imitating their favorite players. Former NHL defenseman and current Bruins Assistant General Manager Mike O'Connell recalls street hockey pick-up games in his small town of Cohasset. "I think every one of the kids that I grew up with, when we played street hockey, we could identify with one of them, one of their styles, whether it be Bobby Orr, Johnny McKenzie, Fred Stanfield," O'Connell says. "We had all the moves down: what they did, how they handled the puck. We had it all."

On January 7, 1970 in Oakland, Johnny Bucyk scored his 300th career goal, capping a 6-1 win over the Seals. It was a well-deserved moment for the Chief, who was playing in his 15th National Hockey League season (13th with the Bruins). The man was a study in longevity. He finished his career with 23 seasons in the NHL — 21 of them for Boston. He went on to amass career totals of 556 goals and 813 assists, scoring 20 or more goals in 16 of the 23 seasons he played. His involvement with the Bruins continued as a color-commentator on their radio broadcasts.

The regular season was now half over, and so far the Big, Bad Bruins had given their fans lots to cheer about and plenty of reason to look forward to more of the same.

It was also around this time that the Massachusetts high school hockey season was in full swing. The Bay State League, one of the first schoolboy hockey leagues before the boom, had some teams with future college and pro stars on their rosters. Seniors for powerhouse Needham High included future pro Robbie Ftorek, future Harvard star Steve Dadgian and goalie Cap Raeder, who went on to play for the University of New Hampshire before turning pro. Norwood High had future Boston College Eagle Mike Martin, and Walpole High had a senior defenseman by the name of Mike Milbury.

The 40th-annual NHL All-Star Game was held in St. Louis on January 20. The Bruins were well represented, as four members of the squad were chosen to participate. For the third year in a row, Bobby Orr and Phil Esposito made the first team, Johnny McKenzie was voted to the second team, and Johnny Bucyk was one of the eight players selected to round out the East roster. The East outshot the West by a record-setting margin of 44-17, cruising to a 4-1 victory.

In a mid-February game at Los Angeles, Bobby Orr broke another of his own records. This time it was for goals by a defenseman, with his 22nd of the year. As noted earlier, these records were definitely inflated by the fact that expansion had watered down the talent level of the league. But considering it was only mid-February, Bobby would certainly have broken them by season's end, if not sooner, had he been playing in the old six-team league.

Later that month, the Rangers came to town for what turned out to be a defining game for the young Boston team. The Bruins won 5-3 against an undermanned New York squad that was missing two of its best defensemen, Brad Park and Jim Neilson. But the injuries seemed moot when, after the game, Ranger coach Emile Francis noted that his team was intimidated by the Bruins. This admission told it all. When the top teams in the league came into the Boston Garden to face the Big, Bad Bruins, they were not exactly brimming with confidence, and the lesser teams were beaten before they took the ice.

In early March, the Bruins took over first place with a 3-1 win at home over the St. Louis Blues. They then traveled to the Gateway City to play those same Blues and ended up singing them instead. They were handed their first loss of the year against an expansion team. But the Bruins had nothing of which to be ashamed. They had gone an incredible 32 games in a row against the West without a loss. It was only a matter of time.

Speaking of the law of averages, the Bruins had been virtually injury-free since they lost "Terrible" Teddy Green back in the preseason. That came to an end March 7, in Philadelphia, the day of a total solar eclipse, when Ace Bailey broke his ankle and Gerry Cheevers cracked his ribs.

Steve Babineau

Harry Sinden coached the B's to Cup glory in 1969-70.

With Cheevers out, veteran netminder Eddie Johnston was called upon to carry the load of the team's goaltending responsibilities. He responded by shutting out the Canadiens in what was only his second start in 14 games, then dueling Tony Esposito to a 0-0 tie in Chicago.

It wouldn't have been as much fun for fans and emulators if the Bruins were running away with the East Division race and were a shoe-in for the Cup. What helped to make them so exciting to follow was the tough competition that the other five franchises from the original six were providing. With just nine games left in the regular season, the race was tighter than ever before in NHL history. Only six points separated the top five teams, with the Bruins holding a one point lead over Chicago for the top spot.

If there was a Most Valuable Player award given for the month of March, Eddie Johnston would have been the recipient. E.J. blanked the North Stars at home to earn his third shutout in seven games. Whatever panic there was in the Bruins camp after Cheevers went down had long subsided. The 34-year-old veteran was turning in gem after gem of a performance down the homestretch. The same night, Orr got his 78th assist, breaking the single-season record set by teammate Phil Esposito the previous season. After the announcement, the Boston crowd began chanting "WE WANT ORR!"

On March 25, the Bruins invaded New York's Madison Square Garden to take on the fading Rangers. Coming into the game, the B's were a miserable 0-11-5 against the East on the road. This time, the law of averages worked in their favor: they took it to the Broadway Blueshirts by the score of 3-1. Derek Sanderson iced it with a shorthanded goal in the third when he blocked a Rod Gilbert shot from the right point, went in on a breakaway and beat Ed Giacomin from the left side.

The East Division race was coming right down to the wire, and with only two games remaining, Boston and Chicago were tied for first with 95 points each. The Bruins picked the perfect time to break the Maple Leaf Garden hex, while Chicago won at Montreal. Now it was down to one. On *Goal Bruins*, a record album that was put out to celebrate the '69-70 season, narrator Don Earle had the perfect description for the tightest race in NHL history: "It was a spine-tingling, thriller-diller, photo-finish, made for Hollywood."

If Hollywood had made a movie of it, they probably would have altered the script slightly to create a Bruins-Blackhawks finale to decide it all. Reality, however, dictated that Boston would host Toronto and Chicago would host Montreal.

The Bruins rocked the Boston Garden with 54 shots, for a 3-1 result over the last place Leafs. After the game, the Bruins anxiously awaited news from the Windy City. A Montreal win or tie would give the B's first place, but the news got worse. Chicago won and was awarded first place because they had more wins, which, according to league rules, was the first tiebreaker.

Boston and Chicago were not the only teams that needed a tiebreaker to decide their postseason fate. Because of their loss to the Blackhawks, Montreal ended in a tie for fourth with New York. Both teams had the same amount of wins, and according to league rules, the next tiebreaker was total goals scored. With eight minutes left in the final game, and victory out of reach, Canadiens coach Claude Ruel pulled his goaltender in an attempt to score three more goals and claim fourth place. They failed, and the Rangers won the tiebreaker. It was the first time in 22 years that the Habs missed the playoffs.

The regular season was finally over. Although the Bruins had to settle for second, the momentum they had accumulated down the home stretch had them brimming with confidence about their chances in the playoffs. The Stanley Cup was for the taking, and the Big, Bad Bruins were poised to bring it back to Boston, and end the 29-year drought.

It wasn't just the Bruins who believed in their chances — so did their fans. There was a feeling around the Boston area that this was the year. Fans were camping out on the streets of the North End, waiting for playoff tickets to go on sale. Tickets were like gold dust. Either you were lucky enough to know somebody who had season tickets, or you waited in long lines for hours if a scalper wasn't within your budget.

The Bruins opened the post-season at home, pounding the Rangers 8-2. Phil Esposito scored Boston's first two goals en route to a hat trick, but what opened the floodgates in this one was a Rangers power play. Early in the second period, with the B's a man short, Bobby Orr circled through center ice, crossed the blue line, and rifled a bullet past Giacomin to the short side. Before the penalty expired, Derek Sanderson took a loose puck at center ice, bolted in and lifted the puck into the upper right corner. It was one of the few times in NHL history that a team scored two short-handed goals on one two-minute penalty.

For a change of pace, the Rangers started 21-year veteran Terry Sawchuck in goal for Game Two. The Bruins got off to a slow start, then exploded for four unanswered goals and cruised to a 5-3 win. They now had a 2-0 series lead, and headed to Madison Square Garden for Games Three and Four.

Early in Game Three, two Rangers ganged up on Derek Sanderson in the corner and a huge brawl broke out. The Rangers didn't like the Turk too much, and chose their own building as the right place to get at him. It was their chance to intimidate the Bruins with their raucous crowd and beeping horns, knowing they'd never get away with such a tactic at the Boston Garden. The strategy worked as the Blueshirts won both games to tie the series at two games apiece.

It wasn't just the high level of competition provided by the original six that made following the Bruins so much fun at the time. It was also the intensity of rivalries between cities like Boston and New York, or Boston and Chicago, that made it more interesting to watch, and more enticing to get on the bandwagon.

The series shifted back to Boston for the pivotal Game Five. Orr wasted no time, giving his team the early lead with one of his brilliant end-to-end rushes. The Rangers fought back, through what became a marvelous display of clutch goaltending by Cheevers and Giacomin, and took a 2-1 lead into the third period. The Rangers were riding the momentum they had gotten from Games Three and Four, and were poised to spoil not only the Bruins' night, but perhaps their Cup hopes. Then Phil Esposito came to the fore. Just seconds after Bobby Orr hit the post with a blazing slapshot, Wayne Cashman dug the puck out of the right-wing corner and fed Esposito in the slot. Espo wristed one by Giacomin, and it was a new game. Later in the period, Orr threaded the needle with a perfect blue line-to-blue line pass, sending Espo in alone for the game-winner. The game was a real gut-check for the Bruins, who kept their composure when the chips were down.

After pulling out the nail-biter in Boston, the B's cruised into New York, hoping for a better outcome than their last visit to the Big Apple. Ranger fans attempted once again to intimidate Boston's heartthrob center, holding signs that read "Derek is Dead." But in the

end, Sanderson had the last laugh. After Brad Park gave the Rangers an early 1-0 lead, the Bruins struck back with successive tallies by McKenzie, Cashman (the game-winner), Orr and Sanderson. The Bruins won the series four games to two, and it was on to the Eastern Conference Finals to face the torrid Chicago Blackhawks.

Everybody knew this was really the big series, because St. Louis was just not good enough to beat the best of the East in a seven-game series.

Chicago had home-ice advantage by virtue of their first place finish, and were riding their own wave of momentum heading into the series. They had just completed a four-game sweep of the Detroit Red Wings, winning each game by the score of 4-2.

Game One was televised nationally. Hockey fans across the land were treated to a head-to-head showdown between the two hottest teams, called by legendary announcer Dan Kelly. The Hawks came out smoking early, but were kept off the scoreboard by some sensational goaltending by Gerry Cheevers. At the other end, Tony Esposito was struck on the side of the face by a Ken Hodge shot from the right wing corner. Tony shook it off and stayed in the net for what turned out to be a tough afternoon for his team as older brother Phil notched his second straight opening-game hat trick of the playoffs, leading the Bruins to a 6-3 win and a 1-0 series lead. It was also an exemplary defensive performance by Orr, who blocked shots while Cheevers was out of the net — including a Bobby Hull slapper he took on the chest.

Orr put the Bruins up early in Game Two, on a perfectly executed give-and-go with Fred Stanfield. Cheevers continued to have the hot

Steve Babineau

Esposito's large frame and deft scoring touch made him a constant threat in front of the opposition's goal.

hand, while Stanfield, Marcotte, and Esposito added goals and the Bruins cruised to a 4-1 victory. The B's had come into Chicago hoping for a split, and left with a 2-0 series lead. In both games, they managed to keep the deafening roar of the enemy crowd to a minimum by getting an early lead and adding to it. By the time the Hawks scored and the Chicago Stadium fog horn went off, the Bruins were already in control of the game. Now it was back to Beantown in quest of a sweep.

In Game Three, the Bruins started slow and trailed 2-1 at the end of the first period. Pie McKenzie provided the wake-up call with a pinpoint pass through the crease to Bucyk, perfectly positioned on the doorstep, and the game was tied. The B's then took the lead on a great individual effort by Cashman.

At the other end of the ice, Gerry Cheevers was putting on a clinic that could have been titled Acrobatic Goaltending 101. Cheesy leaped through the air to stop a Dennis Hull rocket with his shoulder, speared a point-blank Keith Magnuson shot with his glove and swatted a Magnuson redirection out of mid-air with his stick. The Bruins won the game 5-2, taking a commanding 3-0 series lead.

On April 26, the Bruins took the ice with a chance to pull off an unlikely four-game sweep and clinch a berth in the finals. But the Blackhawks, who were facing the near-impossible task of coming back from a three-love series deficit, weren't about to concede.

Despite some standout goaltending by Tony Esposito, the Bruins scored twice in the first frame to take a two-goal lead into the locker room. But Chicago showed heart, and battled back to take a 3-2 lead on a Magnuson slapper and two Dennis Hull tallies before Fred Stanfield tied it up again. Bryan Campbell gave the Hawks their first third period lead of the series before Ken Hodge redirected a Phil Esposito pass with under seven minutes left in regulation to knot it at four. With un-

der two minutes left, McKenzie intercepted Stan Mikita's clearing pass, got the puck to Stanfield who returned it as Pie cut in on the right side. He held it until the moment Tony-O was screened and pulled the trigger, firing a perfect shot — top-shelf, short-side. Game! Match! Series!

What a showcase this was for the game of hockey. A nationally-televised audience got to see what many experts considered to be one of the finest Stanley Cup games ever played. They saw the game's newest superstar and his surging young team take a giant step toward the top by once again shutting down Bobby Hull and outscrapping the high-powered Blackhawks.

The sweep assured the Bruins of some rest before the finals, since St. Louis and Pittsburgh were still battling it out in the West. The Blues eventually prevailed in six games, earning a shot at the Big, Bad Bruins.

It was Boston's first finals appearance since 1958. Although it seemed anticlimactic to be facing the Blues after tangling with the powers of the East, Beantown was nevertheless revved up for what many anticipated to be a championship celebration.

The league awarded the Blues home-ice advantage because of their expansion status, so Games One and Two were held at The Arena in St. Louis. A scary moment occurred early in the second period of Game One. With the score tied 1-1, Fred Stanfield took a slapper that hit Blues goalie Jacques Plante in the mask. Plante was stunned by the shot and fell to the ice. He was okay: the mask, which he pioneered back in 1959, apparently saved his life, or at least his looks.

The Blues hung tough and after two periods, it was 2-1 Boston, thanks to two goals by Johnny Bucyk. In the third, the Bruins broke it open with four unanswered tallies (including the hat trick for the Chief) and Boston won 6-1.

The Blues were never in Game Two. The Bruins dominated, cruising to a 6-2 win. Once again the Bruins found themselves up 2-0 in a series and headed back to the Hub for a chance at a sweep.

St. Louis drew first blood in Game Three with a power play goal by Frank St. Marseille early in the first period. Later in the period, Bucyk tied the game on the power play with his 10th goal of the playoffs. McKenzie put the B's ahead for good in the second before Wayne Cashman put it away with a couple of third period tallies. The Bruins now stood on the threshold of their first Stanley Cup since 1941, leading three games to none. Game Four was scheduled for three days later on Sunday, Mother's Day, May 10 — a date that Boston sports fans will always remember.

The NHL awards banquet was held on Saturday, and Bobby Orr cleaned up by winning the Hart Trophy as the league's Most Valuable Player, the Art Ross Trophy as the league's leading scorer, and, for the third straight year, the Norris Trophy, as the league's top defenseman. The next day, he was awarded the Conn Smythe Trophy as the MVP of the playoffs, becoming the first player ever to win four individual trophies in a single season.

Although the Blues were down 3-0 in the series, and outscored by a total of 16-4, they were not ready to surrender. St. Louis coach Scotty Bowman had his team mentally prepared for battle in Game Four. At the end of two periods, the score was tied at two. Then Larry Keenan gave the Blues a 3-2 lead, and time began to wind down on

Boston. The expansion Blues were threatening to ruin the Garden party and force a fifth game back in St. Louis when, with less than seven minutes remaining, Johnny Bucyk tipped in a McKenzie shot to force sudden-death overtime.

The stage was set for Cup-winning heroics. People throughout New England were glued to their television sets in anticipation of a long-awaited moment of glory. If the Blues scored, the series would go back to St. Louis for a fifth game and the champagne would be put on ice. If the Bruins scored, New Englanders would jump for joy and the party would begin.

B's coach Harry Sinden put the so-called checking line out to open the overtime. After St. Louis won the draw, the Bruins got it right back and began to apply the pressure. Awrey's drive was blocked, Sanderson's drive was wide and Sanderson again shot wide. Then Orr took charge. He blocked Keenan's attempted clear along the right wing boards, passed the puck to Derek behind the net and cut for the net. Sanderson fed Orr a perfect pass in front and he slipped it between Glenn

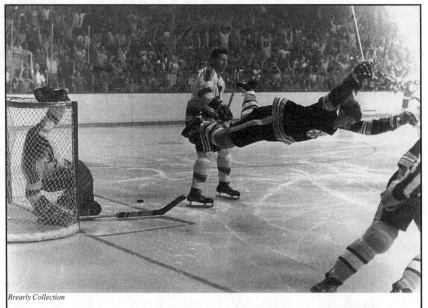

Brearly Collection

Ray Lucier's classic photo of Bobby Orr in flight after scoring the Stanley Cup-winning goal for Boston in 1970.

Hall's pads. Boston's 22-year-old hero flew through the air in jubilation — with a little help from Blues defenseman Noel Picard's stick. Sports photographer Ray Lucier caught the moment in what is considered to be one of the all-time great sports photographs. Posters were immediately printed up and kids all over New England stuck it on their bedroom walls.

The locker room celebration was televised locally, with Don Earle interviewing the triumphant Bruins in a crossfire of champagne and celebratory yells. When locker room coverage ended, many young fans anxiously reached for their equipment and took to the streets. "I remember coming home after they won the Cup in '70 from the Garden," Jack Parker says. "Driving through Charlestown, and you had to avoid the kids in the street. The game was about an hour old and everybody was out in the street playing street hockey."

These kids knew there would be no more Bruins games for the next five months and no frozen ponds for at least six months. Usually, by this time of year, most youngsters had long forgotten about hockey and were out in the fields playing baseball. But not this year. A lot of kids didn't want the hockey season to end, so streets and rinks became the place to go after school and on the weekends.

The next day Bruins fans showed their appreciation by staging what the Boston Globe called a "love-in" for their beloved heroes. The team traveled through Boston in a motorcade that stopped in Government Center for a ceremony to honor the champs. School teachers in the Boston area wondered not why there were so many empty seats in their classrooms. A record 140,000 people turned out for this unique event. Never before had there been a celebration of this magnitude for a sports team in the Hub.

The love-in officially marked the end of a magical hockey season. A season that began in near-tragedy with the Ted Green incident; and ended gloriously with a ten-game winning streak that set a playoff record and culminated in the Stanley Cup's long-awaited return to Boston. And speaking of playoff records, Orr and Esposito set some of their own. Bobby's 9 goals and 20 points were new records for defensemen, while Phil's 13 goals and 27 points were new overall highs.

This championship brought a sense of satisfaction and civic pride to many Boston fans. But for the kids who were hungry to learn how to play hockey and get good at it, there was no time to bask in the glory of their favorite team. Although the kids enjoyed playing street hockey, they knew that if they were to have any chance at the high school or college level, they needed ice time. Fortunately for these kids, there were local organizers and Massachusetts District Commission (MDC) officials who realized their needs and set out to remedy the situation.

The MDC had already built approximately 20 open-air rinks from 1954 to 1969 within Boston's beltway, Route 128. Most of these rinks were built primarily as recreational outlets for public and figure skating. They served certain practical purposes, offering a good place to exercise in the winter and a place for kids to go to where they could be supervised. When most of these rinks were built, the MDC had no idea that within a few years they would be full 24 hours a day. Ice time became a very precious commodity.

The first thing the MDC did to give the kids a chance to practice hockey was to put roofs on the open-air rinks. They couldn't totally enclose them, because they were refrigerated by ammonia and needed ventilation; otherwise, if they ever had a line break, there would be instant fatality. By the late '70s, the ammonia was replaced with freon, which allowed the rinks to be enclosed on the sides as well.

This meant no more rainouts or snowouts. The roofs also provided better lighting and sound, while benches and locker rooms were added for hockey compatibility.

While the MDC was adapting the existing rinks to accommodate organized ice hockey, they continued to build more to help satisfy the increased demand for ice time. The private sector followed suit. Many privately owned rinks popped up around the area and beyond. Longtime hotbeds of baseball and football were getting interested in hockey. Cities and towns started building rinks with their high and elementary schools: when a new school complex was proposed, a skating rink was usually part of the plan.

As these rinks went up, many more high school and youth hockey programs were organized and existing programs were upgraded. There were 59 Massachusetts youth hockey programs listed in the 1971 Official Guide of the Amateur Hockey Association of the United States (AHAUS). From '71 to the early '80s, the number of programs continued to grow. Today there are upwards of 120 boys programs and as many as 25 girls programs.

There was another reason for Boston's hockey mania, and the Bruins were once again involved. The team had Mondays off, so, beginning in '68, Bobby Orr and other players gave clinics at high schools. They taught kids how to practice fundamentals, then scrimmaged against them. In order to even things out, the squads would switch goaltenders. After the scrimmage, the Bruins would hang around and sign autographs. This was the Bruins way of marketing their own popularity. "When the popularity is there and the team doesn't market it, that's their fault," says Derek Sanderson, who remembers not only how beneficial those Mondays were to the team's image, but how fulfilling it was for him. "We went off to schools and it was a great experience. I mean you get to meet the fans, you talk to the kids, and you're not that much older than the kids you're playing against really." The kids were having the thrill of a lifetime, and the players were having a ball too.

While the hockey boom was enveloping New England, the Bruins and their fans were gearing up for another season. With the new season came changes. Former assistant Tom Johnson was named to replace the retiring Harry Sinden as head coach and center Jim Lorentz was traded to St. Louis.

There were some league changes as well. Expansion franchises had been awarded to Buffalo and Vancouver for the new season, making it a 14-team league. The divisions were realigned in an attempt to balance them. The two new teams joined the East, and the Chicago Blackhawks moved to the West.

High expectations for the '70-71 season were more than fulfilled during the regular season. The juggernaut that won ten playoff games in a row en route to the Stanley Cup the previous spring picked up right where it had left off and crushed everything in its path throughout the 78-game campaign.

The Big, Bad Bruins won 57, lost 14, and tied 7 for a record-setting 121 points. In doing so, they scored an astounding 399 goals, with team members taking the top four spots in the scoring race. In no other regular season had one team been so dominant. When the following year's hockey trading cards came out, kids were amazed to see that the card featuring the top three scorers of the previous season had all Bruins: 1) Esposito, 2) Orr, and 3) Bucyk. And they were also likely to learn — if they didn't already know — that the 4th (Hodge), 7th (Cashman), 8th (McKenzie), and one of the three tied for 9th (Stanfield), were all Bruins.

Many people at the time believed that Espo's 76 goals and 152 points were records that would never be broken — except maybe by him. The same was said about Orr's 37 goals and 102 assists, for 139 points by a defenseman. Exactly one decade later, Wayne Gretzky broke Esposito's record for total points, and his record for goals the year after that. Bobby Orr broke his own record for goals in the 1974-75 season with 46. But, to this day, all three of his single-season scoring records for defensemen stand.

The awards ceremony was once again dominated by Bruins, with Espo winning his second Art Ross. Orr sealed his second-straight Hart, and his fourth-straight Norris. Johnny Bucyk won the Lady Byng Trophy, which is awarded to the player combining the highest degree of sportsmanship and gentlemanly conduct with a high standard of playing ability.

After making mincemeat of the rest of the league during the regular season, the '70-71 Bruins were heavy favorites to repeat as Stanley Cup champions. Their first-round opponent was the Montreal Canadiens. Although the Habs finished a very respectable 42-23-13, for 97 points (good for third place in the East), the Bruins were heavy favorites to dispose of them quickly and romp to a second straight Stanley Cup.

The Canadiens, on the other hand, were waiting to pull out their secret weapon. He was Ken Dryden, a 23-year-old goalie out of Cornell University. Dryden was studying law part time at McGill University, while playing with the Canadiens' Nova Scotia farm team. He was called up to the big club late in the regular season and had looked impressive in the six games he played. He arranged to have his final exams delayed, so he could perform in the playoffs.

The Habs coaching staff was aware that Ken had played for Cornell in the ECAC tournament, held every year at the Boston Garden. They knew he was familiar with its small ice surface and accustomed to the funny caroms and bounces the puck would take off the boards.

After the Bruins took the first game at Boston Garden and were leading 5-1 late in the second period of Game Two, it seemed they were well on their way to making quick work of the Canadiens. But then came the comeback. The Habs got one back before the end of the second period to cut the lead to 5-2 as they headed for the dressing room. The third period was dominated by the Canadiens. They came all the way back to stun the Bruins and their fans, and even the series at one game apiece.

That second game was the turning point in the series. The young law student out of Cornell proceeded to stone the frustrated Bruins. Dryden's 6'4", 215-pound frame covered much of the net and, for a rookie, he showed

Steve Babineau

Former Cornell netminder Ken Dryden spoiled a record-breaking season for Boston in 1970-71.

Kevin Hubbard's drawing depicting the playoff series in 1988 when Boston finally broke Montreal's streak of 19 consecutive playoff series victories over the Bruins dating back to 1942.

amazing poise in tight situations. He admitted after the series was over that he was quite fearful every time he had to face the potent Boston attack, but he responded to the pressure by making some extraordinary saves, almost singlehandedly leading the Canadiens to the shocking upset.

Fans across New England were stunned as the dreaded Habs, whose dynasty had supposedly ended in favor of Boston's, derailed the Big, Bad Bruins and advanced to the semifinals. The Canadiens went on to beat Minnesota and Chicago to win their 17th Stanley Cup. They accomplished this with the help of some more great goaltending by Dryden (who earned himself the nickname "Octopus" on his way to winning the Conn Smythe), and the leadership of classy captain Jean Beliveau, who retired at season's end.

It would be a long summer of regret for the Bruins, who couldn't wait until training camp opened in September to begin their quest to regain the Cup.

Meanwhile, the hockey boom in New England continued to grow. The ever-increasing

demand for rinks was met in Massachusetts by the State Department of Natural Resources, which, in collaboration with the Department of Public Works, began the construction of 13 more facilities outside the Boston beltway.

These two agencies had already built five rinks in the late '60s in some of the state's larger cities, to complement what the MDC did around Boston. The Worcester and Brockton rinks were completed by December 1968; Greenfield and North Adams by February 1969; and Springfield by March. Seven of the 13 new rinks were finished by the end of '72 and the other six were completed by the end of '74.

Bobby Orr and his teammates continued to reach out to the communities, setting up games against men's league teams. Part of the evening would include letting the kids from the local youth hockey programs suit up and skate onto the ice to have their pictures taken with Bobby and the other Bruins. These events drew large crowds, and sometimes there wasn't enough room to squeeze everybody in. "I remember one night in Auburn, in '73, and the place was packed for miles down the road," says Ted Butler, a Department of Environmental Management official recalling an event 50 miles west of Boston.

In the off-season of '71, the Bruins lost leftwinger Wayne Carleton to the Seals in the intra-league draft. With Carleton's departure, they lost some size and goal production, but the previous year's mid-season acquisition of center Mike Walton from Toronto spelled potential, allowing for a full season where Walton could gel with his new team.

The Bruins opened the '71-72 season at home with a loss to the New York Rangers. They returned the favor three days later in New York, then proceeded to tear up the league once again.

From mid-to-late November, the Beantowners went on a seven-game winning streak that ended when they tied the Blues in St. Louis.

Wins were now coming easy in places where the Bruins had experienced trouble in years past. In a mid-December meeting with Toronto at Maple Leaf Gardens, they exploded for three goals in less than two minutes, and went on to beat the Leafs 5-3. After Espo scored his 300th career goal against Oakland, the Bruins beat the Blackhawks in Chicago, 5-1. It was their first win at Chicago Stadium since the '70 playoffs.

The Causeway Street Crusaders then invaded the Aud in Buffalo for an early January encounter with the Sabres. Boston won the game, and, by doing so, took over first place.

The All-Star Game was held January 25, during sub-zero temperatures in Minnesota. The Bruins were well represented with Espo, Orr, Bucyk, McKenzie and Dallas Smith all making the squad, and dominated the game as well. The East came back from a 2-0 deficit to win 3-2, when Pie tied it late in the second and Espo scored the game-winner from Orr and Smith early in the third.

The Bruins continued their winning ways after the All-Star break. They beat the Rangers again in New York to stretch their unbeaten streak to 11 games, and had now lost only two of their last 36. They were the picture of consistency.

In late February, the Bruins' brass pulled the trigger on a deal they'd been working on for some time. They sent Rick Smith, Reggie Leach and Bob Stewart to the California Seals for highly-coveted defenseman Carol Vadnais.

It was ironic that Carol's first game with Boston would be against his former team. It seemed as if California had gotten the better of the deal when they jumped to a 6-1 lead, but the Bruins came storming back. In the sec-

ond period, they netted six unanswered tallies to go up 7-6, and never looked back. Esposito scored the tying and game-winning goals in the 8-6 win.

Espo was having yet another marvelous season and hat tricks were becoming commonplace. "The old lamplighter was raising the electric bill at an alarming rate," said Bruins' radio voice Bob Wilson on *The Avengers*, a record album made to commemorate the Big, Bad Bruins' quest to regain the Cup. And if you happened to be riding in a motor vehicle around the Boston area back in those days, you might have seen a bumper sticker that read: "Jesus Saves and Esposito Scores on the Rebound."

On March 8, the Bruins were short on defensemen for their home date with Minnesota, and called up Detroit-born Doug Roberts from their minor league team, the Boston Braves. Roberts came up big in the pinch when he tied the game on the rebound of an Orr shot that hit the post. Then Bucyk gave the Bruins the lead when he potted the rebound of a shot taken by Orr as he laid flat on his back. The result: another Boston win.

The Bruins clinched first place overall at home against the Canadiens to win a second straight Prince of Wales Trophy. Beating Montreal made it even sweeter, for it was the dreaded Habs who had broken the hearts of New Englanders a year ago.

It was playoff time again and the wait for a shot at redemption was finally over. To win the regular season was nice, but it was the Cup that the Bruins coveted. In 1970, they missed first place, but won the Cup. In '71 they took first, but missed the Cup. This year, they were determined to win both.

The playoff format was changed so that the first place team in each division would play the team that finished fourth and second would play third. Therefore, Boston's first playoff opponent was the Toronto Maple

Leafs, who finished with 80 points, just four more than fifth place Detroit.

The Leafs were coached by Hall of Fame defenseman King Clancy, who had his team focused on upsetting the injury-plagued Bruins. Esposito had a knee problem, Stanfield was hurting, Sanderson was battling ulcerative colitis, and Orr's left knee was injured so badly that he was already scheduled for surgery at season's end.

The Bruins, however, were ready to put their injuries aside, and get down to business. They came out in Game One and ran the Leafs off the ice by a 5-0 count. After dropping the second game in overtime, the B's went into Toronto and took both Games Three and Four. Sanderson, who shuttled between the Boston Garden and Massachusetts General Hospital during the first two games, even made the trip.

Game Three was a penalty-filled, scoreless affair until Mike Walton broke the ice by firing one by Bernie Parent on a feed from Orr. In the third, Orr scored to put it away for a 2-0 final. Game Four was a high-scoring affair and Bobby led the way again, playing about 34 minutes and making some big plays. It's hard to imagine what he could have done with two good knees instead of one.

The Bruins put the Leafs away in Game Five and earned a few days to rest their nagging injuries while awaiting the outcome of the St. Louis-Minnesota series. Another change in the playoff format had the two divisions crossing over to play each other in the semi-finals instead of waiting until the finals. If the league had done this when expansion began, it would have produced a much more competitive finals.

St. Louis prevailed over Minnesota, so it would be the Blues in the semis. Fred Stanfield

Steve Babineau

Left wing Wayne Cashman was one of the more intimidating players ever to don the Black and Gold.

notched a hat trick to lead the Black and Gold to an easy win in Game One. The next game was even easier, as the Bruins demolished the Blues to the tune of 10-2. The 10 goals tied a team playoff record for goals in a game, set in 1969 when they beat Toronto 10-0.

The series shifted to St. Louis and the Blues hoped a little home cookin' might turn things around. But the friendly confines of the St. Louis Arena were of no help. Boston won Game Three in another rout, 7-2, and completed the sweep with a 5-3 victory in Game Four.

Meanwhile, the red-hot New York Rangers, who eliminated the defending champion Canadiens in round one, were completing a sweep of the Chicago Blackhawks. This set the stage for a Boston-New York showdown to begin April 30 for all the marbles.

The Bruins had the home-ice advantage because of their first place overall finish. The Rangers went up early in Game One on a goal by Dale Rolfe, but the Bruins responded with four unanswered tallies, including two by Ken Hodge, to take a 4-1 lead into the locker room. Midway through the second period, Hodge completed his hat trick on a feed from Espo and Game One was beginning to look like a blowout. The Rangers, however, were not about to quit as Rod Gilbert scored to cut the Boston lead to 5-2.

In the third, the Rangers began to chip away at the Boston lead and by mid-period tied it on a score by Bruce MacGregor. Panic struck in Boston as the Bruins and their fans witnessed a comfortable lead wither away to nothing.

The score remained tied until, with just over two minutes to go in regulation, Ace Bailey scored the biggest goal of his career. He took a pass from Walton on the left wing side, moved around Brad Park, cut in front of the goal, and flipped a backhander over Ed Giacomin.

Both coaches decided to change their goal-keepers for Game Two. The Bruins started Eddie Johnston and the Rangers went with Gilles Villemure. The result was a low-scoring contest that was tied at one halfway through the third when the Rangers took a couple of penalties, giving the Bruins a five-on-three advantage. Again it was Mike Walton who made it happen, as he found Hodge open on the doorstep. The Bruins had a commanding 2-0 series lead.

The Rangers sucked it up and put on a show for the Madison Square Garden faithful in Game Three, breezing past the Bruins 5-2, on the strength of three power-play goals in the first period.

Number Four led the way for Boston in Game Four with two first period scores to give the B's a 2-0 lead. Late in the second, he set up Don Marcotte for the eventual game-winner, as the Bruins held on to win 3-2. They were now only one win away from bringing the Stanley Cup back to Beantown.

The stage was set for another home-ice Cup celebration when the series returned to Boston for Game Five. The Bruins appeared destined to sip the bubbly by evening's end. They held a 2-1 lead after two periods. But Bobby Rousseau spoiled the party by beating Eddie Johnston twice in the third, sending the series back to the Big Apple.

As in Game Four, Bobby Orr got things going in the right direction in Game Six for the visiting black shirts. The Bruins went on a power play midway through the first. From the right point, Orr moved to his left to save a pass that was heading out of the zone, and faked out MacGregor, bluffing to his right and spinning around to his left before wristing a shot past Villemure on the near side. It was another piece of artistry by the 24-year-old sensation and Boston had the all-important first goal of the game.

The score remained 1-0 through the rest of the first and all of the second, as the two evenly matched teams continued the hard-hitting, fast-paced, aggressive style they'd

Steve Babineau

Two bad knees never stopped the courageous Orr from sacrificing his body when needed.

played throughout the series. Five minutes into the third, the Bruins got a big insurance goal when Wayne Cashman tipped in a shot by Orr. Cashman added another late in the third, and the Bruins — behind the shutout goaltending of Gerry Cheevers — won their second Stanley Cup in three years.

Bobby Orr won his second Conn Smythe Trophy, and Gerry Cheevers once again lived up to his reputation as a money goaltender who came up big when the chips were on the line.

The Bruins took extra pleasure in parading the Stanley Cup around Madison Square Garden. Many experts had doubted their ability to beat the Rangers twice in a row in their own building. The Bruins found it most gratifying to prove to their detractors that they could clinch the championship away from the Boston Garden.

After the locker room celebration, the Bruins boarded a bus for La Guardia Airport. The team took a police escort through the streets of New York to the Queens-Midtown Tunnel. Bobby Orr later told Mike Shalin of the *Boston Herald* that when the two parties reached the tunnel, and the police cars broke off to head back to town, the Bruins waved to thank them and one of the New York cops gave them the finger.

The incident was symbolic of how the Bruins-Rangers clashes of the early '70s had taken on the same kind of bitter intensity as that of the Red Sox-Yankees rivalry.

When the Bruins' flight to Boston landed at Logan Airport around 2:30 A.M., thousands of manic fans charged the Eastern Airlines terminal, causing destruction in their path. When the team and its entourage got off the plane, they were besieged by fans both rowdy and jolly, all chanting "We're number one!"

After another grand celebration at Government Center's City Hall Plaza, the 1971-72

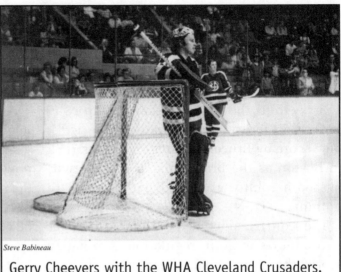

Steve Babineau

Gerry Cheevers with the WHA Cleveland Crusaders.

hockey season was over and the Bruins and their fans had the rest of spring and all of summer to bask in the glory of another Stanley Cup triumph. While they basked, the inspirational seeds that this charismatic team had planted continued to bloom. Streets continued to teem with games of ball hockey. Rinks were so booked that parents had to wake up at four o'clock in the morning to drive their kids out to the only available ice time.

At the same time, a rival league with 12 franchises, the World Hockey Association (WHA), emerged. Owners from the new league lured 70 NHL players away from their former teams during the offseason of '72 by offering them big money contracts. The Bruins were hit hard by the exodus, losing three key players. Gerry Cheevers signed with Cleveland, Ted Green went to the New England Whalers, and John McKenzie and Derek Sanderson left to join the Philadelphia Blazers. Sanderson, however, was bought back by the Bruins after playing only eight games for Philly.

While the new league was stocking its rosters with former NHL players, the NHL added two more expansion teams — the New York Islanders and the Atlanta Flames. The Bruins lost Ed Westfall to the Islanders in the expansion draft. Although they were fortunate enough to get Sanderson back, they lost the guy who teamed so well with him on the third line and on penalty killing.

Hockey fans in Boston were disappointed to see some of their favorites leave town to join the new league, but the flip side was that there would be more opportunities to see pro hockey now that the Whalers were coming to town. The New England Whalers, who split their home games between the Boston Garden and the old Boston Arena, were brought to the Hub to accommodate the thousands of hockey fans who had a hard time getting Bruins tickets.

The Bruins dropped to second place in the East Division behind Montreal in the 1972-73 regular season, despite finishing a very impressive 51-22-5, for 107 points. The B's were hampered by injuries when they opened the playoffs against the New York Rangers. It only got worse when Phil Esposito went down early in the series on a Ron Harris bodycheck. The Rangers avenged their loss in the finals the previous year by taking the Bruins out in five games.

The Black and Gold rebounded the following year by finishing first overall in the regular season and advancing to the Stanley Cup finals against the up-and-coming Philadelphia Flyers. Boston was the favorite to win its third Cup in five years, but a rough, pesky Flyers team — led by the outstanding goaltending of former Bruin Bernie Parent and a masterful, stop-Orr game plan by coach Fred Shero — did them in.

A popular bumper sticker in New England at the time was "The Cup Stops Here." It stopped twice, but compared to people's expectations, its stop was all too brief.

After two Stanley Cups, three finals appearances and three first-place-overall finishes in five years, the reign of the Big, Bad Bruins was over. What is now considered the "glory days" had come to an end. Yet while the Bruins fell short of their desired mark, they had already inspired an entire generation of hockey talent.

During their reign some future NHL stars were either just learning to skate or beginning to develop their skills in youth hockey programs. In 1972, Bobby Carpenter, a member of the 1995 Stanley Cup Champion New Jersey Devils, was part of a Peabody, Mass. squirt team that won the state tournament.

Carpenter's mother, Ann, recalls his early years, when Bobby Orr was his biggest influence. "He always wore number four when he was just a mite, but when he played squirts, another kid had already claimed it," she says. Every kid wanted to wear number four.

Carpenter went on to star at St. John's Prep

Steve Babineau

Don "Grapes" Cherry, seen here with his best friend, Blue, coached the Bruins of the mid to late 1970s to considerable success.

in Danvers, which borders Peabody about 20 miles north of Boston. At the end of his senior year, he was touted as "The Can't Miss Kid" on the cover of *Sports Illustrated*. He went right from St. John's to the National Hockey League, where he scored 32 goals for the Washington Capitals in his rookie season of 1981-82.

Meanwhile, about 35 miles south of Boston at the Hobomock Arena in Pembroke, future Pittsburgh Penguins and Bruins star Kevin Stevens played his first game of organized hockey ever on an instructional mite team. His father, Arty, relates of his son's standout debut: "They dropped the puck, and he skated in and scored. He did it six straight times. They'd drop the puck and he'd skate by everybody. Finally, they took him off center and put him on a wing."

It was also around this time that future Pittsburgh Penguin teammate Tom Barrasso — then age seven — was playing on several mite and squirt teams in the suburban Boston area. One of them was the Assabet squirt team with future pros Bob Sweeney and John Carter, who also played on Tom's Woburn team. Barrasso had learned to skate at age four. "That was around the time of the '69-70 Stanley Cup for Boston," says Tom's mother Lucy. "He got to watching Gerry Cheevers and he was his big hero at that time, so he decided he wanted to skate."

In Barrasso's youth hockey travels, he competed in tournaments held in Canada against such future greats as Patrick Roy and Steve Yzerman. He went on to play for Acton-Boxborough High in the Dual County League, where he once again teamed with Bob Sweeney. Other stars of that team included Mike Flanigan, a defenseman who was drafted by Edmonton and Allen Bourbeau, who broke Robbie Ftorek's state record for goals his senior year.

Like Bobby Carpenter, Barrasso opted to go directly from high school to the pros. A wise decision: he was a standout in his first season with the Buffalo Sabres. He won the Calder Memorial Trophy as Rookie of the Year, the Vezina Trophy as the league's most valuable goalie, and was named to the NHL All-Star first team and All-Rookie team. He later went on to win two Stanley Cups with Pittsburgh.

Another future star who learned to skate in the early to mid-'70s was Chicago Blackhawks center Tony Amonte. When Tony was only three years old, his father Lewis, who followed the Big, Bad Bruins, recommended that his two sons learn to skate. One afternoon Amonte's mother, Kathleen, took the initiative and brought him and his five-year-old brother Rocco to nearby Pilgrim Arena in Hingham on Boston's South Shore. The boys took to it immediately and soon got involved in the Hingham Youth Hockey program.

Tony went on to play high school hockey at Thayer Academy in suburban Braintree. In his first three years at Thayer, his linemate was future Blackhawk teammate Jeremy Roenick, who hails from Marshfield. In Amonte's freshman year, they won the New England Prep school championship by beating future New York Ranger Brian Leetch and his undefeated Avon Old Farms (of Connecticut) team in the finals. "We were big-time underdogs, but it seemed like everything was coming together and we won the game," recalls Amonte of the upset. The next year they repeated by beating Choate Academy in the finals.

Tony then went on to play for Boston University, and was part of the 1990-91 team that lost to Northern Michigan in triple overtime in the NCAA finals. His teammates at BU included future NHL players Shawn McEachern, Ed Ronan, David Sacco, Scott Lachance and Keith Tkachuk, all of whom come from the Boston area.

Of the five other New England states, Rhode Island was probably most driven by the boom.

In the late '60s, Chris Terreri of the Chicago Blackhawks started playing street hockey with his older brother Pete in Warwick. At age 4, Chris was considered too small to play up on the front lines with Pete and his friends, so they put him in goal.

Chris soon learned to skate in the family's mini-rink in the back yard, and began playing organized hockey at age six. In 1975, his squirt team emerged victorious from the national championships that were held in Melvindale, Mich. After playing high school hockey at Pilgrim High in Warwick, he took Providence College to the 1985 NCAA finals, but lost to a very strong RPI team that had Adam Oates, Darren Puppa and John Carter.

Another of the handful of Rhode Islanders who made the bigs is David Emma, who won the Hobey Baker Award at Boston College as the country's outstanding collegiate player, then joined the New Jersey Devils.

The influence of Orr and the Bruins extended to the farmost reaches of New England. The first-ever Vermont native to make the NHL is John LeClair of the Philadelphia Flyers. LeClair was born and raised in St. Albans, located less than 20 miles from the Quebec border and is actually a lot closer to Montreal than to Boston. "Bobby Orr was a great influence on a lot of kids growing up," Leclair says, "because St. Albans considers itself a New England town more than the Canadiens but they're both there. He had a huge impact on every kid before me and up to my age group."

From 1970 to the present, the New England area has produced over 150 players who went on to play in either the NHL or the now-defunct WHA.

The Orr era also produced something unprecedented in the collegiate ranks: two Hobey Baker Award winners from the same family. In 1983, Harvard's Mark Fusco became the first ECAC player to win the award. Mark joined the Hartford Whalers the following year but soon retired from the pro ranks. In 1986, his brother Scott, who also played for the Crimson, won the award. Scott, however, decided not to turn pro.

There are hundreds of New England kids who grew up during the Big, Bad Bruins era who excelled at the collegiate level, but never turned pro. Examples of these are former Harvard stars Allen Bourbeau, Jack Hughes, Joey Cavanaugh, Steve Dadgian and Hockey East Commissioner Joe Bertagna. Other notables include Eddie Riordan (Boston College), Ralph Cox (New Hampshire), and Brian "Dukie" Walsh (Notre Dame).

Many of the ex-college players who didn't turn pro went on to play in the now-defunct New England Amateur Hockey League (NEAHL). Teams such as the

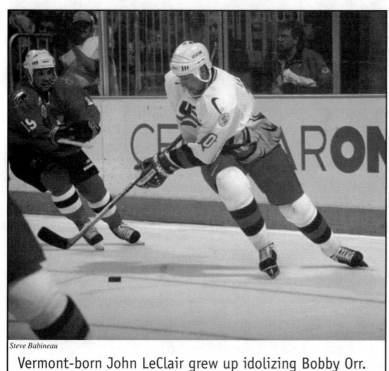

Steve Babineau

Vermont-born John LeClair grew up idolizing Bobby Orr.

Braintree (MA) Hawks and the Manchester (NH) Blackhawks drew well, and provided hockey fans around the area with some quality play.

Because of the abundance of kids who learned to play at a young age in the late '60s and early '70s, New England colleges had more quality local players to pick from by the early '80s. This is the biggest reason that eastern colleges became a lot more competitive with the powerhouses of the midwest. The 1995 NCAA final saw Boston University take on Maine. It was the first time two Hockey East schools had met in the finals.

BU was led by sophomore Mike Grier of Holliston, Massachussets, who, upon being drafted by the St. Louis Blues, became destined to be the first African-American hockey player to turn pro.

Another aftermath of the Orr era in the Boston area was the increase in popularity of the Beanpot, an annual round-robin tournament held at Boston Garden between Harvard, Northeastern, Boston University and Boston College. It's become a real Boston tradition and has sold out well in advance for years, despite being aired on local TV (and later on ESPN 2).

"'Snooks' Kelley, the late, great coach of BC, called it 'the social event of the season,'" recalls Bill Cleary, who has been involved in the tournament in just about every fashion. "I think it's one of the greatest collegiate tournaments of its kind in the country, in any sport."

Four of the key players on the gold medal-winning 1980 Olympic team that pulled off "The Miracle on Ice" at Lake Placid, were

Steve Babineau

Left: Massachusetts native Bobby Miller played six NHL season with Boston, Colorado and Los Angeles. *Right:* Ted Donato is one of many fine hockey players to come out of Massachusetts perennial high school power, Catholic Memorial.

former BU stars Mike Eruzione, Dave Silk, Jack O'Callahan and Jim Craig, all of whom were born and raised in the Boston area. The oldest of the foursome is Eruzione, a forward who scored the game-winning goal against the Russians.

Eruzione began skating in 1963 at age eight before joining pee-wees and then bantams (there were no mites or squirts back then). He skated for Winthrop High from 1970-72 and credits the Big, Bad Bruins for keeping him inspired to play. "I think they made me more of a hockey fan," he says. "I was older at that time and was already playing, but it got me interested more in the game, and if they weren't there, I wonder whether I would've kept pursuing the sport."

Dave Silk grew up in suburban Scituate, where he played in the youth hockey program started by the late Ed Taylor, who later ran the Pilgrim Arena in Hingham. The best youth hockey in the Boston area in the late '60s was played on the South Shore, largely thanks to Taylor. Silk was part of a pee wee team that advanced to the state finals one year and to the New England finals the next.

Silk also attributes much of his development to the summer hockey he played in his early teens. "Between bantams and high school, there isn't a whole lot you can do," he says. "I always played a lot of summer hockey. It was better than midget hockey because you got to play against older kids. I was always able to play against older kids in the summer, and that was where you could really make some hay."

Defenseman Jack O'Callahan of Charlestown and goalie Jim Craig of North Easton played against each other in high school as sophomores back in 1972, when O'Callahan's Boston Latin squad played a pre-season scrimmage against Craig's Oliver Ames team.

When Craig was a senior, his Oliver Ames team played future Norris Trophy winner Rod Langway and his Randolph High team in the semi-finals of the 1975 state tournament. Langway — who was all-scholastic in hockey, football and baseball at Randolph — went on to hockey stardom at the University of New Hampshire and the NHL.

Over the years, the number of New England players on Olympic squads has grown. Out of the 20 players chosen for the 1992 Olympic team, 14 of them came from Massachusetts and two from Rhode Island, which can be attributed to the tremendous high school and prep school system in the New England area.

Massachusetts high school hockey hotbeds such as Catholic Memorial of West Roxbury, Matignon of Cambridge, Arlington and Arlington Catholic and Mount St. Charles of Woonsocket, R.I., are perennial powers that produce a wealth of college, Olympic and pro talent, year after year.

A few examples of the many prep school powers in New England are Thayer Academy of Braintree (MA), St. John's of Danvers (MA), and Avon Old Farms of Avon (CT). Many fine players have come out of these schools and gone on to excel at the higher levels.

In the early '80s, a local television show called *Hockey Night in Boston* debuted. It featured highlights and interviews of local high school players. The show eventually evolved into an annual summer tournament featuring high school all-star teams from all over the United States.

There are also some fine hockey players from New England who chose to pursue careers in different sports, particularly baseball. Tom Glavine of the Atlanta Braves was Division I High School Hockey Player of the Year at Billerica High (MA). He was then drafted by the Los Angeles Kings, but chose baseball instead. In 1993, Glavine lived a dream when, much to the chagrin of the Braves' brass, he spent a week in Los Angeles and practiced with Gretzky and the Kings.

Other New England hockey players who chose major league baseball are catcher Mike LaValliere and pitcher Jason Bere. LaValliere played hockey at Trinity High in Manchester, New Hampshire before skating for the University of Lowell (MA). Bere was a standout forward at Wilmington High (MA).

It wasn't just boys who were inspired by The Big, Bad Bruins. In 1970, a man from East Boston by the name of Tony Marmo ran an ad in a local paper encouraging any girl who would like to play organized ice hockey to show up at the Porazzo MDC Rink in East Boston for a meeting and tryouts. The response was overwhelming: more than 85 girls of all ages showed up. A team was formed called the Massport Jets, named after the Massachusetts Port Authority, which ran Logan Airport in East Boston. Other communities formed their own teams, and girls hockey began to take off.

"The most important factor that made the success of girls hockey what it is today was the influence of the Orr-Esposito era," said Marmo, who coached and directed this landmark team. "They created new fans for this growing sport, especially young girls who became ardent hockey fans, thus creating a desire on their part to participate as competitors in ice hockey."

Women's ice hockey has been approved by the International Olympic Committee to begin competition at the 1998 Winter Games in Nagano, Japan. Team USA will include a considerable New England contingent.

The effect that the Bruins of the Orr era had on the New England area was perhaps best described by Dick Johnson, the Senior Curator and co-founder of the New England Sports Museum. "What they did was galvanize an area that already had a long tradition in hockey, but only in concentrated pockets. They took a tradition and magnified it tenfold."

Because of the national television contract

Steve Babineau

Bobby Orr's retirement ceremony in 1979 was an emotional moment in Boston sports history.

Steve Babineau

When Orr retired, the torch was passed to Ray Bourque, who has dutifully held up the Boston tradition of star defenseman.

the NHL had at the time, the Bruins' influence reached beyond New England to other parts of the United States and Canada. Phil Esposito recalls what his team did for hockey in the U.S. "We had a big influence on not only the Mass. area alone, but also on the whole country. We've been compared to the Oakland Raiders — look what they did for football."

Bobby Orr and the Big, Bad Bruins set New England ablaze in a hockey wildfire, leaving a legacy for future generations.

Chapter 6

The Flyers — An Expansion Success Story

Philly Fans Go Wild Over the "Broad Street Bullies"

Expansion of the NHL from six to twelve teams in 1967-68 inspired many questions about the viability of new franchises such as the Philadelphia Flyers. Could big-league hockey succeed in the City of Brotherly Love where once (1930-31) it had failed? The answer was affirmative. Hockey mania evolved in the Delaware Valley, which encompasses Southeastern Pennsylvania, Southern New Jersey and Delaware and the Flyers were responsible for this mania.

Philly hadn't had an NHL franchise since the inept Quakers (formerly the Pittsburgh

Pirates) set a futility record that still stands by winning only four games. The team's dismal performance that winter resulted in poor attendance and the rapid folding of the Quakers.

By contrast, the Flyers were an instant hit. In their inaugural season (1967-68) they finished first in the new Western Division (which included the six new teams), with a 31-32-11 record. This was accomplished despite having to play some "home" games in neutral sites such as New York, Toronto and Quebec City because the roof of their new arena, The Spectrum, blew off twice in late season. Although the team lost its first playoff series in seven games to the St. Louis Blues, attendance was good and the season was considered a success.

After that impressive first campaign the Flyers slipped in the standings. In their second season they dropped to third place at 20-35-21, and once again lost to the Blues in the first round of the playoffs — this time in four straight games.

General manager Bud Poile had built a team with some talent, including The French Line of Andre Lacroix, Simon Nolet and Jean-Guy Gendron, but it was a small, finesse club that lacked muscle and grit. Help, however, was on the way.

In the 1969 amateur draft Poile and coach Keith Allen drafted a prospect from Flin Flon, Manitoba, named Bobby Clarke, whose zestful work ethic would epitomize the

Steve Babineau

Bobby Clarke.

franchise's philosophy. Clarke, a high-scoring center with the Flin Flon Bombers of the Western Canada (Amateur) Hockey League was passed over by many clubs because he suffered from diabetes. But the Flyers' high command gambled, choosing him in the second round as the 17th pick overall. It was the best choice the club ever made. In their continued search for size and strength Poile and Allen also drafted hefty forwards Dave Schultz (52nd) and Don Saleski (64th).

Another off-season maneuver was the hiring of Vic Stasiuk as head coach replacing Allen, who was promoted to assistant general manager. The team's downward trend continued through the first two months of the new season, and it was apparent that more changes had to be made. In December of 1969, owner Ed Snider made a move that would later pay dividends when he fired general manager Poile and replaced him with Allen.

The 1969-70 season ended in bitter disappointment when the Flyers missed the playoffs by dropping their last six games. The club set a record for ties that season with 24, thereby acquiring the nickname "Flying Tyers." Heading into the season finale at Minnesota, the Flyers needed either a win or another deadlock to secure a post-season berth. But disaster struck when in the third period of a scoreless battle, Minnesota's Barry Gibbs flipped the puck into the Flyers' zone. Goalie Bernie Parent, busy sweeping ice chips from his goal crease, never saw the bouncing rubber, and the fluky goal stood up as the game's lone tally.

The Flyers rebounded the following season with a third-place finish, but suffered a quick playoff exit by losing four straight to the Chicago Blackhawks. Stasiuk, who had alienated many players and fans with his outspoken criticism and screaming from behind the bench, was fired at season's end. Fred Shero, whom Allen called "The only man I really ever considered,"[1] was hired from the New York Rangers' system on June 2.

Shero was one of a kind. He was innovative and unorthodox. He had studied the Soviet style and was one of the first to bring the Russian technique to North America. He immediately implemented a system, which unlike the standard three-forward system, modified the five-man attack to

Steve Babineau

Fred "Fog" Shero.

include the defensemen into the scoring unit. Shero also stressed the importance of winning the battles in the corners and behind the net, which was the perfect philosophy for the Flyers of the early to mid-seventies. To this day they are known as one of the hardest-working teams in NHL history. Shero also became the first NHL coach to use an assistant when he convinced the Flyers' brass to hire Mike Nykoluk.

Just prior to the beginning of the 1971-72 season, Allen, in an attempt to trim some finesse and add some muscle, traded speedy center Andre Lacroix to Chicago for 6-4, 225 pound defenseman Rick Foley. The move, however, did not pay off as Shero wound up suspending Foley for three weeks because of lack of effort and being overweight. Foley spent the next season in the minors and never again became an NHL regular.

A blockbuster deal with the Los Angeles Kings in January 1972 brought wingers Ross Lonsberry and Bill Flett to town. It was one of six successful trades by Allen, who also

obtained Rick MacLeish, Barry Ashbee, Terry Crisp and Andre Dupont, as well as Bernie Parent, whom he reacquired from Toronto. The additions of Lonsberry and Flett paid immediate dividends. Both forwards made valuable contributions to a team that showed marked improvement over the second half of the 1971-72 campaign.

Heading into the season finale at Buffalo, the Flyers needed only a tie to secure the fourth and final playoff position in the West. But with only four ticks left on the game clock, the Sabres' Gerry Meehan fired a desperation 60-foot shot that beat goalie Doug Favell and the nightmare of 1970 had recurred. After the game Shero made a statement that revealed just how much the game of hockey meant to him when he said, "I feel the same way I did when my mother and father died!"[2]

Although the 1971-72 season ended in heartwrenching fashion there was good reason for Flyers fans to be optimistic about the future. In the 1972 amateur draft Allen landed left wing Bill Barber and defensemen Jimmy Watson (whose brother Joe was part of the Flyers blue line corps) and Tom Bladon. Wingers Don Saleski and Dave Schultz, who each had two years of minor league experience under their belts, were now ready for prime time. These five players would soon become key contributors to a team that was on the verge of Stanley Cup contention.

At the time there wasn't much ice hockey played in the Philadelphia area. There were less than a dozen rinks in the entire Delaware Valley and some of them were used primarily for public skating. This, however, would soon change, as this exciting team with their gritty leader and unique coach were rapidly catching the interest of sports fans throughout the area.

The team began to develop a personality which somewhat resembled that of the Big, Bad Bruins: Rough, tough, at times brutal, and hated in every city but their own. For visiting teams Philadelphia was no longer the City of Brotherly Love, but a journey into the hockey's alligator tank. The 1972-73 team set an all-time record with 1,756 penalty minutes during the regular season. Their ruffian style of play was so flagrant they were highly criticized by hockey experts everywhere.

Like the Big, Bad Bruins, they were a colorful group of characters with nicknames such as Moose (Andre Dupont), The Hammer (Dave Schultz), Hound (Bob Kelly), Cowboy (Bill Flett), Big Bird (Don Saleski), Bomber (Tom Bladon), Little O (Orest Kindrachuk) and Fog (Fred Shero). Their leader was Clarke, who while constantly battling diabetes, played every game as if it was his last. Game after game, his teammates followed his example. It was as if the club had been molded after the city it represented. Philadelphia was a blue-collar town and people could relate to the work ethic of this team.

Philadelphians also could relate to the Flyers of the early to mid-'70s because of their accessibility. Many players patronized Rexy's Bar after practice and games. "People would go in there and drink and be able to socialize with some of the Flyers, whereas the players from the other pro teams weren't as accessible," recalls Fred Popelick, a former youth hockey organizer and longtime Flyers follower from Southern New Jersey.

Philly, at that time, was a city that craved a winner. The basketball 76ers, who had won the city's last professional sports championship by taking the NBA title in 1967, were in a rebuilding process; the football Eagles hadn't appeared in a playoff game since they had won the NFL Championship in 1960; and the baseball Phillies had finished in or near the cellar since 1968. But during the 1972-73 season, the Flyers not only caught the interest of sports fans in Southeastern Pennsylvania, but also made them realize that their hockey team

was rapidly becoming their best hope for bringing home a championship.

For the first couple of months in the new season the Flyers continued a trend from the previous year that was a guaranteed recipe for mediocrity — they dominated at home but had little success on the road. The reason for their poor road record was that they were reluctant to play rough outside of their own building, until an incident that occurred during the third period of a late December contest at Vancouver seemed to turn the tide. Don Saleski had a choke-hold on Canucks rookie Barry Wilkins when a fan reached over the glass and started yanking on Saleski's hair. "I thought he was going to pull me right off the ice,"[3] Big Bird said later. Backup goalie Bob Taylor jumped into the stands after the fan and nine other Flyers followed. It was an ugly scene. But for some reason the altercation seemed to cure the team of its unwillingness to mix it up away from the Spectrum. From that point on the Flyers began to win their share of games on enemy ice.

Several nights later they rolled into Atlanta and roughed up the first-year Flames at the Omni. In his game story, *Philadelphia Bulletin* beat writer Jack Chevalier referred to them as "The Broad Street Bullies," and the name stuck.

Midway through the season Shero named Clarke as his captain. At age 23, Bobby became the youngest NHL player ever to wear the "C." By season's end the Broad Streeters had won a franchise record 37 games, finishing second in the West behind only the Chicago Blackhawks, the only original-six team to join the Western Division when the NHL realigned in 1970. Five Flyers scored 30 or more goals: MacLeish (50), Flett (43), Clarke (37), Gary Dornhoefer (30), and Barber (30). Clarke justified the captain's "C" on his sweater by becoming the first player from the Western Division to win the Hart Trophy as the

Steve Babineau

Bob "Hound" Kelly.

Steve Babineau

Don "Big Bird" Saleski.

Stan Fischler collection

Left: Dave "Hammer" Shultz. Right: Shultz (center) wound up in the middle of many of the Broad Street Bullies' brawls.

league's MVP.

The Flyers not only buried the skeletons of 1970 and 1972 by qualifying for the postseason, but they also won their opening round series by outlasting the Minnesota North Stars in six games. It was the franchise's first-ever playoff series victory.

Their next opponent was the powerful Montreal Canadiens. Although they fell to the Habs in five games, the Flyers made a statement by going into the Forum and taking the first game, 5-4 on Rick MacLeish's wrister at 2:56 of sudden-death overtime.

The Flyers led throughout most of Game Two before Yvan Cournoyer stuffed home a rebound to tie the score with just over eight minutes remaining in the third period. With nearly seven minutes gone in overtime, Montreal rookie defenseman Larry Robinson spoiled the Broad Streeters' gutsy attempt to take a 2-0 series lead back to Philly when he blasted a 55-footer past Doug Favell. Robinson's game-winning tally proved to be pivotal. The Canadiens went on to beat the Flyers in five games before defeating Chicago in the finals to win their 17th Stanley Cup.

Having just completed the most successful season in the franchise's young history, the Flyers were now only a player or two away from being considered serious Cup contenders. The team now had balanced scoring, solid defense, the league's MVP and had shown they could win on the road. The final piece of the puzzle was added just days after the 1972-73 season ended when Keith Allen reacquired goalie Bernie Parent by shipping Favell to Toronto for Parent's NHL playing rights. Parent had spent the previous season backstopping for the WHA Philadelphia Blazers. A money dispute had caused him to walk out on the WHA team during the playoffs.

Meanwhile, hockey interest was rapidly growing throughout Pennsylvania. Since there was a lack of rinks and outdoor ice, kids be-

gan playing street hockey. It was similar to the craze that had swept the Boston area several years earlier. New York Ranger goalie Mike Richter, who grew up in the Philadelphia suburb of Flowertown and attended Germantown Academy, recalled what an influence the Flyers were to him and his friends as a kid:

"They were the team that my family and friends used to watch constantly from as early as I can remember. They were having a lot of success in the early 1970s, just when I was getting into hockey, and a lot of the kids around the area were playing street hockey. It was pretty much the biggest thing, and we would imitate every single guy on the team. Of course, Bernie Parent was my favorite, and a good guy to imitate right there."

The Flyers opened the 1973-74 regular season at home on October 11 against the Toronto Maple Leafs. A red carpet was rolled out for legendary vocalist Kate Smith, who sang "God Bless America" to the delight of the sellout crowd. The ritual had begun in 1969 when Spectrum president Lou Scheinfeld surprised Flyers fans by playing Smith's famous recording of "God Bless America" as a change of pace from the traditional "Star Spangled Banner." When he did it the team usually won. This time Scheinfeld pulled the ultimate surprise by bringing Kate Smith in unannounced. She did not disappoint. The Flyers, with Parent back between the pipes, blanked the Leafs by a score of 2-0.

The opening night performance set the standard for what proved to be a glorious season for the young franchise. Throughout the 78-game schedule the Flyers relentlessly worked hard and mixed it up with their opponents, finding the winning formula by blending roughness, superb goaltending and timely scoring. The result was an outstanding record of 50-16-12, which sprang them to the top of the Western Division, seven points ahead of Chicago. They also went 22-10-7 on the road, dispelling any doubts about their ability to win away from The Spectrum.

In the first round of the playoffs the Flyers breezed past the Atlanta Flames in four straight games, outscoring them 17-6.

After easily winning the first two games at home, they traveled to Atlanta for the first Stanley Cup playoff game ever played in the South. With the help of a Rick MacLeish shot that hit the crossbar but was ruled a goal, the Flyers won the brawl-filled affair 4-1, and were now only one game away from a return trip to the semifinals.

The next day Fred Shero allegedly was "mugged" in downtown Atlanta and was forced to return to Philly and miss the fourth game.[4]

Assistant coach Mike Nykoluk filled in for Shero and saw his team fall behind 3-0. The Flyers then came roaring back to tie and force overtime. With just over five and a half minutes gone in the extra frame, Dave "The Hammer" Schultz — known as the meanest Bully of the bunch — took a perfect pass from Clarke and flipped in the series-clinching goal.

Next up for the Broad Streeters was the New York Rangers, who had eliminated the defending Stanley Cup champion Montreal Canadiens in six games. After coasting to 4-0 and 5-2 wins at The Spectrum, the Flyers traveled to the Big Apple where they had a dismal 1-12-6 all-time record on Madison Square Garden ice.

While the Flyers were waiting for the Rangers-Canadiens series to be decided, Schultz uttered a remark that stirred the wrath of the Rangers and their fans when he said to Wilmington, Delaware hockey writer Don McDermott: "I hope we play New York because they have a reputation of choking in the past."[5] The result, needless to say, was a rabid Garden crowd that helped inspire their Blueshirts to two straight victories and a tied series.

Back in Philly for Game Five, the Flyers rebounded by whipping the New Yorkers 4-1. Defenseman Tom Bladon was the hero at both ends of the ice, scoring a goal and making a superb defensive play that denied the Rangers a three-on-one rush.

The Flyers took the ice for Game Six looking for their first win at Madison Square Garden since 1969. No such luck as the Rangers broke open a 1-1 tie in the third period with a three-goal outburst that gave them a 4-1 victory and a trip back to Philadelphia for the seventh and deciding game.

The New Yorkers carried their momentum into Game Seven as Bill Fairbairn scored to give them an early lead. Less than a minute later the Flyers answered when MacLeish converted on a power-play to even the score. The Broad Streeters began to dominate the play, getting scores from Kindrachuk and Dornhoefer to go up 3-1. Steve Vickers cut the deficit to one at 8:49 of the third period, but the Flyers again answered quickly when Dornhoefer scored only 12 seconds later.

Ranger center Pete Stemkowski struck fear in the hearts of the 17,000-plus by scoring with 5:26 left to cut the lead to 4-3. But then Philly proceeded to shut the door with ferocious forechecking and tight defense until the clock expired. The home ice advantage that the Flyers had worked so hard for all season was the difference in a series that saw the home team win every game. It earned them the franchise's first trip to the Stanley Cup Finals.

The finals were a marquee matchup if ever there was one: the "Broad Street Bullies" versus the "Big, Bad Bruins." Both teams were known for their rough and tough style. The Bruins, who were Cup champions in 1970 and 1972, had more talent but the Flyers were hungrier.

On May 7, the Flyers invaded Beantown with only one day of rest, knowing that in order to have any chance of winning the series, they had to win at least one of the first two games at Boston Garden, where they had not won in six and a half years. And they had to do it against a well-rested Bruins squad that easily blew by Toronto and Chicago in the first two rounds.

Game One saw the Bruins jump out to a 2-0, second period lead. It appeared as if it was going to be the lopsided series the oddsmakers had predicted. But Philly rallied to tie the score on goals by Kindrachuk and Clarke. With regulation time winding down, Bill Flett missed on an opportunity to win the game when he had Boston goalie Gilles Gilbert dead to right in front of the net but hit the post. Moments later Bobby Orr took a pass from Ken Hodge and let go a 35-foot slapper that beat Parent for the game-winner. The Flyers winless streak now stood at 19 (0-17-2) on

Steve Babineau

Andre "Moose" Dupont.

Boston Garden ice.

The second game was another hard-fought battle that found the Bruins clinging to a 2-1 lead in the waning minutes. With a minute to play Shero pulled Parent for an extra skater and the Flyers attacked the Boston zone. MacLeish fed the puck from left wing into a crowd of players. Dupont took it, fired it through a screen past Gilbert and jumped into the "Moose Shuffle," a celebratory dance he would perform after one of his rare tallies. At 12:01 of overtime Bobby Clarke flipped home a rebound and the Flyers had finally broken the Garden jinx.

With their Game Two triumph the Flyers had now taken that all-important home ice advantage away from the Bruins, and with the momentum on their side, they returned home brimming with confidence and feeling on the verge of something special.

Home proved to be sweet again as the Broad Streeters recorded back-to-back wins to take a commanding 3-1 series lead. The key to the Flyers success in Games Three and Four was a clever "Stop-Orr" strategy crafted by Shero. George Michael, host of "The Sports Machine," who at the time was Flyers' team photographer, remembers the game plan: "Fred Shero said, 'Let him (Orr) go, let him skate and we'll get him at center ice.' The idea was to let him wear himself out because they knew he was playing 35-36 minutes a game."

In Game Five the Big, Bad Bruins got back down to business with a little home cooking of their own, thrashing the Flyers with a vengeance by a score of 5-1. The teams set a playoff record by combining for 43 penalties, 20 of which were for roughing or fighting. With men from both teams constantly serving time in the box, Orr had plenty of room to roam and lead his team victory.

For Philadelphia, the Game Five blowout underscored the importance of seizing the opportunity to win the next game on home ice because the Bruins had come alive again. If the Flyers lost, it would be much tougher for them to win a seventh game at Boston Garden.

When the teams suited up to take the ice for Game Six, there were two good luck omens present for the Flyers — the referee and the singer; In 1973-74 the Broad Streeters were undefeated (11-0-2) when Art Skov refereed their games, and a perfect 9-0 when Kate Smith appeared in person.

This time Kate was greeted with more than just the usual rousing applause she always obtained when she walked out to sing "God Bless America." Her presence sent a charge through the building that boosted the confidence of both the players and the fans.

Boston came out smoking and dominated the game's early moments with constant pressure in the Flyers end. Parent, however, was sharp and turned aside everything the Bruins threw at him.

Later in the first period with Philly on a power play, Clarke and Orr received matching penalties that gave the hosts a four-on-three advantage. MacLeish won a faceoff back to Dupont at the center of the blue line. Moose moved in toward the crease and let go a shot that MacLeish redirected over Gilbert's right arm and into the net. At period's end, the Flyers took a 1-0 lead into the dressing room.

Throughout the second and third periods the Bruins relentlessly fought for the equalizer, but Parent was unbeatable. With two and a half minutes remaining in the third period and Boston desperately trying to tie the score, the puck caromed into the neutral zone to Clarke who broke away toward the Boston net. Orr chased him down and took him out of the play, causing Clarke to fall to the ice. Skov called the Boston superstar for a two-minute penalty with only 2:22 left and the Beantowners were done.

As the final seconds ticked away the crowd

Steve Babineau

MacLeish, once Bruins' property, notched the Cup-winning goal against Boston in Game Six.

went wild. When the buzzer went off fans spilled from the stands and onto the ice towards Parent, who was being mobbed by his teammates. After the teams shook hands Clarke and Parent proudly paraded the Cup around the Spectrum ice.

They were a team of many heroes, each playing his role and pitching in at crucial times throughout the course of the regular season and the playoffs. But on Sunday, May 19, it was the spectacular goaltending of Bernie Parent (a former Bruin, ironically) that made the difference for hockey's new champions — The Broad Street Bullies.

The season ended almost exactly the way it had begun back on opening night, with "God

Bless America" and a Parent shutout. Kate Smith, whose overall record now stood at 39-3-1, had a perfect 10-0 for the season. Parent won the Conn Smythe Trophy as the Most Valuable Player of the playoffs. And Keith Allen, who assembled the team from a combination of sources including the expansion draft, the annual amateur drafts, trades and free agents, was named the 1974 *Sporting News* Executive of the Year.

The next day Philly fans showed their gratitude with a tremendous turnout for the Cup parade. Two million people lined Broad Street to honor the new holders of hockey's Holy Grail. "You would not believe what it was like," said Greg Scott, lifetime Flyers fan and present director of fan development for the team. "The whole city was just wall-to-wall. You couldn't see a street, you couldn't see a sidewalk. All you could see was just a mass of humanity."

The new champs rode in open convertibles from the Spectrum to Independence Mall. It took nearly three hours for the cars to make their way through the enormous midday gathering, which was actually a continuation of the wild bash that began when Game Six ended the night before. When the team finally arrived at the Mall, they were greeted by Kate Smith, who from a nearby podium sang "God Bless America" six times. Needless to say, hockey interest was at an unprecedented high in the City of Brotherly Love.

This ultimate taste of success did nothing to stunt the hard work ethic of the Broad Street Bullies. The following year they went out and proved that their Cup victory was no fluke by finishing first overall in the regular season

Steve Babineau

Left: Former Bruin Bernie Parent stopped everything that came his way in Game Six. *Right:* The line of Clarke, Barber and Leach led Philly to its second straight Cup in 1974-75.

and repeating as Stanley Cup Champions.

This time their final round opponent was the Buffalo Sabres, who were led by the French Connection Line of Gilbert Perreault, Rick Martin and Rene Robert. It was the first all-expansion team final in league history. The Flyers once again clinched the Cup with a Game Six shutout, beating the Sabres 2-0. With four shutouts and a goals-against average of 1.89, Parent became the first player ever to win back-to-back Conn Smythe Trophies.

In the spring of 1976, the Flyers' bid for a third consecutive Stanley Cup was thwarted by the Montreal Canadiens, who swept them in four straight games. Despite the sweep, Flyers right winger Reggie Leach won the Conn Smythe Trophy by scoring an NHL record 19 playoff goals.

The Flyers Cup reign was over, but the hockey interest that the Broad Street Bullies inspired throughout the Delaware Valley during the early to mid-seventies was only beginning to manifest itself. Over the years it has steadily produced an increasing amount of participation in ice, street and now roller hockey.

Before the Broad Street Bullies came along there were only a handful of ice skating facilities in the area. Older rinks such as Cherry Hill, Wissahickon, and Old York Road were enough to satisfy the small number of figure skaters and hockey players in the area at the time. From the time the Flyers caught on to the end of the '70s, the demand grew and more rinks were built. Among those were Radner, the Skatium, Springfield Ice Rink, Winter Sport Skating Rink, Cobb's Creek Skate House, Scanlon, Rizzo Rink, Simons Rink, and the University of Pennsylvania's Class of '23 Rink.

The growth continued throughout the '80s and into the '90s, and the number of ice rinks is now up to about 40. Overall there are now roughly 120 facilities in the Delaware Valley that house some form of organized hockey; 40 skating rinks, 30 roller rinks and 50 street hockey program centers. Some of the complexes are multi-facilities, with two or three ice rinks and a roller rink. The street hockey program centers are part of Flyers Street Fleet, which falls under the umbrella of Nike NHL Street.

In 1976 Flyer owner Ed Snider created a department called Hockey Central. The department's purpose was to assist the amateur ice hockey community in becoming more organized by keeping statistics and getting exposure through newspapers, etc.

In 1992 the name Hockey Central was changed to the Flyers Youth Hockey Department, but it basically has the same mission: The promotion of youth hockey in the Delaware Valley.

In the late '70s Hockey Central organized an annual tournament called the Flyers Cup, which was the area's scholastic championship. Ice hockey was — and still is — a club sport at most of the high schools in the Delaware Valley. Like many scholastic programs in other states, they are run as a varsity sport, but they have to do their own fundraising.

The success of the Flyers Cup led to other breakthroughs. "That was really our jumping off point," said Greg Scott. "It evolved into doing some clinics, producing things like the Delaware Valley Rink Guide, which we still produce, and that evolved into different types of community oriented programs."

By the early '80s there were a fair amount of youth hockey programs in the Delaware Valley area. Two of the more notable leagues at that time were the Delaware Valley Hockey League and the Atlantic Hockey League, both of which are still in existence.

The DVHL included teams from Wilkes Barre (PA), Howard County (MD), East Windsor (NJ) and the popular Southern New Jersey Gladiators. The Gladiators' popularity stems from the fact that they began as far back as the early '60s, and that some of the Flyers' kids have played for them.

Former Gladiators include Bobby Clarke's son Wade, Darryl Sittler's son Ryan and daughter Megan, Bill Barber's son Brooks, and Mark Howe's son Travis. Dave Schultz, who at one time coached the squirts, also had two sons who played — Dave and Chad. Today's Gladiators squad includes Ron Hextall's son Bret and Keith Acton's son Willy.

Over the years the Gladiators have also competed against teams from the Atlantic Hockey League, which includes the Little Flyers, who have the same logo and uniform as their NHL counterpart. Other league programs are located in Ramapo, Essex and Brick Township, New Jersey.

One could draw a parallel between the effect that the Big, Bad Bruins had on the Boston area and the Broad Street Bullies' influence on the Delaware Valley. So it comes as no surprise to learn that during the 1980s there was a youth hockey exchange program between Boston and Philadelphia area kids. The program was set up by Medford, Massachusetts youth hockey organizer Tony Bova.

"We had an exchange with the Philadelphia area from 1984 to 1988," Bova recalls. "We were trying to get a Canadian exchange — going hours at end — and so I sent letters all over Canada and the U.S. A program from Southern New Jersey contacted us and wanted to exchange with us. They called themselves the Southern New Jersey Gladiators."

Another notable youth hockey program in the Philly area is the Junior Flyers, who practice and play at the Iceline Rink in West Chester, Pennsylvania. The Junior Flyers were founded in 1986 by their first and only head coach Bud Dombrowski, and Tom Koester, who currently serves as president of USA Hockey's Atlantic District (area encompassing a 75-mile radius stretching from Southern

Steve Babineau

Right wing Reggie Leach's 19 goals during the 1975-76 playoffs earned him Conn Smythe honors in a losing cause.

New York through the Delaware Valley to Washington, D.C., including Eastern Pennsylvania, all of New Jersey and Delaware).

The growth of ice hockey has increased tenfold in the Atlantic District since the advent of the Broad Street Bullies. It went from less than 2,000 participants back then to 11,000 in 1988, and to 26,500 in 1997. The Stanley Cup championships won by the 1994 Rangers and the 1995 Devils, as well as the advent of Flyers' superstar Eric Lindros and the "Legion of Doom" line have helped to inspire the recent flood of entries.

Unlike other hockey hotbeds around the U.S., there is very little college hockey in the Philadelphia area. The Villanova ice hockey program is classified as Division I Independent, but plays a Division III schedule. The closest Division I program is at Princeton, about 40 miles away.

The rise in participation inspired by the Broad Street Bullies has also harvested some excellent talent. Aside from Mike Richter, there have been other fine hockey players to come out of the Philadelphia area.

The first player from Philly to make the bigs was Ray Staszak, a stocky right winger who played for the University of Chicago. Staszak was drafted by the Detroit Red Wings, who made him the first player to be given a million dollar bonus in the NHL. His career, however, ended quickly when he blew his knee out after playing in only four games for the Wings in 1985-86.

The next Philadelphia kid to turn pro was Jay Caufield, a big rugged right winger. After a short stint with the New York Rangers in 1986-87 and a cup of coffee with the Minnesota North Stars the following season, Caufield found a home with the Pittsburgh Penguins, where he was part of two Stanley Cup championship teams in 1990-91 and 1991-92.

More recently there was Brady Kramer, a left winger out of Haverford (PA) High. Kramer attended Providence College, where in his junior year of 1993-94, he scored 38 points in 36 games. That stellar junior season earned him the role of captain as a senior. While finishing his last year of college, Kramer joined the Fredericton Canadiens of the American Hockey League for their 1995 Calder Cup playoffs. After a fine playoff performance for the Habs' affiliate he retired from organized hockey.

A young and promising talent is Havertown's Ryan Mulhern. Mulhern, a forward and captain at Brown, was drafted by the Calgary Flames, but did not receive an offer. In 1996-97 Ryan split time between the Hampton Roads Admirals of the East Coast Hockey League and the AHL Portland Pirates. He made his NHL debut with the Washington Capitals early in the 1997-98 season.

As the area continues to produce talent, from youth hockey to college and pro prospects, other parts of the legacy are held intact. The packed houses that the Flyers played for during the '70s didn't stop when the Broad Street Bullies disbanded. The Spectrum continued to sell out over the years and the crowds that have poured in and out it have had the honor of passing a statue erected in memory of a lady who will always hold a special place in Flyers history — Kate Smith.

After the Flyers moved across the parking lot to the new CoreStates Center in 1996, the Spectrum, now called the CoreStates Spectrum (both facilities are part of the CoreStates Complex), became home to the Flyers' American Hockey League affiliate, the Phantoms.

The Phantoms, who averaged 8,000 a game (second in AHL) in their maiden season of 1996-97, are directly attributable to the Flyers' success and help to make up for the lack of a Division I college program in the Philly area. Philadelphia is now the only city to have both NHL and AHL franchises.

The impact of the Broad Street Bullies turned the Delaware Valley into a hockey hotbed that has not only grown over the years, but is still thriving and will continue to do so for years to come.

1. Jack Chevalier, *The Broad Street Bullies* (New York: Macmillan Publishing Company, Inc., 1974) p. 23.
2. Ibid., p. 23.
3. Ibid., p. 48.
4. Ibid., p. 146.
5. Ibid., p. 148.

Chapter 7

Americans Make the Grade

*U.S-Born-and-Raised Players Star in College
and Make the Pros*

Apart from the emergence of the Big,
Bad Bruins in 1970 and the Broad Street Bullies four years later, the decade
of the 1970s also marked the beginning of a new hockey trend — more
Americans were making the grade at higher levels, including the game's
premier circuit — the National Hockey League.

NHL expansion and the World Hockey Association's birth, coupled with the irre-
sistible growth of the sport in the States, found Uncle Sam making his presence known
among hockey's elite.

During the NHL's "Original Six" era (1942-1967) there were only 108 roster spots available at the game's top level. By the mid-'70s there were 18 NHL teams. If one were to add the 14 World Hockey Association clubs, there were now as many as 576 positions available to aspiring big-league stickhandlers.

The increase in opportunities coincided with a boost in quality talent developed in such traditional hotbeds as Minnesota, Michigan and New England. Minnesota, which has been the nation's foremost hockey development area, got a shot in the arm with the arrival of the NHL North Stars in 1967. Michigan, thanks to the inspiration of "Mr. Hockey" himself, Gordie Howe, also became a spawn-ing ground for the ice game. And New England, which turned "hockey crazy" over Bobby Orr, was only beginning to reap the fruits of its boom. It comes as no surprise that the top three states for producing NHLers during the 1970s were Minnesota (46), Massachusetts (23) and Michigan (14).

These areas also produced many fine skaters who excelled at the college level. The top collegiate programs now boasted a larger and higher-caliber talent pool from which to recruit. The result was better college hockey and an eventual balancing of power between eastern and midwestern schools.

The following player profiles feature 12 of the best American-born-and-raised players to make the NHL during the 1970s:

ROBBIE FTOREK

Steve Babineau

Born and raised in the Boston suburb of Needham, Mass., Robbie Ftorek began organized play in his hometown's youth hockey program during the mid-1950s. As a teenager, Ftorek further developed his skills — which were far superior to anyone else his age — on an intramural team at Needham's Newman Junior High.

He graduated to Needham High, where his older brother, Steve, had been part of a state championship team in 1965. Following in his brother's footsteps, Robbie stepped in as a sophomore and led the Rockets to the semifinals of the state tournament. This was followed by two consecutive state championships. In the final game of Robbie's schoolboy career, Needham defeated perennial state-power Auburn before a sellout crowd at the Boston Garden.

Needham was a member of the highly-competitive Bay State League, which at the time included such future hockey stars as Walpole's Mike Milbury and Norwood's Michael Martin. "Ftorek was just a lot smarter than everybody else," recalls Milbury. "He was a great skater but he moved the puck so well, distributed it well and he had a good supporting cast that could work it out. He was just a long way ahead of the rest of high school hockey in terms of seeing the ice."

Ftorek's supporting cast included future Harvard star Steve Dadgian and future WHA netminder Cap Raeder. Their coach was John Chambers, who in 1995 received the "John Mariucci Award," created by the American Hockey Coaches Associaton to honor a sec-

ondary hockey coach who best exemplifies the spirit, dedication and enthusiasm of "The Godfather of U.S. Hockey," John Mariucci.

Fresh out of high school, Ftorek joined the 1972 Olympic Team and helped them win a silver medal at the Winter Games in Sapporo, Japan. In 1972-73 he made his NHL debut for the Detroit Red Wings, but only played in three games and did not record a point. Then, after appearing in 12 games the following season, the Wings gave up on him, claiming he wasn't big enough to succeed at the NHL level.

It was at that point, however, that the talented little center from Needham's pro career got untracked. He signed with the Phoenix Roadrunners of the offensive-oriented WHA. Phoenix gave Robbie a chance to display his talents and prove himself as a worthy pro.

During his three seasons with the Roadrunners Ftorek scored 298 points in 213 games. His best season was 1976-77, when he recorded a career-high 117 points along with his tenacious checking and relentless forechecking. Not surprisingly he won the League's Most Valuable Player Award.

After the Phoenix franchise folded Ftorek enjoyed two highly productive WHA seasons with Cincinnati. And when the WHA merged with the NHL in 1979, Robbie returned to the NHL with the Quebec Nordiques, one of the four WHA franchises to join the NHL. In 1981-82 the Nordiques traded him to the Rangers where he finished his playing career as a Broadway Blueshirt.

His coaching career has included stints as head coach of the Los Angeles Kings and his current position, assistant coach for the New Jersey Devils. In 1994-95 he led the Albany River Rats to the Calder Cup (AHL) championship.

Born: Needham, MA, 1/2/52
5-10, 155
C, shoots left

Season	Team	GP	G	A	Pts	PIM
72-73	Detroit	3	0	0	0	0
73-74	Detroit	12	2	5	7	4
74-75	Phoe (WHA)	53	31	37	68	29
75-76	Phoe (WHA)	80	41	72	113	109
76-77	Phoe (WHA)	80	46	71	117	86
77-78	Cin (WHA)	80	59	50	109	54
78-79	Cin (WHA)	80	39	77	116	87
79-80	Quebec	52	18	33	51	28
80-81	Quebec	78	24	49	73	104
81-82	Quebec-NYR	49	9	32	41	28
82-83	NY Rangers	61	12	19	31	41
83-84	NY Rangers	31	3	2	5	22
84-85	NY Rangers	48	9	10	19	35
NHL Totals		334	77	150	227	262
WHA Totals 373		216	307	523	365	
NHL Playoff Totals		19	9	6	15	28
WHA Playoff Totals		13	6	10	16	10

THE HOWE BROTHERS

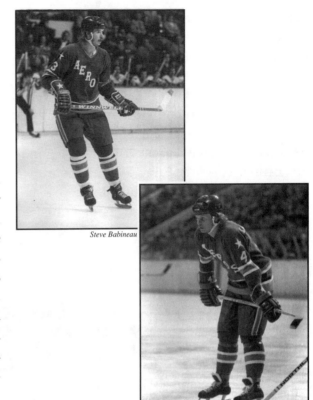

Steve Babineau

Gordie and Colleen Howe's two oldest sons, Marty and Mark, were taught to skate by their father on the ice of Olympia Stadium, the Red Wings' original home rink. They would skate before Red Wings practices during the mid-'50s and learned by holding on to the backs of chairs while Gordie would push them around the ice. Soon the boys had sticks in their hands and learned how to play hockey. In 1959 Marty and Mark, at ages five and four, respectively, joined a minor league team called the Teamsters' 299. It was their first taste of organized hockey.

A year later the Howes — due to a shortage of ice in the Detroit area — followed the lead of many families in Canada and the northern United States. They built an ice rink in their front yard on which the kids could skate.

Of the two, Mark was more intense about becoming a star. This excerpt from Colleen Howe's book, "My Three Hockey Players," explains:

"Marty was an end on his high school football team until his coach dismissed him for missing practice one day to play in a key hockey game. I blew my cork. Gordie told Marty to tell his football coach to shove it. But Marty enjoyed football, had wondered if he might be good enough to play in college, and felt badly about giving it up.

"Mark, on the other hand, never thought about anything else but hockey. As long as I can remember, he was banging a puck against the garage door, or out in the neighborhood trying to recruit some little kid to play goalie. He thought about being a goalie for a time, but there was just no way, with his speed and moves, a coach was going to leave him in the net."[1]

After progressing through youth hockey ranks the boys played for the Detroit Junior Red Wings in 1970-71. In February of 1971 their dad played with them in a benefit game at the Olympia against the rest of the Red Wings squad. The game, which marked the first time the boys played with their dad, raised $30,000 for the March of Dimes.

When Marty qualified to play amateur hockey in Canada, he chose the team Mark would most likely want to play for the following year — the Toronto Marlboros of the Ontario Hockey Association. This was indicative of their tight bond. By 1972-73 they were teammates again: Marty, Mark — and, incredibly, their dad — signed with Houston of the World Hockey Association.

Despite earning big money with the Aeros the boys chose to live at home. Their parents charged them $30 per week. On the ice the boys called their father Gordie — at home they called him Dad. It was a closely-knit bunch.

The three Howes played splendidly together and the Aeros rolled to two straight Avco World Cups. In 1973-74 Mark was named WHA Rookie of the Year. After four years in Houston the Howe Brothers moved on to the New England Whalers for two years before teaming up one more time with their dad — back in the NHL again — in Hartford for what was to be the last year of his legendary career. In 1982 Marty left the Insurance City to join the Boston Bruins for a year before returning to Hartford where he finished his major league career two years later.

In August of 1982 Mark was traded by Hart-ford to Philadelphia where he would spend ten productive seasons on the Flyers' blue line. During his Philly tenure he was named to the NHL All-Star First Team in 1983, 1986 and 1987. His solid defensive play and scoring touch helped the Flyers advance to the Stanley Cup Finals in 1985 and 1987.

In July, 1992 Mark was signed as a free agent by his dad's old team, the Detroit Red Wings. He remained a Wing until finally hanging up his skates after the 1994-95 season. Like his dad, he was the very soul of longevity, playing 22 years as a pro.

Steve Babineau

Gordie Howe came out of retirement to play with his two sons in Houston.

Left to right: Gordie, Mark, and Marty (far right).

MARTY HOWE
Born: Detroit, MI, 2/18/54
6-1, 195
D, shoots left

Season	Team	GP	G	A	Pts	PIM
70-71	Detroit (SOJHL)	-	-	-	-	-
71-72	Toronto (OHL)	56	7	21	28	-
72-73	Toronto (OHL)	38	11	17	28	-
73-74	Hou (WHA)	73	4	20	24	90
74-75	Hou (WHA)	75	13	21	34	89
75-76	Hou (WHA)	80	14	23	37	81
76-77	Hou (WHA)	80	17	28	45	103
77-78	NE (WHA)	75	10	10	20	66
78-79	NE (WHA)	66	9	15	24	31
79-80	Hartford	6	0	1	1	4
80-81	Hartford	12	0	1	1	25
81-82	Hartford	13	0	4	4	2
82-83	Boston	78	1	11	12	24
83-84	Hartford	69	0	11	11	34
84-85	Hartford	19	1	1	2	10
NHL Totals		197	2	29	31	99
WHA Totals		449	67	117	184	460
NHL Playoff Totals		15	1	2	3	9
WHA Playoff Totals		75	9	14	23	85

MARK HOWE
Born: Detroit, MI, 5/28/55
5-11, 185
D, shoots left

Season	Team	GP	G	A	Pts	PIM
70-71	Detroit (SOJHL)	44	37	70	107	-
71-72	Detroit (SOJHL)	9	5	9	14	-
	US Olympic Team		*stats unavailable*			
72-73	Toronto (OHA)	60	38	66	104	-
73-74	Hou (WHA)	76	38	41	79	20
74-75	Hou (WHA)	74	36	40	76	30
75-76	Hou (WHA)	72	39	37	76	38
76-77	Hou (WHA)	57	23	52	75	46
77-78	NE (WHA)	70	30	61	91	32
78-79	NE (WHA)	77	42	65	107	32
79-80	Hartford	74	24	56	80	20
80-81	Hartford	63	19	46	65	54
81-82	Hartford	76	8	45	53	18
82-83	Philly	76	20	47	67	18
83-84	Philly	71	19	34	53	44
84-85	Philly	73	18	39	57	31
85-86	Philly	77	24	58	82	36
86-87	Philly	69	15	43	58	37
87-88	Philly	75	19	43	62	62
88-89	Philly	52	9	29	38	45
89-90	Philly	40	7	21	28	24
90-91	Philly	19	0	10	10	8
91-92	Philly	42	7	18	25	18
92-93	Detroit	60	3	31	34	22
93-94	Detroit	44	4	20	24	8
94-95	Detroit	18	1	5	6	10
NHL Totals		929	197	545	742	455
WHA Totals		426	208	296	504	198
NHL Playoff Totals		101	10	51	61	34
WHA Playoff Totals		74	41	51	92	48

GORDIE ROBERTS

Steve Babineau

Born in Detroit in October, 1957 — and named after Gordie Howe — Gordie Roberts was the youngest of four hockey-playing brothers. The boys logged many hours of ice time on the family's back yard rink where Gordie first learned to skate at the age of three.

After playing on a mite team when he was seven, Gordie moved up through the youth hockey ranks playing squirts, pee wees and bantams. At age 15 he played for a Junior-B team called the "Detroit Big D," which was comprised mostly of players in their late-teens.

In 1973 Roberts joined the same program that produced the Howe brothers — the Detroit Junior Red Wings of the Southern Ontario Junior Hockey League. It was then that he got a taste of the Canadian prejudice that his brothers had earlier experienced.

"I came along in 1974 and played with the Junior Wings out of Detroit, which was in the Southern Ontario Junior League. We played against all Canadian teams. It was definitely tough being an American player at that time knowing what all my brothers went through. Detroit was so close to Canada we used to play in a lot of Canadian rinks and towns. We all thought our first name was 'Yankee.'"

The following season Roberts left for British Columbia to play for Victoria of the Western Canadian Hockey League. After one season in the WCHL, he opted to turn pro at the ripe age of 17 and signed with the New England Whalers of the WHA in September, 1975. Gordie joined the team at training camp but could only practice because he had to wait until October 2, the date of his 18th birthday, to be eligible to play his first game. His second-oldest brother Doug, a ten-year NHL veteran who had also recently joined the Whalers, was now his teammate.

An excellent rushing defenseman, Roberts immediately proved himself at the pro level playing steady "D" and contributing in the scoring column while remaining extremely durable. During his first 11 seasons as a pro he rarely missed a game.

In December, 1980, 15 months after the Whalers joined the NHL, they traded him to Minnesota for American-born left wing Mike Fidler. Gordie's addition to the club helped the North Stars advance all the way to the Stanley Cup Finals in 1980-81 before losing to the New York Islanders in five games. After what amounted to seven productive season with the Stars, two trades sent him to St. Louis via Philadelphia midway through the 1987-88 season.

In October, 1990 the Blues traded him for future considerations to Pittsburgh where he joined Mario Lemieux and Company to become part of two Stanley Cup championship teams in 1990-91 and 1991-92.

When his tenure in the Steel City was over Roberts signed with the Boston Bruins. Beantown brought yet another highlight to what had already been a long and illustrious career. During the 1992-93 season he reached a milestone, becoming the first American to play 1,000 games in the NHL. Roberts finished his playing days in 1994-95 as a player-assistant coach for the Chicago Wolves of the International Hockey league. He currently serves as director of player personnel for the Phoenix Coyotes.

Born: Detroit, MI, 10/2/57
6-0, 190
D, shoots left

Season	Team	GP	G	A	Pts	PIM
73-74	Detroit (SOJHL)	70	25	55	80	-
74-75	Victoria (WCHL)	53	19	45	64	-
75-76	NE (WHA)	77	3	19	22	102
76-77	NE (WHA)	77	13	33	46	169
77-78	NE (WHA)	78	15	46	61	118
78-79	NE (WHA)	79	11	46	57	113
79-80	Hartford	80	8	28	36	89
80-81	Hart-Minn	77	8	42	50	175
81-82	Minnesota	79	4	30	34	119
82-83	Minnesota	80	3	41	44	103
83-84	Minnesota	77	8	45	53	132
84-85	Minnesota	78	6	36	42	112
85-86	Minnesota	76	2	21	23	101
86-87	Minnesota	67	3	10	13	68
87-88	Minn-Phil-StL	70	3	15	18	143
88-89	St. Louis	77	2	24	26	90
89-90	St. Louis	75	3	14	17	140
90-91	StL-Pitt	64	3	13	16	78
91-92	Pittsburgh	73	2	22	24	87
92-93	Boston	65	5	12	17	105
93-94	Boston	59	1	6	7	40
94-95	Chicago (IHL)	68	6	22	28	80
NHL Totals		1097	61	359	420	1582
WHA Totals		311	42	144	186	502
NHL Playoff Totals		153	10	47	57	273
WHA Playoff Totals		46	4	20	24	81

PAUL HOLMGREN

Many fine hockey players can thank their parents for allowing them the opportunity to learn to skate at a very early age. Thanks to his dad, who flooded the empty lot next door to their house in St. Paul, Minnesota each winter, Paul Holmgren began skating as early as age two. Paul, his older brother Mark and all the kids from the neighborhood would frequent the frozen vacant lot throughout those early years.

Paul began playing organized hockey at age six. He and Mark became teammates and continued through the ranks. The boys lived a hockey life: "The playground that we played at was four blocks from our house," recalls Holmgren. "In the winter time we didn't have to take our skates off. We'd just put our skates on and skate up to the playground where the hockey rinks were and skate home for dinner and skate back up after dinner. My mom made us put our skate guards on to come in the house."

Beginning in 10th grade Paul played for Harding High School on the East side of St. Paul. In his junior and senior years the team qualified for the Minnesota State High School Tournament, but each year was eliminated early in the competition. As a senior, however, Holmgren's team managed an upset of powerhouse Minneapolis Southwest before losing the next two games.

When his schoolboy days were over, Paul played a year of Junior Hockey with the St. Paul Vulcans of the Midwest Junior Hockey League. The highlight of the season came when Paul was selected to be part of a team

Steve Babineau

comprised of a MJHL players to compete in the World Junior Tournament in Leningrad, USSR.

In late summer of 1974 Paul enrolled at the University of Minnesota where he played in 37 games for the Gophers that season, scoring 11 goals and assisting on 21 scores for 32 points.

The following year he left college to sign with the Minnesota Fighting Saints of the WHA. When the franchise folded in March of 1976, Paul moved to the Philadelphia Flyers who had drafted him the previous year. Just prior to season's end Paul made his NHL debut.

For Holmgren it was a dream come true putting on a Flyers uniform. In 1967, at age 11, Paul's dad had taken him to see a North Stars game. The opposition was the Flyers and

Gary Dornhoefer soon became his role model. "I remember seeing Gary Dornhoefer playing an up and down physical style," says Holmgren, "and then I got to play with Dorny for a couple of years too, so it was great."

Paul's most memorable season with Philly was 1979-80 when the club compiled a 35-game unbeaten streak. "It was a tremendous year because we also finished first overall," recalls Holmgren. "Then to have a situation where we made it to the Finals and lost in six games to the Islanders. It left a bad taste in everybody's mouth, but still the year as a whole was a tremendous experience."

Despite suffering a knee injury during the final round, the fearless right winger could not be kept out of the lineup. And it was against the Isles that Holmgren became the first American-born player to record a hat trick in a final-series game. A 30-goal scorer during the regular season, Paul finished the post-season with 10 goals and 10 assists.

Holmgren spent the better part of seven seasons with Philadelphia before returning to his home state in 1984 where he finished his playing career with the North Stars a year later.

In 1988 Paul returned to the Flyers organization as head coach, a position he kept until 1992. He then coached the Hartford Whalers off and on from 1992 to 1996. He's now back in the Flyers organization where he serves as director of pro scouting.

Born: St. Paul, MN, 12/22/55
6-3, 210
RW, shoots right

Season	Team	GP	G	A	Pts	PIM
74-75	U Minn (WCHA)	37	11	21	31	108
75-76	Minn (WHA)	51	14	16	30	121
75-76	Philly	1	0	0	0	2
76-77	Philly	59	14	12	26	201
77-78	Philly	62	16	18	34	190
78-79	Philly	57	19	10	29	168
79-80	Philly	74	30	35	65	267
80-81	Philly	77	22	37	59	306
81-82	Philly	41	9	22	31	183
82-83	Philly	77	19	24	43	178
83-84	Phil-Minn	63	11	18	29	151
84-85	Minnesota	16	4	3	7	38
NHL Totals		527	144	179	323	1684
WHA Totals		51	14	16	30	121
NHL Playoff Totals		82	19	32	51	195

MIKE MILBURY

When Mike Milbury was a kid, his family moved from the Boston suburb of Brookline to Walpole, located approximately 20 miles southwest of the city. Walpole was sprinkled with lots of ponds and owned a rich hockey tradition which included state championship high school teams as well as such athletic legends as former Boston College hockey coach Len Ceglarski and Joe Morgan, who went on to manage the Boston Red Sox.

While his older brothers played basketball, Mike toyed with pond skating and at the age of 13, he signed up for the town pee wee team.

After competing at both the pee wee and bantam levels Mike played varsity hockey for coach Charlie Sinto at Walpole High, which was a member of the powerful Bay State League. A multi-sport athlete at Walpole, it was football that earned Mike a scholarship to Colgate where he eventually turned his focus to hockey and the prospects of a pro career.

It turned out the team he grew up loving — the Big, Bad Bruins — soon took an interest in him. Mike's entry into the NHL was slightly different from most. Instead of drafting Mike, the Bruins put him on a negotiation list, which was a way of keeping other clubs from tampering with their free agents. After playing in a couple of tryout games for the Bruins' Boston Braves farm club during his senior year, Mike returned in the fall without a contract but came to terms by mid-October. That season the Bruins moved their AHL affiliate from Boston to Rochester where Mike spent two seasons before being called up to the big club

Steve Babineau

late in the 1975-76 season.

Although he was not blessed with speed nor flashy offensive moves, Mike always played with heart and was very adept at keeping rival forwards from stationing themselves in front of the net. Such attributes kept him a Bruin blueliner for the remaining 11 seasons of his career before he called it quits after the 1986-87 campaign.

Following his retirement as a player, Mike remained in the Bruins organization as a coach for their Portland, Maine AHL affiliate. After two years in Maine, Mike was hired to coach the Bruins in 1989-90. Under the direction of their assertive rookie coach, the Bruins advanced all the way to the Stanley Cup Finals where they bowed to the Edmonton Oilers in five games.

The following season Mike left the bench to move upstairs as the Bruins assistant general manager. After leaving Beantown in 1994 and serving a brief stint as a hockey analyst for ESPN, Mike was hired as coach of the New York Islanders. He later added the general manager's role to his repertoire. Early in the 1996-97 season he yielded his coaching duties to Rick Bowness (also his Boston replacement) in order to concentrate on front office responsibilities.

Born: Brighton, MA, 6/17/52
6-1, 200
D, shoots left

Season	Team	GP	G	A	Pts	PIM
75-76	Boston	3	0	0	0	9
76-77	Boston	77	6	18	24	166
77-78	Boston	80	8	30	38	151
78-79	Boston	74	1	34	35	149
79-80	Boston	72	10	13	23	59
80-81	Boston	77	0	18	18	222
81-82	Boston	51	2	10	12	71
82-83	Boston	78	9	15	24	216
83-84	Boston	74	2	17	19	159
84-85	Boston	78	3	13	16	152
85-86	Boston	22	2	5	7	102
86-87	Boston	68	6	16	22	96
Totals		754	49	189	238	1552
Playoff Totals		86	4	24	28	219

REED LARSON

Reed Larson first skated at age four on a frozen lake nearby his Minneapolis home. He began organized play two years later, playing center for a local pee wee team. After moving up the ranks through cubs and bantams he attended Roosevelt High in Minneapolis.

As a 15-year-old sophomore defenseman Reed made the "Teddies" varsity squad. The following season the Teddies, coached by Bucky Freeberg, won the first of back-to-back Minneapolis City Championships. In Larson's senior year the team also qualified for the State High School Tournament at the Met Center in Bloomington but lost its first game in double overtime to Grand Rapids.

"For playoffs or big rivalry games we had 6,000 people," Larson remembers. "Then when we made it to the state high school tournament, which was everybody's goal or dream, we were playing in front of 16,000 and on TV, so we could feel the pressure. Everybody was a little nervous."

Playing in front of such a large crowd was a primer for his next step — the University of Minnesota. Having grown up watching the Gophers, Reed was thrilled to don the maroon and gold. As a freshman he helped lead his team to the WCHA Championship and a trip to the NCAA Finals where they bowed to Michigan Tech. The following season the Gophers returned to the NCAA Championship Game where they defeated Michigan Tech to win the National Championship.

It marked the third year in a row the two schools had met in the finals.

A strong skater with a sizzling slap shot,

Steve Babineau

Reed caught the attention of the Detroit Red Wings who drafted him in the second round of the 1976 Entry Draft. After being suspended from college hockey for a fighting incident near the end of the 1976-77 season, Reed was given a 14-day tryout with the Wings. He didn't leave until nine years later.

In his first full season (1977-78) he made the All-Star Team and experienced the biggest thrill of his career:

"The first All-Star Game I played in was at Buffalo. There I was, sitting in the dressing room and looking around," recalls Larson. "I was remembering that I was in college and high school just a few short years earlier. Now I was looking at Guy Lafleur, Yvon Cournoyer, Larry Robinson, Borje Salming, Gilbert Perreault, Richard Martin, Ken Dryden, Jacques Lemaire, Serge Savard, Marcel Dionne. My team picture of my first All-Star Game to me was an incredible hockey team."

Reed not only provided the Wings with a stocky presence in front of the net but added a lot of offense to their attack. His most productive season was 1982-83 when he banged home 22 goals and notched 52 assists.

Another big thrill came later in Larson's career when he helped the Boston Bruins stage a Stanley Cup run in 1987-88 before losing to Edmonton in a controversial five-game series.

It was a historic year for Boston, which ended its longtime "Montreal jinx" by rebounding to win four straight from the Canadiens after dropping the opening game of the series. For Bostonians 45 years of bleu, blanc et rouge domination had mercifully come to an end.

After helping Boston get a monkey off its back, Reed left the Bruins for short stints with

four other clubs before hanging up his NHL skates at the end of the 1989-90 season. He then left North America to play in Italy for five seasons with Alleghe, Aosta and Hockey Club Milano.

Larson now works for a company that creates and sells web pages on the internet. He also helps run hockey schools. And like many of the fine people who have played this game, he gives his time to charity events.

Now Larson looks look back on his career with a humorous perspective: "You know, it's funny, I tell people I played for the Roosevelt Teddies, the Minnesota Gophers and the Detroit Red Wings. Not the most masculine team names. Kind of like a boy named Sue!"

Born: Minneapolis, MN, 7/30/56
6-0, 195
D, shoots right

Season	Team	GP	G	A	Pts	PIM
76-77	Detroit	14	0	1	1	23
77-78	Detroit	75	19	41	60	95
78-79	Detroit	79	18	49	67	169
79-80	Detroit	80	22	44	66	101
80-81	Detroit	78	27	31	58	153
81-82	Detroit	80	21	39	60	112
82-83	Detroit	80	22	52	74	104
83-84	Detroit	78	23	39	62	122
84-85	Detroit	77	17	45	62	139
85-86	Det-Bos	80	22	45	67	117
86-87	Boston	66	12	24	36	95
87-88	Boston	62	10	24	34	93
88-89	Edm-NYI-Minn	54	9	29	38	68
89-90	Buffalo	1	0	0	0	0
Totals		904	222	463	685	1391
Playoff Totals		32	4	7	11	63

DAVE LANGEVIN

The fourth of eight children, Dave Langevin started skating on the family's back yard rink in St. Paul at age five. The rink was built by his dad, a former Cretin High School star forward. Shortly after those first lessons, Dave played his first organized hockey on a pee wee team at nearby Hazel Park Playground.

After pee wees and bantams, Dave attended a nearby Catholic school named Hill High School. After making the junior varsity as a freshman, he played varsity hockey for coach André Beaulieu, a former college player who built the program which is now regarded as one of the elite programs in Minnesota. Langevin helped the Pioneers win two state championships while setting his sights on higher goals before graduating in 1972.

"I realized in high school that some of the kids in the upper grades were trying to get scholarships," explains Langevin. "At that point I decided that maybe that was the way I wanted to go."

And that he did. Dave attended the University of Minnesota-Duluth where he played his first three years for coach Terry Shercliff and his final season under the direction of Shercliff's replacement, Gus Hendrickson.

In 1974 he was drafted by both Edmonton of the WHA and the New York Islanders. Seeing a chance to immediately step into the lineup with the Oilers, Dave chose Edmonton. "They gave me a better opportunity to play on their club," explains Langevin. "I think New York was going to put me in the minors at first."

After graduating from Duluth, Dave joined

Steve Babineau

the Oilers in 1976-77. As the only American on the team at the time, he felt he had to prove himself.

"I went in and showed that I could play tough and physical," says Langevin. "We had guys who could score and guys who could fight. As more guys showed they could play, it opened up for everybody."

In 1978-79 Dave had the honor of playing with a 17-year-old rookie phenom by the name of Wayne Gretzky. His association with Gretzky, however, was short-lived. After the season ended the WHA folded. Although the Oilers were one of the four clubs merged into the NHL, Langevin joined the New York Islanders who exercised their option to reacquire him as a former draft pick.

For Langevin it was a blessing. He was separated from "The Great One," but was extremely fortunate to become part of an Islanders dynasty that included four consecutive Stanley Cups, beginning with 1979-80, his first season. Langevin, who for his hard-hitting style of play was also known as "Bam-Bam," gave the Isles much-needed extra muscle — something they had lacked in previous playoffs.

After six quality seasons on the Island, Langevin was placed on waivers at the end of the 1984-85 campaign. Soon after, Minnesota claimed him and Dave found himself back in his home state for one season before heading to Los Angeles in 1986. He hurt his chronically injured knee in L.A. and decided to call it a career. The knee had bothered him over the course of six seasons but the rugged Minnesotan still managed to play in 70 or more games each year.

After retirement Langevin returned to school for a teaching degree. He now has his own business as a residential appraiser in the St. Paul area where he still resides and is coaching the (Boise) Idaho Steelhawks in the West Coast Hockey League.

Born: St. Paul, MN, 5/15/54
6-2, 200
D, shoots left

Season	Team	GP	G	A	Pts	PIM
76-77	Edm (WHA)	77	7	16	23	94
77-78	Edm (WHA)	62	6	22	28	90
78-79	Edm (WHA)	77	6	21	27	76
79-80	NY Islanders	76	3	13	16	109
80-81	NY Islanders	75	1	16	17	122
81-82	NY Islanders	73	1	20	21	82
82-83	NY Islanders	73	4	17	21	64
83-84	NY Islanders	69	3	16	19	53
84-85	NY Islanders	56	0	13	13	35
85-86	Minnesota	80	0	8	8	58
86-87	Los Angeles	11	0	4	4	7
NHL Totals		513	12	107	119	530
WHA Totals		216	19	59	78	260
NHL Playoff Totals		87	2	15	17	106
WHA Playoff Totals		23	2	4	6	44

ROD LANGWAY

Steve Babineau

Rod Langway is an exception to the rule that if a boy wants to grow up to become a professional hockey player he must learn to skate by the age of seven. Rod didn't learn until he turned 11.

Born in Taiwan, Langway moved to the Boston area when he was a youth. Inspired by Bobby Orr and the Big, Bad Bruins, Rod first used figure skates. "The guys who I played hockey with wouldn't let me play unless I got regular hockey skates," he recalls, "and that was the following winter. I got my first pair of hockey skates when I was 12 and-a-half. I played mostly baseball and football. Then all of a sudden all my buddies who played baseball and football got me interested in hockey."

Soon Rod joined a winter house league and lied about his age so he could play with his buddies who were at least a year older. One of his close pals was future University of Vermont star and Pittsburgh Penguins draft choice Joey Oslin, who later was killed in car accident. It was Oslin who played a key role in getting Rod interested in hockey.

Rod then played on a local bantam team coached by Jack Foley, who went on to succeed Arthur Valescenti at Thayer Academy. Foley was Valescenti's assistant when Tony Amonte and Jeremy Roenick led Thayer to two consecutive New England Prep School Championships during the mid-'80s.

"Probably my biggest influence — to give credit where it's due — would be Jack Foley," says Langway. "He took an interest in me. I think I'd only gone to two or three Boston Bru-ins games when I was a kid. You couldn't get tickets and our family never went to sporting events. We just listened on the radio and watched it on TV. Jack Foley took me to a Bruins exhibition game. For a coach to take an interest in a player — it's something that I'll always remember. And to this day I think he's probably one of the better coaches around."

Following two years of bantams Rod played both center and defense for Randolph High of the Old Colony League. Secondary school highlights included playing in State Championship Tournaments at Boston Garden in 1973 and 1975. In the 1975 semifinals they went head-to-head with future Olympic star Jim Craig and his Oliver Ames team.

Langway was both a football and baseball star for Randolph but it was a football scholarship that sent Rod to the University of New Hampshire, which promised him he could play hockey too. After a shoulder separation ended his football career, Langway devoted his athletic efforts to the varsity hockey team as a freshman and sophomore. Some 18-20 players from these squads went on to play some form of pro hockey. His teammates included Cliff Cox, Jamie Hislop, Bobby Gould, Bruce Crowder, Bobby Miller, Paul Powers, Joey Rando, Ralph Cox, Bobby Francis, Dave Lumley, Gary Burns, and Timmy Burke.

Drafted by Montreal in the second round of the 1977 NHL Entry Draft and the WHA Birmingham Bulls in the first round, Langway opted to leave UNH to play for Birmingham in 1977-78. After only one season with the Bulls he signed with the Canadiens.

Under the able tutelage of future Hall of Fame defenseman Larry Robinson, whom Rod credits for a large part of his development, he helped the Habs win their fourth straight Stanley Cup in 1978-79.

Langway's most significant achievement as a pro came in both the 1982-83 and 1983-84 seasons, when he won consecutive Norris Trophies as the league's best defenseman. Today the Norris Trophy is often awarded to the best offensive defenseman, but Rod's steady yet tenacious "stay at home" style was a true testament to the fine art of pure defense play.

Born: Formosa, Taiwan, 5/3/57
6-3, 218
D, shoots left

Season	Team	GP	G	A	Pts	PIM
77-78	Birm (WHA)	52	3	18	21	52
78-79	Montreal	45	3	4	7	30
79-80	Montreal	77	7	29	36	81
80-81	Montreal	80	11	34	45	120
81-82	Montreal	66	5	34	39	116
82-83	Washington	80	3	29	32	75
83-84	Washington	80	9	24	33	61
84-85	Washington	79	4	22	26	54
85-86	Washington	71	1	17	18	61
86-87	Washington	78	2	25	27	53
87-88	Washington	63	3	13	16	28
88-89	Washington	76	2	19	21	65
89-90	Washington	58	0	8	8	39
90-91	Washington	56	1	7	8	24
91-92	Washington	64	0	13	13	22
92-93	Washington	21	0	0	0	20
NHL Totals		994	51	278	329	849
WHA Totals		52	3	18	21	52
NHL Playoff Totals		104	5	22	27	97
WHA Playoff Totals		4	0	0	0	9

MIKE O'CONNELL

Steve Babineau

Mike O'Connell was born in Chicago, but his family moved from the Windy City to Buffalo where Mike started skating at the age of four. A year later the family moved to the Boston suburb of Cohasset, Massachusetts. While in first grade O'Connell began skating at the recently-constructed Cohasset Winter Gardens. It was at the Winter Gardens where Mike began playing his first organized hockey, competing at the pee wee level.

As he moved up through the youth hockey divisions (playing bantam, midget and junior) he also played football in the fall. His former coach Jim Harrington recalls an early heroic moment in Mike's sports career: "In eighth grade football Mike played defensive and offensive end," recalls Harrington. "In the last game of the year in West Bridgewater it was getting dark and we were behind 3-0 and this team was striking at us again. But Michael stole the ball and ran 75 yards for a touchdown to win the championship. I always kid him about that."

When Mike reached the ninth grade he enrolled at Archbishop Williams High, a Catholic school in nearby Braintree, which competed against such powerhouses as Catholic Memorial, BC High, Severian, Matignon and Malden Catholic. After starring on the varsity hockey squad as both a freshman and sophomore, Mike opted to continue his schooling at Williams, but play hockey for a semi-pro team called the Braintree Hawks of the old New England Hockey League.

Most of the players in the NEHL were former collegians. "I was playing with men as opposed to playing with kids," says O'Connell. "For my development it was the best route to take." The League, which had been around since the late '60s, folded after that season, forcing O'Connell to take a different route. The following season he headed to Canada to compete at the Junior level for Kingston of the Ontario Hockey League.

Apart from the 70-game seasons and the higher caliber of play, O'Connell claims that the rougher style of play was just what he needed to become NHL stock:

"It was tough. There were more bodychecks and there was fighting. It was not 'goon' hockey. It was good, hard North American hockey, which was a great training for me. I learned that getting hit and being hit didn't hurt. It was a training that I'll never forget and if I had not done it I probably wouldn't have played in the National Hockey League. I needed it! I needed to toughen up! I realized that the threat of being punched in the nose wasn't that bad. My strengths were skating and passing, but I became aware of the physical part of the game and not to let it affect me. You learn that it's always going to be there and you face up to the fact that it's a tough game. I learned it at an earlier age and a lot of times it takes players a long time to understand that they should experience it at a young age. A lot of players still haven't faced up to the fact that it's a tough game. You have to be trained. For some people it comes naturally and some people have to be trained and I was trained. They just can't handle it. Not that they're not big enough or strong enough, but just the threat of being punched in the nose in front of millions of people and how to react to it — it's pretty powerful."

After spending two seasons playing Canadian Junior hockey, Mike was drafted by the Chicago Blackhawks. He played three and a half years in the minors with Dallas and Moncton before being called up in December,

1977 making his NHL debut for the team that represents the city of his birth.

For more than two seasons Mike was a strong addition to the Hawks defense before a trade brought him back to Boston in late 1981. It was with the Bruins that Mike added a scoring touch to his repertoire, potting at least 14 goals in three of his four full seasons with the B's. During the 1985-86 season Mike was traded to the Detroit Red Wings where he finished his career in 1989-90.

"It was very fortunate," says O'Connell, when asked to sum up his 13-year pro career. "I stayed away from the big injuries and I had a lot of fun doing so."

O'Connell is now assistant general manager for the Boston Bruins. It is expected that when Harry Sinden retires Mike will take over the reigns as key decision-maker for the Black and Gold.

Born: Chicago, IL, 11/25/55
5-9, 180
D, shoots right

Season	Team	GP	G	A	Pts	PIM
77-78	Chicago	6	1	1	2	2
78-79	Chicago	48	4	22	26	20
79-80	Chicago	78	8	22	30	52
80-81	Chi-Bos	82	15	38	53	74
81-82	Boston	80	5	34	39	75
82-83	Boston	80	14	39	53	42
83-84	Boston	75	18	42	60	42
84-85	Boston	78	15	40	55	64
85-86	Bos-Det	76	9	28	37	63
86-87	Detroit	77	5	26	31	70
87-88	Detroit	48	6	13	19	38
88-89	Detroit	66	1	15	16	41
89-90	Detroit	66	4	14	18	22
Totals		860	105	334	439	605
Playoff Totals		82	8	24	32	64

CHRIS NILAN

Chris Nilan learned to skate at age five on a large frozen puddle in the middle of a large parking lot near his home in West Roxbury, Massachusetts. He then began public skating at a nearby rink where he soon became a regular. At age seven he played his first organized hockey in a youth hockey program called the Charlie Doyle League, named after a local politician. "I played in that league but every time I could go public skating I would go," says Nilan. "It cost a quarter to get in and I used to skate on Friday night. Then, I'd be up there Saturday night and I'd skate every chance I got." Other favorite spots for logging ice time included the Charles River and a nearby swamp which is now the site of West Roxbury High School.

The next step for Chris was the Boston Neighborhood Hockey League, where his West Roxbury pee wee team won the league championship under coach Steve Curtin. In the championship game Chris contributed by scoring a goal in a 9-5 win over Charlestown.

Nilan then was selected to play for the Hub City Team, an all-star squad coached by the late Judge Paul King (brother of former Massachusetts governor Ed King) and was comprised of boys from around the Boston area. Judge King was influential in Nilan's development. "He was the man who backed me and opened doors for me that might otherwise not have been opened based on my talents alone," claims Nilan. "He knew there was something else there other than my limited skills at the time."

Judge King was responsible for Chris get-

Steve Babineau

ting an opportunity to go to Northeastern University on a full scholarship. King was good friends with Northeastern University coach Fernie Flaman, a former NHL defenseman with the Bruins and Maple Leafs. Flaman came to see Chris play on a couple of occasions and liked what he saw. He later gave Nilan a full scholarship to Northeastern.

During his early teens Nilan attended Catholic Memorial High School in West Roxbury and made the freshman team in his first year but sat on the bench. As a sophomore Chris was sent back and forth between varsity and junior varsity, but during his junior and senior years Chris saw a lot of ice time. After his final year at CM assistant coach Bill Hanson (now the head coach) encouraged Chris to play a year of prep school hockey before heading for college.

Nilan took Hanson's advice and went to Northwood Prep in Lake Placid, New York for a year on a half-scholarship. Northwood competed against junior varsity squads from colleges such as Clarkson, St. Lawrence and Elmira. At season's end Chris was named Most Improved Player and was fully prepared to play at the next level.

In the fall of 1976, Chris enrolled at Northeastern where he played for three years under the guidance of Flaman. At the end of his sophomore season Chris was drafted by the Montreal Canadiens. He wanted to leave school then, but stayed to please his father who wanted him to finish. But after Chris's junior year he told his father he was leaving.

Nilan showed up at the Canadiens training camp in late summer of 1979 without a contract. The Habs sent him to Halifax and gave him a ten-game tryout at $200 per game. He sat out the first three games but in the fourth game in Portland, Maine against Philadelphia's affiliate, the Maine Mariners, Chris was not going to let an opportunity slip away.

"I went out on the first shift I played and got into a fight with Glen Cochrane, a big tough kid from Western Canada who played in the NHL too," Nilan recalls. "He was about 6-3, and an animal. I cut him open and he went nuts. We both got kicked out of the game and they had a contract offer for me two days later."

The Canadiens weren't going to miss an opportunity either. They knew they had the reincarnation of their quintessential enforcer John Ferguson.

Nilan played 50 games for Halifax that season, scoring 15 goals, adding 10 assists and accumulating 304 penalty minutes. "I played with Rick Meagher who also went to BU," says Nilan with a chuckle. "I protected his little ass."

The next season began a seven and one half year stretch where Nilan saw regular action with the Canadiens. The highlight of his career came while playing with Montreal in 1985-86 as the stocky right winger chipped in 19 goals while keeping star forwards off their game to help the Habs coast to their 23rd Stanley Cup.

After short stints with the Rangers and Bruins, Chris returned to Montreal for the remainder of the 1991-92 season to finish his career in the city where his NHL loyalties reside. It was somewhat ironic that Nilan had grown up loving the Big, Bad Bruins, but became the tough guy of Boston's dreaded nemesis — Les Habitants.

Anyone who trifled with Chris on the ice had to pay the price. Steal one of his shoes and you're really in trouble. While Nilan was catching a little "shut-eye" on a plane trip back from Buffalo during his Rangers days, teammates Darren Turcotte and John Vanbiesbrouck stole one of his shoes and never returned it. Upon awakening, a peeved Nilan searched in vain for the missing shoe before reluctantly walking through the airport terminal in only his socks!

Eventually Chris was tipped off about the identity of the culprits and set out to avenge the act. He and a teammate drove to Turcotte's Greenwich, Connecticut residence one evening and slashed all four of the rookie's tires. The next day at practice Chris overheard Turcotte complaining about how he thought he had "picked a safe neighborhood" in which to live.

For Vanbiesbrouck a different punishment was in order: Chris broke into Beezer's Volvo, opened up the back seat and inserted a bag of dead fish. Before long Beezer was complaining about the terrible smell coming from inside his car. He thought he might have unknowingly hit a skunk. Finally John had his mechanic take the car apart, at which time the nearly decomposed fish were discovered.

Nilan later admitted to each of his teammates that it was he who was responsible for the acts of revenge. They told him they thought it was a rather dramatic way to pay them back for the stolen shoe.

"That's right," responded Nilan in typical Chris fashion, "I am the judge, the jury and the executioner!"

Born: Boston, MA, 2/9/58
6-0, 205
RW, shoots right

Season	Team	GP	G	A	Pts	PIM
79-80	Montreal	15	0	2	2	50
80-81	Montreal	57	7	8	15	262
81-82	Montreal	49	7	4	11	204
82-83	Montreal	66	6	8	14	213
83-84	Montreal	76	16	10	26	338
84-85	Montreal	77	21	16	37	358
85-86	Montreal	72	19	15	34	274
86-87	Montreal	44	4	16	20	266
87-88	Mont-NYR	72	10	10	20	305
88-89	NY Rangers	38	7	7	14	177
89-90	NY Rangers	25	1	2	3	59
90-91	Boston	41	6	9	15	277
91-92	Bos-Mont	56	6	8	14	260
Totals		688	110	115	225	3043
Playoff Totals		111	8	9	17	541

JOEY MULLEN

Raised in Manhattan's Hell's Kitchen neighborhood on the island's West Side, Joey Mullen and his younger brother, Brian, also a former NHLer, grew up playing street and roller hockey. During the 1970s Joey, Brian and their other brother Kenny, played in the Fort Hamilton Roller Hockey League, which at the time was considered the highest caliber circuit of its kind in the country.

After playing four years in the New York Major Junior Hockey League, including his MVP season of 1974-75, Joey attended Boston College where he became a standout goal-scorer earning ECAC All-Star honors in both his junior and senior years. As a junior Joey helped lead the Eagles to the 1978 NCAA Championship Game against Boston University. One of his more memorable performances came earlier that season against RPI in the first game of the ECAC Tournament when he scored the tying goal and then the winning goal in overtime.

When his college days were over Mullen was one of a handful of players highly coveted by Herb Brooks for the 1980 Olympic Team. Knowing that his dad was ill, Joey opted for the pros to get a sizable paycheck in order to help his dad. In August, 1979 he signed with the St. Louis Blues.

The Blues sent him to their CHL Salt Lake City affiliate for the season before calling him up to the big club for post-season action. For his 40-goal performance at Salt Lake that season Mullen was voted the recipient of the Ken McKenzie Trophy as the CHL's top rookie and was thrown into playoff action with the Blues

for one game. He followed that performance with a league-leading 117-point season in 1980-81, which made him the clear choice for the Tommy Ivan Trophy as the CHL's MVP.

In 1982-83 a long and prolific NHL career got underway for the tough little right winger. Through four and one half seasons in St. Louis Mullen averaged better than one point per game. In February, 1986 the Blues sent him to Calgary as part of six-player blockbuster deal. It was with the Flames that he enjoyed his most productive years.

His best season ever was 1988-89 when, while helping the Flames to the first Stanley Cup triumph in franchise history, Mullen led the league in plus-minus, won the Lady Byng Trophy, was named to the NHL First All-Star Team and led all playoff goal-scorers with 12.

In June 1990 the Flames surprisingly dealt him to Pittsburgh for a second round choice (Nicolas Perreault) in the 1990 Entry Draft.

The move to Western Pennsylvania worked

out well for the New York City native, who saw his name inscribed on Lord Stanley's Cup after each of the next two seasons.

On February 7, 1995 Joey made hockey history by becoming the first American-born player to score 1,000 points in an NHL career with an assist in a 7-3 victory over Florida — his 935th career game.

Later in 1995 Joey, his brother Brian and amateur hockey executive Bob Fleming were each awarded the 1995 Lester Patrick Award for outstanding contributions to U.S. hockey.

In September 1995 Mullen signed as a free agent with the Boston Bruins. After an injury-riddled year in Beantown, Joe returned to Pittsburgh the following season to become the first American-born NHLer to score 500 goals. He retired at season's end.

With 502 goals and 1,063 points, Mullen stands alone as the most prolific American-born goal-scorer and point-producer in NHL history as well as a future Hall of Famer.

Born: New York, NY, 2/26/57
5-9, 180
RW, shoots right

Season	Team	GP	G	A	Pts	PIM
77-78	Boston College	34	34	34	68	-
78-79	Boston College	25	32	24	56	-
79-80	Salt Lake City	75	40	32	72	-
79-80	St. Louis		(playoffs only)			
80-81	Salt Lake City	80	59	58	117	-
81-82	St. Louis	45	25	34	59	4
82-83	St. Louis	49	17	30	47	6
83-84	St. Louis	80	41	44	85	19
84-85	St. Louis	79	40	52	92	6
85-86	StL-Calg	77	44	46	90	21
86-87	Calgary	79	47	40	87	14
87-88	Calgary	80	40	44	84	30
88-89	Calgary	79	51	59	110	16
89-90	Calgary	78	36	33	69	24
90-91	Pittsburgh	47	17	22	39	6
91-92	Pittsburgh	77	42	45	87	30
92-93	Pittsburgh	72	33	37	70	14
93-94	Pittsburgh	84	38	32	70	41
94-95	Pittsburgh	45	16	21	37	6
95-96	Boston	37	8	7	15	0
96-97	Pittsburgh	54	7	15	22	4
Totals		1062	502	561	1063	241
Playoff Totals		143	60	46	106	42

U.S.-BORN/RAISED PLAYERS (BY STATE) WHO
MADE THE NHL FROM 1970-71 TO 1979-80

MINNESOTA: (46)

	Place of Birth	Pos	Turned Pro
Stan Gilbertson	Duluth	LW	(71-72)
Bob Paradise	St. Paul	D	(71-72)
Henry Boucha	Warroad	C	(71-72)
Gary Gambucci	Hibbing	C	(71-72)
Bruce McIntosh	Minneapolis	D	(72-73)
Phil Hoene	Duluth	LW	(72-73)
Mike Antonovich	Calumet	C	(72-73)
Jim McElmury	St. Paul	D	(72-73)
Dale Smedsmo	Roseau	LW	(72-73)
Butch Williams	Duluth	RW	(73-74)
Jim Watt	Duluth	G	(73-74)
Robert Collyard	Hibbing	C	(73-74)
Earl Anderson	Roseau	RW	(74-75)
Dean Talafous	Duluth	RW	(74-75)
Pete LoPresti	Virginia	G	(74-75)
Jack Carlson	Virginia	LW	(74-75)
Al "Hank" Hanglesben	Warroad	D	(74-75)
Mike Baumgartner	Roseau	D	(74-75)
Craig Sarner	St. Paul	RW	(74-75)
Doug Palazzari	Eveleth	C	(74-75)
Bill Butters	St. Paul	D	(74-75)
Steve Jensen	Minneapolis	LW	(75-76)
Bill Nyrop	Wash. DC	D	(75-76)
Mike Wong	Minneapolis	C	(75-76)
Steve Carlson	Virginia	C	(75-76)
Warren Miller	South St. Paul	RW	(75-76)
Paul Holmgren	St. Paul	RW	(75-76)
Gary Sargent	Red Lake	D	(75-76)
Dave Langevin	St. Paul	D	(76-77)
Joe Micheletti	Hibbing	D	(76-77)
Reed Larson	Minneapolis	D	(76-77)
Tom Younghans	St. Paul	RW	(76-77)
Mark Heaslip	Duluth	RW	(76-77)
Steve Short	Roseville	LW	(77-78)
Steve Alley	Anoka	LW	(77-78)
Mike Polich	Hibbing	LW	(77-78)
Don Jackson	Minneapolis	D	(77-78)
Jim Cunningham	St. Paul	LW	(77-78)
John Taft	Minneapolis	D	(78-79)

Jim Warner	Minneapolis	RW	(78-79)
Tom Gorence	St. Paul	RW	(78-79)
Rob McClanahan	St. Paul	C	(79-80)
Steve Christoff	Richfield	C	(79-80)
Mike Ramsey	Minneapolis	D	(79-80)
Dave Christian	Warroad	RW	(79-80)
Steve Janaszak	St. Paul	G	(79-80)

MASSACHUSETTS: (23)

Robbie Ftorek	Needham	C	(72-73)
Paul O'Neil	Charlestown	C	(73-74)
Dave Hynes	Cambridge	LW	(73-74)
Bob McManama	Belmont	C	(73-74)
Fred Ahern	Boston	RW	(74-75)
Don Wheldon	Falmouth	D	(74-75)
Mike Milbury	Brighton	D	(75-76)
Kurt Walker	Weymouth	D	(75-76)
Dwight Schofield	Waltham	D	(76-77)
Paul Stewart	Boston	LW	(76-77)
Mike Fidler	Everett	LW	(76-77)
Tom Rowe	Lynn	RW	(76-77)
Rod Langway	Formosa, Taiwan	D	(77-78)
Mike O'Connell	Chicago, IL	D	(77-78)
Bob Miller	Medford	C	(77-78)
Richie Dunn	Boston	D	(77-78)
Tom Songin	Norwood	RW	(78-79)
Dick Lamby	Auburn	D	(78-79)
Jim Craig	North Easton	G	(79-80)
Dave Silk	Scituate	RW	(79-80)
Chris Nilan	Boston	RW	(79-80)
Steve Baker	Boston	G	(79-80)
Jon Fontas	Arlington	C	(79-80)

MICHIGAN: (14)

Jim Niekamp	Detroit	D	(70-71)
Craig Patrick	Detroit	RW	(71-72)
Bob Johnson	Farmington	G	(72-73)
Mark Howe	Detroit	D	(73-74)
Marty Howe	Detroit	D	(73-74)
Rob Palmer	Detroit	C	(73-74)
Ronald Sarafini	Detroit	D	(73-74)
Gord Buynak	Detroit	D	(74-75)
Gordie Roberts	Detroit	D	(75-76)
Dave Debol	Clair Shores	C	(77-78)

Dean Turner	Dearborn	D	(78-79)
Mike McDougal	Port Huron	RW	(78-79)
Ken Morrow	Flint	D	(79-80)
Gary Morrison	Detroit	RW	(79-80)

NEW YORK: (9)

Glenn Patrick	New York	D	(73-74)
Pete Scamurra	Buffalo	D	(75-76)
Dave Reece	Troy	G	(75-76)
Nick Fotiu	Staten Island	LW	(76-77)
Richie Hansen	Bronx	C	(76-77)
Jack Brownschidle	Buffalo	D	(77-78)
Craig Norwich	New York	D	(77-78)
Earl Ingarfield, Jr.	Manhasset	C	(79-80)
Joey Mullen	New York	RW	(79-80)

RHODE ISLAND: (4)

Curt Bennett	Regina, Sask.	C	(70-71)
Tom Mellor	Cranston	D	(73-74)
Harvey Bennett, Jr.	Cranston	C	(74-75)
Bill Bennett	Warwick	LW	(78-79)

OHIO: (3)

Doug Volmar	Cleveland Hts	RW	(70-71)
Curt Fraser	Cincinnati	LW	(78-79)
Ed Hospodar	Bowling Green	D	(79-80)

CALIFORNIA: (2)

Mike Lampman	Hamilton, Ont.	LW	(72-73)
Chris Ahrens	San Bernardino	D	(73-74)

COLORADO: (2)

Joe Noris	Denver	D	(71-72)
Mike Eaves	Denver	C	(78-79)

WISCONSIN: (2)

Dave Hanson	Cumberland	D	(76-77)
Mark Johnson	Madison	C	(79-80)

WASHINGTON ST: (2)

Duane Wylie	Spokane	C	(74-75)
Bob Attwell	Spokane	RW	(79-80)

PENNSYLVANIA: (1)

Gerry O'Flaherty	Pittsburgh	LW	(71-72)

ILLINOIS: (1)

Lee Fogolin	Chicago	D	(74-75)

TEXAS: (1)

Mike Christie	Big Spring	D	(74-75)

MAINE: (1)

Dan Bolduc	Waterville	LW	(75-76)

IOWA: (1)

Russ Anderson	Des Moines	D	(76-77)

MISSOURI: (1)

James Boo	Rolla	D	(77-78)

OREGON: (1)

Jere Gillis	Bend	LW	(77-78)

MARYLAND: (1)

Jeff Brubaker	Hagerstown	LW	(78-79)

1. Colleen Howe, *My Three Hockey Players*
   (New York: Hawthorne Books, 1975), p. 82.

Chapter 8

The Miracle on Ice and Its Impact

The 1980 U.S. Olympic Team Pulls Off the Miracle in Lake Placid and Fans the Flames Lit in the Late '60s

In 1977 the United States Olympic Committee began searching for coaching candidates for the 1980 Olympic Hockey Team.

The first choice was Michigan Tech's John MacInnes, whose resume consisted of three NCAA titles and 532 wins (most ever in collegiate hockey history). However, in mid-1978, diabetes and related ailments forced MacInnes to withdraw his name. The USOC then looked to Harvard's Bill Cleary, but Cleary refused, not wanting to spend time away from his family. The next choice was a man who was assembling his third

National Championship team at the University of Minnesota — Herb Brooks.

Brooks grew up on the east side of St. Paul and was a standout hockey player at St. Paul Johnson High School during the mid-1950s. He enrolled at the University of Minnesota in the fall of 1958 where he starred at wing and defense for the Gophers before graduating in 1962 with a degree in Psychology. Brooks also played on the 1964 and 1968 Olympic Teams, was a member of five U.S. National Teams, and coached a college team from the bottom of its conference to the National Championships in two years.

Apart from the fact that Brooks' resume was as impressive as anyone else's, he was the perfect man for the job because of who he was — an intense person, who feared failure. A perfectionist who was always well-prepared, Brooks was willing to take all the steps necessary in assembling the best possible team to represent the USA. His three Titles as Gopher coach had been splendid works of art — but this would be his piece de resistance.

Like former Flyers and Rangers coach Fred Shero, Brooks was a student and admirer of the Soviet system. He and assistant coach Craig Patrick looked to combine certain elements of the Russian game such as puck control, a wide-open style of play and superb conditioning, with the toughness and aggressive forechecking of the North American game. They called this combination of both styles "American Hockey."

"We developed a style with the puck where the forwards were more interchangeable and more creative," said Brooks. "We tried to get more puck control and to get into more of a high-tempo skating type of game. It was based upon some of the European thoughts and the Canadian thoughts; the Canadian thought was basically without the puck and the European thought was with the puck. So we developed that hybrid style which I thought was crucial. We had to throw their (Russians, Czechs, Swedes) game at them as best we could."

In the early summer of 1979 regional tryout camps for the 1980 Olympic Hockey Team were conducted at various sites across the United States. Each player who tried out would be rated by Brooks and assistant coach Patrick with the help of a special advisory committee chosen by Brooks.

Committee members included Harvard's Bill Cleary, New Hampshire's Charlie Holt, Colorado College's Jeff Sauer and former rivals "Badger Bob" Johnson of Wisconsin and Boston University's Jack Parker. "I didn't want an 'I, me, myself' organization," said Brooks. "There's a wealth of hockey talent in terms of expertise around the country, so I wanted to get those people involved."[1]

In selecting his committee, Brooks acted responsibly by burying the hatchet with his former rivals for the sake of choosing the very best judges of talent. After the Gophers defeated BU in the 1976 NCAA semi-finals, Parker accused Brooks of playing "Goon" hockey. To which Brooks responded that if he had the time and the money he would have sued. But Parker and Johnson were the best men for the jobs and Herbie wasn't going to let past tiffs keep them out of the loop. "It would have been stupid for me not to listen to their thoughts because they were good, proven hockey people." Brooks said. "They were very successful and I respected their opinions. Yes, we did have some real heated battles but because I did respect their opinions they were on that committee."[2]

Out of the more than 400 players who auditioned, 68 were invited to the National Sports Festival at Colorado Springs in July for the next round of tryouts. Out of those 68 players, a dozen were picked for Brooks' nucleus. All of them either had offers from or were being sought out by NHL teams. These players all had concerns about jeopardizing their pro careers by joining the Olympic team. They were fearful that the pro clubs wouldn't wait or that a career-threatening injury might occur. They also needed money in the interim.

Those concerns were mitigated thanks to an arrangement that New York agent-attorney Arthur Kaminsky set up with the United States Olympic Committee. It provided insurance, a modest salary ($7200 for the six-month period) and expenses for the players. Only Boston College star Joey Mullen couldn't be wooed because his father was seriously ill. Joey signed with the St. Louis Blues in order to help his dad.

From the Sports Festival tryouts, a 26-man touring squad was chosen for a five-month exhibition tour through Europe and North America. All of the selections were current or former collegians and each of the eight defensemen and 15 forwards chosen were speedy skaters. Brooks and his staff also chose a four-man taxi squad which consisted of skaters who were playing for various colleges. The taxi squad served as a reserve unit in case the squad was hit with a rash of injuries.

The team left New York's Kennedy Airport on the first day of September for Oslo, Norway, to begin a three-week European tour that would be followed by a four-month road trip through North America. The trip's highlight would be the Pre-Olympic Tournament at Lake Placid, New York (site of the Games) in mid-December.

The tour schedule, which was devised by Brooks, consisted of games against pro and international opponents. It would be the toughest competition ever faced by an American Olympic team. Before it was over, six more cuts would be made in order to trim the squad down to the final 20-man roster for the Games.

From the beginning Brooks made it a point to keep apart from his team in order to remain fair and objective. "I had a lot of Minnesota kids on the squad and I didn't want to display any favoritism," explains Brooks. "By design I was withdrawn — could've been construed as aloof — and did not get real close to the players. Craig Patrick did that and did a tremendous job. I stayed away because they're all good guys, and I didn't want their personalities to influence the decision I had to make. So I treated them all the same — all bad."

Knowing the differences in background between his players, Brooks warned them against what he called "regionalism," or separation into cliques, i.e. — Gopherism, Badgerism, Terrierism, etc. Whenever a player started talking up his former school someone would jump in: "Don't get regional."[3]

A three-week tour of Europe was just what the doctor ordered. Aside from providing the inevitable competition to earn a roster spot, it would be a unique (first for most) travel experience they would share. It was the first step in developing a tightly-knit team.

While in Norway Brooks made it clear that lack of hustle would not be tolerated. Moments after a 3-3 tie with Norway, he ordered his squad back out on the ice for an exhausting practice. The next night they routed the Norwegians 9-0. Except for the Gophers on the team, it was the squad's first taste of Brooks and his unpredictability.

Brooks was known to do anything from putting his players through grueling two and a half hour practices to treating them to beer and pizza instead. He always kept his players off balance. They didn't know what to expect — except Monday practices, which were brutal.

When the Olympic squad was formed, only the University of Minnesota players knew what to expect. The others would approach them and ask if this was what Brooks was always like. After he'd sing the praises of a prospect during the recruiting process, Brooks would greet him with a harsh dose of reality

159

at the first practice: "I'm not going to be your friend; nobody's guaranteed anything here." If he thought you were an excellent player, he would never want you to know it.[4]

Ironically, this created a camaraderie between the players on his various teams. "Every team I played on for five years always felt a common bond," said Steve Janaszak. "Twenty guys who all hated Herb. You knew the guy sitting next to you had been through all the same crap."[5]

Although most of Brooks' players considered him to be a pain in the neck, they also — at times — got a kick out of him and some of his slogans, which he would read from a crumpled piece of paper fished out of his pocket. Some of the players called them "Brooksisms":

"Don't dump the puck in. That went out with short pants."

"You're playing worse every day, and right now you're playing in the middle of next month."

"Passes come from the heart and not from the stick."[6]

When the European trip was over, the team had won seven and tied one of the 10 games

Steve Babineau

The Olympic experience was a lonely one for Herb Brooks, who kept his distance from his players off of the ice.

it played, outscoring its opponents by 53-22. In the wake of its cross-Atlantic success the team returned to the States and lost its next four games, all to NHL clubs.

After their NHL humbling, Team USA rebounded by winning 15 of their next 16 games, which were played mostly against college and minor league opponents.

In mid-December the squad took first place at the Pre-Olympic Tournament in Lake Placid with impressive victories over teams from Sweden, Canada, Czechoslovakia and the Soviet Union. The tournament triumph served as a confidence-builder for the young team as they went 12-3-2 over their next 17 games.

With the Olympic Games approaching, Brooks made his final six cuts. Released were Bruce Horsch, Les Auge, Jack Hughes, Gary Ross, Dave Delich and New Hampshire's Ralph Cox, the all-time leading scorer in UNH history.

No one in the world could better empathize with them than Brooks. He was the last man cut from the 1960 team that went on to win the gold medal at Squaw Valley.

The final game of the tour was held at Madison Square Garden in late January against the Soviet Union. The Russians handed the Yanks an ugly 10-3 beating, putting a damper on the confidence Herb's skaters had been enjoying. It didn't faze their captain. After the lopsided loss, Mike Eruzione went to dinner with his family and predicted that his team would defeat the Russians at Lake Placid.

Another parallel that could be drawn between the 1960 and 1980 Winter Games is that they were both held in the United States. It was Team USA's hope that once again the home-crowd advantage would produce success.

For the tournament's preliminary round, the field was divided into two six-team leagues — the Blue Division and the Red Division. By way of a round robin format, the top two teams from each division would advance to medal round. Team USA was put in the Blue Division with Sweden, Czechoslovakia, West Germany, Norway, and Romania. The Red Division was comprised of the Soviet Union, Canada, Finland, Poland, Japan and Holland.

Team USA entered the tournament with the 20-man roster listed below.

The preliminary round began on February 12, a day before the opening ceremonies were held. Team USA's first opponent was Sweden. Although the Swedes were favored to win, they hadn't played together very long as a team. In fact, their entire preparation consisted of only six practices and no games. The

Name	Age	Hometown	College
Goalies:			
Jim Craig	22	North Easton, MA	Boston University
Steve Janaszak	22	White Bear Lake, MN	Minnesota
Defensemen:			
Bill Baker	22	Grand Rapids, MN	Minnesota
Dave Christian	20	Warroad, MN	North Dakota
Ken Morrow	22	Davison, MI	Bowling Green
Jack O'Callahan	21	Charlestown, MA	Boston University
Mike Ramsey	18	Minneapolis, MN	Minnesota
Bob Suter	22	Madison, WI	Wisconsin
Forwards:			
Neal Broten	19	Roseau, MN	Minnesota
Steve Christoff	21	Richfield, MN	Boston University
John Harrington	22	Virginia, MN	Minn.-Duluth
Mark Johnson	21	Madison, WI	Wisconsin
Rob McClanahan	21	St. Paul, MN	Minnesota
Mark Pavelich	21	Eveleth, MN	Minn.-Duluth
Buzz Schneider	24	Babbitt, MN	Minnesota
Dave Silk	21	Scituate, MA	Boston University
Eric Strobel	21	Rochester, MN	Minnesota
Phil Verchota	22	Duluth, MN	Minnesota
Mark Wells	21	St. Clair Shores, MI	Bowling Green

Herb Brooks, Head Coach	St. Paul, MN	
Craig Patrick, Assistant Coach	Wellesley, MA	
Warren Strelow, Goalie Coach	Mahtomedi, MN	
Ralph Jasinski, Manager	Mounds View, MN	
Gary Smith, Trainer	Minneapolis, MN	
Dr. V.G. Nagobads, Physician	Edina, MN	
Bud Kessel, Equip. Manager	St. Paul, MN	

Americans, of course, were well prepared but were minus their most mobile defenseman, Jack O'Callahan.

The Swedes carried the play throughout the first period but goalie Jim Craig kept his team close by stopping 17 of the 18 shots he faced. Team USA was off to a bad start — but then came the turning point:

During the period Rob McClanahan took a vicious check into the boards from a Swede and limped to the locker room with a charley horse. Trainer Bruce Kola recommended that he sit out the rest of the game, but Brooks would have none of it. During the intermission Brooks chewed out his players for their lackluster play and in the process ordered McClanahan to put his skates back on and be ready to play. The two engaged in a shouting match before Brooks had to be restrained by O'Callahan. When tempers settled McClanahan laced 'em up again and returned to the ice. From the outset of the second period Team USA began to dominate the play. The incident had awakened them.

Throughout the period the U.S. continued to get chances but could not solve Swedish goalie Pelle Lindbergh, a second-round pick of the Philadelphia Flyers in the 1979 NHL draft. Finally, with 28 seconds left Dave Silk broke over the blue line and fired home the tying score.

Sweden regained the lead in the third period on a goal by Thomas Eriksson and Team USA once again found itself looking for the equalizer. With 41 seconds left Brooks pulled Craig for an extra attacker and the Yanks desperately swarmed the Swedish zone. Buzz Schneider sent a pass from the corner that made its way to Bill Baker just inside the blue line. Baker let go a one-timer that found the net with only 27 ticks remaining to give the U.S. a hard-earned 2-2 tie. Although they had only narrowly escaped defeat, Brooks' speedy young squad had shown heart and was ready

for bigger challenges.

Two days later Team USA faced off against Czechoslovakia, the tournament's number two seed. The Czechs went up early on a goal by Jaroslav Pouzar. The U.S. answered back with goals by Eruzione and Pavelich to take a 2-1 lead. Before the period had ended Peter Stastny set up brother Marian to knot the game at two apiece after one period of play.

The second period went to the Americans. Schneider converted on a pretty feed from Pavelich to put the U.S. in the lead. Then Mark Johnson — on a superb individual effort — walked in and beat Czech goalie Jiri Kralik with a backhander to give them a 4-2 lead at the end of two.

A two-goal lead with a period to play was not enough to comfort this hungry young group. With a raucous crowd rooting them on, Team USA went right to work. Verchota banged in a rebound, then Schneider struck again on a pass from Harrington. Czechoslovakia scored to cut the lead to 6-3, but then McClanahan put it away with one for the highlight films. He took a pass from Johnson and made a beautiful conversion by falling to the ice and flipping the puck into the net for a 7-3 final.

With only two minutes left a Czech player showed his frustration by chopping Mark Johnson across the shoulder with his stick. The former Badger had to be carried off the ice but x-rays later showed no dislocation and Johnson was cleared for action the following Saturday against Norway.

When the final buzzer sounded, the team converged around Craig and the crowd proudly applauded. It was February 14, 1980. The United States was mired in an economic recession and demoralized by the Iran hostage crisis. But against all odds the U.S. Olympic hockey team had now tied Sweden and upset Czechoslovakia. Tim Wendel best described the moment in his book *Going For*

Mark Johnson, son of "Badger" Bob, led all U.S. Olympic scorers with five goals and six assists.

the Gold: "On Valentine's Day 1980, America found a new bunch of sweethearts."[7]

Now it would be interesting to see how Brooks' feisty squad would respond to the role of favorites. They were outplayed by Norway in the first period and went to the locker room trailing 1-0. During the intermission Dave Silk stood up and suggested that everyone say nice things to each other. They took his advice and spent the rest of the break exchanging compliments. Evidently the ploy worked. Team USA owned the second period. Eruzione, Johnson and Silk each scored goals and Craig stopped everything, including a breakaway by Stephen Fronst. Former Bowling Green teammates Mark Johnson and Ken Morrow each added third period tallies and the U.S walked away with a decisive 5-1 victory.

Despite the strong recovery and five unanswered goals, Brooks was not happy with his team's play. "I better take a whip to these guys," he said after the game. "Some of them are backing up to the pay window."[8]

On Monday February 18, the U.S. took on Romania. Bolstered by the return of defenseman Jack O'Callahan, Team USA routed the underdogs, 7-2, and in doing so

earned itself a berth in the medal round.

The "Iron Rangers" line broke the ice with just under eight minutes left in the first when Pavelich executed a give-and-go on the right with Harrington and fed a pretty pass across to a streaking Schneider who deflected it home. Minutes later Strobel scored on a brilliant individual effort in front of the net and the rout was on.

Team USA's final game of the preliminary round was against West Germany. Although the game had no significance in the standings, it was a grudge match. The West Germans had denied the Americans a bronze medal at the 1976 Olympics by belting them 4-1 in the final game. Since then the two countries had engaged in chippy contests when tangling in World Championship tournaments. This one was no exception. The teams combined for 24 minutes in penalties and several fights nearly erupted.

West Germany got two scores in the first period and held a 2-0 lead into the second until McClanahan got the Yanks on the board. Later in the stanza Broten tied the count and after two periods the game was deadlocked at two.

In the third period McClanahan struck again for what proved to be the game-winner. Phil Verchota added an insurance goal to seal the 4-2 victory. Team USA finished the preliminary round tied with first-place Sweden in points (9), and still was undefeated at 4-0-1.

In order to remain unbeaten and get a shot at the gold medal, Team USA would have to beat the Russians, who had not lost an Olympic hockey game since 1968. Friday's other medal round matchup would match Sweden against Finland.

Despite their awesome Olympic win streak,

Steve Babineau
Steve Christoff

Steve Babineau
Mike Ramsey

the Soviet team did not suggest world-beaters during the preliminary round. The Finns and Canadians both had them on the ropes but blew third period leads. Word soon got around that the once-imposing Russian team was starting to show its age.

Before the game Brooks asked Bill Cleary, who happened to be at the game, to visit the locker room and say something to his team. Cleary obliged: "I'm sure you have no idea of the impact you have on not only the American public, but the whole world with what you've done," said Cleary, whose 1960 team won the gold medal by beating the Russians in the semifinals. "We played them in 1960 and I'll tell ya, you fellas are a much better hockey team than we were. There's no doubt in my mind or in anyone else's mind that you're gonna win this game."

Brooks followed Cleary's words of inspiration with some of his own: "You were born to be a player," he said to his team. "You were meant for this moment. You were meant to be here. So let's have poise and possession of ourselves at this time."[9]

Despite the pep talks, the Americans got off to a shaky start. Brooks' defense was sloppy in its own end but Craig, who continued to look sharp, bailed them out. Midway through the first period the Russians took the lead when Aleksei Kasatonov grabbed a loose puck and fired a slapper that was deflected home by Vladimir Krutov.

Moments later Schneider took a pass from Pavelich and drove a slapper past goalie Vladislav Tretiak to tie the game. The Soviets proceeded to apply the pressure but Craig kept it tied. Their efforts finally paid off at the

17:34 mark when Vladimir Golikov set up Sergei Makarov to give the Russians another one-goal lead that they hoped to take into the intermission. But with only seconds remaining, Johnson grabbed the rebound of a long drive by Christian, made a nice move on Tretyak and knotted the game with only one second left. Johnson's pivotal goal gave the Americans a big lift and prompted Russian coach Viktor Tikhonov to pull Tretiak and replace him with backup goalie Vladimir Myshkin.

The last-second goal was a huge morale-booster for the Americans. "That sent us into the locker room on Cloud Nine rather than being a goal behind," O'Callahan said. "Instead of them going in a goal up and laughing, and us a goal down and worrying, we're tied and the Russians are beginning to doubt themselves. That's quite a turnabout, and things like that just don't happen naturally. It's almost like the parting of the Red Sea."[10]

In the second period the Soviets once again took the lead when Alexsandr Maltsev broke through the American defense and put the puck past Craig.

Inspired by Maltsev's go-ahead goal, the Russians stepped up their assault looking to add insurance, but again Craig stood tall. The U.S. goalie continued to make big saves when his team needed them most and after two periods — despite being outshot 30-10 — Team USA was still within striking range, trailing 3-2.

At 8:39 of the third period Johnson — who on this night always seemed to be in the right place at the right time — struck again. Silk skated the puck over the Russian blue line but was knocked to the ice by a hip check. As he fell, Dave pushed the puck forward. It caromed off a Soviet player's skate and over to Johnson who drove it past Myshkin. Silk's extra effort paid off and the U.S. had once again tied the score.

Moments later Pavelich made an outstanding play by knocking the puck past a Russian defenseman toward the slot. It bounded over to Eruzione who moved in on the right and fired a wrister through a screen to give Team USA a 4-3 lead with exactly ten minutes remaining. "I knew either the defenseman had to come at me and if that happened I'd give it to Baker, or the defenseman would go down and try to block the shot," Eruzione said. "He tried doing that and I used him as a screen. It went by him and I don't think the goalie saw it either."[11]

The Russians countered by changing lines every 45 seconds in an attempt to surprise the worn out American squad. But whenever the Americans found themselves back on their heels Brooks wasted no time in replacing those players with fresh legs and telling them to "play your game." The strategy worked and with five minutes to play the Russians panicked and began dumping the puck in.

As the final seconds ticked away ABC play-by-play commentator Al Michaels enthusiastically asked: "Do You Believe In Miracles?" Many at home, watching the tape-delayed telecast answered — at least in his or her mind — "Yes, I do now!"

When the game ended Team USA members piled on top of Craig and wildly celebrated around the U.S. net while the raucous crowd of 10,000 chanted "USA! USA!" A little less than a month earlier the young American squad had been taken to school by a seemingly invincible Soviet Team. Now it was celebrating one of the biggest upsets in Olympic hockey history.

As was the case in 1960 when the United States knocked off the Russians, there was still one more game to win in order to attain the gold medal. On Saturday Brooks arrived at practice where he found his team signing autographs and posing for pictures. At that point he knew he was facing his biggest challenge.

He had to bring his team down from Cloud Nine and get them mentally prepared for one last obstacle — Finland.

"Trying to get them down to earth and focused was not an easy task," explained Brooks. "It was probably the most difficult time of the whole thing. I had to turn them against me by reminding them that it was an upset and they were too young to do it again because they weren't good enough. I said it to bring them down to reality and get them focused on their next game. I sort of banged up the locker room a little bit and reminded them two or three times at practice that they weren't good enough. I just said 'you are too young to pull it off.'"

The gold medal game began at 11 a.m. on Sunday. Nearly midway through the first period the Finns scored and the Americans found themselves in a position to which they had grown accustomed — down by a goal. When the period ended the U.S. still trailed 1-0, thanks to a sparkling performance by Finland's 33-year-old veteran goalie Jorma Valtonen.

Five minutes into the second period Neal Broten forced a Finnish defenseman to cough up the puck in his own end. It went to Christoff who flipped a backhander through Valtonen's legs and Team USA had the equalizer.

Moments later Buzz Schneider took a penalty for slashing. On the power play center Mikko Leinonen tipped home a pass from defenseman Hannu Haapalainen and the Finns regained the lead. At the end of two periods Team USA found itself in the same position as the 1960 team did in their gold medal game — down a goal with 20 minutes to play.

During the intermission Brooks — ever the psychologist — gave what would be his last locker room pep talk. "20 minutes, gentlemen," he told them. "If it's not 20, you'll never live it down. This will haunt you the rest of your lives."[12]

Less than three minutes into the final stanza Dave Christian, whose father Bill had assisted on the tying goal in the 1960 gold medal game against the Czechs, fed a pass to Phil Verchota streaking down the left side. Verchota released a 15-footer that found the back of the net to tie the game at 2-2.

Minutes later Johnson fed McClanahan from behind the net. The former Gopher faked, waited for Valtonen to commit himself and slid the puck between his legs.

With a one-goal lead and the gold medal within their grasps the Americans surprised everybody — including themselves — by taking three cheap penalties. Team USA killed off each of the infractions and maintained its slim advantage. Finally, with 3:35 remaining, Johnson provided the coup de grace by whipping a backhander past Valtonen. The United States had won its second Olympic Gold Medal in ice hockey.

In the dressing room after the game Vice President (and former Minnesota Senator) Walter Mondale was dialing up President Jimmy Carter on the phone when he displayed some regionalism of his own by asking: "Where are the players from Minnesota?" Brooks responded: "We have no players from Minnesota, Mr. Vice President. We have only Americans."[13]

At the medal presentations later that afternoon team captain Mike Eruzione was called up to the medal stand to accept the gold. After he received the hardware and the anthems were played, the U.S. captain spontaneously waved his teammates up to join him. "It was just a reaction on my part." Eruzione says. "I felt all along that one person should never be up on the podium. It was the 20 players that won the gold medal, not just me." There they were, all 20 of America's new heroes on the medal stand together. An Olympic moment

Steve Babineau

Team USA Captain Mike Eruzione gets a word of inspiration from Harvard coach and former Olympic gold medalist Bill Cleary.

for the ages!

The next day the hockey team and the rest of the Olympic squad flew to Washington to be honored by the President and the First Lady at the White House. During a short speech from the White House steps President Carter said: "For me, as President of the United States, this is one of the proudest moments I have ever experienced."[14] This marvelous group of young athletes had reinstated a great spirit and pride in the United States of America and for just a few days the American people were joyously distracted from the woes of the times.

Within a week after the "Miracle at Lake Placid" nine members of the U.S. Olympic team went directly into the National Hockey League and four others joined minor league clubs for the final weeks of the 1979-80 season. Three others would later turn pro.

Steve Christoff became the first 1980 Olympian to play in the NHL when he suited up for the Minnesota North Stars February 28 in Montreal. In the final 20 regular season games he scored eight goals and assisted on seven. In the playoffs the former University of Minnesota star set an NHL rookie playoff scoring record with eight goals and four assists, for 12 points in 14 games. While setting the record he also helped the Stars upset the defending Stanley Cup champion Montreal Canadiens. Christoff played two more seasons with Minnesota and one with the Calgary Flames before finishing his career with the Los Angeles Kings in 1983-84.

Dave Christian, a defenseman for the Olympic team, had the most memorable debut of any of the Olympians as a center for the Winnipeg Jets. It took him all of seven seconds to score his first NHL goal. The instant success began a torrid streak for the former University of North Dakota sharpshooter. In the season's final 15 games Christian collected eight goals and 10 assists for 18 points. He spent three more years in Winnipeg before being traded to Washington in 1983-84. With the Caps he enjoyed his finest season in 1985-86 with 41-42-83 numbers. In late 1989 he was dealt to Boston where he played right wing on a line with former Flyer Dave Poulin and helped the Bruins earn a trip to the 1989-90 Stanley Cup Finals. Dave also played for St. Louis and Chicago before finishing in the IHL.

Defenseman Mike Ramsey was the first American ever selected in NHL's first round when Buffalo made him the 11th overall pick in the 1979 entry draft. Ramsey certainly lived up to that billing. He spent 14 seasons with the Sabres as a force behind the Buffalo blue line. He was named to the All-Star team in 1982, 1983, 1985 and 1986. In late March of

1993 the Sabres dealt him to the Pittsburgh Penguins for left wing Bob Errey. During the summer of 1994 Mike was signed as a free agent by Detroit and was a vital cog for the Red Wings defense machine.

Jim Craig was signed by the Atlanta Flames on February 29 and won his first game the next day, a 4-1 victory over the Colorado Rockies. He was acquired by Boston in 1980-81 and played in 23 games for them that season, recording a 3.68 goals-against-average. After spending a season in the minors Craig returned to the scene in 1983-84 with Minnesota but played in only three games before retiring.

For defenseman Kenny Morrow, the glory was just beginning. Morrow joined the New York Islanders and within three months became the first and only player ever to win an Olympic gold medal and the Stanley Cup in the same year.

The Flint, Michigan native was part of four successive championship teams with the mighty Islanders from 1979-80 to 1982-83. And in what has become a rarity in professional sports Ken played his entire career with the Isles before retiring after the 88-89 season.

Mark Johnson played 11 NHL seasons with Pittsburgh, Minnesota, Hartford, St. Louis and New Jersey before retiring after the 1989-90 season. His best year was with the Penguins in 1983-84 when he put up 35-52-87 numbers.

Olympic backup goalie Steve Janaszak played in only one game with the Minnesota North Stars just after the Games before bouncing around the minor leagues (Oklahoma City, Tulsa of Central Hockey League and Baltimore of Eastern Hockey League). He returned to the NHL scene in 1981-82 with a short stint in Colorado before deciding to hang up the pads.

Neal Broten was Minnesota's third choice (42nd overall) in the 1979 entry draft. Neal finished his senior year at the University of Minnesota in 1980-81 before breaking in with the North Stars at the end of the 1980-81 season. In the 1981 playoffs the former Olympian helped his team advance to the Stanley Cup Finals by contributing a goal and seven assists in 19 games. In 1994-95 the Stars traded him to the New Jersey Devils. In that season he became part of the Stanley Cup championship team with the most Americans ever. His finest season was 1985-86 when he broke the 100-point barrier with 29 goals and 76 assists.

On November 21, 1980 Craig Patrick was hired as general manager of the New York Rangers. The next day Patrick fired coach Fred Shero and took over behind the bench for the rest of the 1980-81 season. When the season ended Patrick hired Herb Brooks as the new coach of the Rangers.

Under Brooks, the Broadway Blues qualified for post-season play each of the three full seasons the former Olympic mentor was at the helm. In the opening round of the 1984 playoffs, Brooks' Rangers brought their rivals — the defending Stanley Cup Champion New York Islanders — to the brink of elimination. The chance for an upset

Steve Babineau

Goalie Jim Craig poses in the comfort of his Massachusetts home.

was spoiled, however, when former Olympian Kenny Morrow won it for the Isles by scoring in sudden-death overtime of the fifth and deciding game.

When Brooks began coaching the Rangers he and general manager Craig Patrick implemented the same style that brought them Olympic success. "It was a distinctly different style than anything else in the National Hockey League," Brooks says. "Edmonton was doing a little bit of it but nobody else.

"Of course, Craig and I were under great scrutiny and that style was under great scrutiny, but as the NHL evolved over the last 10-12 years that now is the style the league is playing with the puck. More of a North-South-East-West game as opposed to just a straight line North-South game. It has opened the game up to give the players a better environment to showcase their talents. That was a very key thing and nobody's really made too much of a point on that. If we would have been a typical North American team I don't know if we would've gotten past the Soviet Union, much less the Czechs or the Swedes or any of those other teams."

During his tenure with the Rangers, Brooks had the pleasure of once again coaching former Olympians Dave Silk, Mark Pavelich and Rob McClanahan.

Dave Silk first joined the Rangers a week after the Olympics but after only two games, he was sent down to New Haven of the AHL. Dave spent most of the next season making a solid contribution with the big club and in 1981-82 scored 15 goals and fed 20 assists in 64 games with the Blueshirts. When his Ranger days were over, Silk continued his NHL career with relatively short stints in Boston, Detroit and Winnipeg. In the fall of 1986 the former BU star set out to play a season with Mannheim in a German pro league and ended up staying for five years.

After completing his senior year at the Uni-

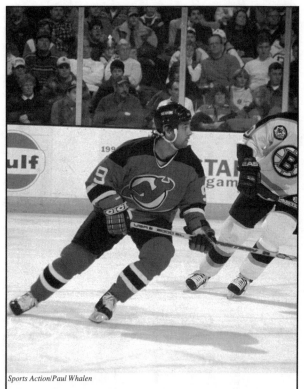

Sports Action/Paul Whalen

Regarded by many as the greatest player ever to emerge from Minnesota, Neal Broten followed his Olympic glory by playing 17 NHL seasons.

Steve Babineau

Mark Pavelich.

versity of Minnesota-Duluth, Mark Pavelich joined the Rangers in 1981-82. Over the course of five seasons with New York, Pavelich was the picture of consistency, scoring 133 goals and notching 185 assists for 318 points in 341 games. In 1986-87 the Eveleth native returned

Steve Babineau

Jack O'Callahan

John Harrington's minor league stint was not a pleasant one. In a game against Hershey, Harrington became the object of Canadian resentment towards the U.S. Olympians when he was attacked from behind by Hershey left winger Lou Franceshetti. Harrington suffered a broken nose, fractured jaw, a concussion and four loosened teeth. "Some Canadian-born kids resent the fact that the Americans did so well in the Olympics and they're a little bit jealous of them," charged Buffalo defenseman Larry Playfair.[15] Despite the cheap shot, Harrington showed grit and hung in with Rochester to score four goals and seven points in 12 games.

Bill Baker was Montreal's third-round choice in the 1978 draft. The stocky defenseman from Grand Rapids, Minnesota began with the Hab's Nova Scotia affiliate where he earned a call to the big club during the following season of 1980-81. After a cup of coffee with the Canadiens he journeyed to Colorado, St. Louis and New York. In his final season, 1982-83, he appeared in 70 games for the Rangers scoring four goals and adding 14 assists.

Jack O'Callahan became the last of the 1980 Olympians to reach the pro ranks when he broke in with the Chicago Blackhawks in 1982-83. The Charlestown, Massachusetts native played steady defense for the Hawks through 1986-87 before finishing his career in New Jersey.

The impact of the "Miracle on Ice" produced a modest revival in ice hockey participation on a nationwide basis. AHAUS team registration had gone down from 10,933 in 1978-79 to 10,490 in 1979-80, but by 1981-82 it went up to 11,094. More importantly, Team USA's stunning triumph put ice hockey in the national spotlight and for a few days it was the number one sport in the United States. It also left a trail that remains to this day.

"It's an ongoing exciting moment in Ameri-

to his home state to play in 12 games for the Minnesota North Stars before calling it quits. He made a brief return to the NHL in 1991-92 with San Jose before retiring for good.

Over the course of five NHL seasons speedy forward Rob McClanahan played for Buffalo and Hartford before joining the Rangers. His best season was with the Rangers under Brooks in 1982-83 when he lit the lamp 22 times and assisted on 26 scores for 48 points.

Mark Wells, Eric Strobel and John Harrington were each drafted by pro teams but never competed beyond the minor league level. After the Olympics, Wells played for the Canadiens' AHL affiliate in Nova Scotia but scored only one goal in nine games. Strobel and Harrington, both of whom were draftees of Buffalo, each played for Rochester of the AHL.

can sports history," says USA Hockey's Art Berglund. "Some people aren't hockey fans but they all watched that. It's an identification for the game of hockey and we gained a lot of hockey fans because of it."

When *Sports Illustrated's* 1980 "Sportsman of the Year" issue was released the cover did not contain a picture of the world's favorite sports individual. More appropriately, the award that year should have been called "Sportsmen of the Year," because they gave it to the 1980 U.S. Olympic Hockey Team.

SCORES OF ALL U.S. GAMES

Exhibition Games:

	USA	Opponents		USA	Opponents
Holland Nationals	8	1	Salt Lake City	6	4
Holland Nationals	11	4	Canada	6	7
Reipas (Finland)	1	2	Canada	2	6
Saipa (Finland)	4	1	Canada	3	4
Sapko (Finland)	6	0	Canada	1	2
Karpat (Finland)	5	4	Cincinnati	6	1
Lukko (Finland)	5	3	North Dakota	6	1
Jokerit (Finland)	1	4	Oklahoma City	5	3
Norway Nationals	3	3	Yale	6	1
Norway Nationals	9	0	Adirondack	0	1
Minnesota North Stars	2	4	Gorki Torpedo	4	2
St. Louis Blues	1	9	Gorki Torpedo	5	1
Atlanta Flames	1	6	Gorki Torpedo	10	3
Washington Capitals	4	5	Indianapolis	2	2
Maine Mariners	4	2	Gorki Torpedo	2	3
Canada	7	2	Oklahoma City	4	3
Canada	6	0	Tulsa	5	2
Salt Lake City	7	5	Houston	5	3
Colorado College	10	1	Tulsa	7	4
U Minnesota-Duluth	4	0	U Wisconsin	6	2
U Minnesota	8	2	Fort Worth	3	4
Indianapolis	1	0	Dallas	4	3
Flint	15	0	IHL All-Stars	4	4
Birmingham	5	2	U Wisconsin	4	2
Houston	3	4	Fort Worth	3	5
Birmingham	5	2	Dallas	10	6
Harvard	5	0	Warroad Lakers	10	0
RPI	9	3	Russia	3	10
Cincinnati	3	2			

Pre-Olympic Tournament:

Sweden	4	2
Canada	3	1
Czechoslovakia	3	0
Russia	5	3

Preliminary Games:

Sweden	2	2
Czechoslovakia	7	3
Norway	5	1
Romania	7	2
West Germany	4	2

Medal Round Games

Russia	4	3
Finland	4	2

Overall Record: 48 wins, 16 losses, 4 ties

FINAL STANDINGS

Blue Division:	W	L	T	PTS
Sweden	4	0	1	9
United States	4	0	1	9
Czechoslovakia	3	2	0	6
Romania	1	3	1	3
West Germany	1	4	0	2
Norway	0	4	1	1

Red Division:				
Soviet Union	5	0	0	10
Finland	3	2	0	6
Canada	3	2	0	6
Poland	2	3	0	4
Holland	1	3	1	3
Japan	0	4	1	1

Medal Round: *(Includes preliminary round games between medal-round teams)*

United States	2	0	1	5
Soviet Union	2	1	0	4
Sweden	0	1	2	2
Czechoslovakia	0	2	1	1

FINAL RANKINGS

Gold — United States
Silver — Soviet Union
Bronze — Sweden
4) Finland
5) Czechoslovakia
6) Canada
7) Poland
8) Romania
9) Holland
10) West Germany
11) Norway
12) Japan

SCORING SUMMARY:

	Goals	Assists	Pts	PIM
Mark Johnson	5	6	11	6
Buzz Schneider	5	3	8	4
Rob McClanahan	5	3	8	2
Mark Pavelich	1	6	7	2
Dave Christian	0	7	7	6
John Harrington	0	6	6	2
Mike Eruzione	3	2	5	2
Phil Verchota	3	2	5	8
Dave Silk	2	3	5	0
Mark Wells	2	1	3	0
Neal Broten	2	1	3	2
Steve Christoff	2	1	3	6
Ken Morrow	1	2	3	6
Eric Strobel	1	2	3	2
Mike Ramsey	0	2	2	8
Bill Baker	1	0	1	4
Jack O'Callahan	0	1	1	2
Bob Suter	0	0	0	6
Jim Craig	0	0	0	2
Team USA	33	48	81	70
Opponents	15	19	34	64

Goaltending

	GP	W	L	T	GA	Ave.	Svs.	Ave.
Jim Craig	7	6	0	1	15	2.14	183	26
Opponents	7	0	6	1	33	4.71	194	28

SCORING BY LINES:			
	G	**A**	**Pts**
Schneider-Pavelich-Harrington	17	20	34
McClanahan-Johnson-Silk	14	14	28
Eruzione-Broten-Christoff	7	4	11
Verchota-Wells-Strobel	6	5	11

1. Tim Wendel, *Going For the Gold* (Westport, CT: Lawrence Hill & Co., 1980), p. 8.
2. Ibid., p. 8.
3. John Powers and Arthur C. Kaminsky, *One Goal* (New York: Harper & Row Publishers, 1984), p. 58.
4. Ibid., p. 21.
5. Ibid.,p. 22.
6. Wendel, p. 12
7. Ibid., p. 30.
8. Ibid., p. 31.
9. Ibid., p. 34
10. Ibid., p. 35.
11. Ibid., pp. 38-39.
12. Powers and Kaminsky, , p. 225.
13. Ibid., p. 228.
14. Wendel, p. 45.
15. Edited by Zander Hollander, *The Complete Handbook of Pro Hockey*, 1981 Season (New York: Signet, 1980), p. 48.

Chapter 9

The Islander Dynasty Spreads the Boom

The New York Islanders Win Four Consecutive Stanley Cups and Give Long Island a Case of Hockey Fever

While the Philadelphia Flyers of the mid-'70s were shocking the hockey world by achieving the ultimate as a seventh-year expansion team (winning two consecutive Stanley Cups), another expansion success story was evolving on Long Island.

The New York Islanders were born on December 30, 1971, when entrepreneur Roy Boe and 19 partners bought the franchise for six million dollars (three times as much as the 1967 entries paid) plus a four-million dollar indemnification fee for invading the territory of the team that would soon become their arch-rival — the New York Rangers.

On February 15, 1972 Boe hired former Oakland Seals vice president Bill Torrey as general manager. Torrey's strategy for building a successful team was to bite the proverbial bullet and draft young players, knowing that this would mean losing for at least a couple years. "I committed myself to youth," said Torrey. "We decided to draft people who will be around for years rather than those who will not be with us after a year or two."[1]

Torrey's first move was the hiring of two scouts. Former Toronto goalie Ed Chadwick and ex-Rangers center Earl Ingarfield were signed to assist Torrey in the building process. The three men combed the continent for talent at the same time realizing they had to compete with the newly-formed World Hockey Association for prospects.

With the first overall choice in the 1972 amateur draft the Islanders chose right winger Billy Harris, who years later would be part of an important trade that would lead the franchise to its first big taste of glory.

The second and third choices, respectively, were center Lorne Henning and right wing Bobby Nystrom, both of whom would play key roles in what was destined to be one of the greatest teams of all time.

Later in the same draft Torrey also acquired 5-9, 170-pound left winger Garry Howatt. Despite being small and suffering from epilepsy, Howatt would soon become known as one of the most ferocious forwards in the league.

Most critics would agree that the general manager of a brand-new team would have to be considered both clever and lucky to obtain the "franchise goaltender" before the team ever played a game. But that's what happened to Bill Torrey! In the 1972 expansion draft Torrey selected 21-year-old netminder Billy Smith from the Los Angeles Kings. Thus, success between the pipes was guaranteed.

The new team's home arena was the recently-constructed Nassau Veterans Memorial

Steve Babineau

Billy Smith.

Coliseum, better known as the "Nassau Coliseum," located in Uniondale, New York, approximately 20 miles outside of Manhattan.

On opening night, October 7, 1972, a crowd of 12,221 turned out to see the Isles lose to the NHL's other new entry, the Atlanta Flames, by a score of 3-2.

The Islanders' first coach was former NHL center Phil Goyette. After the team won only six of its first 50 games Goyette was fired and temporarily replaced by team scout Earl Ingarfield.

The Islanders finished their inaugural season of 1972-73 with only 12 wins and set a new record for losses with 60 (12-60-6). Although the dismal record was an embarrassment — even for an expansion club — it turned out to be a blessing in disguise. Torrey now had a better chance of drafting the highly-touted Denis Potvin, a stocky 6-0 205-pound

Steve Babineau

Denis Potvin.

worthy of Denis, he was quite different from Boston's fabulous number four. While Orr displayed more offensive firepower as a defenseman and was responsible for revolutionizing The Game in that way, Potvin was a better hip checker who frequently softened opponents with tremendous hits in the neutral zone.

Another big off-season coup for Torrey was the landing of a superior coach. Ingarfield wanted out of coaching to return to scouting, so Torrey offered the job to former NHL defenseman and coach Al Arbour. Arbour was familiar with the sweet smell of success and well schooled in what it took to be a winner, having been part of three successive Stanley Cup championship teams with the Punch Imlach-coached Toronto Maple Leafs of the early 1960s. After finishing his playing career with the expansion St. Louis Blues in the late 1960s, Arbour also coached the Notes for parts of two years in the early '70s.

The following season the club showed signs of promise under its new coach. Although the young Isles again wound up in the East Division cellar, the club's record improved to 19-41-8 for 56 points, 26 points more than its maiden season.

As coach of the Islanders, Arbour was a strict disciplinarian who did not waste any time getting the point across that he was the boss. Bobby Nystrom remembers opening day of training camp in 1973: "When you take your photos and have your medicals done," says Nystrom, referring to a normal first day of training camp, "usually you go out on the ice and go for a light skate just to get a feel for the equipment that you've been given. He (Arbour) said 'we're just going to go out for a light skate' and we were still out there two and a half hours later."

The 1974 amateur draft was another prosperous one for the young franchise. In the first round Torrey chose left winger Clarke Gillies.

defenseman from Ottawa, Ontario, who could score, carry the puck and deliver thunderous body checks.

Near the end of the 1972-73 campaign Torrey made a move that would almost insure the signing of Potvin when the Isles' clever GM sent Terry Crisp to Philadelphia for Denis' older brother Jean. Torrey knew that Denis would be delighted to have Jean as his teammate.

As planned, the Islanders made Potvin their first choice in the 1973 amateur draft. Denis rejected an offer from the WHA and flew to New York with his parents to sign with the Islanders. He made it known what his preferences had been when he admitted: "I always wanted to play in the NHL and only the NHL."

Observers have often compared Potvin to Bobby Orr. Although such lofty praise was

Steve Babineau

Bryan Trottier.

as a steady fixture behind the Isles blue line during their heyday.

For the 1974-75 season, the NHL realigned into four divisions. The Islanders were placed in the Patrick Division with Philadelphia, Atlanta and their Manhattan rivals — the New York Rangers. It was also the franchise's first winning season. The Isles improved to 33-25-22, good for a second-place tie in points with the Rangers. The Blueshirts, however, claimed the runner-up spot with more wins.

To put in perspective how much the Islanders improved from their first season to their third, their goals-for went up from 170 to 264 and their goals-against decreased from an NHL all-time worst 347 in 1972-73, to third best in the league at 221 by 1974-75.

The Islanders followed their first winning season with a magical playoff run. In their first postseason appearance they won nine games and made it all the way to the seventh game of the semifinal round. They drew the Rangers in the first round and upset them two games to one. J.P. Parise's goal just 11 seconds into overtime of the decisive Game Three lifted the upstarts from Long Island over their Manhattan rivals.

The franchise's next big highlight came in the second round of the playoffs when the Isles rebounded from a three-games-to-none series deficit to win four straight games from the Pittsburgh Penguins. This arresting comeback marked only the second time in the history of professional sports that a team was able to rebound from a 3-0 series deficit and win. The only other happened in the 1942 Stanley Cup Finals when the Toronto Maple Leafs rallied to overtake the Detroit Red Wings.

When they were down 3-0, coach Al Arbour replaced Smith in goal with Glenn "Chico" Resch. In Game Four Resch helped the Isles break the sweep by turning aside 27 of 28 shots en route to a 3-1 victory. With their Game

Gillies was a big, intimidating forward whose physical play in the corners would help lead to many a goal. He also became the team's enforcer, but not by design; Gillies was not known for instigating fights, but when provoked he could finish one quickly.

In the second round Torrey landed the sleeper of the draft in 17-year-old center Bryan Trottier. "Trots," soon to be considered the league's best two-way center, would score 30 or more goals 11 times and crack the 100-point barrier six times during his illustrious career with the Isles.

Having already landed two permanent fixtures, Torrey wasn't finished. Later in the draft he grabbed Swedish defenseman Stefan Persson with the 214th pick. Persson, who did not join the club until the 1977-78 season, became a point man on the power play as well

Four victory the Isles felt confident that if they observed the bromidic advice and "take it one game at a time," they could salvage the series. Arbour, however, reduced the classic slogan to "one shift at a time," insisting that if they could just go out and try to win each shift, they could win the series.

Resch continued his stellar netminding and the Islanders won two more games to set up a seventh and deciding match at Pittsburgh. Former Bruin Ed Westfall scored at 14:42 of the third period to break a scoreless tie and write the third-year expansion club into the record books.

In the semifinals the Isles again fell behind 3-0 in games, this time to the defending Stanley Cup Champion Philadelphia Flyers. But there would be no quit in Arbour's troops. The miracle workers went to work once again and incredibly came roaring back to even the series at three games apiece. Back-to-back miracles would have been too much to expect, however, as they lost the seventh game in Philly to a Flyers team that went on to defeat the Buffalo Sabres in six games to earn its second straight Cup triumph.

Amazing! In just three seasons the expansion Islanders went from NHL doormats to a near trip to the Stanley Cup Finals. They were young and on the rise. Such accolades earned Bill Torrey the Sporting News NHL Executive of the Year award for 1975.

Excitement was building and interest on Long Island was beginning to stir throughout Nassau and Suffolk Counties. The Isles' thrilling and improbable playoff run had put them on the map and earned them an identity as Long Island's own. Meanwhile, their young aces matured.

During the 1975-76 regular season center Bryan Trottier won the Calder Trophy and, in doing so, set an NHL rookie scoring record with 95 points on 32 goals and 63 assists. Denis Potvin took home the Norris Trophy as the league's best defenseman and Al Arbour was rated as best coach in several independent surveys.

In the playoffs the scrappy Isles again reached the semifinals and gave the eventual Stanley Cup champion Montreal Canadiens their toughest competition of the 1975-76 post-season. After the series Montreal goalie Ken Dryden praised his opponents. "Believe me," insisted Dryden, "they're going to be just as good — or better — in years to come. They've got pride and they're not going to be psyched out in any situation. They've developed a certain amount of mental toughness. It's obvious that this is one team that doesn't discourage easily and it proves that they've developed considerable maturity."[2]

The next big step in the Islanders building process came in the 1977 amateur draft when Torrey chose right wing Mike Bossy with the 15th overall pick. Bossy, a pure goal-scorer, would go on to be one of the all-time magnificent snipers to play the game. The "Boss" would score at least 50 goals in each of his nine seasons with the Isles, an NHL record. It didn't take Mike very long to adapt to the NHL's level of play. As part of what became known as the famous "Trio Grande" line with Gillies and Trottier, he scored a record-setting 53 goals as a rookie and became the third Islander in four years to win the Calder Trophy.

Although it appeared the Isles now had all the pieces in place to become a championship team they continued to get outmuscled in the playoffs, ousted by Toronto in 1977-78 after a brutal seven-game series. In 1978-79 they tore the league apart, finishing with a league-best 116 points (51-15-14). They were paced by Trottier, who led the league in scoring and won the Hart Trophy as the league's MVP. There were high hopes around the Islanders camp that this might be the year, but they once again fell short of their ultimate goal. This time they were upset at the hands of their

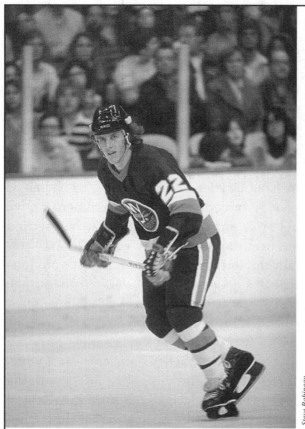

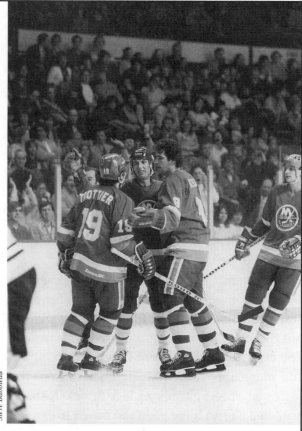

Steve Babineau

Mike Bossy scored a remarkable 573 goals and collected 1,126 points in only 752 NHL regular season games.

The famous "Trio Grande" line of Trottier, Bossy and Gillies celebrates a goal.

hated rivals from Gotham, the Rangers, who eliminated them in six games.

At the time there was not much organized hockey played on the Island. In Nassau County there was the Cantiague Park Rink where the Islanders practiced, Racquet and Rink in Farmingdale and the New Bridge Ice Rink, home of the Oyster Bay Gulls (A level) and the Nassau Lions and Nassau Arrows (B level) youth hockey programs. All Suffolk County had was the Superior Ice Rink, located in King's Park which housed the Suffolk Police Athletic League (PAL) youth hockey program.

During the next five years, however, this would change because the Islanders were on the verge of becoming one of the all-time great

dynasties in the history of professional hockey. Like the Bruins of the early '70s and Flyers of the mid-'70s, the Islanders would soon become the talk of their territory and kids would want to emulate them. The Island was about to transform from an area where ice hockey participation was just a rumor, into a place where every kid wanted to shoot like Bossy, skate like Trottier, hit like Potvin and make clutch saves like Smith.

For most of the 1979-80 regular season the Islanders struggled to attain the level of play they had achieved in the previous year. A big young defenseman was added in Ken Morrow, who joined the team fresh off his Olympic gold medal triumph at Lake Placid. Morrow was a meaningful addition to the Isles blue line corps, but was not enough to inspire Cup thoughts at the time.

As the regular season wound down Torrey searched for the missing ingredient that would put his team over the hump. With only 12 games left in the season the savvy GM sent right winger Billy Harris and defenseman Dave Lewis to Los Angeles for versatile center Butch Goring. It took only one game for Goring to feel that he could be that missing ingredient. "Logistically and realistically I think we can win the Cup this year,"[3] Goring said immediately following his debut as an Islander.

Goring, like Trottier, was a fine defensive center who could win faceoffs and kill penalties. His six goals and five assists over the last 12 games of the regular season sparked the Isles to an 8-0-4 finish and gave them some much-needed confidence entering the playoffs.

After dispatching Goring's former team, Los Angeles, in the first round, the Islanders came of age against the rugged Boston Bruins. Excellent goaltending by Billy Smith and the refusal to be intimidated made the difference.

The series began with the Isles pulling off two overtime wins at the dreaded Boston Garden. At their hotel before the first game some of the team's members overheard a Boston sportscaster predict that the Bruins would easily win the series. Such boasting only served to stoke the fire in the bellies of the Islanders who boarded the team bus determined to prove their detractors wrong.

The Bruins immediately attempted to intimidate the visitors but this time the Islanders were not going to back down. Boston soon learned that intimidation was not the recipe for winning the series. A huge brawl broke out at the end of the first period and it was clear that this time the Isles were in it together. "Everyone came into the locker room afterwards,"

recalled Bobby Nystrom. "Bobby Lorimer, the guy who was probably beat up the most, he just sort of stood there and said: 'Hey, listen, this isn't gonna bother me, I'm ready to go,' and, we really hung together in that series."

The teams split the next two games on the Island and returned to Boston for Game Five. Up three-games-to-one, the Isles looked to deliver the knockout punch. When the Bruins got out to a quick 2-0 lead, however, it looked as if the New Yorkers would have to wait until they returned to Nassau Coliseum to try and dispose of the feisty Bruins. Smith, however, settled down and held Boston scoreless the rest of the game. The Isles slowly chipped away, and before they knew it were heading out of Beantown with a series victory and another trip to the semifinals, their fifth in the last six seasons. They were once again knocking on the door to a trip to the Stanley Cup Finals. But this time — thanks to their Boston conquest — they truly believed they could win the whole ball of wax.

The determined Islanders finally opened that door by taking the Sabres out in six games. Their final round opponents would be their divisional rivals, the Philadelphia Flyers, who enjoyed an NHL record 35-game unbeaten streak during the 1979-80 regular season.

Philadelphia held a 3-2 lead late in the third period of Game One when they took a penalty, giving the lethal Islander power play a chance to tie it up. The Isles capitalized to forced overtime. Two minutes into the extra session, the Flyers took a rare overtime penalty when Jimmy Watson was called for holding. The Isles made Philly pay for their mistake. Denis Potvin took a perfect pass from John Tonelli and beat Flyers' goalie Pete Peeters to give the New Yorkers a crucial road victory and a leg up in the series. Potvin's tally marked only the third time in Stanley Cup finals history that an overtime game was decided by a power play goal.

Philly rebounded by routing the Isles 8-3 in Game Two to even the series. The Flyer attack was paced by Paul Holmgren, who became the first American-born player to score a hat trick in a final-series match.

After coming away with a split the Isles returned to Nassau and dominated Games Three and Four, recording 6-2 and 5-2 wins to take a 3-1 series lead. Back at the Spectrum for Game Five the Flyers staved off elimination by belting the Isles 6-3 to cut the series lead to 3-2.

Game Six would feature the first network telecast of an NHL game since 1975. Due to a scheduling conflict the opening faceoff time was moved from evening to the afternoon in order to accommodate CBS. The Isles knew that a Game Six loss would set up a seventh game back in Philadelphia, a scenario they badly wanted to avoid. As the second period was drawing to a close Bobby Nystrom scored to give the hosts a two-goal lead heading into the third period. With their backs to the wall, the Flyers quickly battled back with two third period scores to tie the game at four apiece and send it into overtime.

Seven minutes into the extra session utility forward Lorne Henning — a replacement for the injured Anders Kallur — got the puck near center ice, shifted back towards the New York blue line and fed a pass over the red line to John Tonelli who was cutting across from left to right. Tonelli brought the puck over the Flyers blue line, moved in on the right and slid a perfect pass through both Philly defensemen on to the stick of a streaking Nystrom who one-timed a backhander to the left of Pete Peeters and into the net. The Coliseum erupted and Nystrom was mobbed by his teammates. Pandemonium struck the Island. The Islanders were Stanley Cup Champions!

In a recent interview Nystrom described the moment and how he felt: "More than anything

Steve Babineau

Bob Nystrom's scrappy play was a big contribution to the Isles' success.

else it was just relief," recalls Nystrom. "It's so hard to get to the Stanley Cup Finals, let alone winning it, and I just remember how exhausted I was and how glad we were to get it over. We had a couple of disappointments in '78 and in '79 when we lost to the Rangers. So this kind of took the monkey off our backs and we had finally accomplished what we wanted to. It's got to be one of the most difficult sports to win because the injuries are such a major factor, and playing that kind of sport where it's very physical you do get your injuries and aches and pains. But I was just ecstatic to get it over and then as soon as I saw the guys coming over to pile on — then it was just exhilaration."

It was a record-setting postseason for the Islanders' special teams. During the finals the devastating power play converted on the man-advantage an NHL-record 15 times during the six games. Some of the credit for this accomplishment should go to the organist at the Coliseum, who assisted the power play unit by playing the "Jaws" theme. This had to wear on the psyche of the visiting team.

While the power play was delivering goals, the penalty-killing unit was contributing to the scoring column as well. During the 1980 playoffs, Goring, Trottier, Bourne, and Henning, et al., set an NHL record with seven shorthanded tallies.

Trottier, who amassed a record-breaking 29 points throughout the playoffs, won the Conn Smythe Trophy. For American-born defenseman Ken Morrow it was his second championship in three months. When asked which was the bigger thrill, winning the Olympic gold medal or sipping from Lord Stanley's Cup, Morrow could not say. "I really don't think it's fair to compare the two," he said. "In the Olympics you play for your country; In the Stanley Cup you play for your team. Sometimes I do think this was all a dream and it's hard to realize it really happened to me. It is incredible!"[4]

The Islanders Cup-winning squad was comprised of 17 players who were acquired from the draft and five by way of trade. The championship club also included four original members — Billy Smith, Lorne Henning, Bobby Nystrom and Garry Howatt.

Early in the 1980-81 regular season Lorne Henning retired as a player and became assistant coach. Center Bill Carroll replaced him as part of the penalty-killing unit. When the trading deadline arrived Torrey once again made his bold move. He sent Chico Resch to the Colorado Rockies for veteran defenseman Mike McEwen. A former Ranger, McEwen helped bolster the Isles blue line corps through the rest of their Cup reign.

After finishing with the league's best record at 48-18-14, Arbour's troops knocked off Toronto and Edmonton before sweeping the hated Rangers to earn a second straight trip to the finals. Their opponents this time, the Minnesota North Stars, had finished ninth overall and were simply no match for the defending champs who beat them in five games.

Mike Bossy set an NHL playoff record with 35 points and Butch Goring, whose timely scoring and relentless forechecking spelled doom for the Cinderella Stars, captured the Conn Smythe Trophy.

The Isles power play set another record, scoring 31 man-advantage goals during the playoffs. The penalty-killers scored nine shorthanded goals, eclipsing their own record of seven from the previous season.

In 1981-82 the defending two-time champions tore the league apart during the regular season compiling a handsome 54-16-10 record. In doing so, the Isles put together a string of 15 straight victories to break Boston's record of 14 straight set back in 1929-30. Smith won

Steve Babineau

Kenny Morrow followed his Olympic glory with four Stanley Cup rings.

the Vezina Trophy with a 2.97 goals-against average, and Mike Bossy set a new NHL mark for right wingers by amassing 147 points on 64 goals and 83 assists.

In the opening round of the playoffs the Islanders posted two consecutive blowouts over Pittsburgh. It looked as if nothing could stop the orange and blue juggernaut. Then, overconfidence set in. The Pens stayed alive by pulling out Game Three in overtime and coasting to an easy 5-2 victory in Game Four. It was now a dog fight that would be settled by a fifth and deciding game back on the Island.

The Isles hoped home ice would provide an answer for the surging Pens, but Pittsburgh's momentum was unrelenting. After 54 minutes of hockey battle the Penguins held a 3-1 advantage and doubts began to loom throughout the jam-packed Nassau Coliseum. Moments later defenseman McEwen scored to cut the lead in half and the "Never Say Die" Islanders were still alive.

Still trailing by a goal, the Islanders needed a savior. Someone had to step up or golf season was going to prematurely arrive. Then Tonelli came to the fore: With just over two minutes left in regulation time Tonelli scored to tie the game and force a series-deciding sudden-death overtime. At 6:19 of the extra stanza, the hero of the hour, Tonelli, banged home a rebound. The defending champs had dodged the bullet.

The playoff disappointments suffered in earlier years had developed a "fear of losing," which is a vital component of many great teams. It was the fear that helped to pull them through in situations like this. "That's why we win," said Bob Bourne. "Because we never forget what it was like to lose."[5]

Having survived the Pittsburgh scare, the Islanders next took aim at the Rangers. This series posed a problem for many middle-aged and elder-set New Yorkers who were torn as to their rooting interests. Although a lot of them grew up bleeding Ranger blue, many of them could not resist the temptation to embrace this gutsy team from suburbia. Although many Rangers fans converted, "most of them," as Chico Resch once said, "still had a Rangers cap in the back of their closets."

"The young kids identified with this new young team that was coming in," recalls Nystrom. "And there were some of the older Ranger fans, when we beat them in 1975, who all of a sudden got so discouraged they said: 'Hey, the heck with it, we're gonna become fans of the team out on the Island.' Ranger rooters are pretty loyal fans, but we had a little bit of a turnover there in 1975 when we made a real run at it in our third year of existence. People jumped on the bandwagon there a little bit."

It wasn't just the winning that attracted new fans to the Islanders. Their accessibility and strong sense of community made people want to embrace them.

"There wasn't a whole lot of mystique about

Steve Babineau

John Tonelli.

our team," says Nystrom. "I mean, the fact is we had a group of guys who were out in the community and we developed a very close relationship with our fans. It was like we were the brothers and sons of a lot of the people who were in the stands."

No matter which side a New York fan selected — Isles or Rangers — he or she was treated to a hard-fought series that saw Arbour's skaters defeat the Blueshirts in six games. Then, after sweeping the Quebec Nordiques in the Wales Conference Finals, the Islanders found themselves in another finals mismatch, this time with the Vancouver Canucks, who finished the regular season under .500 at 30-33-17. A Cinderella team, the Canucks were backed by Richard Brodeur's outstanding work between the pipes.

The Isles wiped out Vancouver in four straight games to become the first American-based NHL franchise to win three consecutive Stanley Cups. Mike Bossy tied Jean Beliveau's final-series record by lighting the lamp seven times during the four games. His 17 playoff goals (for the second straight postseason) earned him Conn Smythe Trophy honors.

With three straight Cups under their belts, the Islanders' fan following — like that of other dynasties — spread beyond their immediate geographic boundaries. NHL forward and Southern Connecticut native Ted Drury remembered how he became an Islanders fan during his youth.

"The Islanders had character and were a fun bunch to watch. I knew I was seeing some of the best people in the game," recalled Drury. "They had the best goal-scorer in Bossy and Trottier was the best all-around player. They had Gillies, who was the best big man at the time. They had Billy Smith who was a little different too. He was a great goaltender and a little wacky. They had Denis Potvin who was the best defenseman. They had a really interesting team. When I think about it I realize

that they really should've been winning those Cups because they had an unbelievable team."

The Islanders — like any championship organization — also had role players who made valuable contributions to the club's success. Those included forwards Brent and Duane Sutter, Anders Kallur, Billy Carroll and Wayne Merrick as well as defensemen, Stefan Persson, Ken Morrow, Dave "Bam-bam" Langevin, Gord Lane and Bob Lorimer.

The Sutter brothers, with their scrappy, hard-working and hard-hitting style fit right into the Isles' scheme. Beginning in 1981-82 Brent scored 20 or more goals for 10 consecutive seasons with the club, while Duane pitched in with four 17-plus goal seasons from 1981-82 to 1985-86.

Kallur banged home 76 lamplighters in three seasons, including 1980-81 when the Swedish star put up 36-28-64 numbers. Carroll only saw limited action at center but was a valuable asset to the Isles' stingy penalty-killing unit. Merrick, a veteran center who joined the club during the 1977-78 season, played six years with the club before retiring after the 1983-84 campaign. Wayne's best season was 1978-79, when he potted 20 goals and added 21 assists.

Persson was a mobile, slick-passing blueliner who, as mentioned earlier, became known for his role playing the left point on the awesome Islanders' power play. Aside from being a steady fixture on the Isles defensive unit, Kenny Morrow was known to score a big goal occasionally, including the series-winner in sudden-death overtime against the Rangers in the 1983-84 playoffs. Langevin, a St. Paul native, was known for his pounding hits along the sideboards and his physical play behind the net. Lorimer was a good, steady defenseman who rarely made mistakes in his own end, as was Lane, who was also known for his shot-blocking capability.

The 1982-83 regular season saw the three-time champs fall to sixth place overall at 42-26-12. But despite their sub-par regular season performance the Isles were able to turn it on in the playoffs.

In the first round of the Patrick Division playoffs they drew the upstart Washington Capitals, who were making their first-ever playoff appearance. The defending champs spoiled the Caps' post-season debut by taking them out in four games. Next up was the injury-riddled Rangers who they disposed of in six games to earn their fifth straight Patrick Division title.

A big test came in the Wales Conference finals against the Boston Bruins, who finished first overall in the regular season standings with an impressive 50-20-10 record. The Isles met the challenge by ousting the B's in six games. Their biggest challenge, however, was yet to come as their final-round opponents would be the high-flying Edmonton Oilers, an offensive powerhouse that was busy rewriting the NHL record books in the Campbell Conference.

After battling the Bruins for six games, the physically exhausted Islanders flew to Edmonton to face the favored Oilers in Game One. At first the fatigued champs looked sluggish and played sloppily, but Billy Smith bailed them out with a masterpiece netminding performance. His extraordinary Game One shutout gave the Islanders an early series lead and, more importantly, a chance to catch their breaths.

"The greatest game that I think Billy Smith ever played was our 2-0 win up in Edmonton that first game," assesses Nystrom. "We were very, very tired as a team and we flew up there and nobody had any legs. It was one of those nights where you get out there and you've got 'two columns of cement.' That's pretty much the whole story. I mean we were just awful, and I remember Smitty just making save-after-save-after-save, and he just really held us

in that game. He stood on his head and in my mind that was the greatest game that Billy Smith ever played."

In Game Two the Islanders — with their legs back — scored three first period goals and never looked back, outscoring the Oilers 6-3, to take an improbable two-games-to-none series lead back to the Island.

The Isles continued their defensive mastery of Gretzky and Company with a convincing 5-1 victory in Game Three. Game Four, however, was a much tighter contest. The Isles held a 3-2 lead in the third period when Edmonton desperately sought the equalizer. Once again "Battlin' Billy" held the fort and the Isles were soon indulging in their annual rite of spring — sipping champagne from a big silver bowl.

With their fourth Cup-triumph, the Islanders joined the Montreal Canadiens as one of only two teams to win as many as four consecutive Stanley Cups.

Billy Smith deservedly won playoff MVP honors, allowing only six goals in the final series. Mike Bossy, the previous year's playoff MVP, was awarded the Lady Byng Trophy. Defenseman Ken Morrow, an unlikely scoring threat, pitched in with three goals and two assists in the finals while "The Great One," Wayne Gretzky, was held to no goals and four assists.

"To win that series four games straight was probably our greatest accomplishment," says Nystrom. "I think it was the best Cup — from my standpoint anyhow. We competed against one of the greatest teams that the National Hockey League has ever seen and we were able to beat them four straight. That, in my mind, was quite an accomplishment."

Despite being decimated by injuries during the regular season, the Islanders returned to the finals in 1983-84 and once again faced the Oilers. In their "Drive For Five," however, the Isles would have to overcome a handicap. For the first time ever, the National Hockey League changed the finals to a 2-3-2 format, meaning that the team that earned home-ice advantage would have to play three games in a row in their opponent's building.

After splitting the first two games at Nassau Coliseum, the Oilers won all three games in Edmonton to win their first Stanley Cup. Whether the Islanders would have fared better by the old format (2-2-1-1-1) is something we will never know. But what is for sure is that the Oilers were truly a great team that deserved to be Stanley Cup champions. The 1983-84 finals marked the change of the guard. The Islanders had passed the torch to hockey's next dynasty. The Cup would visit Edmonton four more times by 1990. The Oilers' five Cups earned them "Team of the Decade" honors and tied them with the Bruins for third place in all-time Stanley Cup triumphs.

Steve Babineau

Billy Smith and Denis Potvin fight off Boston's Terry O'Reilly.

For the Islanders, the final-series loss to Edmonton also ended a string of 19 consecutive playoff series wins (a standing NHL record) which began in 1980, the year they won their first Stanley Cup.

Although the Islanders have not yet again reached the Stanley Cup finals, they continued to show guts and perseverance over the years. On Easter morning, 1987, the Isles won one of the longest Stanley Cup playoff games ever when Pat LaFontaine scored at 8:15 of the fourth overtime in Game Seven to defeat the Washington Capitals. In the 1992-93 playoffs David Volek's overtime goal in Game Seven of the Eastern Conference semifinals prevented Mario Lemieux and the Pittsburgh Penguins from going on to win a third straight Stanley Cup.

Throughout their Cup reign the Islanders were the picture of stability, keeping 16 common members from 1980 to 1984. That is a tremendous credit to the players as well as the organization. Former Ranger coach Herb Brooks perhaps best summed up why the Islanders of the early '80s were so successful:

"They were a balanced team. On the ice they had a lot of balance, a lot of different styles and they really meshed. They played a good skating game, they played a real physical game, they had good goalkeeping, they played well with the puck, they played well without the puck. And also I think that balance goes into their overall management team. With Bill Torrey and Al Arbour it was just a tremendous organization at that time and obviously when you win that many Cups it almost goes without saying."

With their four consecutive Stanley Cups the Islanders' place in NHL history is assured, but what is more important is the lasting trail they left in their community. Like the legacies left by the Big, Bad Bruins and the Broad Street Bullies on their respective areas, the Islanders left a positive imprint on Long Island.

From the time the Isles won their first championship to the present the number of rinks on Long Island has grown from roughly four to more than 20. Most of these rinks serve as venues for which youth hockey and high school programs compete. The Rinx in Hauppauge, owned by former Islander Gerry Hart, is where the Islanders hold their rookie camp. During the season the Isles practice at the Long Island Skating Academy in Syosset which is partly owned by former Islander Gerald Diduck.

Other indoor facilities that have been constructed in Nassau and Suffolk Counties since the advent of the Islander dynasty are Iceland in New Hyde Park, Freeport Ice Rink, Dix Hills Ice Rink, Long Beach Arena and Sports Plus in Smithtown. Outdoor rinks include Christopher Morley in Searingtown and Syosset/Woodbury Park in Woodbury.

Other former Islanders who have helped in the expansion of amateur hockey on the Island are Wayne Merrick, Mike Hordy, Bryan Trottier, John Tonelli and Bob Nystrom.

After Merrick retired in 1984 , he coached his son Andrew's teams in PAL Hockey through pee wees and Bantams before moving back to Toronto. Hordy currently conducts clinics as a paid roving instructor for high school teams.

Back in the mid-'80s Trottier invested in the construction of the Bryan Trottier Skating Academy in Port Washington (now called the Port Washington Skating Academy), located in Northwest Nassau County. Trottier also sponsored travel teams that played there called the Bryan Trottier Select.

John Tonelli is another former player who has been very visible in the community, donating his time and energy to the advancement of youth hockey in the Long Island area. In 1995-96 Tonelli coached the Long Island Gulls (formerly the Oyster Bay Gulls)

bantams to the USA Hockey National Championship.

What is impressive is that Long Island had two national champions and a New York State Champion in 1995-96. A youth hockey organization called the New York Apple Core of the Metropolitan Junior Hockey League iced a junior age level (20 & under) team that won the USA Hockey national title and St. Mary's of Manhasset repeated as state champions of high school club hockey.

Such accomplishments speak volumes about the level of ice hockey being played on the Island and it will only get better. Some of the roughly 100 high school hockey programs in Nassau and Suffolk Counties do not have a varsity team yet because kids from the "Islander Boom" have yet to reach that age. Before the Islander craze there were no more than 20 high schools with hockey programs.

There has also been growth in street and roller hockey in the area since the early '80s. Street hockey, of course, was convenient and inexpensive and therefore fairly popular. The New York metropolitan area has a history of roller hockey dating back to the '70s and the days of the Fort Hamilton Roller Hockey League, which had teams from all over New York City. The league, which was managed by Ray Miller, produced such ice hockey stars as Joey and Brian Mullen. And with the advent of in-line skates, roller hockey — as it is in most places — is growing in popularity on the Island and all over the New York area.

Two Long Island natives to make the NHL are the Ferraro twins, Peter and Chris. The pair from Port Jefferson began in the Rangers organization but now play for the Pittsburgh Peguins. A couple of top prospects from the Island to look for are the Scuderi brothers, Robby and Kenny, who both play defense and hail from Bethpage. Robby, who captained his St. Anthony's team to the Suffolk County high school title and was a part of the New York

Apple Core junior B team that won the national championship, is a freshman at Boston College. Kenny, a senior at St. Anthony's, was part of John Tonelli's Long Island Gulls bantam team that won the national championship.

Bobby Nystrom, who currently serves as Director of Amateur Hockey Development for the Islanders, recently described the give-and-take relationship his team had with its community:

"This was a team that had tremendous character and I'm not talking only on the ice. This team was very community-oriented. We felt it was important to be out there and be a part of it and share it with our fans. Also, we just had an attitude that no matter how bad the situation we could find a way to overcome it. So many of us have gone into the business community now and everything that we learned while we were players applies directly to what we are doing in business. If you went across the board and looked at the individuals on that team I think that you would see a lot of successful guys. We did some things for Long Island, but Long Island has been pretty good to all of us. So it's been a real nice partnership."

The result of this partnership is that an area which had very little hockey interest — let alone participation — is just beginning to harvest a crop of talent that began growing over a dozen years ago. And this crop will be cultivated and harvested for years to come.

1. Stan Fischler, *Golden Ice* (Scarborough, Ontario: McGraw-Hill Ryerson Limited, 1990), p. 32.
2. Ibid., p. 38.
3. *The Sporting News Great Dynasties*, chapter titled "New York Islanders, Bring Forth the Cup," by Pat Calabria, co-editors: Joe Hoppel, Mike Nahrstedt, Steve Zesch (St. Louis: The Sporting News Publishing Company, 1989), pgs. 335-336.
4. *The Complete Handbook of Pro Hockey, 1981 Season*, chapter titled "The Olympians' Fiery Baptism in the Pros," by Hugh Delano (New York: Signet, published by the American Library, Inc., 1980), p. 40.
5. Calabria, p. 354.

Chapter 10

The College Game

Eastern Colleges Become National Powers and Rival the Historically-Dominant Schools of the Midwest

"The whole purpose of college athletics is to instill an appreciation and understanding of teamwork and expression of individual efforts. That is, the whole is bigger than the combination of its parts." — Jim Murray, American Council of Education.

For more than a century fans of the ice game — primarily in the Northeastern and Midwestern United States — have enjoyed the highly-spirited and less-expensive alternative to the pro game: college hockey.

A natural "rah-rah" atmosphere and lower ticket prices set the college game apart

Boston University coach Jack Parker (center) guided his Terriers to national championships in 1978 and 1995.

Former University of Michigan and NHL forward Red Berenson returned to his alma mater to coach and led the Wolverines to the NCAA title in 1996.

DIVISION I CONFERENCES

WEST:

Central College Hockey Association (CCHA):

Alaska-Fairbanks, Bowling Green, Ferris State, Lake Superior State, Miami (Ohio), Michigan, Michigan State, Notre Dame, Ohio State, Western Michigan, Northern Michigan.

Western College Hockey Association (WCHA):

Alaska-Anchorage, Colorado College, Denver, Michigan Tech, Minnesota, Minnesota-Duluth, North Dakota, St. Cloud State, Wisconsin.

Independent:

Air Force, Nebraska, Mankato State.

EAST:

Eastern College Athletic Conference (ECAC):

Brown, Clarkson, Colgate, Cornell, Dartmouth, Harvard, Princeton, Rensselaer, St. Lawrence, Union, Vermont, Yale.

Hockey East:

Boston College, Boston University, Maine, UMass-Amherst, UMass-Lowell, Merrimack, New Hampshire, Northeastern, Providence.

Independent:

Army, Niagara.

from the pros — and the rules are quite different: There are no red-line offsides. This opens the ice for more breakaways and odd-man rushes; icing is called as soon as the puck crosses the goal line, which helps limit end-of-rink injuries; and there is much less fighting. If a player is involved in a fracas, he's thrown out of that game and the next.

At the Division I level, men's college hockey is divided into four conferences — two in the West and two in the East. The West is comprised of the Central Collegiate Hockey Association (CCHA) and the Western Collegiate Hockey Association (WCHA). The East is made up of The Eastern Collegiate Athletic Conference (ECAC) and Hockey East. The ECAC, which began in 1938, was the only conference in the region until the creation of Hockey East in 1984.

At the end of the regular season each conference holds a tournament to determine its champion. When the conference tournaments conclude, college hockey's biggest event of the season — the NCAA Division I Championship Tournament — takes the spotlight.

Twelve teams receive berths in the tournament. The regular season and playoff champions from each of the four conferences are awarded automatic bids. A team winning both its regular season and playoff championship earns an automatic bye to the quarterfinal round. The four winners emerging from the quarterfinals win a trip to college hockey's version of what NCAA basketball calls the "Final Four," which is played at one site.

The event has grown over the years from very little exposure (during the 1950s and 1960s) to being televised nationally. For the first ten years of the tournament's existence the Broadmoor Hotel in Colorado Springs was the site of both the semifinals and the championship game. Beginning with Minneapolis in 1958, the event has been held at various eastern and midwestern sites. The tournament celebrated its 50th anniversary in March of 1997 when record crowds packed Milwaukee's Bradley Center. Included in the pageantry was the introduction of the Golden Anniversary Team during the second intermission of the championship game between Boston University and North Dakota.

In 1997-98 Boston's FleetCenter will play host. In 1998-99 college hockey will move west when Arrowhead Pond, home of the Mighty Ducks of Anaheim, will be the site. NCAA brass expect that this move will give the sport more exposure and help it reach the level of popularity that college football and basketball now enjoy. "It's the first time it's in a non-traditional hockey area and it's a bit of a gamble," says Hockey East commissioner Joe Bertagna. "We think the game is exciting enough and with Disney out there and the Ducks with Paul Kariya, Teddy Drury — guys who were college players. We hope that it's going to sell and it's going to show we're taking that next step."

From the tournament's inception until the mid-1980s, college hockey was dominated by the powerhouse programs of the WCHA and the CCHA. When Cornell defeated Clarkson in 1970, it marked the first time two Eastern schools had squared off in the final round of the NCAA Tournament since Boston College defeated Eddie Jeremiah's Dartmouth squad in 1949, the tournament's second year. Boston University emerged as a power during the 1970s, winning three titles (1971, 1972, 1978), but it wasn't until after the formation of Hockey East in January 1984 that the balance of power between East and West began to even out.

"It used to be that if an Eastern school made the top ten they would have to have a great won-lost record," says Jeff Sklar, a BU season ticket holder and RPI alumnus. "Whereas a western school could make it with a lesser

NCAA DIVISION I CHAMPIONSHIP TOURNAMENT RESULTS

Year	Champion	Score	Runner-Up	Site
1948	Michigan	8-4	Dartmouth	Colorado Springs
1949	Boston College	4-3	Dartmouth	"
1950	Colorado College	13-4	Boston Univ.	"
1951	Michigan	7-1	Brown	"
1952	Michigan	4-1	Colorado College	"
1953	Michigan	7-3	Minnesota	"
1954	Rensselaer	5-3	Minnesota	"
1955	Michigan	5-3	Colorado College	"
1956	Michigan	7-5	Michigan Tech	"
1957	Colorado College	13-6	Michigan	"
1958	Denver	6-2	North Dakota	Minneapolis
1959	North Dakota	4-3	Michigan State	Troy, NY
1960	Denver	5-3	Michigan Tech	Boston
1961	Denver	12-2	St. Lawrence	Denver
1962	Michigan Tech	7-1	Clarkson	Hamilton, NY
1963	North Dakota	6-5	Denver	Boston
1964	Michigan	6-3	Denver	Denver
1965	Michigan	8-2	Boston College	Providence
1966	Michigan State	6-1	Clarkson	Minneapolis
1967	Cornell	4-1	Boston Univ.	Syracuse
1968	Denver	4-0	North Dakota	Duluth
1969	Denver	4-3	Cornell	Colorado Springs
1970	Cornell	6-4	Clarkson	Lake Placid
1971	Boston Univ.	4-1	Minnesota	Syracuse
1972	Boston Univ.	4-0	Cornell	Boston
1973	Wisconsin	4-2	Denver	Boston
1974	Minnesota	4-2	Michigan Tech	Boston
1975	Michigan Tech	6-1	Minnesota	St. Louis
1976	Minnesota	6-4	Michigan Tech	Denver
1977	Wisconsin	6-5	Michigan	Detroit
1978	Boston Univ.	5-3	Boston College	Providence
1979	Minnesota	4-3	North Dakota	Detroit
1980	North Dakota	5-2	Northern Michigan	Providence
1981	Wisconsin	6-3	Minnesota	Duluth
1982	North Dakota	5-2	Wisconsin	Providence
1983	Wisconsin	6-2	Harvard	Grand Forks
1984	Bowling Green	5-4	Minnesota-Duluth	Lake Placid
1985	Rensselaer	2-1	Providence	Detroit
1986	Michigan State	6-5	Harvard	Providence

1987	North Dakota	5-3	Michigan State	Detroit
1988	Lake Superior St.	4-3	St. Lawrence	Lake Placid
1989	Harvard	4-3	Minnesota	St. Paul
1990	Wisconsin	7-3	Colgate	Detroit
1991	N. Michigan	8-7	Boston Univ.	St. Paul
1992	Lake Superior St.	5-3	Wisconsin	Albany
1993	Maine	5-4	Lake Superior St.	Milwaukee
1994	Lake Superior St.	9-1	Boston Univ.	St. Paul
1995	Boston Univ.	6-2	Maine	Providence
1996	Michigan	3-2	Colorado College	Cincinnati
1997	North Dakota	6-4	Boston Univ.	Milwaukee

Steve Babineau

BU star forward Chris Drury (younger brother of Ted) is considered to be one of the top pro prospects in college hockey.

record because the voters considered the competition to be much greater in the West."

Shortly after its inception, Hockey East added Western opponents to its regular season schedule and counted them as league games. At first the Western schools dominated but within two or three years the Eastern schools began winning and won considerable respect.

Of the 24 teams to advance to the Division I championship game over the 12-year stretch from 1985 to 1997, half were from the East. During the 12 previous years (1973-1984) only three of the 24 teams to appear in the final game were from the East. Subtract 1978 and the Eastern schools had made only one championship appearance during that period.

It's not surprising that college hockey, which celebrated its 100th birthday during the 1995-96 season, has many keen rivalries. In the West, Michigan-Michigan State, Minnesota-Wisconsin and Colorado College-Denver are the most intense. Two of the top rivalries in the East are Boston University-Boston College and Harvard-Cornell.

In the "rivalry madness" category there are none crazier than the fans at Cornell's Lynah Rink. They represent the ultimate example of how far fans will go in carrying out rituals. Whenever the Crimson visit Ithaca, a large percentage of the Big Red followers who attend come equipped with props — mostly newspapers. When the Harvard lineup is introduced before the game and whenever Harvard carries the play or scores a goal, the fans open their newspapers and pretend to be reading them while ignoring the action.

Some folks smuggle in dead fish. When the Zamboni machine finishes cleaning the ice, Cornell players — in cooperation — wait in their dressing room until the Harvard squad takes the ice. As soon as the Cambridge boys begin to exit the visitors' dressing room (located 15 feet from the ice) the fish come flying from everywhere.

Bob Hines, a former season ticket holder and brother of Big Red Hall of Famer Cheryl Hines, once witnessed an even more bizarre gag. "One of the memories I have is of a guy they called 'Chicken Man,'" Hines recalls. "He would come out on the ice and tie a live chicken to the Harvard goal. He tied its leg to the pipe and set it on the top of the net. I remember the Harvard goalie getting booed

Steve Babineau

A BU Terrier hoisting the Beanpot Trophy has become a familiar sight in Boston.

pretty loudly when he took a swipe at it with his stick."

With such a psyche job to overcome, a Crimson victory at Lynah is difficult. "Nothing more gratifying than to go in there and win," says Harvard coach Ron Tomassoni. And year after year the visitors from Cambridge relish the opportunity to meet the challenge.

Another part of college hockey's rich tradition is its annual round robin tournaments. In early February of each year Boston University, Boston College, Harvard and Northeastern square off in "The Beanpot," the most colorful of college hockey's annual events. Since 1952 the four schools have clashed, with BU winning it a record 20 times.

The state of Michigan, which embraces six Division I schools, also is home to a couple of popular annual tournaments. The Joe Louis Arena in Detroit is the site of The Great Lakes Invitational, which pits Michigan, Michigan Tech, Michigan State and a designated fourth team against each other. The College Hockey Classic, which takes place on Thanksgiving weekend, matches Michigan, Michigan State, Wisconsin and Minnesota.

Other round-robin classics include Milwaukee's Badger Showdown, The Mariucci Classic in Minneapolis, The Denver Cup at McNichols Arena, The RPI Invitational at Troy, NY, and The Syracuse Invitational.

Although the college game has not yet spread into the warmer climates in the manner of the NHL, minor league and in-line hockey, it has shown considerable growth over the past 10 to 15 years. During that time some schools have either added ice hockey as a club sport or made the jump from club to varsity. Some schools with club programs are located in what have always been considered non-hockey areas. Although these schools have not yet moved up to varsity status they have managed to cultivate strong followings.

"When somebody would say club hockey I

196

used to picture guys renting a van and going out at two in the morning to rent ice somewhere," says Bertagna. "What I didn't realize is that Iowa State, Penn State, Arizona and Arizona State have club hockey where you'll see 3 or 4,000 people a game and at the national club championship they'll draw 5 or 6,000. Club hockey in the East, where there's a lot of hockey played at the varsity level, is like that — a bunch of guys getting together and nobody in the building. But in the non-traditional areas where club hockey is very big it has a huge following."

Of the schools to make the transition from club to varsity the University of Alabama-Huntsville is perhaps the most noteworthy because of its location in the Deep South. Also known as "The Hockey Capital of the South," UAH began its club program in 1979 and made the jump to Division II varsity in 1985.

In March, 1994, UAH's Von Braun Civic Center was the site of the NCAA Division II Championships. A team record 6,451 fans paid to see the Chargers finish second. The tournament also included the program's first live television broadcast. UAH Hockey has also been featured on NBC Nightly News with Tom Brokaw, ESPN, and in Sports Illustrated and Southern Living magazines.

There have been discussions recently concerning the possible formation of a fifth Division I conference. Schools such as Holy Cross, Connecticut, Fairfield and Canisius, which are NCAA Division I in other sports but not in hockey, are among the schools that would like to be considered Division I. "If enough of them get together and play enough games against each other," explains Bertagna, "by definition they would become the fifth Division I league. They wouldn't have any illusions about being as strong as the existing four, but it would change the landscape for the first time. Some 17, 18 or 19 different schools have taken part in the discussions

about this new league. My guess is that it may start with a modest six or eight teams in 1998-99. That's a very significant change in the landscape because for the first time you have a fifth conference that would not purport to be at the same level as those other four.

"There are leagues playing Division I basketball that are not at the same level as the Big East or the ACC or the Pac Ten," Bertagna adds. "But when they have the national tournament they all get some representation and occasionally a Princeton beats a UCLA. In hockey we don't have those other Division I leagues that are Division I in name but don't play at that same level on a regular basis. What that does is it keeps teams on the sidelines. They've got to jump from club to one of the top leagues in the country because there is no I-AA-type league or a half step to get into."

Two other factors have slowed the growth of men's college hockey — economics and gender equity. Ice hockey, to begin with, is a very expensive sport for a school to add. Title IX (Federal law stating that a school must spend as much money on women's sports as it does on men's sports and that opportunities for scholarships must be equal between both genders), makes it much harder for a school to justify starting up a men's program in such a costly sport. "Once the schools get their acts together and rectify some imbalances," predicts Bertagna, "The popularity that's going on elsewhere in the hockey world (pros, minor leagues, etc.) will spread into the men's college hockey programs."

Title IX has, however, fostered the evolution of women's college hockey. (The growth of the women's game is covered in Chapter 15.)

What benefits both the men's and women's game is the NCAA rule allowing small schools to "play-up" in one male sport and one female sport. There are some Division I college hockey powers competing in Division II or III

Steve Babineau

Above: Notre Dame coach Lefty Smith confers with an official in a mid-'70s contest against Harvard. *Right:* Former Notre Dame and NHL star center Dave Poulin returned to South Bend to coach the Fighting Irish in 1995-96.

in all sports except ice hockey. A good example is St. Lawrence University, a Division III school that plays Division I men's and women's ice hockey. About one-third of men's college hockey's Division I membership are comprised of small schools that have opted to "play up."

Former stars of the men's college game have made an impact at the pro level within the past five years. The 1993-94 Stanley Cup Champion New Jersey Devils had 13 former collegians on its roster. When the Rangers won the Cup in 1993-94 the Conn Smythe Trophy winner was Brian Leetch, who played at Boston College and the goalie was former Wisconsin netminder Mike Richter. Of the 12 NHL All-Stars chosen for the 1995-96 season, seven were from the college ranks; in each of the three Stanley Cup Conference Quarterfinal seventh games played on April 29, 1997, the winning goalie and the player to score the game-winning goal were all former collegians.

NHL front office personnel are also coming from college hockey. The general managers of both the 1993-94 (Rangers) and 1994-95 (Devils) Stanley Cup champions are from the college ranks (Neil Smith of Western Michigan and Providence's Lou Lamoriello). Other NHL GMs from the college ranks include former Colgate defenseman Mike Milbury of the Islanders and Craig Patrick of the Penguins.

The impact that college hockey is having on the pro ranks is even more remarkable when one considers that the Canadian and U.S. Junior leagues are not its only competition these days. Considerable talent comes from across the Atlantic. "It's hard to tell what effect college hockey will have on the pros in the late-1990s," says Boston University coach Jack Parker. "There are so many Russians and Europeans coming into the NHL." So far the influx of Russian and European talent has not overshadowed the growing influence of the American college alumni.

As college hockey has grown, competition between it and the Junior ranks has heightened. In previous decades, if a teenager had pro aspirations, he would play Junior hockey. If he wanted an education he went to college. Now college recruiters can offer both.

In a move to try to maintain its status as the NHL's primary feeder, Junior leagues are now offering to pay for players' educations. According to Bertagna those who choose to go that route are taking a risk.

"What they don't tell the kid is that you can be traded in junior hockey," claims Bertagna. "You can start to go to school in that area and get traded to another town. So you're uprooted from not just the hockey team but from whatever academic pursuits you had going at the same time. They can't really claim to be in the education business. If they want to say that they provide a better opportunity to be a pro, we're not going to battle them on that. If the kid has no academic aspirations at all, maybe he should go to junior hockey. But when you have 60 games, long bus trips and the possibility of being traded there's no way they can claim that their educational opportunities can come close to the stability that a four-year college provides."

With a stable education as a selling tool NCAA recruiters have lured more and more kids from the growing American talent pool.

"There are a lot of good U.S. kids," says University of Michigan coach Red Berenson. "We signed five kids in 1996 for 1997 and all of them are U.S. kids. We're not saying we're just looking for U.S. kids because that's not true. We're looking for the best players. In a lot of cases there are more and more U.S. players who are capable and want to go to college and play pro hockey."

As the number of American kids playing ice and roller hockey increases, college hockey must grow to create more opportunities for the young players to compete at the collegiate level.

Harvard athletic director Bill Cleary credits the influence of Boston Bruins ace Bobby

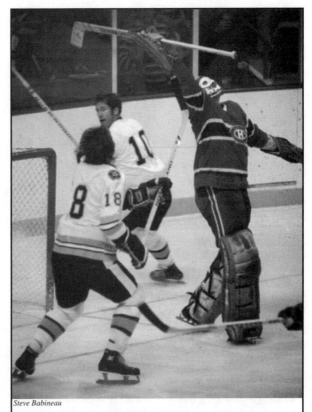

Steve Babineau

Above: Former Cornell goalie Ken Dryden backstopped the Montreal Canadiens to six Stanley Cups in eight years. *Below:* After a standout career at Michigan State, forward Bryan Smolinski potted 31 goals as an NHL rookie in 1993-94.

Steve Babineau

Steve Babineau

The NHL draft has become a familiar setting for college hockey players. Here Boston College scoring machine Marty Reasoner holds up the jersey of his future team, the St. Louis Blues.

Sports Action/Robert Rooks

Former Providence College standout Ron Wilson went on to coach in the NHL for Anaheim and now Washington.

Orr for starting the American boom. "In the 1970s the level of play rose," says Cleary. "Before that college rosters were dominated by Canadians, but now there are more Americans. There were schools out west that had all Canadians and they still have a number of them but now all of them have some American players and that all started with Orr. He created the interest; there's no doubt about it. We have Canadian kids and they're great kids — they're wonderful players — but the American kids are as good as the Canadian kids."

How much of an influence Orr had on a nationwide basis is debatable. What is certain is that his impact on the New England area during the early-'70s was one of several factors that helped increase participation in the Northeast. Also contributing was the Philadelphia Flyers' influence on the Delaware Valley during the mid-'70s, the "Miracle On Ice" of 1980 and the interest sparked in Long Island and parts of the Tri-State area by the New York Islanders dynasty of the early-'80s. These catalysts were all partly responsible for tilting the balance of power between Eastern and Western schools which began to evolve after the formation of Hockey East in 1984.

The following are 34 college hockey highlights dating back to the beginning of the NCAA Tournament in 1948. They were obtained courtesy of "50 Memorable Moments in College Hockey History," presented by the American Hockey Coaches Association and One XCEL:

• *March 20, 1948: Michigan takes the first NCAA Championship by sweeping Boston College and*

Steve Babineau

The Fuscos, Mark (left) and Scott, are the first brother tandem to win Hobey Baker Awards.

Dartmouth, 6-4 and 8-4 respectively. In the championship game the Wolverines break a 4-4 tie with four third period goals. Wolverine forward Wally Gacek is 5-3-8 over the two days.

• *March 24, 1951: At the annual meeting of the American Hockey Coaches Association, Dartmouth's Eddie Jeremiah is named the first AHCA Coach of the Year. Sometime later, when a College Division Coach of the Year award is created, it is named after Jeremiah.*

• *December 26-27, 1952: Boston's Beanpot Tournament is launched at the Boston Arena and Harvard is inaugural winner with 3-2 (OT) and 7-4 wins over Boston College and Boston University, respectively. The event became a fixture on the first two Mondays in February starting in 1954 and moved on to the Boston Garden where it remained until 1995. A new era began with the opening of the FleetCenter in February, 1996.*

• *March, 1956: Michigan wins its sixth NCAA title in nine years by sweeping Harvard, 7-3, and Colorado College, 5-3.*

• *March, 1959: RPI's Field House is the site of the first NCAA tournament where all four games are decided in overtime. In the semifinals, Michigan State and North Dakota take 4-3 OT wins over Boston College and St. Lawrence, respectively. BC is a 7-6 second OT consolation winner over SLU and North Dakota wins its first NCAA title with a 4-3 overtime win over Michigan State.*

• *March 1961: Tournament host Denver becomes the second school (after Michigan) to win back-to-back NCAA titles, destroying St. Lawrence, 12-2 in the title game. The tournament's Most Outstanding Player is future NHLer Bill Masterton, for whom the Masterton Trophy is named. The award, given to the player who best exemplifies the qualities of perseverance, sportsmanship and dedication to hockey, was named for Masterton who died as a result of a collision in an NHL game between Minnesota and Oakland.*

• *March 10, 1962: St Lawrence downs Clarkson, 5-2, to win the first ECAC Championship game at the Boston Arena. The tournament's leading scorer is SLU forward Ron Mason, now head coach at Michigan State and college hockey's winningest coach.*

• *December 19, 1964: A modern-day standard for*

saves is established when Minnesota-Duluth's Bill Halbrehder makes 77 stops against Michigan.

- December 22, 1965: The University of Toronto defeats Michigan Tech, 6-2, in the first championship game of the Great Lakes Invitational Tournament at Detroit's Olympia Stadium. Scoring both goals for the Huskies is Rick Yeo, current MTU athletic Director and a member of the NCAA Rules Committee. The event continues at Joe Louis Arena in Detroit.

- The 1967-68 Season: This became the first season to feature intercollegiate hockey for women as Brown University was defeated by Queen's University in the first such recorded game.

- March 15, 1969: Denver defeats Cornell, 4-3, at the Broadmoor in Colorado Springs, to win its second straight NCAA championship. The game marks the end of the collegiate career of Cornell goaltender Ken Dryden who finishes with a 1.59 goals against average, a .939 save percentage, and a .946 winning percentage over 83 games.

- March 21, 1970: Cornell defeats Clarkson, 6-3, at Lake Placid, to win the 1970 NCAA Championship and conclude the only perfect NCAA championship season at 29-0-0.

- November 12, 1971: The first ever CCHA game is hosted by the Billikens of St. Louis University, 3-2 winners over Ohio State.

- November 13, 1971: Denver's Peter McNab scores three goals in 31 seconds v. Colorado College. McNab later shines for the Boston Bruins (and others) before launching a successful broadcasting stint in New Jersey and then Denver.

- November 14, 1971: The first CCHA hat trick is scored by Ohio State's Jerry Welsh in a 6-5 OT loss at St. Louis. Welsh later becomes head coach at Ohio State.

- March 4, 1972: Ohio State defeats St. Louis, 3-0, to capture the first CCHA Championship at St. Louis Arena.

- March 1972: Boston University becomes the third school to win back-to-back NCAA titles when Tim Regan stops all 39 shots to blank Cornell, 4-0, before an NCAA record 14,995 at the Boston Garden.

- March 1973: Wisconsin wins its first NCAA title with a stunning 6-5 OT semifinal win over Cornell at Boston Garden. Down 4-0 in the second period, the Badgers rally to tie the game at 5-5 on Dean Talafous' goal at 19:55 of the third period. When Talafous scores at 9:27 of OT, Wisconsin is en route to a 4-2 final win over Denver and the school's first NCAA crown.

- March 1974: Mike Polich's shorthanded goal at 19:47 of the third period lifts Minnesota to a 5-4 win over Boston University in the NCAA semifinals at Boston Garden and the Gophers go on to beat Michigan Tech, 4-2 in the final. It is the first of three straight Minnesota-Michigan Tech finals, with the Huskies winning in 1975 and the Gophers taking the third game in 1976.

- Providence defenseman Ron Wilson sets an NCAA mark for blueliners with 8 points v. Norwich. Wilson later surfaces in the NHL as head coach of the Anaheim Mighty Ducks.

- March 5, 1978: Dana Decker of Michigan Tech scores at 0:05 of the first period against Minnesota-Duluth. Decker is the first of five players to accomplish this and the record remains.

- March 18, 1978: Merrimack wins the first NCAA Division II Championship Final, defeating Lake Forest, 12-2, in Springfield, MA.

- April 10, 1980: The American Hockey Coaches Association sponsors the first of five annual senior All-Star games, with the East and West playing to a 3-3 draw at St. Paul Civic Center. MVP for the game is St. Cloud goalie Doug Randolph. Coaches are Lou Lamoriello of Providence for the East and the late Bob Johnson of Wisconsin for the West. The game is disbanded after the 1984 game and brought back in 1993 as the Shrine East-West College Hockey Classic.

- December 28, 1980: In an exhibition against Sweden's Vasby Hockey Club, Maine goalie Jim Tortorella scores a goal. Tortorella is now head coach at Colby College.

- April 1, 1981: Neal Broten of Minnesota is presented the first Hobey Baker Award by the Decathlon Club of Bloomington, MN.

- *November 13, 1982:* On the night after he scores a hat trick against Notre Dame, Illinois-Chicago forward Colin Chin has three goals disallowed for, a) being in the crease, b) using a high stick, and c) a penalty is called on UIC.
- *January 18, 1984:* In a press conference at Boston's Parker House, the official formation of Hockey East Association is announced.
- *March 17, 1984:* Babson wins the first NCAA Division III Championship Final, defeating Union, 8-0, in Rochester, NY.
- *March 24, 1984:* Bowling Green outlasts Minnesota-Duluth, 5-4, in four overtimes, when Gino Cavallini scores to give the Falcons the NCAA title at Lake Placid.
- *December 14, 1985:* Michigan State's Mike Donnelly scores five goals against Ohio State en route to an eight-goal weekend. Donnelly finishes his career as the CCHA's all-time scoring leader.
- *March 16, 1985:* Providence goalie Chris Terreri makes 65 saves in a 2-1 double overtime thriller as the Friars win the first Hockey East Championship. Terreri later shines for the New Jersey Devils.
- *March 30, 1991:* Northern Michigan University captures the NCAA Championship in perhaps the most exciting NCAA final ever, downing Boston University, 8-7, in triple overtime at St. Paul. The Wildcats set an NCAA mark with 283 goals during the season.
- *March 12, 1993:* Michigan State's Ron Mason becomes college hockey's winningest coach. He entered the 1997-98 season with 775 victories.
- *April 3, 1993:* Scoring twice in the third period to overcome a 4-3 deficit, Maine brings the NCAA championship trophy "Down East" with a thrilling 5-4 win over defending champion Lake Superior State before 17,704 at Milwaukee. Future NHL stars figure in this one with Paul Kariya (Anaheim) setting up the winning goal against Blaine Lacher (Boston). Maine sets an NCAA win mark in its 41-1-2 season.

- *April 9, 1993:* The first AHCA College Player of the Year Award is presented to Ray Alcindor of Middlebury College. The next day, Alcindor is among 42 seniors who suit up for the first Shrine College Hockey East-West All-Star Classic, won by the East, 5-4, at Maine's Alfond Arena.
- *November 26, 1993:* Steve Shields of Michigan becomes college hockey's winningest goalie with a 6-0 shutout of Minnesota. He would graduate with 111 career victories.
- *March, 1993:* Providence forward Cammi Granato wins her third straight ECAC Women's Hockey Player of the Year Award. Granato, who was also ECAC Rookie of the Year as a freshman and the sister of NHL star Tony Granato, would lead Providence to two ECAC team titles during her tenure. The Lady Friars have won six of the 12 ECAC championships for women, including the first two in 1984 and 1985.
- *October 28, 1994:* Hockey East introduces the "Shootout" to conference games. Tied 4-4 at the end of regulation, Northeastern wins the shootout, 3-2, to get the better of Maine (game is still a tie for NCAA purposes).
- *March 30, 1995:* In what many call the greatest hockey game they've ever seen, Maine downs Michigan, 4-3, in triple overtime, in a nationally televised NCAA Semifinal matinee at Providence (though ESPN misses the winning goal live).

NCAA TITLES WON

Michigan	9
North Dakota	6
Denver	5
Wisconsin	5
Boston University	4
Lake Superior State	3
Michigan Tech	3
Minnesota	3
Cornell	2
Michigan State	2
Rensselaer	2
Boston College	1
Bowling Green	1
Colorado College	1
Harvard	1
Maine	1
Northern Michigan	1

HOBEY BAKER AWARD WINNERS
(Given to the outstanding college hockey player in the nation)

1981	Neal Broten, Minnesota, F
1982	George McPhee, Bowling Green, F
1983	Mark Fusco, Harvard, D
1984	Tom Kurvers, Minnesota-Duluth, F
1985	Bill Watson, Minnesota-Duluth, F
1986	Scott Fusco, Harvard, F
1987	Tony Hrkac, North Dakota, F
1988	Robb Stauber, Minnesota, G
1989	Lane MacDonald, Harvard, F
1990	Kip Miller, Michigan State, F
1991	David Emma, Boston College, F
1992	Scott Pellerin, Maine, F
1993	Paul Kariya, Maine, F
1994	Chris Marinucci, Minnesota-Duluth, F
1995	Brian Holzinger, Bowling Green, F
1996	Brian Bonin, Minnesota, F
1997	Brendan Morrison, Michigan, F

NCAA CHAMPIONSHIP GAME 50TH ANNIVERSARY ALL-STAR TEAM

Goaltenders:

Marc Behrend, Wisconsin, 1981-83
Ken Dryden, Cornell, 1967-69
Chris Terreri, Providence, 1983-85

Defensemen:

Chris Chelios, Wisconsin, 1982-83
Bruce Driver, Wisconsin, 1981-83
George Konik, Denver, 1960-61
Dan Lodboa, Cornell, 1970
Keith Magnuson, Denver, 1968-69
Jack O'Callahan, Boston University, 1976-78

Forwards:

Tony Amonte, Boston University, 1990-91
Lou Angotti, Michigan Tech, 1960-62
Red Berenson, Michigan, 1962
Bill Cleary, Harvard, 1955
Tony Hrkac, North Dakota, 1987
Paul Kariya, Maine, 1993
Bill Masterton, Denver, 1960-61
John Matchefts, Michigan, 1951-53
John Mayasich, Minnesota, 1953-54
Jim Montgomery, Maine, 1990-93
Tom Randall, Michigan, 1955-57
Phil Sykes, North Dakota, 1979-82

THE COLLEGE HOCKEY CENTENNIAL ALL-TIME EAST AND WEST SQUADS

EAST TEAM

	School	Final Year
The Goaltenders		
Ken Dryden	Cornell	1968-69
Daren Puppa	Rensselaer	1984-85
Chris Terreri	Providence	1985-86
The Defensemen		
Ed "Butch" Songin	Boston College	1949-50
Tom "Red" Martin	Boston College	1960-61
Dan Lodboa	Cornell	1969-70
Vic Stanfield	Boston Univ.	1974-75
Ron Wilson	Providence	1976-77
Jack O'Callahan	Boston Univ.	1978-79
Mark Fusco	Harvard	1982-83
Brian Leetch	Boston College	1986-87
Chris Imes	Maine	1994-95
The Forwards		
Bob Marquis	Boston Univ.	1959-60
Jack Garrity	Boston Univ.	1950-51
Bill Riley	Dartmouth	1948-49
Bill Cleary	Harvard	1954-55
Gene Kinasewich	Harvard	1963-64
Joe Cavanaugh	Harvard	1970-71
Dave Taylor	Clarkson	1976-77
Joe Mullen	Boston College	1978-79
Rick Meagher	Boston Univ.	1976-77
Scott Fusco	Harvard	1985-86
Lane MacDonald	Harvard	1988-89
Joe Nieuwendyk	Cornell	1986-87
Adam Oates	Rensselaer	1984-85
Paul Kariya	Maine	1993-94
Coaching Staff		
Jack Parker	Boston Univ.	Active
Ned Harkness	Cornell*	1969-70
Jack Kelley	Boston Univ.	1971-72
Eddie Jeremiah	Dartmouth	1966-67
Snooks Kelley	Boston College	1971-72

* Also coached at Rensselaer and Union

WEST TEAM

	School	Final Year
The Goaltenders		
Lorne Howes	Michigan	1956-57
Tony Esposito	Michigan Tech	1966-67
Robb Stauber	Minnesota	1988-89
The Defensemen		
Ken Yackel	Minnesota	1955-56
Bill Steenson	North Dakota	1958-59
Lou Nanne	Minnesota	1962-63
Ken Morrow	Bowling Green	1978-79
Craig Norwich	Wisconsin	1976-77
Keith Magnuson	Denver	1968-69
Tom Kurvers	Minnesota-Duluth	1983-84
Chris Chelios	Wisconsin	1982-83
Norm Maciver	Minnesota-Duluth	1985-86
The Forwards		
John Mayasich	Minnesota	1954-55
John Matchefts	Michigan	1952-53
Reg Morelli	North Dakota	1959-60
Bill "Red" Hay	Colorado College	1957-58
"Red" Berenson	Michigan	1961-62
Bill Masterton	Denver	1960-61
Lou Angotti	Michigan Tech	1961-62
Tom Ross	Michigan State	1975-76
Mike Eaves	Wisconsin	1977-78
Neal Broten	Minnesota	1980-81
Mark Johnson	Wisconsin	1978-79
Brett Hull	Minnesota-Duluth	1985-86
Tony Hrkac	North Dakota	1986-87
Greg Johnson	North Dakota	1992-93
Coaching Staff		
Ron Mason	Michigan State*	Active
Murray Armstrong	Denver	1976-77
John MacInnes	Michigan Tech	1981-82
Bob Johnson	Wisconsin	1981-82
Vic Heyliger	Michigan	1956-57

* Also coached at Lake Superior and Bowling Green

COACHES WITH MOST WINS

Name	School	Wins
Ron Mason	Lake Sup. St., BG, Mich. St.	775
Bob Peters	North Dakota, Bemidji State	700
Len Ceglarski	Clarkson, Boston College	674
John MacInnes	Michigan Tech	555
Jack Parker	Boston University	549
Jeff Sauer	Colorado College, Wisconsin	545
Jack Riley	Army	542
Don Roberts	Gustavus Alolphus	532
Jerry York	Clarkson, BG, Boston College	509
Ed Saugestad	Augsburg	503
John "Snooks" Kelly	Boston College	501
Rich Comley	Lake Sup. St., Northern Michigan	490
Don Brose	Mankato State	482
Murray Armstrong	Denver	462
Charlie Holt	Colby, New Hampshire	412
"Badger" Bob Johnson	Colorado, Wisconsin	394
Gino Gasparini	North Dakota	392
Amo Bessone	Michigan Tech, Michigan State	387
Ned Harkness	Rensselaer, Cornell, Union	385
Bill Riley	Lehigh, Lowell	376

Chapter 11

The Floodgates Open

The "Can't Miss Kid" Opens the Door for a Whole New Crop of U.S. Talent

The decade of the 1980s was a breakthrough era for Americans at the pro level. The turning point came during the autumn of 1981 when Bobby Carpenter went directly from St. John's Prep School in Danvers, Massachusetts to instant success with the Washington Capitals. This happened only months after Carpenter was labeled "The Can't Miss Kid" on the cover of *Sports Illustrated* magazine.

The *Sports Illustrated* "jinx" did not apply here because Bobby did not miss. He scored 32 goals in each of his first two seasons and averaged 34 goals and 71 points over his first five seasons while not missing a single game! In doing so, he opened the eyes of pro scouts everywhere and made them aware of the talent that was hiding on the rosters of New England high school teams.

Michigan, which experienced a boom of its own during the '80s, also was busy breeding hockey talent. Youth programs such as Little Caesar's, sponsored by Red Wing owner Mike Ilitch, and the Peter Karmanos-backed Compuware teams were where some of the game's future stars were developing their skills.

The 1983 NHL Entry Draft saw five U.S. natives picked in the first round. A total of 65 Americans were chosen in the Draft, compared to 35 Europeans and 144 Canadians.

The third overall pick was Detroit native Pat LaFontaine, who was chosen by the New York Islanders. LaFontaine was a product of the Compuware program. The fifth overall pick was Tom Barrasso, who followed in Carpenter's skatemarks by going directly from Acton-Boxborough (MA) High School to the Buffalo Sabres. In Barrasso's first season he won the Vezina Trophy as the NHL's best goalie.

Players such as Barrasso opened the eyes of scouts and served as inspirations for others to follow. "I remember watching Barrasso at the old Boston Garden in high school when Acton-Boxborough lost to Matignon 4-2 in the finals," says Boston Bruins goalie Jim Carey, who grew up in nearby Weymouth, Mass. "Just seeing him play there and then make the jump to Buffalo in one year. You've got to look up to a guy like that. Especially when there aren't many American goaltenders in the league."

The following player profiles feature 12 of the best American players to make the NHL during the 1980s:

BOBBY CARPENTER

Born in Beverly and raised in Peabody, Massachussets, Bobby Carpenter first laced up a pair of skates at age four. He took a liking to skating and before long, post-kindergarten winter afternoons were spent on a little pond at end of his street.

Bobby began organized play as a mite at the age of six. Inspired after witnessing the Boston Bruins' 1970 Cup-clinching game in person, Bobby donned a jersey with number four on the back in honor of his hero Bobby Orr. With Orr as his inspiration, Carpenter played hockey all year long while still managing to compete at Little League Baseball.

Early accomplishments include leading the Peabody squirts team to the state championship and winning the Catholic League title with St. John's Prep. After graduating from St. John's in 1981 Carpenter made the big decision to turn pro immediately and play for the Caps. It was the right choice and an historic one as well. He scored at least 27 goals in each of first his four seasons, including 53 in 1984-85.

After trades sent Carpenter to the Rangers and Kings, Bobby was brought back to his hometown of Boston in 1989 when a deal sent him to the Bruins for veteran Steve Kasper. Carpenter spent three fairly productive years with the B's, helping them to a Stanley Cup Finals appearance and a President's Trophy in 1990.

In the summer of 1992 the stocky center decided to leave Beantown and return to Washington when he signed as a free agent with the Capitals. After a brief stint with his old team, Bobby moved to the New Jersey Devils just prior to the 1993-94 season. The following year he helped the Devs to a convincing Stanley Cup triumph over regular season powerhouse Detroit. Still going strong, "The Can't Miss Kid" continues to hit bulls-eyes.

By the end of the 1996-97 season he had become acknowledged as one of the NHL's best penalty-killers and defensive forwards.

Born: Beverly, MA, 7/13/63
6-0, 190
C/LW, shoots left

Season	Team	GP	G	A	Pts	PIM
81-82	Washington	80	32	35	67	69
82-83	Washington	80	32	37	69	64
83-84	Washington	80	28	40	68	51
84-85	Washington	80	53	42	95	87
85-86	Washington	80	27	29	56	105
86-87	Wash-NYR-LA	60	9	18	27	47
87-88	Los Angeles	71	19	33	52	84
88-89	LA-Boston	57	16	24	40	26
89-90	Boston	80	25	31	56	97
90-91	Boston	29	8	8	16	22
91-92	Boston	60	25	23	48	46
92-93	Washington	68	11	17	28	65
93-94	New Jersey	76	10	23	33	51
94-95	New Jersey	41	5	11	16	19
95-96	New Jersey	52	5	5	10	14
96-97	New Jersey	62	4	15	19	14
NHL Totals		1056	309	391	700	861
NHL Playoff Totals		127	20	38	58	134

JOHN VANBIESBROUCK

Considered to be one of the best goalies ever produced in North America, John Vanbiesbrouck started playing organized in a community hockey program in Detroit's Grosse Point area. He later made the transition to AAA Hockey with Little Caesar's of the Michigan National Hockey League.

After bantams John played only one year of midgets before heading north to Sault Ste. Marie of the Ontario Hockey League. After posting an impressive 31-16-1 record in his first OHL season, "Beezer" was ready for bigger things. The New York Rangers made him their fifth choice (72nd overall) in the 1981 Entry Draft.

Vanbiesbrouck continued to improve his netminding skills while spending two more seasons with Sault Ste. Marie and a year with Tulsa of the CHL. In 1984-85 the Rangers called him up to stay and made him their number one goaltender, a status he would keep for the next nine seasons.

Three shutouts and a 3.32 goals-against-average in 61 appearances earned Beezer the Vezina Trophy and a First Team All-Star selection in 1985-86.

During the 1993 off-season John was traded by the Rangers to the Vancouver Canucks for future considerations (Doug Lidster). Shortly thereafter he was claimed by the Florida Panthers from Vancouver in the Expansion Draft.

As a Panther, John has enjoyed some of his finest seasons. His goals-against-average has dipped from the 3.30 range to well below three goals per game. In 1995-96 Vanbiesbrouck was virtually unbeatable while leading a starless Panthers squad to playoff upsets of Philadelphia and Pittsburgh en route to the Stanley Cup Finals. His best season to date was 1996-97 when he recorded a career-low 2.29 GAA.

The essence of puckstopping quality, Beezer keeps getting better with age.

Born: Detroit, MI, 9/4/63
5-8, 176
G, catches left

Season	Team	GP	Mins	GA	SO	Avg
80-81	SS Marie (OHL)	56	-	-	0	4.14
81-82	SS Marie (OHL)	31	-	-	0	3.62
81-82	NY Rangers	1	60	1	0	1.00
82-83	SS Marie (OHL)	62	-	-	0	3.61
83-84	Tulsa (CHL)	37	-	-	3	3.46
83-84	NY Rangers	3	180	10	0	3.33
84-85	NY Rangers	42	2358	166	1	4.22
85-86	NY Rangers	61	3326	184	3	3.32
86-87	NY Rangers	50	2656	161	0	3.64
87-88	NY Rangers	56	3319	187	2	3.38
88-89	NY Rangers	56	3207	197	0	3.69
89-90	NY Rangers	47	2734	154	1	3.38
90-91	NY Rangers	40	2257	126	3	3.35
91-92	NY Rangers	45	2526	120	2	2.85
92-93	NY Rangers	48	2757	152	4	3.31
93-94	Florida	57	3440	145	1	2.53
94-95	Florida	37	2087	86	4	2.47
95-96	Florida	57	3178	142	2	2.68
96-97	Florida	57	3347	128	2	2.29
NHL Totals		657	37432	1959	25	3.14
NHL Playoff Totals		65	3600	168	4	2.80

PHIL HOUSLEY

———————

Most hockey observers consider Phil Housley one of the most gifted Minnesota products. Born and raised in St. Paul, Housley played both Junior and high school hockey before turning pro. After a brief stint with St. Paul of the United States Junior League in 1980-81, Phil put up stellar numbers for South St. Paul High School the following season. Playing in only 22 games, he scored 31 goals and amassed 65 points for the Packers.

Housley was the Buffalo Sabres' first choice (sixth overall), in the 1982 NHL Entry Draft. Before joining the Sabres he played for Team USA in both the 1982 World Junior and World Cup Tournaments.

In 1982-83 he stepped into the Sabres' lineup and as a defenseman immediately added scoring punch to the Buffalo attack. During his eight seasons with the Sabres, Housley scored 178 goals and accumulated 558 points while playing in a total of 608 games. His outstanding play has earned him six All-Star appearances and the honor of being named

to the 1983 NHL All-Rookie Team.

In June, 1990 he was traded to the Winnipeg Jets as part of a multi-player deal. In 1991-92 and 1992-93 Phil enjoyed his two most productive seasons as a pro, amassing 86 and 97 points, respectively.

After the Jets traded him to St. Louis in September, 1993, the crafty blueliner has had short stays with the Blues, Flames and Devils before signing as a free agent in July, 1996 with his present team, the Washington Capitals.

Born: St. Paul, MN, 3/9/64
5-10, 185
D, shoots left

Season	Team	GP	G	A	Pts	PIM
80-81	St. Paul (USHL)	6	7	7	14	-
81-82	S. St. Paul HS	22	31	34	65	-
82-83	Buffalo	77	19	47	66	39
83-84	Buffalo	75	31	46	77	33
84-85	Buffalo	73	16	53	69	28
85-86	Buffalo	79	15	47	62	54
86-87	Buffalo	78	21	46	67	57
87-88	Buffalo	74	29	37	66	96
88-89	Buffalo	72	26	44	70	47
89-90	Buffalo	80	21	60	81	32
90-91	Winnipeg	78	23	53	76	24
91-92	Winnipeg	74	23	63	86	92
92-93	Winnipeg	80	18	79	97	52
93-94	St. Louis	26	7	15	22	12
94-95	Calgary	43	8	35	43	18
95-96	Calg-NJ	81	17	51	68	30
96-97	Washington	77	11	29	40	24
NHL Totals		1067	285	705	990	638
NHL Playoff Totals		59	13	38	51	28

TOM BARRASSO

Tom Barrasso's first experience tending goal came when he was three years old on his own street in Burlington, Massachusetts. He joined some older kids on the block who played street hockey regularly. Since Tom wasn't big enough by his neighbors' standards to play up front, he wound up in goal. "The kids used to say 'You get in the goal because you're too small,'" recalls his father Tom.

Playing in the street and watching the Bruins' goalie Gerry Cheevers on TV warmed Tom's appetite for ice hockey. Shortly thereafter his parents took him to a nearby rink so he could learn how to skate. It was love at first glide; the boy wanted to skate all the time.

At age five he began playing organized hockey in the Burlington intramural program and a year later he skated for Burlington as a mite. That summer he went to a summer camp at nearby Stoneham Arena where he began to learn the fundamentals of goaltending from a man named Bill Bergland.

At seven he played in several youth hockey programs, including the Assabet Valley squirt team with future NHLers John Carter and Bob Sweeney. According to Tom's parents, Tom and Lucy, the kid loved to play hockey, he had it in him and he couldn't get enough of it. "Now let me get one thing straight," insisted his father Tom, "we did not push him ('Oh God no!,' his mother Lucy injected). He pushed us!"

Soon the Barrassos were making trips to Canada and the Midwest to watch their son compete in various youth hockey tournaments. In the final game of the Mosquito Tournament Barrasso's team faced a Canadian team called the North Shore All-Stars, which featured a young French boy by the name of Patrick Roy in goal.

In the ninth grade Tom attended Acton-Boxborough Regional High School where, as a freshman, he tried out for the varsity squad and made the team as a back-up. The next year he became the school's number one backstopper and started in almost every game through his senior year. In his final season at AB he recorded a remarkable 0.73 goals-against-average. Complementing Barrasso's stellar play between the pipes those years were Tom's former squirt teammates Bob Sweeney, and Alan Borbeau, who broke Robbie Ftorek's record for goals during his senior year, and Mike Flanigan, a defenseman, who was later drafted by Edmonton.

Although Barrasso had accepted a scholarship to Providence College and was chosen for the 1984 Olympic Team, he decided to turn pro instead and join the Buffalo Sabres who had made him their first-round pick in 1983.

In Tom's first season with Buffalo he won the Vezina Trophy as the League's outstanding goaltender; was named to the NHL First All-Star Team; won the Calder Trophy as the NHL's top rookie; and was named to the NHL All-Rookie Team.

In November, 1988, he was traded to Pittsburgh along with a third-round draft choice for Doug Bodger and Darrin Shannon. In the Steel City Tom enjoyed his most glorious moments. In both 1990-91 and 1991-92 his solid netminding helped lead the Penguins to two straight Stanley Cups.

Born: Boston, MA, 3/31/65
6-3, 211
G, catches right

Season	Team	GP	Mins	GA	SO	Avg
81-82	Acton-Box. HS	23	-	32	7	1.86
82-83	Acton-Box. HS	23	-	17	10	0.73
83-84	Buffalo	42	2475	117	2	2.84
84-85	Buffalo	54	3248	144	5	2.66
85-86	Buffalo	60	3561	214	2	3.61
86-87	Buffalo	46	2501	152	2	3.65
87-88	Buffalo	54	3133	173	2	3.31
88-89	Buff-Pitt	54	2951	207	0	4.21
89-90	Pittsburgh	24	1294	101	0	4.68
90-91	Pittsburgh	48	2754	165	1	3.59
91-92	Pittsburgh	57	3329	196	1	3.53
92-93	Pittsburgh	63	3702	186	4	3.01
93-94	Pittsburgh	44	2482	139	2	3.36
94-95	Pittsburgh	2	125	8	0	3.84
95-96	Pittsburgh	49	2799	160	2	3.43
96-97	Pittsburgh	5	270	26	0	5.78
NHL Totals		602	34624	1988	23	3.44
NHL Playoff Totals		94	5418	281	5	3.11

Lucy Barrasso's beautiful, action-packed painting depicting her son's early netminding heroics.

Tom Barrasso

CHRIS CHELIOS

Chris Chelios grew up in the Chicago suburb of Evergreen Park, Illinois. In 1975 he attended Mount Carmel High School where he played varsity hockey in both his freshman and sophomore seasons.

Mount Carmel is a member of the Chicago Catholic League (oldest high school hockey league in Illinois) which includes such schools as Brother Rice, Fenwick, St. Rita, St. Lauwrence, and Notre Dame. Each year they compete for the Kennedy Cup, named after the late President John F. Kennedy.

After winning the 1976-77 regular season championship Mount Carmel squared off against Brother Rice in a best-of-three playoff for the Kennedy Cup. With the series tied at one game apiece and the rubber game also knotted at one, Chelios — all 110 pounds of him — scored the Cup-winning goal with only 10 seconds left in the game. It was the school's first of six consecutive Kennedy Cups, making Chris's clutch tally one of the biggest goals in Mount Carmel hockey history.

After that magical sophomore season Chris's family moved to San Diego. Since Southern California at the time had little to offer in the way of competitive amateur hockey, Chris left the Golden State for Moose Jaw of the Saskatchewan Junior Hockey League.

His superb play in the SJHL was enough to induce the Montreal Canadiens to take a chance on the underage Junior as their fifth choice, 40th overall, in the 1981 Entry Draft. Next would be many "great days for hockey" at the University of Wisconsin under the guidance of "Badger" Bob Johnson.

In 1983 Chelios produced an average of one point per game while playing steady defense to help lead the Badgers to the NCAA Championship. He was chosen to the NCAA All-Tournament Team and WCHA Second All-Star Team. It was a busy year for the Chicago native who also played on both the U.S. National and Olympic Teams as well as appearing in 12 games for the Canadiens. He appeared uncertain and unsteady at first in the NHL, but the best was yet to come.

In 1984-85 Chris became a regular part of the Hab's blue line corps. A year later his name was inscribed on the Stanley Cup. As a valuable addition to a team led by poised veterans Bob Gainey and Larry Robinson, Chelios pitched in with two goals and nine assists during Montreal's magical 1985-86 playoff run. In 1988-89 Chel's excellent play in the Montreal end and the highest point production of his career earned him the Norris Trophy.

In late June, 1990, a trade sent him back to

his hometown when the Habs dealt Chelios and a 1991 second-round draft choice to Chicago for Denis Savard. Since the day he arrived in his hometown Chris has been one of the most popular Blackhawks. He now owns a bar/restaurant near the United Center called Cheli's Chili Bar where fans congregate before and after games.

In his second season with the Hawks Chelios anchored the defense in front of standout goalie Ed Belfour while Jeremy Roenick lit the lamp early and often. The combination led the Blackhawks to an 11-game winning streak during the first three rounds of the playoffs. The streak, however, was derailed by the surging Pittsburgh Penguins who swept the Hawks four straight in the Finals.

Since settling into the Windy City again Chelios has won two more Norris Trophies (1993, 1996) and has played in six All-Star Games.

A glorious highlight in his career came in September, 1996, when Chelios was a key part of the Team USA squad that defeated Team Canada in two straight games to win its first World Cup.

Born: Chicago, IL, 1/25/62						
6-1, 186						
D, shoots right						
Season	Team	GP	G	A	Pts	PIM
79-80	Moose Jaw (SJHL)	53	12	31	43	-
80-81	Moose Jaw (SJHL)	54	23	64	87	-
81-82	U Wisconsin	43	6	43	49	-
82-83	U Wisconsin	26	9	17	26	-
83-84	US Nat'l	60	14	35	49	-
83-84	US Olympic	6	0	4	4	-
83-84	Montreal	12	0	2	2	12
84-85	Montreal	74	9	55	64	87
85-86	Montreal	41	8	26	34	67
86-87	Montreal	71	11	33	44	124
87-88	Montreal	71	20	41	61	172
88-89	Montreal	80	15	58	73	185
89-90	Montreal	53	9	22	31	136
90-91	Chicago	77	12	52	64	192
91-92	Chicago	80	9	47	56	245
92-93	Chicago	84	15	58	73	282
93-94	Chicago	76	16	44	60	212
94-95	Chicago	48	5	33	38	72
95-96	Chicago	81	14	58	72	140
96-97	Chicago	72	10	38	48	112
NHL Totals		920	153	567	720	2038
NHL Playoff Totals		163	28	88	116	319

PAT LAFONTAINE

Born in St. Louis and raised in Waterford, Michigan, Pat LaFontaine is far and away the most productive NHL center to emerge from the Detroit area. Pat and his older brother, John, played for the Waterford Lakers of the Michigan National Hockey League, which was coached by their dad, John.

When Pat reached his mid-teens he joined the Compuware team of the MNHL, coached by Real Turcotte. His teammates included such future NHLers as Turcotte's son, Alfie, and Al "The Planet" Iafrate.

"Pat was always a superior player," says Neil Carnes, general manager for all Compuware youth teams. "He always had tremendous speed, great skills and could see the whole ice. He was always a step above everybody else in the area."

After only one year at the midget level, LaFontaine left the Great Lake State to play for Verdun of the Quebec Major Junior Hockey League. His league-leading 104 goals and 234 points earned him Canadian Major Junior Player of the Year honors for 1983. Remarkable, considering that Mario Lemieux played in the same league that season.

Pat's shining performance prompted the New York Islanders to make him their first choice (third overall) in the 1983 Entry Draft. Pat spent most of the next season playing for both the U.S. National and Olympic Teams before making his Islanders debut at the tail end of the 1983-84 campaign.

Beginning in 1984-85 LaFontaine enjoyed seven straight productive seasons with the Isles. His best season as a member of the Or-

ange and Blue was 1989-90, when he scored 54 goals and recorded 51 assists. The highlight of his stay on the Island came when he potted the game-winning goal at 8:15 of the fourth overtime of Game Seven against the Washington Capitals on Easter morning, 1987.

Early in the 1990-91 season a multi-player deal sent Pat to the Buffalo Sabres. It was with the Sabres in 1992-93 that he enjoyed his best season as a pro when he banged home 53 lamplighters and recorded an incredible 95 assists for 148 points.

He missed most of the following season due to a knee injury but his return in 1994-95 earned him yet another accolade — the Bill Masterton Memorial Trophy, given to the NHL player who best exemplifies the qualities of perseverance, sportsmanship and dedication to hockey.

After a solid 1995-96 campaign, LaFontaine

was forced to sit out most of the 1996-97 season because of a head injury he sustained as a result of a concussion. He was traded to the New York Rangers on the eve of the 1997-98 season.

Born: St. Louis, MO, 2/22/65
5-10, 180
C, shoots right

Season	Team	GP	G	A	Pts	PIM
82-83	Verdun (QMJHL)	70	104	130	234	-
83-84	US Nat'l Team	58	56	55	111	-
83-84	US Olympic Team	6	5	10	15	-
83-84	NY Islanders	15	13	6	19	6
84-85	NY Islanders	67	19	35	54	32
85-86	NY Islanders	65	30	23	53	43
86-87	NY Islanders	80	38	32	70	70
87-88	NY Islanders	75	47	45	92	52
88-89	NY Islanders	79	45	43	88	26
89-90	NY Islanders	74	54	51	105	38
90-91	NY Islanders	75	41	44	85	42
91-92	Buffalo	57	46	47	93	98
92-93	Buffalo	84	53	95	148	63
93-94	Buffalo	16	5	13	18	2
94-95	Buffalo	22	12	15	27	4
95-96	Buffalo	76	40	51	91	36
96-97	Buffalo	13	2	6	8	4
NHL Totals		798	445	500	951	516
NHL Playoff Totals		69	26	36	62	36

BRETT HULL

Brett Hull is the son of NHL Hall of Famer Bobby Hull and nephew of ex-NHLer Dennis Hull. Unlike each of his four siblings (Bobby Jr., Blake, Bart and Michelle), who were all born in their native Chicago, Brett was born in 1964 in Belleville, Ontario, where the family spent summers.

Brett was taught how to skate at age five by his mother, Joanne, who was a professional figure skater for Hilton Hotel shows. "I wasn't exactly a natural at hockey, early in my career," recalls Hull. "I tried to quit teams more than once because I was cold. And sometimes, I wouldn't participate in pre-game warmups because I thought they were a waste of time.

"Even after mom taught me how to skate, dad and two teammates, Chico Maki and Phil Esposito, had to hold me down to force skates on me, at a Chicago Blackhawks Christmas party."[1]

Hull played his first organized hockey at age seven for the Elmhurst Huskies with future NHL forward Tony Granato and Tommy Stapleton, son of Blackhawks defenseman Pat Stapleton.

In 1972 his dad, "The Golden Jet," joined the Winnipeg Jets for the 1972-73 WHA season. Brett began playing for a team called the Tuxedo Jets. After a couple of years with the Jets, Brett joined the Canadian Professional Hockey School's team. When he was 12 he helped the Winnipeg Southside Monarchs win the Quebec Pee Wee Tournament.

Meanwhile, Brett and his brothers were also logging ice time at the Winnipeg Arena skating after Jets practices. Sometimes Jets' goalies

Ernie Wakely and Joe Daley would stay on the ice and face their shots. In 1976 Kent Nilsson came to the Jets and gave Brett lessons on shooting accuracy. He would line up 10 pucks at center ice and bet the kids five bucks that he could hit the crossbar at least seven times. Then, to their disbelief, Nilsson would hit it eight or nine times.[2]

When Brett's parents became separated in 1979, he, his brother Blake and his sister Michelle moved to Vancouver with their mom. Brett played bantams then midgets at the North Shore Winter Club as well as competing at football and baseball.

When Brett was 18 he was offered a chance to play with the Penticton Knights of the British Columbia Junior Hockey League, mostly because of his father. "If my name was Brett Smith or Brett Jones," Hull points out, "I never would have made the Penticton Knights that season."[3] It was at least partly a ploy by Knights management to put people in the seats.

In his second season with the Knights he

raised more than a few brows by scoring a league-leading 105 goals. After that impressive second season with the Knights, Hull was drafted by the Calgary Flames in the sixth round of the 1984 Entry Draft.

He was also recruited by American colleges. For several reasons, he chose the University of Minnesota-Duluth. He was attracted to the low-key, small-town atmosphere of the area; he was impressed with coach Mike Sertich; and he was assured by his recruiter, assistant coach Tim McDonald, that despite a roster laced with talent — they had lost to Bowling Green in four overtimes in the final game of the NCAA tournament the previous year — the Bulldogs would find room for him to play.

Before Hull accepted the scholarship he told coach Sertich: "When I come to Duluth, I'm coming as Brett Hull, not Bobby Hull's son."[4]

Hull's two seasons at Minnesota-Duluth followed the same pattern as the two at Penticton. He scored an impressive 32 goals in his freshman year, which earned him WCHA Freshman-of-the-Year Award. The next season he tore the league apart with 52 goals. In the spring of 1986 Brett made his NHL debut with the Flames, appearing in two playoff games.

After spending most of the next season with Moncton of the American Hockey League, Hull began to see regular action for the Flames in 1987-88. He looked like a winner but disagreements with the general staff intervened. In early March he was dealt to St. Louis with Steve Bozek for Rob Ramage and Rick Wamsley.

In St. Louis, Brett found his niche. He has since emerged as one of the great pure snipers the game has seen. After slapping home 41 goals in his first full season (1988-89) with the Blues he found the back of the net 72 times the next season and a remarkable 86 times in 1990-91. His 86-goal season is second only to Wayne Gretzky's 92-goal season in 1981-82.

Other NHL accolades for "The Golden Brett" include seven All-Star Game appearances, winning the Lady Byng Trophy in 1990, receiving the Lester B. Pearson Award in 1991 and being awarded the Hart Trophy as League MVP in 1991. Brett also is the only son of an NHL 50-goal scorer to record a 50-goal season.

One of the biggest goals in Brett's career came late in the third period of the final game of the 1996 World Cup between the United States and Canada when he tipped home a Brian Leetch shot to tie the score at two apiece. Team USA went on to win the game, 5-2, and in doing so claim its first-ever World Cup.

Born: Belleville, Ont., 8/9/64
5-10, 201
RW, shoots right

Season	Team	GP	G	A	Pts	PIM
82-83	Penticton (BCJHL)	50	48	56	104	-
83-84	Penticton (BCJHL)	56	105	83	188	-
84-85	Minn-Duluth	48	32	28	60	-
85-86	Minn-Duluth	42	52	32	84	-
86-87	Moncton (AHL)	67	50	42	92	-
85-86	Calgary	-	-(playoffs only)-			-
86-87	Calgary	5	1	0	1	0
87-88	Calg-StL	65	32	32	64	16
88-89	St. Louis	78	41	43	84	33
89-90	St. Louis	80	72	41	113	24
90-91	St. Louis	78	86	45	131	22
91-92	St. Louis	73	70	39	109	48
92-93	St. Louis	80	54	47	101	41
93-94	St. Louis	81	57	40	97	38
94-95	St. Louis	48	29	21	50	10
95-96	St. Louis	70	43	40	83	30
96-97	St. Louis	77	42	40	82	10
NHL Totals		735	427	388	915	272
NHL Playoff Totals		98	66	48	114	49

CHRIS TERRERI

When Chris Terreri was only four years old he learned how to skate on his family's backyard rink in Warwick, Rhode Island. Organized hockey began for Chris in instructional squirts at age six at Thayer Arena in Warwick.

As kids, Chris and his older brother, Peter, grew up living hockey. When they weren't competing they watched Boston Bruins games and NHL hockey on Sundays called by Dan Kelly. Their thirst to see live hockey was quenched by their dad who regularly brought them to the Providence Auditorium to see the Providence Reds of the AHL.

In the late 1960s when Peter and his friends began playing street hockey Chris would join them and play goal. "Chris was always the smallest kid around so we always threw him in net," recalls Peter. "He played a lot of street hockey against a lot of the bigger guys like myself and some neighbors who were bigger than me. He wouldn't have been able to compete outside of the net, so we just kind of threw all the pads on him and put him in there. He did pretty well against some of the older guys."

In 1975 Chris' squirt travel team advanced all the way to the national championships which were held in Melvindale, Michigan, just outside of Detroit. They played a Michigan team in the finals and won.

After advancing through the youth hockey ranks Chris played high school hockey at Pilgrim High in Warwick, a Metropolitan B division school. Although Pilgrim did not compete at the state's top level, Chris' excel-lent backstopping was good enough to earn him All-State honors above all of the Met-A goalies during his junior and senior years. He also caught the attention of Providence College coach Lou Lamoriello who recruited him to play for the Friars.

During his first two years at Providence, Chris served as backup to Mario Prouix. At the end of his freshman year he was chosen by the New Jersey Devils in the third round (87th overall) in the 1983 Entry Draft.

In his junior season of 1984-85 Chris almost singlehandedly carried the Friars to the Hockey East Championship and to the final game of the NCAA Championship Tournament. In the final game the Cinderella Friars lost a hard-fought 2-1 contest to an RPI squad that featured future NHLers Darren Puppa, Adam Oates, Craig Neinhaus and John Carter. Despite the loss, Chris was named the Tournament's Most Valuable Player. Other accolades received by the Warwick native that season were Hockey East Player of the Year, Hockey East All-Star First Team, NCAA All-America East Team and NCAA All-Tournament Team.

After graduating from Providence College Chris made his debut with the Devils early in the 1986-87 season. After seven games with the big club, Chris was sent to the Devils' AHL Maine affiliate for the remainder of the season.

His progression continued in the following season when he played for the U.S. National and Olympic Teams before finishing the season with Utica of the AHL. After splitting time between Utica and New Jersey in 1988-89, Chris landed a permanent spot on the Devils roster in 1989-90. Although he was a backup to Sean Burke throughout most of the regular season, he improved down the stretch and was the starting netminder in four of the club's six playoff contests. For his impressive postseason performance he became the team's number one goalie in 1990-91.

His finest season as a pro came in 1993-94 when he posted a 2.72 goals-against-average. More than that, he heroically bailed out the Devils who had lost the first two games of their playoff series with Boston. Terreri then replaced Martin Brodeur and the Devils won four straight. His only starts in the series were in all three of the games played at Boston Garden and he won them all, including the sixth game clincher.

The following season Brodeur emerged as the team's number one goaltender and helped lead the Devils to their first Stanley Cup in franchise history. Although he saw limited action during the Devs' Cup-run, Chris recorded the lowest goal-against-average (2.53) of his pro career during the regular season and most deservedly saw his name inscribed on Lord Stanley's coveted hardware.

In November, 1995, he was traded by the Devils to San Jose. In the middle of the 1996-97 season the Sharks dealt him to his current team, the Chicago Blackhawks.

Born: Providence, RI, 11/15/64
5-8, 160
G, catches left

Season	Team	GP	Mins	GA	SO	Avg
82-83	Prov. (ECAC)	11	-	-	2	1.93
83-84	Prov. (ECAC)	10	-	-	0	3.07
84-85	Prov. (H.E.)	33	-	-	1	3.35
85-86	Prov. (H.E.)	22	-	-	0	3.74
86-87	Maine (AHL)	14	-	-	0	4.47
86-87	New Jersey	7	286	21	0	4.41
87-88	U.S. Nat'l Team	26	-	-	0	3.40
87-88	U.S. Olym. Team	3	-	-	0	6.56
87-88	Utica (AHL)	7	-	-	0	2.71
88-89	Utica (AHL)	39	-	-	0	3.42
88-89	New Jersey	8	402	18	0	2.69
89-90	New Jersey	35	1931	110	0	3.42
90-91	New Jersey	53	2970	144	1	2.91
91-92	New Jersey	54	3186	169	1	3.18
92-93	New Jersey	48	2672	151	2	3.39
93-94	New Jersey	44	2340	106	2	2.72
94-95	New Jersey	15	734	31	0	2.53
95-96	NJ-San Jose	50	2726	164	0	3.61
96-97	SJ-Chicago	29	1629	74	0	2.72
NHL Totals		343	18876	988	6	3.14
NHL Playoff Totals		29	1523	86	0	3.39

BRIAN LEETCH

Steve Babineau

Shortly after Brian Leetch was born in Corpus Christi his family moved from Texas to California, which is where he first laced on a pair of skates. At about the time Brian turned five the Leetch family once again relocated, this time to Connecticut where he started playing ice hockey on a regular basis.

When Leetch wasn't on the ice shooting a puck around, he was throwing and hitting baseballs. During the mid-1980s he attended Avon Old Farms School For Boys where he excelled at both sports.

His prep school hockey career began with a bang. With his team trailing by a goal late in his first game, he took the puck from behind the net and skated the length of the ice and scored. In his junior season of 1984-85 he scored 30 goals and recorded 46 assists for 76 points in only 26 games. The following season he improved to 84 points in 28 games while leading Avon Old Farms to the finals of the New England Prep School Championship Tournament. In the final game Avon bowed to a highly-talented Thayer Academy squad that featured future NHL aces Tony Amonte and Jeremy Roenick.

Brian's outstanding play at the prep school level enticed the New York Rangers to make him their first choice (9th overall) in the 1986 Entry Draft.

Meanwhile offers from colleges and universities were rolling in. Brian decided to attend college and chose Boston College because his dad, Jack, had been an All-American there. In his only year as an Eagle Leetch collected 47 points in 37 games, including an amazing 38 assists. His end-to-end puck-rushing, racing-back style along with fellow Connecticut-raised teammate Craig Janney's pretty passing made the Eagles a lot of fun to watch in 1986-87. At season's end Leetch was named both Hockey East Player of the Year and Rookie of the Year and made the NCAA East First All-American Team.

Brian left BC after one year to play on the U.S. National Team which became the 1988 U.S. Olympic Team. After a failed attempt by Team USA to win a medal, Leetch moved to the Rangers as soon as the Olympics were over.

In Brian's first full season as a member of the Broadway Blues he set an NHL record that still stands for most goals by a rookie defenseman, 23. It helped to earn him the Calder Trophy as the League's best rookie, the first of a growing collection of awards for the well-rounded, playmaking defenseman.

In 1991-92 he won the Norris trophy as the league's best defenseman and in 1993-94 a terrific postseason performance made him the first American to win the Conn Smythe Trophy as playoff MVP. With 11 goals and 23 assists in 23 games he was the driving force behind the Rangers' "curse breaking" season.

Of the many attributes that Brian Leetch has demonstrated as a hockey player, the most important is his postseason performance rate. You can count on him to make big plays and his career playoff scoring average proves the point — 1.25 points-per-game.

Born: Corpus Christi, TX, 3/3/68
5-11, 190
D, shoots left

Season	Team	GP	G	A	Pts	PIM
84-85	Avon Old Farms	26	30	46	76	-
85-86	Avon Old Farms	28	40	44	84	-
86-87	Boston College	37	9	38	47	-
87-88	US National	50	13	61	74	-
87-88	US Olympic	6	1	5	6	-
87-88	NY Rangers	17	2	12	14	0
88-89	NY Rangers	68	23	48	71	50
89-90	NY Rangers	72	11	45	56	26
90-91	NY Rangers	80	16	72	88	42
91-92	NY Rangers	80	22	80	102	26
92-93	NY Rangers	36	6	30	36	26
93-94	NY Rangers	84	23	56	79	67
94-95	NY Rangers	48	9	32	41	18
95-96	NY Rangers	82	15	70	85	30
96-97	NY Rangers	82	20	58	78	40
NHL Totals		649	147	503	650	425
NHL Playoff Totals		82	28	61	89	30

KEVIN STEVENS

To call Kevin Stevens' organized hockey debut auspicious would be an understatement. At age seven he was chosen to play center on the instructional mites "B" team at the Hobomock Arena in Pembroke, Massachusetts. At the beginning of his first game he took six faceoffs, and, after winning each one to himself, he waltzed in on goal and scored. The early-game heroics immediately caught the attention of the "A" team's coach. "Where the hell did I miss this guy?" said the coach in utter disbelief. "I mean, what the hell's going on? He's better than anybody I've got in A's."

Little did the coach know that Kevin had a head start on the rest of the kids. A year earlier he learned to skate on the cranberry bogs across from his house with his mom, Pat, and his two sisters.

After instructional mites came mites, squirts and bantams. At each level he traveled to nearby towns and competed in tournaments as far away as Montreal. As a squirt, at age 10, Kevin scored 135 goals in one season.

As a freshman at Silver Lake Regional High School he made the varsity team and played midgets during the summer. Later in his schoolboy years he began to receive numerous offers from colleges and universities. His clear choice was Boston College because he fell in love with the campus atmosphere while visiting his older sister, Kelly, who attended before him.

Just prior to his high school graduation, the Los Angeles Kings selected Kevin in the sixth round of the June, 1983, Entry Draft. Three months later, however, the Kings traded his

Steve Babineau

rights to the Pittsburgh Penguins.

During his four years as a BC Eagle under the guidance of coach Len Ceglarski, Kevin improved his overall hockey skills. His offensive numbers steadily climbed from six goals and 14 assists in 37 games as a freshman, to 35 goals and 35 assists in 39 games as a senior.

After graduating from BC Kevin toured with the U.S. National Team which became the 1988 Olympic Team. At the conclusion of the Winter Olympic Games at Calgary he made his NHL debut with the Pens. The following season (1988-89) he split time between the Penguins and their IHL Muskegon affiliate.

Returning to The Steel City the next season, Stevens was put on a line alongside Mario Lemieux. The result was a four-year stretch in which he scored 40, 54, 55 and 41 goals, helping the Pens win two consecutive Stanley Cups. In the first period of Game Seven of the 1992-93 Wales Conference semi-finals against the New York Islanders Kevin sustained a career-threatening head injury as a result of a collision with Isles defenseman Rich Pilon.

Stevens' presence was sorely missed and the upstart Isles defeated the Penguins, spoiling Pittsburgh's chances for a third straight Cup.

During the summer of 1995 the Penguins traded Stevens to his hometown, Boston, where high expectations awaited his homecoming. But after Kevin scored only 10 goals in 41 games the Bruins' brass gave up on him and dealt him to the Los Angeles Kings. After a mediocre 1996-97 campaign with the Kings, he was traded to the New York Rangers.

Born: Brockton, MA 5/15/65
6-3, 217
LW, shoots left

Season	Team	GP	G	A	Pts	PIM
83-84	Bos. Col. (H.E.)	37	6	14	20	36
84-85	Bos. Col. (H.E.)	40	13	23	36	36
85-86	Bos. Col. (H.E.)	42	17	27	44	56
86-87	Bos. Col. (H.E.)	39	35	35	70	54
87-88	U.S. National	44	22	23	45	52
87-88	U.S. Olympic	5	1	3	4	2
87-88	Pittsburgh	16	5	2	7	8
88-89	Pittsburgh	24	12	3	15	19
88-89	Muskegon (IHL)	45	24	41	65	113
90-91	Pittsburgh	80	40	46	86	133
91-92	Pittsburgh	80	54	69	123	254
92-93	Pittsburgh	72	55	56	111	177
93-94	Pittsburgh	83	41	47	88	155
94-95	Pittsburgh	27	15	12	27	51
95-96	Boston-LA	61	13	23	36	71
96-97	Los Angeles	69	14	20	34	96
NHL Totals		588	278	319	597	1135
NHL Playoff Totals		86	43	57	100	150

JEREMY ROENICK

On the very first day Jeremy Roenick put on a pair of skates he proved he was a gamer. Clad in football helmet and double-runner skates and holding a plastic hockey stick, Jeremy went skating with some neighbors on the Nawgatuck River. Splash! Right through the partially-frozen surface he fell. His dad, Wally, came to his rescue and pulled him out of the hole in the ice.

How did the boy react? Was he discouraged? Quite the contrary, he went home, changed his clothes and returned. He already had the mental makeup to play in the NHL.

In fact, he was only ten years old when he tied one of Wayne Gretzky's records. Jeremy scored six goals in one game at the acclaimed Quebec Winter Carnival pee wee tournament in Quebec City, equalling the mark set by The Great One in that tournament a decade earlier.

The older brother of NHL forward Trevor Roenick, Jeremy was born in Boston but also lived in Texas, New York, Connecticut and Virginia while growing up. At age 14 he attended Thayer Academy, located in the Boston suburb of Braintree.

At Thayer Jeremy played on the same line with Tony Amonte, who later became his teammate with the Chicago Blackhawks. The two helped Thayer win back-to-back New England Prep School championships, the first of which included a final-game victory over Brian Leetch and his heavily-favored Avon Old Farms team. "We were big-time underdogs," Amonte recalls, "but it seemed like everything was coming together and we won

the game."

In the 1988 NHL Entry Draft Roenick was chosen by the Chicago Blackhawks in the first round as the eighth overall pick. The following season, he split time between Chicago and Hull of the Quebec Major Junior Hockey League. His 70 points in 28 games with Hull earned him a spot on the QMJHL Second All-Star Team.

The 1989-90 campaign was Jeremy's first full season as a Blackhawk. His speed, agility and toughness immediately made him a favorite of the Chicago crowd. His 26 goals and 40 assists that season prompted the Sporting News to name him as their NHL Rookie of the Year.

As an NHL sophomore Roenick banged home 41 goals and added 53 assists in helping to lead the Hawks to the Stanley Cup Finals where they bowed to the high-powered

Pittsburgh Penguins. Although the Hawks dropped back to the middle of the pack, Roenick continued to blossom. From 1991-92 to 1993-94 he posted three consecutive 100-plus-point seasons.

In March, 1994, Jeremy was reunited with Amonte, who arrived via a trade from the New York Rangers. The association, however, lasted only two seasons. In August, 1996, the Hawks surprisingly dealt Roenick to his current team, the Phoenix Coyotes, for Alexie Zhamnov, Craig Mills and Phoenix's first round choice in the 1998 Entry Draft.

Surrounded by scoring aces Keith Tkachuk and Craig Janney as well as Russian goaltending sensation Nikolai Khabibulin, Roenick's future looks bright in The Valley of the Sun.

Born: Boston, MA, 1/17/70
6-0, 170
C, shoots right

Season	Team	GP	G	A	Pts	PIM
86-87	Thayer Academy	24	31	34	65	-
87-88	Thayer Academy	-	34	50	84	-
88-89	Hull (QMJHL)	28	34	36	70	14
88-89	Chicago	20	9	9	18	4
89-90	Chicago	78	26	40	66	54
90-91	Chicago	79	41	53	94	80
91-92	Chicago	80	53	50	103	98
92-93	Chicago	84	50	57	107	86
93-94	Chicago	84	46	61	107	125
94-95	Chicago	33	10	24	34	14
95-96	Chicago	66	32	35	67	109
96-97	Phoenix	72	29	40	69	115
NHL Totals		596	296	369	665	685
NHL Playoff Totals		88	37	46	83	57

MIKE MODANO

Steve Babineau

Mike Modano is yet another example of a superior hockey talent produced in Michigan. Born and raised in the Detroit suburb of Livonia, Mike played his youth hockey in the Michigan National Hockey League for both Little Caesar's and Compuware.

At age 16 Mike sought tougher competition in the Canadian Junior circuit and headed west to play in the Western Hockey League. At Prince Albert, Mike followed an impressive first season with a standout performance in 1987-88. His sparkling play caught the attention of the Minnesota North Stars, who made him the first choice overall in the 1988 Entry Draft.

After one more season in Prince Albert, Mike made his NHL debut by appearing in two games for the North Stars in the 1988-89 playoffs. The next season — his first full NHL season — his 29 goals and 46 assists earned him a spot on the NHL All-Rookie Team.

A year later he helped lead the Stars on a Cinderella playoff run by contributing 8 goals and 12 assists en route to the Stanley Cup Finals where the Stars were upended by Mario Lemieux and the Pittsburgh Penguins.

Mike's finest season to date came in 1993-94, the Stars' first year in Dallas. He knocked home 50 goals and added 43 assists in 76 games. In 1996-97 he helped lead the Stars to a first place finish in the Western Conference by posting a most impressive plus-43 in the plus-minus category. This came as evidence that general manager Bob Gainey's efforts to make Modano into a good two-way center had more than materialized.

A favorite of the growing Dallas fan base, Modano has yet to reach his full potential.

Born: Livonia, MI, 6/7/70
6-3, 200
C/RW, shoots left

Season	Team	GP	G	A	Pts	PIM
86-87	Pr. Alb. (WHL)	70	32	30	62	-
87-88	Pr. Alb. (WHL)	65	47	80	127	-
88-89	Pr. Alb. (WHL)	41	39	66	105	-
88-89	Minnesota	-	-(playoffs only)-		-	
89-90	Minnesota	80	29	46	75	63
90-91	Minnesota	79	28	36	64	65
91-92	Minnesota	76	33	44	77	46
92-93	Minnesota	82	33	60	93	83
93-94	Dallas	76	50	43	93	54
94-95	Dallas	30	12	17	29	8
95-96	Dallas	78	36	45	81	63
96-97	Dallas	80	35	48	83	42
NHL Totals		581	256	339	595	424
NHL Playoff Totals		55	23	19	42	48

Steve Babineau

Above: Rhinelander, Wisconsin, native Craig Ludwig has played steady defense for 15 NHL seasons with Montreal, the New York Islanders, Minnesota and now Dallas. *Right:* Michigan native Al Iafrate has perhaps the fastest slap shot of any player ever to emerge from the Great Lake State.

Right: Craig Janney of Enfield, CT, has impressed NHL audiences over the years with his superb playmaking abilities. *Far right:* New Jersey-born Brian Lawton was the first selection overall in the 1983 NHL Entry Draft. *Bottom left:* Elk River, MN, native Joel Otto helped Calgary win the Stanley Cup in 1989. *Bottom right:* Like New York Islanders star defenseman Bryan Berard, NHL blueliner Mathieu Schneider attended hockey powerhouse Mt. St. Charles Academy (RI) before turning pro.

Sports Action/Jon Hayt

Steve Babineau

Steve Babineau

Steve Babineau

AMERICAN-BORN/RAISED NHLers By State From 1980-81 To 1989-90

MASSACHUSETTS: (48)

	Place of Birth	Pos	Turned Pro
Gary Burns	Cambridge	C	(80-81)
Jack Hughes	Somerville	D	(80-81)
Bill McCreary	Springfield	RW	(80-81)
Bill Whelton	Everett	D	(80-81)
Bobby Carpenter	Beverly	C/LW	(81-82)
Paul Miller	Billerica	C	(81-82)
Gerry McDonald	Weymouth	D	(81-82)
Mark Holden	Weymouth	G	(81-82)
Jack O'Callahan	Charlestown	D	(82-83)
Andy Brickley	Melrose	C	(82-83)
Tom Barrasso	Boston	G	(83-84)
Tom O'Regan	Cambridge	C	(83-84)
Dean Jenkins	Billerica	RW	(83-84)
Richard Costello	Farmington	C	(83-84)
Mark Fusco	Burlington	D	(83-84)
Bill O'Dwyer	Boston	C	(83-84)
Phil Bourque	Chelmsford	LW	(83-84)
Bob Brooke	Melrose	C	(83-84)
Frank Simonetti	Melrose	D	(84-85)
Peter Taglianetti	Framingham	D	(84-85)
Cleon Daskalakis	Boston	G	(84-85)
Steve Rooney	Canton	LW	(84-85)
Paul Fenton	Springfield	LW	(84-85)
David A. Jensen	Newton	C	(84-85)
Mark Kumpel	Wakefield	RW	(84-85)
John Carter	Winchester	LW	(85-86)
Jay Miller	Wellesley	LW	(85-86)
Dale Dunbar	Winthrop	D	(85-86)
Steve Leach	Cambridge	RW	(85-86)
Dom Campedelli	Cohasset	D	(85-86)
Bob Sweeney	Concord	C/RW	(86-87)
Doug Brown	Southboro	RW	(86-87)
Brian Noonan	Boston	RW	(87-88)
Scott Harlow	East Bridgewater	LW	(87-88)
Bob Kudelski	Springfield	RW	(87-88)
Jeff Norton	Acton	D	(87-88)
Kevin Stevens	Brockton	LW	(87-88)
Scott Young	Clinton	RW	(87-88)
Jim Vesey	Columbus	C/RW	(88-89)

Tom Fitzgerald	Melrose	C	(88-89)
Jon Morris	Lowell	C	(88-89)
Darren Turcotte	Boston	C	(88-89)
Peter LaViolette	Norwood	D	(88-89)
Michael McHugh	Bowdoin	LW	(88-89)
Jeremy Roenick	Boston	C	(88-89)
Ric Bennett	Springfield	LW	(89-90)
Scott Gordon	Brockton	G	(89-90)
Bob Corkum	Salisbury	RW	(89-90)

MINNESOTA: (39)

Les Auge	St. Paul	D	(80-81)
Aaron Broten	Roseau	LW	(80-81)
Neal Broten	Roseau	C	(80-81)
Mark Pavelich	Eveleth	C	(81-82)
Peter Hayek	Minneapolis	D	(81-82)
Phil Housley	St. Paul	D	(82-83)
Tim Harrer	Bloomington	RW	(82-83)
Scott Bjugstad	St. Paul	RW	(83-84)
Robert Mason	Int'l Falls	G	(83-84)
Bryan Erickson	Roseau	RW	(83-84)
Keith Hanson	Ada	D	(83-84)
Tom Hirsch	Minneapolis	D	(83-84)
David H. Jensen	Minneapolis	D	(83-84)
Mike Lauen	Edina	RW	(83-84)
John Johannson	Rochester	C	(83-84)
Neil Sheehy	Int'l Falls	D	(83-84)
Jon Casey	Grand Rapids	G	(83-84)
Joel Otto	Elk River	C	(84-85)
Tom Kurvers	Minneapolis	D	(84-85)
Jeff Teal	Edina	RW	(84-85)
Chris Pryor	St. Paul	D	(84-85)
Jim Johnson	New Hope	D	(85-86)
Chris Dahlquist	Fridley	D	(85-86)
Jeff Parker	St. Paul	RW	(86-87)
Sean Toomey	St. Paul	LW	(86-87)
Scott Sandelin	Hibbing	D	(86-87)
Todd Okerlund	Burnsville	RW	(87-88)
Steve Martinson	Minnetonka	LW	(87-88)
Guy Gosselin	Rochester	D	(87-88)
Pat Micheletti	Hibbing	C	(87-88)
Robb Stauber	Duluth	G	(89-90)
Paul Broten	Roseau	C	(89-90)

Tom Chorske	Minneapolis	RW	(89-90)
Cory Millen	Cloquet	C	(89-90)
Mike Peluso	Pengilly	LW/D	(89-90)
Dave Snuggerud	Minnetonka	RW	(89-90)
Shaun Sabol	Minneapolis	D	(89-90)
Tim Bergland	Crookston	C	(89-90)
Randy Skarda	St. Paul	D	(89-90)

MICHIGAN: (34)

Bobby Crawford	Long Island	RW	(80-81)
Tony Curtale	Detroit	D	(80-81)
Don Waddell	Detroit	D	(80-81)
Bill Baker	Grand Rapids	D	(80-81)
John Vanbiesbrouck	Detroit	G	(81-82)
David Feamster	Detroit	D	(81-82)
Paul Skidmore	Smithtown	G	(81-82)
John Blum	Detroit	D	(82-83)
Pat LaFontaine	St. Louis	C	(83-84)
Mark Hamway	Detroit	RW	(84-85)
Kevin Hatcher	Detroit	D	(84-85)
Al Iafrate	Dearborn	D	(84-85)
Ken Leiter	Detroit	D	(84-85)
Wayne Presley	Detroit	RW	(84-85)
Kelly Miller	Lansing	LW	(84-85)
Craig Wolanin	Grosse Pointe	D	(85-86)
Ted Speers	Ann Arbor	RW	(85-86)
Chris Cichocki	Detroit	RW	(85-86)
Larry DePalma	Trenton	LW	(85-86)
Brad Jones	Sterling Heights	LW	(86-87)
Mike Hartman	Detroit	LW	(86-87)
Jimmy Carson	Southfield	C	(86-87)
Mike Donnelly	Detroit	LW	(86-87)
Don McSween	Detroit	D	(87-88)
Shawn Chambers	Sterling Heights	D	(87-88)
Patrick Mayer	Royal Oak	D	(87-88)
Adam Burt	Detroit	D	(88-89)
Shawn Cronin	Flushing	D	(88-89)
Kevin Miller	Lansing	C	(88-89)
Danton Cole	Pontiac	RW	(89-90)
Todd Krygier	Northville	LW	(89-90)
Dennis Smith	Detroit	D	(89-90)
Bobby Reynolds	Flint	LW	(89-90)
Mike Modano	Livonia	C	(89-90)

NEW YORK: (12)

Jeff Brownschidle	Buffalo	D	(81-82)
Jim Pavese	New York	D	(81-82)
Brian Mullen	New York	RW	(82-83)
Greg Britz	Buffalo	RW	(83-84)
Edward Lee	Rochester	RW	(84-85)
Dan McFall	Kenmore	D	(84-85)
Dan Dorion	Astoria	C	(85-86)
Mike Lalor	Buffalo	D	(85-86)
Ted Fauss	Clark Mills	D	(86-87)
Max Middendorf	Syracuse	RW	(86-87)
Mike Walsh	New York	LW	(87-88)
Bob Beers	Cheektowaga	D	(89-90)

ILLINOIS: (12)

Tom Fergus	Chicago	C	(81-82)
Chris Chelios	Chicago	D	(83-84)
Robert Janecyk	Chicago	G	(83-84)
Steve Richmond	Chicago	D	(83-84)
Rick Zombo	Des Plaines	D	(84-85)
Ed Olczyk	Chicago	C	(84-85)
Mark LaVarre	Evanston	RW	(85-86)
Brett Hull	Belleville, Ont.	RW	(86-87)
Jeff Rohlicek	Park Ridge	C	(87-88)
Tony Granato	Downers Grove	LW	(88-89)
Mike Rucinski	Wheeling	C	(88-89)
Peter Lappin	St. Charles	RW	(89-90)

RHODE ISLAND: (7)

Paul Guay	Providence	RW	(83-84)
Chris Terreri	Providence	G	(86-87)
Scott Shaunessy	Newport	D/LW	(86-87)
Mathieu Schneider	NY, NY	D	(87-88)
Clark Donatelli	Providence	LW	(89-90)
David Capuano	Warwick	C	(89-90)
Jack Capuano	Cranston	D	(89-90)

CALIFORNIA: (5)

Lee Norwood	Oakland	D	(80-81)
Roy Sommer	Oakland	C	(80-81)
Rik Wilson	Long Beach	D	(81-82)
Craig Coxe	Chula Vista	C	(84-85)

Tim Friday	Burbank	D	(85-86)

PENNSYLVANIA: (3)

Ray Staszak	Philadelphia	RW	(85-86)
Jay Caufield	Philadelphia	RW	(86-87)
Mike Richter	Philadelphia	G	(89-90)

WISCONSIN: (3)

Craig Ludwig	Rhinelander	D	(82-83)
Marc Behrend	Madison	G	(83-84)
Gary Suter	Madison	C	(85-86)

CONNECTICUT: (2)

Craig Janney	Hartford	C	(87-88)
Brian Leetch	Corpus Christi, TX	D	(87-88)

NEW JERSEY: (2)

Brian Lawton	New Brunswick	LW	(83-84)
Randy Wood	Princeton	LW/C	(86-87)

OHIO: (2)

Dave Ellett	Cleveland	D	(84-85)
Pat Jablonski	Toledo	G	(89-90)

NEW HAMPSHIRE: (2)

Kent Carlson	Concord	D	(83-84)
Hubie McDonough	Manchester	C	(88-89)

VIRGINIA: (2)

James Walsh	Norfolk	D	(81-82)
Eric Weinrich	Roanoke	D	(88-89)

FLORIDA: (1)

Val James	Ocala	LW	(81-82)

NORTH DAKOTA: (1)

Bob Bergloff	Dickinson	D	(82-83)

ARIZONA: (1)

Jim Brown	Phoenix	D	(82-83)

INDIANA: (1)			
Alfie Turcotte	Gary	C	(83-84)
OHIO: (1)			
Moe Mantha	Lakewood	D	(80-81)
OREGON: (1)			
Grant Sasser	Portland	C	(83-84)
OKLAHOMA: (1)			
Dan Woodley	Oklahoma City	RW	(87-88)
MISSOURI (1)			
Paul Ranheim	St. Louis	LW	(88-89)

1. Brett Hull and Kevin Allen, *Brett, The NHL's Hottest Star, His Own Story* (Buffalo: Firefly, published by arrangement with Prentice Hall Canada, Inc., previously published under title *Brett: Shootin' and Smilin'*, 1991), p. 2.
2. Ibid., p. 5.
3. Ibid., p. 28.
4. Ibid., p. 37.

Chapter 12

The Gretzky Trade Plants the Seed

The Arrival of "The Great One" in L.A. Ignites the West and Becomes a Catalyst for Expansion

On August 9, 1988, Edmonton Oilers' owner Peter Pocklington traded Wayne Gretzky, Marty McSorley and Mike Krushelnyski to the Los Angeles Kings for Jimmy Carson, the signing rights to first-round pick Martin Gelinas and $15 million in cash. This landmark deal, which sent hockey's best player to Southern California, sparked unprecedented enthusiasm for the ice game on the West Coast. It also led to NHL and minor league expansion into the West and South that has dramatically changed the sports landscape of the Sun Belt.

The Kings, along with the Bay Area's Oakland Seals, were both part of the NHL's original six-team expansion of 1967-68. The two California entries were the farthest west the NHL had migrated into the warmer regions of the United States.

In their early days the Kings drew only about 7,000 people to many of their games. The Seals, who moved to Cleveland in 1976, drew even lower numbers. In 1971-72 the Kings average home attendance was 8,676. The addition of All-Star goaltender Rogie Vachon later that season and the hiring of Bob Pulford as coach the following year helped turn the club in the right direction. The Kings became more competitive and attendance improved.

Steve Babineau

For the better part of 12 seasons, Marcel Dionne thrilled Forum crowds with his exceptional scoring and playmaking abilities.

With the arrival of Marcel Dionne in 1975 the Kings obtained a scoring machine who went on to be the third-leading scorer (behind Howe and Gretzky) in NHL history. For years sports fans in "La-La Land" had the pleasure of watching the famous "Triple Crown Line," anchored by Dionne, who was flanked by snipers Dave Taylor and Charlie Simmer.

Although Dionne became one of the most prolific NHL scorers he was not a box-office idol and never obtained the recognition he deserved. When Dionne was traded in 1987 Los Angeles was without a hockey superstar. Kings owner Bruce McNall was in search of a marketing ploy to ignite hockey interest in the City of Angels so he practically gave away half the franchise to pluck Gretzky from the dynastic Oilers.

"I kept asking myself, 'What can I do to try and make everyone else pay more attention to the team, to really stand up and take notice?'" McNall said at the time. "There was only one way to do it."[1]

And that was to get The Great One.

L.A. at the time was a huge basketball town with the Lakers having just become the first NBA team since the 1968-69 Boston Celtics to win back-to-back world championships. But now sports fans in Tinseltown had another reason to go to the Fabulous Forum (since renamed Great Western Forum) because the man who had already rewritten a large portion of the NHL record book was on his way to town.

Upon Gretzky's arrival the team donned new uniforms in black, silver and white — fashioned after their neighbors, the highly successful football Raiders. For the Raiders, black and silver symbolized intimidation, and the Kings hoped it would produce the same effect for them.

In Gretzky's first season (1988-89) with the Kings he led his new team to a second place finish in the Smythe Division with 91 points (23 higher than the previous season) and a

Steve Babineau

The Great One's arrival in L.A. in 1988 marked the beginning of a new era in American hockey.

Associated Press

LA's newest star proudly holds up the jersey of his new team.

come-from-behind playoff series victory over his former team, the defending champion Oilers. People began to take notice. Attendance skyrocketed to an average of 14,875 per game, an increase of more than 3,000 from the previous season.

Early in the following season Gretzky gave his new fans an encore when he broke Gordie Howe's long-standing record of 1,850 points by scoring the tying and winning goals in a 5-4 overtime victory at — appropriately enough — Edmonton. Gretzky now stood alone as the NHL's all-time leading scorer.

The spark ignited in Southern California by Gretzky's arrival created an interest in hockey

that increased over the course of two seasons, encouraging further NHL expansion into the Sun Belt.

NHL hockey returned to Northern California in 1991 with the inception of the San Jose Sharks, who played their first two seasons at the Cow Palace in San Francisco before moving into the brand-new San Jose Arena in 1993.

Further expansion occurred over the next two seasons. The Tampa Bay Lightning became Florida's first NHL franchise in 1992-93. A year later the Miami-based Florida Panthers entered the league along with the Disney-owned Mighty Ducks of Anaheim.

Gretzky's career hit a snag at the beginning

of the 1992-93 season when he was sidelined by a back injury. A career- threatening herniated thoracic disc forced him to miss the first 39 games of the season. Soon there were rumors of The Great One retiring.

Gretzky put those rumors to rest by returning to the lineup to score 65 points over the final 45 games of the season. Although it was the first minus-100-point season of his 15-year career, Gretzky most certainly would have broken the century mark had he been healthy for most of the season. His career points-per-game average, however, plummeted from 2.26 to 1.44, leaving many concerned that the 32-year-old ace had seen his best days and was now on the down side of his career.

Despite missing Gretzky for nearly half the season and the fact that forwards Dave Tay-lor, Tomas Sandstrom, and Corey Millen missed a total of 121 games during the season, the Kings still managed a third-place finish in the Smythe Division with a record of 39-35-10.

Under the direction of their 36-year-old rookie coach Barry Melrose, who sported shoulder-length hair that was spiky on top, the club finished fifth overall in offense but fourth worst in defense. They were buoyed by sharp-shooting left winger Luc Robitaille, who lit the lamp a career-high 63 times. Complementing Robitaille's scoring touch up front were forwards Tony Granato, Mike Donnelly, former Oiler Jari Kurri and, when healthy, Taylor, Sandstrom and Millen. Defenseman Rob Blake headed up the Kings' blueline corps and in goal was former Islander

Finnish-born Jari Kurri, another former Oiler, rejoined Gretzky in L.A. in 1991.

Steve Babineau

Left winger Tony Granato of Downers Grove, IL, added 37 goals and 45 assists to a potent Kings attack in 1992-93.

Kelly Hrudey, who since 1988-89 had been the team's number one netminder.

During the playoffs a revitalized Gretzky led the Kings to postseason glory. Their first-round opponent was the Calgary Flames, who finished second in the Smythe Division with 97 points, nine points better than the third place Kings. After the teams battled through four games to a 2-2 series tie, the Kings high-powered offense exploded for 18 goals over the next two games. The results were 9-4 and 9-6 triumphs and a trip to the Divisional finals against the first place Vancouver Canucks.

The high-powered Los Angeles attack, which was triggered by Gretzky and Robitaille, was aided by the speedy "Smurf" line of Millen, Granato and Donnelly. These guns combined to help the Kings win games that were shootouts and not the tight, defensive struggles characteristic of Stanley Cup hockey.

The Kings then went to war with the bigger, tougher Canucks. The Canucks outmuscled them in Game One and skated away with a 5-2 victory. Vancouver was hoping that their physical style would disrupt the fluidity of the finesse Kings.

But L.A.'s run-and-gun offense got back on track in Games Two and Three when the Kings posted 6-3 and 7-4 victories. In Game Two The Great One led the way with a goal and two assists, one of which sprang Kurri free for a shorthanded tally. Back at the Forum for Game Three The Great One made playoff history by scoring two goals, the first of which marked the 100th playoff goal of his career.

Luc Robitaille's 22 post-season points helped Los Angeles earn a trip to the Stanley Cup Finals in 1992-93.

Kings goalie Kelly Hrudey tightens his headband during pre-game warmups.

Down 2-1 in the series, the Canucks rebounded with a solid performance in Game Four, pounding Melrose's sextet by a score of 7-2.

Entering Game Five the Kings found themselves in the same situation they had been in against Calgary in the previous series — even at two games apiece. Once again the Kings prevailed, but this time the playoff heroics came from an improbable source. Former University of Wisconsin star Gary Shuchuk nailed the series-turning goal and the Kings went on to wrap it up in six.

The Kings' success — like that of the basketball Lakers — began to attract the attention of Hollywood celebrities. Dyan Cannon, James Woods, Goldie Hawn and Mick Jagger were now among the faces spotted in the crowd at Kings games. It was the fashionable thing to do.

In the Campbell Conference Finals the Kings faced the Toronto Maple Leafs. The series featured a battle of two superstars: Gretzky versus Toronto's Doug Gilmour. Gilmour, who had 32 goals and 95 assists for a team-record 127 points during the regular season, was playing some of the best hockey of his career. His ferocious checking and fancy playmaking were the main reasons that the scrappy Leafs were able to survive back-to-back seven-game battles against both Detroit and St. Louis in the Norris Division

Steve Babineau

Leafs captain Doug Gilmour was all over the ice — even on it at times — during the 1993 Campbell Conference Finals.

playoffs.

The series opened at Maple Leaf Gardens in Toronto where the Leafs took Game One by a score of 4-1. Gilmour, who was now 20 pounds lighter than his training camp weight of 175, had two goals and two assists. His light frame also wound up on opposite ends of the game's two biggest hits. He put a devastating hip check on Kings defenseman Alexei Zhitnik and was nailed with a bruising hit by Kings enforcer Marty McSorley.

Los Angeles fought back by winning the next two games before dropping Game Four. For the third straight series the Kings were deadlocked at two games apiece. Unlike in their first two series, the Kings came up short in the pivotal fifth game, putting themselves in a hole. It looked as if it would be Toronto and Montreal — the NHL's two most storied franchises — battling it out for Lord Stanley's Cup.

The Kings, however, were not quitters. Back in L.A. Game Six was tied 4-4 at the end of regulation time. Early in the extra session the Leafs took a penalty and the stage was set for Number 99 to come through in the clutch. Gretzky delivered by scoring a power play goal 1:41 into overtime to tie the series. After the game a confident Barry Melrose predicted a seventh-game victory by declaring: "We're going to Montreal."[2]

The Great One followed his Game-Six heroics by notching a hat trick and an assist in a 5-4, Game-Seven victory to help earn his sixth trip to the Stanley Cup Finals and the Kings' first.

The dramatic seven-game series triumph over Toronto was an excellent showcase for hockey and its new fans in the West. The success of the Gretzky-era Kings had reached an all-time high. And with the well-rested Montreal Canadiens waiting on deck, the Kings set their sights on even higher goals.

"It took five years of hard work for me to

win a championship with Edmonton," Gretzky said. "This is my fifth year with the Kings. Maybe it's our time."[3]

The Kings took their momentum into Montreal's hallowed Forum and won the first game 4-1. In Game Two the Kings held a 2-1 lead late in the third period when, with 1:45 remaining, Montreal coach Jacques Demers gambled by calling for a measurement of the curve of the blade of Marty McSorley's stick, risking a delay of game penalty if the stick was ruled legal. It was reported at the time that it was Demers who noticed McSorley's stick, but according to Habs right wing Ed Ronan, it was actually Canadiens captain Guy Carbonneau who spotted the over-curved blade.

"I can remember sitting next to Guy Carbonneau," recalls Ronan. "And I asked him if he knew who made that call. He said that he had noticed it and suggested it to Jacques."

It worked. The curve on McSorley's blade was ruled to be wider than the legal one half inch. The Kings enforcer was sent to the box and the Habs were suddenly in business. "We were desperate and needed a break," added Ronan.

Demers then pulled Patrick Roy to make it a six-on-four advantage. Thirty-two seconds later Canadiens' defenseman Eric Desjardins drove a blast past a screened Hrudey for his second goal of the game. The video tape revealed that John LeClair was in the crease but referee Kerry Fraser refused to call it. For the Habs the goal broke an 0-32 streak on the power play extending back to the Conference Finals against the New York Islanders.

Less than a minute into the overtime Desjardins misfired on a slapper from just inside the right circle. Teammate Benoit Brunet gathered the loose puck from behind the net and fed a pass out to Desjardins who had circled back to the same spot. Desjardins fired the puck through Hrudey's legs to complete

Steve Babineau

When push came to shove, it was Gretzky who delivered the knockout punch in Games Six and Seven against Toronto.

the hat trick and tie the series at a game apiece. The Kings — thanks to their own negligence — had blown a golden opportunity to go up 2-0 in the series and were heading back to Tinseltown tied at a game apiece.

June 5, 1993 marked the date of the first-ever Stanley Cup Finals game played in California. As predicted, a Lakeresque celeb-fest accompanied the sellout crowd. Spotted in the elite seats were Goldie Hawn, John Candy, Michelle Pfeiffer, Michael Eisner and none other than the former president Ronald Reagan and his wife, Nancy.

They witnessed the Canadiens jump to a 3-0 lead before the Kings came fighting back to tie the score after two periods. Another opportunity to gain the upper hand in the series went by the boards late in the third period when Robitaille missed the net on a clean

Steve Babineau

After protecting LA's offensive weapons while amassing a league-leading 399 penalty minutes in 1992-93, McSorley's illegal stick in Game Two of the Finals could very well have cost the Kings their first Stanley Cup.

breakaway. Still tied at three, the game went into overtime.

Early in the extra session the opportunistic Canadiens went right for the jugular. At 0:34 left wing John LeClair, on his third attempt, lifted a rebound into the net to give Montreal another overtime victory — its ninth straight in the post-season.

When regulation time of Game Four expired with the score tied at two, it was a foregone conclusion which team would prevail. And sure enough, Mr. Sudden Death himself, LeClair, came through again. The 3-2 victory made it 10-straight in extended play for the torrid Habs — a record that may never be broken.

Back in Montreal the Canadiens wrapped up the series with a 4-1, Game-Five victory.

After dropping the series opener, the Canadiens had rebounded to win four straight games and earn their NHL-record 24th Stanley Cup. Apart from the momentum-turning stick incident, the keys to the Kings' demise were the neutralization of the Gretzky line by Montreal's checking line of Carbonneau, Brunet and Ronan as well as the clutch goaltending of Conn Smythe Trophy winner Patrick Roy.

Gretzky had arrived in California five years earlier with two goals. The first was to help sell hockey in California. The second was to bring the area its first Stanley Cup. Although he fell short of the latter, he more than fulfilled the first and most important one: his box-office appeal gave a struggling franchise a shot in the arm by consistently packing the Forum; his performance helped his team spark fan interest in a warm-climate market that became a catalyst for further Sun Belt expansion; and he became a role model who inspired youngsters to participate in both ice and roller hockey.

"When I went there," recalled Gretzky, "it was a dream of mine to fill the rink, to make hockey popular and to win a championship. We came close to doing all of that."[4]

Gretzky knew his mission to promote hockey in The Golden State was a success when he saw a sign posted next to a tennis court near his Thousand Oaks home that read: "No hockey allowed here."[5]

In 1987-88 there were 394 ice hockey teams in California registered with USA Hockey. By 1994-95 the count had risen to 931 and by 1996-97 the number had grown to 1,170. Due to its convenience and a lack of ice rinks there are even more kids playing street and roller hockey in California these days. Mighty Ducks forward Teemu Selanne has noticed the growth of hockey in Southern California since his arrival in early 1996.

"In-line hockey is getting bigger and there

are a lot of young kids who want to play street hockey and more and more kids are coming to play ice hockey too," says Selanne. "It's a really good hobby for young kids — to keep those kids out of the streets."

Tampa Bay Lightning general manager Phil Esposito compares his glory days with the Big, Bad Bruins with what happened in L.A. during the Gretzky era:

"I liken what we did in Boston in the late '60s-early '70s to what Gretzky has done for the L.A. area," declares Esposito. "He's done more for hockey in general all over the world than any other player. You go to L.A. and there are people playing street hockey all over the place. You look at those rappers — they're wearing LA Kings jackets and sweaters."

What The Great One began in the southwestern United States is continuing to catch on with the younger set. In truth, we've only seen the tip of the iceberg.

1. *1997 NHL All-Star Game* magazine (New York: NHL Publishing, 1997), article titled "The NHL's Golden Age," by Rick Sadowski, p. 13.
2. *Sports Illustrated*, June 7, 1993 issue, articled titled "King of the Kings," by Jon Scher, p. 32.
3. Ibid., p. 33.
4. Sadowski, p. 14.
5. Ibid., p. 11.

Chapter 13

The Rangers Break the Jinx

*The New York Rangers Finally Break the 54-Year Hex,
Showcasing the First Playoff MVP from the U.S.*

Bryan Hextall's overtime goal in Game Six of the 1940 Stanley Cup Finals gave the New York Rangers their third championship in the franchise's 15-year existence. The Blueshirts' Cup-triumph had broken a seven-year drought which began the year after their 1933 Cup.

But what nobody would have then believed — or even imagined — was that by the spring of 1994 a 54-year drought would be a monkey on the back for many New York hockey fans. Even more amazing is the fact that from 1942 to 1967 there were only six

Steve Babineau

The "Messiah," Mark Messier, was brought to The Big Apple to exorcise the "curse."

teams vying for the coveted hardware.

The 1993-94 New York Rangers were a powerhouse during the regular season. Led by their so-called "Messiah" — captain Mark Messier — who descended from the Edmonton dynasty, the Broadway Blues dominated the entire league.

Adam Graves led the team in scoring with 52 goals. Defenseman Sergei Zubov was team leader in assists with 77 and scoring with 89 points. Goalie Mike Richter won 42 games, had five shutouts and posted a 2.57 goals-against-average. Jeff Beukeboom, who provided muscle and played tough, steady defense, accumulated a team-leading 170 penalty minutes.

On special teams the Rangers were more than adequate. Graves and Steve Larmer each had four shorthanded tallies playing on a penalty-killing unit that had an 84.6-percent success rate. The power play, where Graves scored 20 more of his goals, converted at a very impressive 23 percent.

Providing sparkling play at both ends of the ice for the New Yorkers was their brilliant young defenseman — Connecticut-raised Brian Leetch. Leetch, who had missed a large part of the 1992-93 campaign due to an ankle injury, appeared in all 84 games for the Blueshirts. The speedy blueliner potted 23 goals and assisted on 56 others while rushing the puck from end to end and hurrying back to play steady defense. He also manned the left point on the Rangers' potent power play.

Also contributing to the team's success were some of the club's new acquisitions. Since the Rangers could not keep both Richter and John Vanbiesbrouck, general manager Neil Smith dealt "Beezer" (who was later claimed by Florida in the expansion draft) to Vancouver for defenseman Doug Lidster. For Richter's backup, Smith acquired the rights to former Islander Glenn Healy from Tampa Bay. Healy, a product of Western Michigan University, appeared in 29 games for his new team, posting a 3.03 goals-against average.

Hard-nosed head coach Mike Keenan called for the recruitment of Steve Larmer, a close-checking, offensively-talented two-way player whom he coached in Chicago. Smith obliged and sent James Patrick and Darren Turcotte to the Hawks for Larmer, Nick Kypreos and Barry Richter and a sixth-round choice in the 1994 Entry Draft.

Five more players were acquired just prior to the trading deadline. In five separate deals the Rangers picked up Stephane Matteau and Brian Noonan as well as former Oilers Glenn Anderson and Craig MacTavish at the expense of losing some offensive firepower in former Boston University star Tony Amonte and vet-

Steve Babineau

Boston native Brian Noonan gave the Blueshirts size and added scoring touch up front.

and Graves were named to the Second Team.

The game was typically high-scoring. Each of the four Ranger participants helped the Eastern Conference squad defeat the stars from the West by a score of 9-8. Messier had a goal and an assist and Richter, for his sensational second-period performance, was named the Game's Most Valuable Player.

The 52 wins and 112 points amassed during the regular season by the Rangers were both franchise records. The question remained, however, as to whether this would translate to playoff success. Did they have the right formula to exorcise the 54-year hex? After all, in 1991-92 the Blueshirts finished first overall only to be upended by the defending and eventual Cup champion Pittsburgh Penguins in the second round.

The first-round opponent would be the New York Islanders. The Rangers wasted no time in sending a message to the rest of the league that these playoffs would be different from years past. They posted back-to-back 6-0 shutouts at the Garden to take a 2-0 series lead. Messier's breakaway goal in Game Four sealed a 5-2 victory and a series sweep of the team that not only invaded their territory 22 years ago but then proceeded to steal away a large chunk of the New York hockey spotlight during the early 1980s by winning four consecutive Stanley Cups.

After sending their Long Island rivals to the golf links, the Rangers faced another nemesis — the Washington Capitals. The Caps, who had eliminated the Rangers from postseason play in both 1989-90 and 1990-91, were coming off a first-round conquest of the high-powered Pittsburgh Penguins. It took the Blueshirts only five games to dispose of the overmatched Capitals. This time it was Leetch who delivered the knockout punch by scoring the series-clinching goal with just under three and a half minutes remaining in Game Five.

eran wing Mike Gartner.

This added up to an impressive record of 52 wins, 24 losses and eight ties, good enough to earn the New Yorkers first place in the Atlantic Division and their second Presidents Trophy in three years. The key to the Rangers' division triumph was sweeping the season series from their cross-Hudson rivals, the second place New Jersey Devils, who finished only six points back.

Apart from the Rangers' success, the highlight of hockey's regular season in Manhattan was the 1994 NHL All-Star Game held at Madison Square Garden in February. The Blueshirts were well represented. Richter and Messier were chosen as starters while Leetch

In the Conference Finals the New Yorkers had to look no farther than across the Hudson River. The up-and-coming New Jersey Devils, who had outlasted Buffalo in seven games and Boston in six, were poised to spoil the Cup expectations that were brewing on Manhattan.

In Game One the Rangers held a one-goal lead late in the third when New Jersey coach Jacques Lemaire pulled goalie Martin Brodeur for an extra attacker. With 43 ticks remaining Claude Lemieux banged home a loose puck to tie it up and force overtime. The teams battled relentlessly through more than 35 minutes of sudden-death when Devils sniper Stephane Richer took a pass from Bobby Carpenter and streaked down the left side. Richer cut around Graves and then avoided Richter's pokecheck while flipping the puck over him and into the cage.

The game was a preview of how the series was going to go — a see-saw dogfight to the finish.

Game Two was another hard-fought contest that saw the Rangers grab an early 1-0 lead and cling to it into the third period. Eventually the New Yorkers broke it open with three scores to come away with 4-0 shutout that evened series at a game apiece.

The series shifted to New Jersey's Brendan Byrne Arena (since renamed Continental Airlines Arena) for Game Three. It was another classic. For the second time in the series the teams battled into a second overtime. Finally, at 6:13 of the second extra session, Stephane Matteau scored an unassisted goal and the Broadway Blueshirts had a 2-1 series lead.

With the favored Rangers seemingly in control of the series, the Devils surprised by bouncing back with 3-1 and 4-1 victories to regain the upper hand. The upstarts from New Jersey now had a chance to wrap up the series on home ice in Game Six. The Rangers, on the other hand, suddenly found themselves up against it; it was do or die and they needed a savior. That's when the Messiah came to the fore.

Realizing his team was low in confidence and in need of a morale boost, Messier allegedly told a reporter that the Rangers would go into the Meadowlands and even the series with a Game Six victory. The headline on the cover of the May 25 edition of the *New York Post* read: "We'll Win Tonight." The Devils got out to a 2-0 lead but, thanks to Richter, could not put the Rangers away. Late in the second period Messier set up Alexei Kovalev for his team's first score and the Blueshirts went to the dressing room down by only one goal.

In the third period Messier tied the game at 2:48, taking a pass from Kovalev deep on the right side and sliding a backhander past Martin Brodeur. At 12:12 Messier knocked in a rebound and the Rangers led 3-2. Late in the period Rangers left winger Glenn Anderson took a slashing penalty and Lemaire pulled Brodeur for an extra attacker. The Rangers suddenly found themselves two men short trying to protect a one-goal lead. But once again Messier saved the day by hitting the empty net from 160 feet out to complete a natural hat trick and seal the victory. There would be a seventh game to be played on Madison Square Garden ice.

From the outset Game Seven was a goaltender's duel between Richter and Brodeur. The game remained scoreless until midway through the second period when Brian Leetch scored to give the Rangers the all-important first goal of the game. The lead held until the game's waning moments when Devils left wing Valeri Zelepukin poked home a loose puck with 7.7 seconds remaining to force another sudden-death overtime.

Like Games One and Three, the teams battled through a scoreless overtime period. Just over four minutes into the second extra session, Matteau had the puck to the left of the cage, circled the net and from a tough angle flipped a backhander that trickled past Brodeur and into the net. The Rangers were in the Stanley Cup Finals for the first time since 1979. The surprising Vancouver Canucks, who were led by the "Russian Rocket" (their young superstar Pavel Bure), would provide the opposition.

Although the Neilsen ratings of the Rangers-Devils series averaged only about 1.7 per game, the excitement generated by the games was rapidly catching the attention of sports fans throughout the United States. "The games did very well," said Vic Morren, coordinator of production and research for ESPN's National Hockey Night and Fire On Ice. "Interest was starting to peak because New York had the curse and the 54 years."

Hockey mavens wondered: was there more excitement to come or would the finals be anticlimactic?

In Game One the playoff drama picked up where it had left off in Game Seven against the Devils. After 60 minutes of hard fought hockey the score was tied at two. The Garden crowd braced itself for yet another sudden-death overtime. Canucks center Greg Adams scored at 19:26 of the extra frame to win it. The star of the game was Vancouver goalie Kirk McLean, who turned aside 52 Ranger shots in leading his team to victory.

Once again trailing in a series, the Rangers proceeded to live up to their role as favorites by winning the next three games. After winning the all-important second game at home by a score of 3-1, the Blueshirts went into Vancouver's Pacific Coliseum and took both Games Three and Four by scores of 5-1 and 4-2, respectively. Leetch led the way in Vancouver with two goals in Game Three and a goal and three assists in Game Four. With a three-games-to-one series lead the New Yorkers now stood in the driver's seat — just one win away from their ultimate goal.

When the teams arrived back in the Big Apple for Game Five, New York was primed to celebrate the Rangers' first Cup in more than half a century. The champagne was on ice, the tickertape was ready to fly, the city was ready to rumble and the Garden was surrounded by hordes of police and security.

But the Canucks weren't ready to succumb. McLean came out and stopped everything that was thrown his way and by early in the third period the Canucks had built a 3-0 lead. It looked as if the Blueshirts would have to wait until Game Six at Vancouver for another chance to clinch when suddenly they came alive and rallied for three unanswered goals

Steve Babineau

"The Russian Rocket," Pavel Bure, led Vancouver to a seven-game standoff with Messier and company.

Mike Keenan's one year in Manhattan was a productive one.

Steve Babineau

to tie the score. The Garden was rockin' and a Ranger victory seemed imminent. But Pat Quinn's troops didn't buckle. Instead, they responded with a three-goal flurry of their own to spoil the Garden party and skate away with a 6-3 win.

With the momentum back on their side the Canucks returned to the Pacific Coliseum and treated their fans to a 4-1, Game-Six triumph. The victory set up a winner-take-all seventh game back in Manhattan.

June 14, 1994, marked the first time since 1987 that a seventh-game showdown had occurred in a Stanley Cup Finals. The Rangers broke the ice at 11:02 of the first period when Sergei Zubov fed a beautiful pass across to Leetch who was open at the left circle. Leetch fired a shot that found the back of the cage and the New Yorkers had drawn first blood. Adam Graves added a power-play goal at 14:45 and the Broadway Blues were off and running with a two-goal lead after one period.

Vancouver countered early in the second frame when Trevor Linden's shorthanded goal cut the Ranger lead in half. Mark Messier's power play tally at 13:29 gave the Blueshirts another two-goal advantage going into the second intermission.

Just over four minutes into the third period Rangers left wing Esa Tikkanen went off for hooking and 24 seconds later Linden scored his second goal of the game to cut the Ranger lead to one. The heart of every Rangers fan skipped a beat when, with six minutes left, Vancouver forward Nathan Lafayette clanged one off the goal post behind Richter. The Canucks kept coming but Richter kept them off the board. With 1.6 seconds left and McLean pulled for an extra attacker, Keenan had Craig MacTavish take a faceoff to Richter's right. The helmetless veteran won the draw and flipped the puck into the corner as time expired. Long years of Cup drought had finally come to an end.

On Friday the new champs were honored with a ticker-tape parade up Broadway. Along the parade route the team was wildly applauded by a continuous mass of fans sporting shirts and waving pennants that read "Rangers, Stanley Cup Champions," and "Now I Can Die in Peace." It was the fulfillment of a goal and a dream. Keenan had showed his players videotapes of tickertape parades during the preseason. Now Gotham's newest

Steve Babineau

Left: Philly native Mike Richter was clutch between the pipes. *Above:* The new champs celebrate, relieving Rangers fans from 54 years of frustration.

heroes got to live what they had watched and hoped would happen to them.

The Rangers' Stanley Cup-winning game produced the biggest television audience to watch a hockey game in American history. It received a rating of 5.2 nationally on ESPN and 1.7 on MSG in the New York market for a combined 6.9. It was the best rating ever for an NHL event, surpassing the 5.0 from Game Seven between Philadelphia and Edmonton in 1987.

"Part of the thing that made Game Seven against Vancouver so great was the intrigue. This curse was actually taking on some sort of life form to it," explained Morren. "And I think having the New York team in there certainly helped the ratings along the line."

While it was the excitement of the games and the intrigue of the curse that had attracted new followers, it was the tremendous job that ESPN did covering the games that helped to keep them watching. "We worked hard exposing the quote-unquote 'second tier' of stars in the NHL," claimed Morren. "The Jeremy Roenicks, the Mike Modanos — Pavel Bure was still on his way up the ladder in 1994. We were able to create an identity for these guys that would make people want to tune in. And I think we did that very well."

Apart from the breaking of the curse and the unprecedented ratings of the final game, the Rangers' dramatic playoff run also marked a defining moment in the history of United States hockey. When Brian Leetch was awarded the Conn Smythe Trophy as the most valuable player of the playoffs, he became the first American to win the prize in the award's 30-year history. Leetch was the league's leading scorer during the postseason with 11 goals and 23 assists in 23 games. He also led all scorers in the final series with five goals and six assists during the seven games.

As the playoffs were winding down and the Rangers were heading to their dramatic finish, rumors were heard that Mike Keenan wanted out of New York to accept another coaching job. First the Detroit Red Wings and later the St. Louis Blues were the interested teams. After a contractual dispute between the Rangers and Keenan that had to be mediated by NHL commissioner Gary Bettman, the cantankerous coach left a month later to join the Blues. Keenan, who was signed on to coach the Rangers in April of 1993, had coached two other teams to the Stanley Cup Finals. He came to the Big Apple with a .590 winning percentage but no championship ring. Now that he had his ring he wanted out.

The melodrama that culminated with the Rangers' Stanley Cup victory actually had several equally dramatic sequels. One of them was a thunderous victory march up Manhattan's Canyon of Champions that to this day is considered one of the most tumultuous sports celebrations in the Big Apple's history.

This was followed by the denouement of the Keenan-Neil Smith brouhaha. In the end both were winners. Smith was rid of his nemesis while Keenan signed a fat-cat contract to manage and coach the St. Louis Blues.

But the biggest winners were the long-suffering Rangers fans who finally had their thirst for a championship quenched by the Stanley Cup champagne.

Steve Babineau

Brian Leetch, Gotham's newest hero and the pride of Avon Old Farms (CT), at press conference after Game Seven.

Chapter 14

The Devils — America's Team

The 1995 Stanley Cup Champions Had More U.S. Players Than Any Previous Cup Winner

In 1974 the National Hockey League continued its expansion into the United States by adding two new franchises — the Washington Capitals and the Kansas City Scouts. Two years later the Scouts moved to Denver and became the Colorado Rockies. The Rockies remained in Denver until May 1982 when they were purchased by three men who moved them to New Jersey.

The buyers were New Jersey native and former Houston Astros owner Dr. John J. McMullen; John C. Whitehead, now chairman of AEA Investors, Inc.; and former New

Jersey governor Brendan T. Byrne. Upon purchasing the club the new owners received NHL approval to shift the franchise to its new home — Byrne Arena at the Meadowlands Sports Complex in East Rutherford, New Jersey.

In search of a new nickname the new owners decided to hold a contest. The winning entry was Devils.

The New Jersey Devils failed to make the playoffs their first five seasons. But with the arrival of Lou Lamoriello, whom Dr. McMullen hired as club president and general manager after Bob Butera resigned in April of 1987, the Devils fortunes turned around quickly.

Over a period of 20 years Lamoriello had built a highly successful athletic program at Providence College. He coached the Friars for 15 years beginning in 1968 and in 1982 became the school's athletic director. Lamoriello then went on to become the driving force behind the formation of Hockey East.

"In Lou Lamoriello," said Dr.McMullen, "the Devils have a hockey man who has earned great respect for his accomplishments at and away from the rink and for both his hockey and business acumen. I look forward to working with Lou as we take the Devils franchise through the next steps of our development — the playoffs and the Stanley Cup."[1]

The first of those two steps was taken in Lamoriello's first season with the organization. Midway through the 1987-88 campaign Lamoriello fired head coach Doug Carpenter and replaced him with former NHL defenseman and Buffalo Sabres coach Jim Schoenfeld.

Schoenfeld immediately instilled a positive attitude in his new club and with its newfound confidence the team began to improve over the second half of the season. They finished with a record of 38-36-6 for 82 points, good for fourth place in the Patrick Division, knocking out the Rangers on the final night of the season. It was the franchise's first over-.500 season and first post-season berth. And it wasn't accomplished until John MacLean beat Chicago goalie Darren Pang in overtime to put New Jersey in and New York out.

The Devils were a big surprise in the 1988 playoffs. Disposing of the Islanders and the Capitals along the way, they made it all the way to the Wales Conference Finals before bowing to Boston in seven games.

The Boston series will always be remembered for the remarkably hostile exchange between Schoenfeld and referee Don Koharski after the third game was atrociously officiated by Koharski. Schoenfeld confronted the official, made a derogatory remark about his weight and told him to "have another doughnut." For his comments the fiery coach was suspended, prompting the Devils to go to court and obtain a restraining order prior to Game Four. At that point the officiating crew walked out and amateur officials were summoned as replacements.

The Devils missed the playoffs the following season but rebounded in 1989-90 with their highest finish to date — second in the Patrick Division. From that point on qualifying for the playoffs became a habit they carried into the '90s.

Another franchise-high came in 1993-94 when the club finished the season with a 47-25-12 record for 106 points. The unprecedented numbers placed them second in the Atlantic Division and gave them third seed in the Eastern Conference playoff rankings. A key to their success was the excellent goaltending tandem of Chris Terreri and Calder Trophy recipient Martin Brodeur. The duo combined to allow the second-fewest goals in the league, earning them runners-up to Buffalo's Dominik Hasek and Grant Fuhr for the Jennings Trophy.

In the first round of the playoffs New Jersey outlasted the Buffalo Sabres in seven games, despite an exhausting 1-0 quadruple overtime loss in Game Six. In the conference semifinals the Devs drew the fourth-seeded Boston Bruins. The B's, who had just eliminated Montreal, skated into Byrne Arena and took the first two games of the series. The Devils then traveled to Boston facing a must-win situation. Lemaire switched goalies and started Chris Terreri between the pipes in Games Three and Four. It was at that point that the team graduated to another level of playoff performance. Terreri stoned the Bruins in both games while his teammates played poised, championship-calibre hockey. The result was two clutch victories that were the turning point in a series that saw the Devils come back to win four straight games.

In the conference finals the Devs faced the Rangers, who were favored to finally break their 54-year Stanley Cup drought. Lemaire's troops gave their neighbors from Manhattan all they could handle by taking them to double overtime of Game Seven before losing on a Stephane Matteau wrap-around. It was a heartbreaking loss but the team grew from it. The experience gained in the Boston series showed itself against the Broadway Blueshirts and now the Devils had even more of it to draw from. "Getting that far gave us the experience and the taste," said Devils right wing Tom Chorske, "but you never know until the next year exactly what it's going to mean to you."

It was a considerable accomplishment for the young Devils to win two playoff series and nearly pull an upset over the Rangers, whose payroll was double that of New Jersey.

The 1994-95 season was stunted by a lockout which nearly caused the NHL to forego the entire season. The dispute was finally settled in January. In order to salvage the season an agreement was made to play a 48-game schedule where each team would play only the other teams in its conference.

The shortened season brought a return of the defensive-style play of the 1960s. The league's goals-per-game average dropped considerably; scores were lower and so were sniper's stats. When the abridged campaign was completed, the Devils had crossed the finish line with a record of 22-18-8, which placed them second in the Atlantic Division and fifth in the Eastern Conference.

What was most unique about this edition of the Red and Black was the makeup of the team's roster. Since his arrival in 1987, Lamoriello continued to acquire — by draft, trade or free agency — American-born-and-raised players. Of the 25 players listed on the 1994-95 roster, 12 came from the United States and of the nine Canadians, two attended U.S. colleges.

In the conference quarterfinals the Devils met the Boston Bruins who, for the second year in a row, finished as fourth seed in the Eastern Conference.

Game One was played in Boston on the unusually late date of May 7th. The Devils, behind the solid netminding of Brodeur and some opportunistic scoring, routed the Bruins by a score of 5-0. Lemaire's sextet followed the Game One blowout with a 3-0 victory in Game Two.

Apart from Brodeur, the back-to-back shutouts at Boston Garden were attributable to two factors. One was Claude Lemieux's shadowing and nagging of Boston sniper Cam Neely who was held to only two goals in the series. According to Devils right wing Bill Guerin, Lemieux teased Neely about his role in the movie *Dumb and Dumber*. "He kept asking Neely which one he was, dumb or dumber."[2] The other reason for Boston's anemic output was a defensive style employed by head coach Jacques Lemaire which came to be known as the "trap." It was reminiscent of the style used by Montreal Canadiens teams of the past, of

1994-95 ROSTER

Americans:

	Pos	Born	College or Other
Neil Broten	C	Roseau, MN	Minnesota
Bobby Carpenter	C/LW	Beverly, MA	St. John's Prep
Shawn Chambers	D	Sterling Hts, MI	Alaska-Fairbanks
Tom Chorske	RW	Minneapolis, MN	Minnesota
Danton Cole	C/RW	Pontiac, MI	Michigan State
Kevin Dean	D	Madison, WI	New Hampshire
Jim Dowd	C/RW	Brick, NJ	Lake Sup. St.
Bill Guerin	C/RW	Wilbraham, MA	Boston College
Mike Peluso	LW/D	Pengilly, MN	Alaska-Anchorage
Chris McAlpine	D	Roseville, MN	Minnesota
Brian Rolston	C	Flint, MI	Lake Sup. St.
Chris Terreri	G	Providence, RI	Providence

Canadians:

Martin Brodeur	G	Montreal, Que.	St-Hyacinthe
Ken Daneyko	D	Windsor, Ont.	Seattle
Bruce Driver	D	Toronto, Ont.	Wisconsin
Claude Lemieux	RW	Buckingham, Que.	Trois-Rivieres
John MacLean	RW	Oshawa, Ont.	Oshawa
Randy McKay	RW	Montreal, Que.	Michigan Tech
Scott Niedermayer	D	Edmonton, Alta	Kamloops
Scott Stevens	D	Kitchener, Ont.	Kitchener
Stephane Richer	RW	Ripon, Que.	Chicoutimi

Europeans:

Bobby Holik	LW	Jihlava, Czech.	Dukla Jihlava
Tommy Albelin	D	Stockholm, Sweden	Djurgarden
Valeri Zelepukin	LW	Voskresensk, USSR	Khimik
Sergei Brylin	C	Moscow, USSR	Russian Pen's

which Lemaire and his assistant Larry Robinson were members. It worked quite effectively in shutting down the Bruins attack — especially on the smaller ice surface at Boston Garden.

Ahead in the series by two games, the Devils returned to the Meadowlands to host Games Three and Four. With more room to roam at Byrne Arena, the Bruins were able to generate some offense in Game Three and come through with a much-needed 3-2 victory to get back in the series. But as fate would have it, Boston's bid to tie the series was spoiled by Randy McKay's overtime goal in Game Four.

With the Devils now holding a commanding three-games-to-one lead, the series shifted back to Beantown for what turned out to be the last playoff game ever played at venerable Boston Garden. New Jersey held a 3-1 lead late in the third period when, with about five minutes left, Bruins playmaker Adam Oates scored to cut the Devils' lead to one. Stirred with emotion, the Boston fans suddenly came alive. They didn't want the series to end. But Brodeur held the fort and the Devils wrapped up the series in five games.

The defensive system that had held the Bruins to one-goal-per-game was put to an even bigger test in the conference semifinals when Lemaire's skaters took on the high-powered Pittsburgh Penguins.

Game One was tied 2-2 late in the third period when Pittsburgh's Luc Robitaille scored to give the Pens an early series lead.

But then the Devils took control of the series. Their stingy trap stifled the high-powered Pittsburgh attack and as they did in the Boston series, New Jersey's forwards kept patient and picked their spots. Thanks to Claude Lemieux, Jagr was held to only two goals over the last four games of the series.

To complement his highly-effective defensive strategy, Lemaire rotated four lines. The patient wait-and-snipe strategy of the New Jersey forwards proved even more effective with fresh legs coming off the bench. The result was four straight wins by a combined score of 15-5.

Having displayed all the makings of a championship team the Devils prepared themselves to face an even tougher opponent in the conference finals — the Philadelphia Flyers, led by Eric Lindros and the "Legion of Doom" line.

The Devils skated onto Spectrum ice and took complete control of Game One, beating the Flyers by a score of 4-1. New Jersey's suffocating defense contained Philly's big guns while the offense was paced by former Boston College star Bill Guerin, who scored twice.

For Lemieux it was Eric Lindros' turn to be nagged and harassed. "On the ice," said Devils' enforcer Mike Peluso, "Claude's a consistent pain in the ass."[3] From Neely to Jagr to Lindros, Lemieux was nullifying some of the game's best snipers while scoring clutch goals in big games.

In Game Two the winning goal came as a result of what will never show up on a score sheet: Lemieux held Flyers defenseman Peter Svoboda's stick, allowing Randy McKay to break to the net and score. The Devils rolled to a 5-2 triumph.

Heading back to Jersey with a two-game sweep under their belts, the Devils were in the driver's seat. When Game Three went into overtime they had a chance to run away with the series but an Eric Lindros goal gave Philly a 3-2 win and new life. Breathing easier, the Flyers also won Game Four to even the series at two.

Having blown an opportunity to take command of the series by winning at least one of the two home games, the Devils looked for a positive to take into Philly for Game Five. "We were dwelling on the fact that we won the first two games there," recalls Chorske. "We were trying to get some confidence from that. And also having the experience from the year past. We were able to draw off that too. We never got too excited or too down. We had that experience to fall back on and I think we used that to our advantage."

Game Five — like the series — was tied 2-2 late in the third period. With under a minute to play, Claude Lemieux broke down the right side and fired a rocket that beat Philly goalie Ron Hextall to the upper-far side. The game-winning goal was probably the key play of the Devils playoff run. This time they would not be denied a trip to the Finals. Two days later they clinched the series back at Byrne Arena with a 4-2 win. Their final-round opponents would be Scotty Bowman's powerhouse Detroit Red Wings, who tore apart Dallas, San Jose and Chicago en route to the big dance.

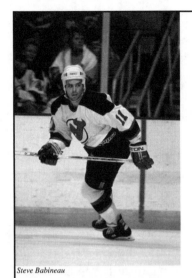

Steve Babineau

The first Jersey native to play his home games at East Rutherford, Jim Dowd did the Garden State proud by notching the game-winner in Game Two of the finals.

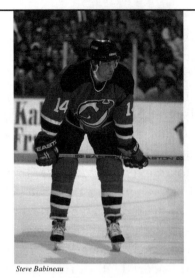

Steve Babineau

Lake Superior State grad Brian Rolston earned a championship ring his rookie season.

Steve Babineau

Minneapolis native Tom Chorske's ten goals during the lockout-shortened regular season gave the Devils some extra scoring punch.

Playing in the Stanley Cup Finals at Detroit's Joe Louis Arena in the spring of 1995 fit perfectly into a ten-year pattern Chris Terreri's career had followed. In 1975 Chris had been a member of a squirt team that competed at the national championships in Melvindale, Michigan (just outside of Detroit) and in the spring of 1985 Chris' Providence College team had played in the NCAA championship game at Joe Louis.

Game One was played on June 17, a new record for the latest date a Stanley Cup game had ever been played. The trap immediately went to work, limiting the scoring chances of the Red Wings' juggernaut offense. The game was scoreless until midway through the second period when, with Detroit's Kris Draper in the penalty box for roughing, Richer scored from Albelin and Broten. Less than two minutes later Bobby Holik was charged with highsticking, giving the Wings their first man-advantage. Detroit's Dino Ciccarelli returned the favor with a power-play tally to tie the score at one-apiece.

The game remained deadlocked into the third period when at 3:17 Lemieux notched what proved to be the game's deciding goal. It was Claude's third game-winner of the playoffs and 14th of his career in the postseason. The Devils, who outshot the Red Wings 28-17, improved their road record in the playoffs to 9-1, setting a new NHL record for most road wins by one team in the playoffs.

Like the first game, Game Two was a scoreless standoff into the second period but this time it was Detroit who drew first blood. Nearly seven minutes into the second period Brodeur was called for a rare delay of game penalty. Just 21 seconds later the Wings capitalized when Slava Kozlov converted to give Detroit their first lead of the series. The Devils answered back at 9:40 when MacLean scored on passes from Niedermayer and Broten.

Steve Babineau

A mid-season trade added more size to the Jersey blue line when Michigan native Shawn Chambers came over from Tampa Bay.

Steve Babineau

The Devils' sturdy defense corps was led by one of the NHL's best, rugged veteran Scott Stevens.

Steve Babineau

Since the Devils' second season, right wing John MacLean has consistently lit the lamp while remaining virtually injury-free.

Early in the third Detroit climbed back on top with a goal by Sergei Fedorov but the Devils tied it up again when Jim Dowd set up Niedermayer at 9:47. The score remained knotted at two until the 18:36 mark when Dowd, the first New Jersey-born player to play for the Devils, potted the game-winner. Bowman pulled Mike Vernon for an extra skater but Richer sealed it with an empty-netter for a 4-2 final. With the win, the Devils extended their playoff record for road victories to ten and tied another postseason record by winning their seventh straight road game. They left The Motor City with a commanding two-games-to-none lead and were headed back to New Jersey brimming with confidence.

Back home the Devils found themselves in the same position they had been in against Philadelphia — up 2-0 in the series with the next two games on home ice. This time, however, they weren't about to let their series lead slip away.

Defenseman Bruce Driver got it rolling for the Devs in Game Three with a power-play goal midway through the first period. Later in the frame Lemieux scored from Carpenter and Stevens and the Devils, who outshot the Red Wings 15-7 over the first 20 minutes, went to the dressing room with a 2-0 lead.

Seven minutes into the second period Neal Broten, who was acquired late in the season from Dallas, scored what turned out to be the game-winning goal. New Jersey then broke it open with scores by McKay and Holik. A couple of Detroit power-play goals by Fedorov and Yzerman late in the third closed out the scoring. With the dominating 5-2 victory the Devils stood just one win away from a drink out of Lord Stanley's Cup.

The word complacency was not in the Devils vocabulary. Just 68 seconds into Game Four, Broten connected on a lamp-lighter from Richer and Chorske. The Wings, who weren't about to roll over and die, fought back to take

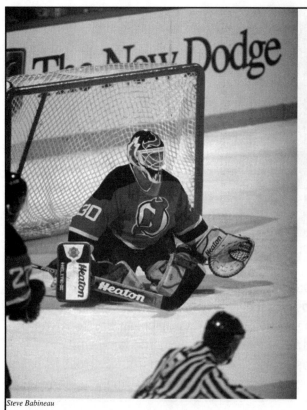

Steve Babineau

When enemy attackers managed to permeate New Jersey's trap, their shots were usually turned aside by Martin Brodeur.

Steve Babineau

Claude Lemieux's Conn Smythe Trophy was earned at both ends of the ice, as he combined clutch goal-scoring with the fine art of distracting the opposition.

a 2-1 lead on goals by Fedorov and Coffey. Nearing the end of what was an evenly-played first period, Driver set up Michigan native Shawn Chambers and the teams went to the locker room tied at two.

Nearly eight minutes into the second period the Devils regained the lead on a goal by Broten. It was the fourth game-winning goal of the playoffs and the first Stanley Cup-winning goal for the former Hobey Baker Award winner.

With a 3-2 lead heading into the third period, the Devils could smell it. They dominated the Wings in the final stanza, outshooting them by 10-1 and sprinting to a 5-2 victory. With about three minutes to play the sellout crowd at Byrne Arena began to roar their appreciation for a team that had rebounded from the

heartbreak of the previous season to come back with a vengeance and execute an unexpected sweep of Detroit in the finals.

Claude Lemieux, who scored only six times during regular season, but did it all in the playoffs, won the Conn Smythe Trophy. Lemieux erupted for 13 goals during the postseason while shadowing the superstars of opposing teams.

All-star Defenseman Scott Stevens led the stingy Devils blue line corps in suffocating the offensive attacks of playoff opponents. And whatever scoring chances opposing teams were able to muster were usually turned aside by standout goalie Martin Brodeur, who allowed only seven goals in the final series for a 1.75 goals-against-average.

Jacques Lemaire, who had won eight Cups

as a player, became only the fourth individual to score a Stanley Cup-winning goal and to coach a Stanley Cup-winning team.

"We had a team that jelled and clicked all at the right time," said Chorske. "Everyone seemed to know their role and everyone enjoyed doing it and everyone played for each other. Everything fell into place and that's usually what happens when you can make a run for the Stanley Cup."

After the Cup-clinching game, owner John McMullen threw a party for the team at the Glenpointe Marriott Hotel in Teaneck, New Jersey, where the Devils players lived during the championship series. Later that evening the party and the Stanley Cup shifted to the Verona Inn where the players celebrated with friends and family into the wee hours.

Amidst rumors that the franchise was leaving for Nashville, the Devils held their official victory celebration three days later in the vast parking lot of the Byrne Arena. More than 25,000 fans — some with faces painted red and black — gathered to show their support. The Nashville rumors were put to rest when, later that summer, McMullen signed a 12-year lease ensuring that the club would remain in New Jersey until at least the year 2007.

The 12 Americans on the 1994-95 Devils squad were the most ever on a Stanley Cup winner. The 1990-91 and 1991-92 Pittsburgh Penguins, as well as the 1937-38 Chicago Blackhawks, each had nine.

1. Stan and Shirley Fischler, *Pain and Progress* (East Rutherford, NJ: The New Jersey Devils, 1992), p. 53.
2. *Sports Illustrated*, June 12, 1995 issue, article titled "Guile and Grateness," by Michael Farber, p. 42.
3. Ibid., p. 40

Steve Babineau

Above: Wilbraham, Mass.' Billy Guerin savors a locker room moment with Lord Stanley's hardware. *Below:* Never before have so many Americans (12) posed for a Stanley Cup team photo.

Steve Babineau

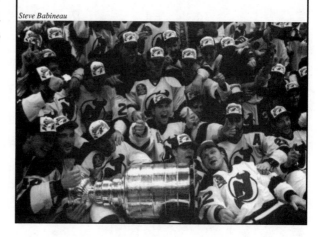

Chapter 15

The Women's Game

The New Olympic Sport is Growing Fast in the U.S.

Women's ice hockey has recently become one of the fastest growing sports in the world. In 1990-91, 5,573 women were registered with USA Hockey. By 1996-97 the number had grown to more than 23,000. And when the sport makes its debut at the 1998 Olympic Winter Games in Nagano, Japan, there's no telling how high participation will skyrocket.

Women's ice hockey dates back to 1890 when the first organized and recorded all-female game was played in Ottawa, Ontario. Canadian women continued to play the

Donald T. Young

Above: Hockey-hungry teenage girls, sporting boy's equipment and figure skates, invade East Boston's Perazzo Rink in 1970: a true indication of the feverish craze that gripped Boston during the Bobby Orr era. *Below:* In the early days of the Massport Jets, Marmo's squads, lacking competition from women's teams, played against men's teams.

Tony Marmo collection

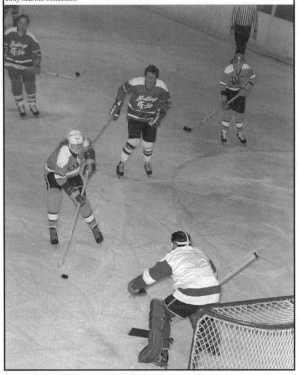

sport into the early part of the 20th century. By 1910, or shortly thereafter, local and provincial women's championships were held in Canada.

Although the sport's American origins are unknown, it is documented that an international women's tournament was held in Cleveland, Ohio, in 1916, featuring both Canadian and American teams.

Women's college hockey dates back to the 1920s when institutions in both the United States and Canada began to organize teams. The growth enjoyed in the United States during the 1920s, however, was stunted by the Great Depression and World War II.

In 1967 the first annual Canadian Dominion Ladies' Hockey Tournament was held in Brampton, Ontario. Today, the Dominion is one of the world's largest women's tournaments with more than 150 teams from North America competing. The sport didn't resurface in the U.S. until 1967-68 when Brown University formed a team and took on Queen's University in the first recorded intercollegiate game.

In November, 1970, Tony Marmo, an ambitious man from East Boston, helped revive the sport in the United States when he founded a team called the Massport Jets. Marmo, a multi-sport athlete, had always felt sorry for his sisters' lack of access to competitive sports. "I always thought my sisters were denied," says Marmo, "I was always out playing sports but they had to stay around and do housework and help with the cleaning."

This was at the height of the Bobby Orr era in the Boston area. Marmo knew that a lot of girls avidly followed the Big, Bad Bruins. He believed it was the perfect time to start a women's program.

"I was the commissioner of the boy's hockey league then," recalls Marmo, "and that was the big, popular thing. I could see that Bobby Orr had made Boston — which had always been a good hockey town — a fabulous hockey town. One day I said to my wife, Didi, 'Those poor girls have to sit and watch. Why can't I start girl's hockey? Now is the time to do it! It's ripe!'"

Marmo placed an ad in a local newspaper announcing an organizational meeting and tryouts for all interested young ladies at the Perazzo Rink in East Boston. The response was far greater than he expected. More than 85 girls of all ages showed up at the first meeting. After several weeks of practice about half of the girls dropped out, leaving Marmo with a devoted core of approximately 40 players with whom to proceed.

The original team was coached by Marmo who was assisted by future Massachusetts state senator Bob Travaglini. The Massport Authority supplied the team with uniforms and they soon became known as the Massport Jets. Since there were no other girls' teams in the area at the time, the Jets played their first games against boys' teams. But it wasn't long before other towns in the area followed suit and organized girls' teams.

After the formation of the Jets the American Girls' Hockey League was formed, with ten charter cities and towns. After ten more cities and towns joined, there were approximately 800 girls from 20 greater Boston communities participating in ice hockey.

By the late 1970s the Jets and the AGHL disbanded, but not without leaving a trail. In 1977 former Jet Christine Yanetti and Donna Sorrentino, who had played for the Watertown team of the AGHL, started women's club hockey at Northeastern University. Three years later the Huskies made the jump from club to varsity. Sorrentino, who also started girl's hockey at Watertown High, also helped initiate the first Women's Beanpot Tournament in 1979.

This was representative of what happened in North America during the 1970s, which saw Canadian provincial and college organizations begin operation as well as the formation of U.S. college varsity and club teams in the East and Midwest.

During the 1970s the sport also grew in Europe and Asia. Norway, Sweden, Finland, Germany, Switzerland, Japan, China and Korea all organized teams.

Girls' youth hockey got a boost in 1980 when USA Hockey hosted the first pee wee and midget National Championships in Taylor, Michigan. The host city captured the inaugural pee wee crown while Wayzata, Minnesota took top honors in the midget division.

A year later USA Hockey included senior women in its National Championships, with Assabet Valley, Massachusetts, winning the Senior A National Championship and Cape Cod, Massachusetts, capturing the Senior B crown.

One of the most significant events in ECAC history occurred in 1983 when the Eastern Association of Intercollegiate Athletics For Women joined the ECAC structure. A year later the ECAC began sponsoring women's hockey. Today the best women's hockey in the United States is played at the collegiate level, where there are more than 65 schools across the East and the Midwest that have either women's varsity or club ice hockey programs.

Sparked by the sport's rapid growth and the help of Title Nine, each year more and more schools are adding the sport to their athletic programs. With a constant influx of teams, changes in the conference alignment are likely. In fact, rumor has it that by the 1998-99 season a new league called the Minnesota Intercollegiate Athletic Conference (MIAC) will form, thereby making the Midwestern Collegiate Hockey Conference (MCWHA) obsolete.

A major breakthrough for women's ice hockey occurred in 1993 when it was recognized by the NCAA as an emerging sport. This

USA HOCKEY NATIONAL CHAMPIONSHIP REVIEW, GIRLS' & WOMEN'S HOCKEY

	Girls' Pee Wee	Girls' Midget
1980	Taylor, Mich.	Wayzata, Minn.
1981	Clarence, NY	Minneapolis, Minn.
1982	Clarence, NY	Massena, NY
1983	Livonia, Mich.	Stoneham, Mass.
1984	Livonia, Mich.	Buffalo, NY
1985	Stoneham, Mass.	Assabet Valley, Mass.
1986	Hartford, Conn.	Assabet Valley, Mass.
1987	Assabet Valley, Mass.	Stoneham, Mass.
1988	Assabet Valley, Mass.	Stoneham, Mass.
1989	Assabet Valley, Mass.	Assabet Valley, Mass.
1990	Chelmsford, Mass.	Team Connecticut
1991	Assabet Valley, Mass.	Team Connecticut
1992	New Hampshire Selects	Assabet Valley, Mass.
1993	Chelmsford, Mass.	Michigan
1994	Chelmsford, Mass.	Assabet Valley, Mass.
1995	Connecticut Polar Bears	Wisconsin Challengers
1996	Connecticut Polar Bears	Alaska Firebirds
1997	Connecticut Polar Bears	Connecticut Polar Bears

	Women's Senior A	Women's Senior B
1981	Assabet Valley, Mass	Cape Cod, Mass.
1982	Minneapolis, Minn.	Cape Cod, Mass.
1983	Stoneham, Mass.	Chelmsford, Mass.
1984	No competition	Cape Cod, Mass.
1985	No Competition	Waltham, Mass.
1986	Assabet Valley, Mass.	Cape Cod, Mass.
1987	Stoneham, Mass	Wayne, Mich.
1988	Stoneham, Mass.	Wayne, Mich.
1989	Stoneham, Mass.	Wayne, Mich.
1990	Stoneham, Mass.	Cheektowaga, NY
1991	Assabet Valley, Mass.	Needham, Mass.
1992	Assabet Valley, Mass.	Hobomock, Mass.
1993	Assabet Valley, Mass.	Needham, Mass.
1994	Hudson, Mass., Nighthawks	Lincoln Park, Mich., Chiefs
1995	Needham, Mass.	Minnesota Northern Lights
1996	Minnesota Northern Lights	Michigan O'Leary Hawks
1997	Team Southwest Capitals	Springfield, MA, She-Devils

CURRENT WOMEN'S COLLEGE HOCKEY ALIGNMENT

ECAC Women's Hockey League (all varsity; all Division I except Colby):
Boston College, Brown, Colby (Division II), Cornell, Dartmouth, Harvard, New Hampshire, Northeastern, Princeton, Providence College, St. Lawrence, Yale.

ECAC Women's Hockey Alliance (all varsity except Vermont):
East: Amherst College, Bowdoin, Connecticut College, Maine, Wesleyan University, Williams.
West: Colgate, Hamilton, Middlebury, Rensselaer, Rochester Institute of Technology, Vermont.

Midwestern Collegiate Women's Hockey Alliance (all club except Minnesota, Augsburg, Gustavus Adolphus and College of St. Benedict):
Augsburg, Carlton, Gustavus Adolphus, * Wisconsin (Red), Wisconsin-Eau Claire, Wisconsin-River Falls, Mankato State, Minnesota, Minnesota-Duluth, College of St. Catherine, College of St. Benedict, St. Cloud State, St. Mary's, St. Olaf, St. Thomas, Iowa State.

Central Collegiate Women's Hockey Alliance (all club):
Bowling Green, Illinois-Champaign, Lake Forest, Michigan, Michigan State, Ohio State, Western Michigan, * Wisconsin (White).

Other Club Teams:
Bates, Boston University, Clarkson, Colorado College, Connecticut, Holy Cross, Massachusetts-Amherst, Michigan Tech, Massachusetts Institute of Technology, Mount Holyoke, North Country Community College, Pennsylvania, Skidmore, Colorado-Boulder, Smith College, Southern Maine, Union, Wheaton.

Independent:
Niagara, Sacred Heart, Skidmore, St. Michael's.

* *Wisconsin has two squads. Red competes in MCWHA and White belongs to CCWHA.*

acknowledgement will enable the sport to graduate from a regional to a national sport at the collegiate level. "It's an important step in women's college hockey," says Maria Dennis, a former Yale star and member of USA Hockey's Board of Directors, "because it's beyond the ECAC now. We're now a national-level sport, which is going to open new doors by providing new opportunities and more scholarships at the scholarship schools."

According to NCAA rules, for a women's sport to hold a national championship tournament it needs at least 40 schools to sustain varsity programs for at least a two-year period. This could happen by the 2000-01 season. "I believe that over the next six years there will be a huge number of schools adding the sport," says Cornell coach Julie Andeberhan. "There have been rumblings from lots of different places around the country."

The main event in women's college hockey is the ECAC Women's Championship Tournament which began in 1984. 1997's finale between Northeastern and New Hampshire at Boston's Matthew's Arena drew 636 spectators who witnessed the Huskies rally to defeat the Wildcats in a 3-2 thriller. Seeded seventh coming into the tournament, Northeastern pulled off a Cinderella run to reach the finals, including a stunning upset of league-leading Brown in the semifinals. The Huskies, however, were playing with an unfair advantage: They were sporting a new line of equipment designed specifically for women by former Northeastern and Team USA goaltender Kelly Dyer, currently product manager of female hockey for Louisville Hockey.

With the exception of special chest pad and pelvic protector gear designed back in the 1970s, female stickhandlers had been forced to compete with equipment made specifically for male players. But thanks to Dyer and Louisville Hockey, a division of Hillerich & Bradsby, women players no longer have to buy their equipment in the less-protective men's junior sizes.

"My motive was to give female hockey players something that was more comfortable and less restricting with better protection," explains Dyer. "Something more geared towards higher performance. I kept a little notebook and documented what people of various shapes and sizes and different playing styles liked and disliked in equipment."

"Don't tell me what I can't do," is the slogan Louisville Hockey is using to encourage women of all ages to compete at what has traditionally been considered a man's sport. Louisville's new female line features shoulder pads, elbow pads, wrist bands, pants, gloves and sticks for forwards and defensemen, as well as pads, gloves, sticks and blockers for goalies. Louisville is also in the process of developing an entire line of inline or off-ice hockey equipment for women.

These new products, along with a women's hockey skate recently released by CCM, will accommodate the needs of women players and help to further accelerate the sport's already frenetic growth.

Over a seven-year stretch from 1990-91 to 1996-97, the number of females registered with USA Hockey grew from 5,573 to more than 23,000. Registrations were broken up into five age categories ranging from "nine and under" to "senior (20 and over)." The category showing the most growth in 1996-97 was the "nine and under" division, which comprised 30 percent of the total number of participants, followed by the "12 and under" division which accounted for 22 percent; more than half of the females playing ice hockey in the U.S. have not yet reached their teens.

They're not only breeding them young, but in warm climate areas as well. "We've gotten calls from places like Texas and Mexico City," says Andeberhan. "You'd be surprised how

USA HOCKEY GIRLS' AND WOMEN'S REGISTRATION FIGURES

Season	Players	Teams
1990-91	5,573	149
1991-92	6,805	232
1992-93	8,991	269
1993-94	12,577	352
1994-95	17,537	498
1995-96	20,555	710
1996-97	23,000	910

Percentage By Age Category For 1996-97

20 & Over (Senior)	17%
19 & Under	11%
15 & Under	20%
12 & Under	22%
9 & Under	30%

many people are playing and they're playing all over the map. I've heard rumblings of new initiatives to get organizations for women's hockey started in southern Florida."

In addition to the female ice boom, many woman are playing in-line hockey. "You see a lot of ice hockey players going to roller," says Dennis. "Everybody roller blades, so even the women, when they see roller hockey they think: 'Oh, I roller blade so why can't I put a stick in my hand?'" As is the case with men's ice hockey, roller hockey will also serve to speed the growth of women's ice hockey.

At the international level, further breakthroughs were made during the late-1980s. In 1987 the first World Invitational Tournament was held in North York and Mississauga, Ontario. Around that time groups began to lobby the International Ice Hockey Federation for the creation of a Women's World Championship. In 1989 IIHF president Dr. Gunther Sabeski attended the European Women's Championship, and plans were drawn for fu-

ture IIHF Women's World Championships.

These plans came to fruition in 1990 when the first IIHF Women's World Championship was held in Ottawa, Ontario. The host team won the gold, Team USA took the silver and Finland the bronze. Andeberhan, a former Harvard star forward and member of the 1990 national team, recalls the thrill of finally getting an opportunity to compete on such a grand stage:

"It was like my dream come true," said Andeberhan, who also heads the American Women's Hockey Coaches Association. "It was something that I always hoped for and now it was happening. A lot of my time playing sports had been spent just trying to pursue excellence and not really having a concrete idea of what I could do. Here was finally a chance to play on the U.S. team with such great players and for the first time understand what it is to play on an international level."

Two years later the second IIHF Women's World Championship was held in Tampere, Finland. Canada, the U.S. and Finland once again finished 1-2-3.

An event that attracted a lot of attention occurred in September 1992 when former Quebec Major Junior League (Draveurs Trois Rivieres) goaltender Manon Rheaume played in an exhibition game for the Tampa Bay Lightning against the St. Louis Blues. A crowd of 27,000 packed the Tampa Thunderdome to witness the Quebec City native backstop the Lightning to a 2-2 tie before she was pulled after the first period.

Although Rheaume's NHL debut was considered by many as a mere publicity stunt by Lightning brass, it increased awareness of the fact that women play ice hockey. Hordes of media showed up to cover the momentous occasion. "I knew it was a big game because a lot of people were there and I felt a lot of pressure," says Rheaume, "but when I stepped out on the ice I just forgot about everything and concentrated on my game. After the game I realized how big a thing I did because of all the media that was there."

After failing to make the Lightning's regular season squad, Rheaume played the rest of the season with the Lightning's IHL Atlanta affiliate. The following year Rheaume was invited back to the Lightning's training camp and appeared in another exhibition game, this time against the Boston Bruins. Since then Rheaume has played for the Knoxville Cherokees and Charlotte Checkers of the ECHL, the Las Vegas Thunder of the IHL and Reno Renegades of the WCHL.

Until recently many were reluctant to accept the fact that women can play hockey.

"It's a cultural thing," says Dennis. "People don't think of putting their daughters on the ice because they don't see a lot of women on the ice. Women's hockey has not been publicized in the U.S. It's not on TV, it's not in the papers a lot and it's never on the radio. People don't see it, so, therefore, when their sons start playing and they have a little daughter, too, they just don't think of putting her on the ice. I don't think they're necessarily doing it consciously, although some people do. I think it's more of a subconscious thing. They just don't realize that it's an opportunity for their daughters.

"When I was growing up playing mostly with the boys in youth hockey programs people would come up to me and say: 'You skate so wonderfully,' and I would say, 'thank you' and they'd say, 'you skate like a guy.' To which I would reply: 'I don't skate like a guy I skate like a hockey player. There are many guys I would not like to skate like.' That was the comment and that's where the culture comes in. I would get angry when I heard it. Now I understand because people can't help their background and what they grew up with. People still say it to me but I don't think they say it as often because women's hockey

is now more accepted. I think people are more conscious of just playing the sport — playing hockey. Not whether you're male or female — just whether you're a hockey player."

The lack of girls' youth hockey programs has made it harder on young women with hockey aspirations. Most girls have had to play on boys' teams. USA Hockey reports that although the number of girls'/women's teams has grown over the past seven years, the majority of females continue to play on mixed-gender teams. Knowing that they are a minority that is not always readily accepted by their male counterparts, some girls have gone as far as to disguise themselves to play on boys' teams in order to either avoid em-

Sports Action/Jon Hayt

Canadian-born Manon Rheaume made sports history by appearing in two exhibition games for the Tampa Bay Lightning.

barrassment or simply to make the team.

"I think that a lot of times girls growing up playing in such a male-dominated sport as hockey feel they have to prove themselves more," says Brown senior forward/defenseman Jodi McKenna, "because they're always being looked at and judged being a girl in a boy's sport. I know I felt that way growing up. I thought that the spotlight was always turned towards me because of comments like: 'What is she doing here? Girls don't belong in this sport.' And I thought I always had to prove myself more so I could earn a place and be accepted."

A breakthrough of major proportions occurred for women's ice hockey in 1992, when the International Olympic Committee voted to include it as a full medal sport. The IOC designated the 2002 Winter Games in Salt Lake City as a date but also gave the organizers of both the 1994 and 1998 Winter Games an option to include it in their competitions. The Japanese committee voted its acceptance for their 1998 Winter Games at Nagano.

In late July of 1993 the sport debuted at the U.S. Olympic Festival in San Antonio, Texas. The United States defeated Canada in a two-game series for the gold medal. The victory marked the only time in the history of the women's game that the U.S. finished ahead of Canada in organized competition.

Near winter's end of 1994, Lake Placid, New York, was the site of the third IIHF Women's World Championship. Team Canada rebounded from its second place finish at the Olympic Festival the previous year to win its third consecutive IIHF gold medal with the U.S. again taking the silver medal and Finland the bronze.

In March 1994 Minnesota became the first state in the U.S. to sanction girl's ice hockey as a high school varsity sport. The number of public high schools to ice teams in the Gopher State has swelled from 24 in 1994-95 to ap-

proximately 85 in 1997-98.

"Minnesota is the model for the other states," says Andeberhan. "There are more public high schools adding women's hockey in Massachusetts and a few in New York, but Minnesota is really the model. They have a huge number of players with organized opportunities to play. I think that as other states follow suit and offer those opportunities to high school girls you'll see a great number of girls who have either been playing on boys teams or on club teams or on ponds. In Minnesota, once the opportunity was there it was amazing how many women came out to play. It's important that it has advanced beyond just eastern prep schools."

In 1994 USA Hockey created the women's equivalent to college hockey's Hobey Baker Award — the USA Hockey Women's Hockey Player of the Year Award. Goaltender Erin Whitten from Glens Falls, NY, now the starting goaltender for Team USA, was the first recipient of this prestigious honor.

Another major international women's ice hockey tournament was held in San Jose, California in April 1995 called the IIHF Pacific Women's Hockey Championship. The event, which featured only teams from the Pacific Rim, pitted the United States, Canada, China and Japan against each other. Canada came away with the tourney's first-ever gold medal by edging Team USA in an overtime shootout. The following year Vancouver, British Columbia served as host for the event which again saw Canada prevail over the U.S. to earn its second straight gold medal.

The fourth IIHF Women's World Championship was held in Kitchener, Ontario, in April 1997 as a qualifier for the 1998 Olympic Winter Games. Under the direction of former Northeastern men's coach Ben Smith, who will also coach Team USA at the Olympics, the United States nearly pulled off an upset of top-seeded Canada. A crowd of 6,247 gathered at

Kitchener Memorial Auditorium to see Canada win its fourth straight Women's World Championship by outlasting the U.S., 4-3 in overtime. Nancy Drolet's third goal of the contest at 12:59 of the extra session won it for the Maple Leafs, extending Canada's record to a perfect 20-0 in Women's World Hockey Championship history.

It was a heartbreaking defeat for Team USA who dominated the play but once again fell short of a gold medal. Despite the loss, the U.S. is optimistic about the upcoming Games at Nagano.

"It was very upsetting," says Dennis, "but we could take a very positive outlook at this whole experience and say: 'Well, this is the closest in competitive level that the two teams have ever been.' So definitely the US has closed the gap that has always existed between it and Canada. We've seen it closing over the past couple of world tournaments and this year was the closest it has ever been."

The game was televised nationally in Canada on TSN, but not in the U.S. Evidence of the fact that although Team USA's program is better funded than its counterparts north of the border, Canada benefits from more media exposure.

Finland, which has finished third behind Canada and the U.S in every international competition to date, is another team that continues to close the gap and China isn't far behind. "Any of the three teams could have won the gold medal," says Dennis. "The teams — in preparing for the Olympics over the past three or four years — have upped their levels of ability. There have been large increases in their competitive levels. I'm sure everybody is just waiting to see what is going to happen

in Nagano because it could go to anybody. Especially since China, the fourth-place team, is really working hard on its training program."

Of the eight teams that competed at Kitchener, Canada, USA, Finland, China and Sweden each earned berths to compete in the Olympic tournament with host Japan, while Russia, Norway and Switzerland failed to qualify for the Games.

The Olympic training process for Team USA began with tryout camps held in Walpole, Massachusetts throughout the winter of 1996-

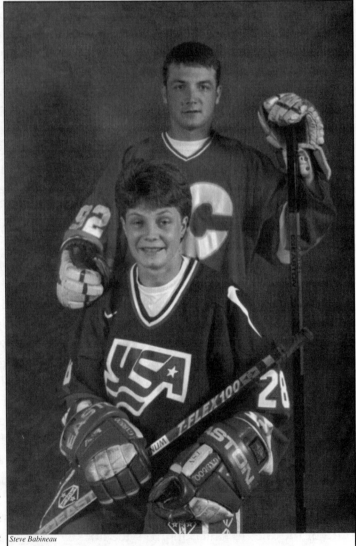

Steve Babineau

Like Tony and Cammi Granato, Chris and Stephanie O'Sullivan of Dorchester, MA are one of hockey's premier brother-sister tandems.

RESULTS OF FOURTH IIHF WOMEN'S WORLD CHAMPIONSHIP
Round Robin

USA 7, Norway 0
China 6, Russia 2
Sweden 2, Norway 2
China 11, Switzerland 3
Finland 10, Norway 0
Switzerland 3, Russia 3

Finland 5, Sweden 0
Canada 6, Switzerland 0
Finland 3, USA 3
Canada 9, Russia 1
USA 10, Sweden 0
Canada 7, China 1

Qualifying Round

Sweden 7, Switzerland 1
Russia 2, Norway 1

Medal Round

Canada 2, Finland 1
USA 6, China 0

Bronze Medal Game
Finland 3, China 0

Gold Medal Game
Canada 4, USA 3 (OT)

97. The camps were ran in between three focal points: 1) The first Three Nation's Tournament held in Ottawa in October between Canada, USA and Finland; 2) The first Friendship Cup held at Harbin, China (Northern Manchuria), in January '97 between China, Finland and the USA; 3) The World Championships at Kitchener.

Throughout the winter college players — mostly from the ECAC — were invited to Walpole to audition for the national team. "All through the year we've been checking on players and watching all the college teams play in the ECAC," says Smith, "which is, right now, probably the heart of the women's program in regards to the development of national or Olympic calibre players."

The Friendship Cup served a dual role for the U.S. squad. "It was a chance for outside competition," explained Smith, "and also to get into that type of time zone and travel mode, if you will, for down the road in Nagano next February. It gave us a feel for the Pacific Rim, if you will."

USA Hockey conducted national camps for its top 15 and 16-year-olds and top 17 & 18-year-olds at Lake Placid during the last week of June and first week of July. At the conclusion of those camps, 54 players were invited to the Women's Hockey Festival at Lake Placid that began August 19. Those 54 were divided into three teams of 18 each (16 skaters & two goalies). The teams played each other four times for a total of eight games for each team. From that group 24 players were named to tour and train throughout the fall. A final squad of 20 will undergo its final month of training and exhibition games by touring the West in January, culminating with its final exhibition game in Anchorage, Alaska, versus Team Canada on January 27.

Leading the charge for Team USA in their quest to win the first-ever women's ice hockey Olympic gold medal will be starting

Steve Babineau

Team USA goalie Erin Whitten.

Coach Smith is confident that the long training process will help his team's chances in Nagano. "Some of the players who played with us on the World Team will have been with us for an extensive period of time," says Smith, "rather than just picking them up at the last minute. I think we are going to be a little bit stronger and a little more cohesive."

The non-checking, finesse-style game played in international women's competitions should help to showcase the sport's appeal via the Olympic tournament and at the same time encourage parents to allow their daughters to compete at ice hockey. Officials from some countries where checking is the norm, however, would like to see checking added to the sport at international competitions. "There are two camps," says Andeberhan, who also heads the American Women's Hockey Coaches Association. "One says we need checking, the other says we have a better game without checking." Coach Smith agrees with the latter:

goaltender Erin Whitten and point-producing forward Cammi Granato.

Whitten, a former University of New Hampshire star and native of Glens Falls, New York, has thrice backstopped the U.S. National Team to silver medals in IIHF World Championship competition. Granato, whose brother Tony recently recovered from brain surgery to make a courageous comeback with the San Jose Sharks, was named ECAC Player of the Year three times at Providence College and was the recipient of the 1996 USA Hockey Player of the Year Award.

"I think women's hockey has a chance to be a wonderful sport at the international level," says Smith, "and I would just hate like hell to see the skill legislated out of it. A lot of the countries don't like getting whupped by other teams, but I don't think that the way to close the gap is to penalize a team for having too much skill. In some places when you mention the word hockey a lot of times it doesn't have the best connotation with people. I don't want that to be an influence on the parents of little girls. I don't want mom and dad to think 'well, we don't want her playing that game because it's a roughhouse game.' I want more people dying to play this game because it's a skilled game. Learning to skate takes skill. Learning to handle a stick takes skill. Learning to handle the puck with a stick on skates takes even more skill. And then doing all of that with five other people takes a very, very high level of skill and we want to make sure that the people who are playing the game continue to view it that way. We've made great strides with equipment. The injury factors are almost negligible and we don't need people being frightened off for the wrong reason."

With teams competing at the youth hockey, high school, college and international levels, the only level left unchartered is professional. The emergence of women's basketball, which now has two pro leagues, may help pave the way for other women's sports such as hockey. But first women's hockey needs to get the exposure that women's basketball has enjoyed.

A step in the right direction is a new magazine called *Women's Hockey*, published by Quint Randle, publisher of *Hockey Player* magazine. It features news coverage at the college, high school and recreational levels, including interviews, tournament reports, recreational league news and playing and coaching tips.

The television coverage the sport will receive from the Winter Games at Nagano will be a giant step. Especially because for the first time the Games will feature NHL stars in the men's competition, a novelty that is sure to attract a great deal of attention.

By the year 2000 there will be upwards of 50,000 women playing some form of organized ice hockey in the United States.

PAST ECAC CHAMPIONS

1984	Providence College
1985	Providence College
1986	New Hampshire
1987	New Hampshire
1988	Northeastern
1989	Northeastern
1990	New Hampshire
1991	New Hampshire
1992	Providence
1993	Providence
1994	Providence
1995	Providence
1996	New Hampshire
1997	Northeastern

TEAM USA IN IIHF COMPETITION

1990 Women's World Championship
Ottawa, Ontario
4-1-0 Overall/Silver Medal

March 19	USA 16, Switzerland 3
March 21	USA 17, Norway 0
March 22	USA 5, Finland 4
March 24	USA 10, Sweden 3 (semifinal)
March 25	Canada 5, USA 2 (Gold Medal Game)

Team USA Leading Scorer: Cindy Curley, 5 GP, 11-12-23

1992 Women's World Championship
Tampere, Finland
4-1-0 Overall/Silver Medal

April 20	USA 17, Switzerland 0
April 21	USA 9, Norway 0
April 23	USA 5, Finland 3
April 25	USA 6, Sweden 4 (semifinal)
April 26	Canada 8, USA 0 (Gold Medal Game)

Team USA Leading Scorer: Cammi Granato, 5 GP, 8-2-10

1994 Women's World Championship
Lake Placid, NY
4-1-0 Overall/Silver Medal

April 11	USA 6, Switzerland 0
April 12	USA 16, Germany 0
April 14	USA 2, Finland 1
April 15	USA 14, China 3 (semifinal)
April 17	Canada 6, USA 3 (Gold Medal Game)

Team USA Leading Scorers: Karyn Bye, 5 GP, 6-6-12; Cammi Granato, 5 GP, 5-7-12

1995 Pacific Women's Hockey Championship
San Jose, Calif.
4-1-0 Overall/Silver Medal

April 3	USA 3, China 2
April 4	USA 14, Japan 0
April 6	USA 5, Canada 2
April 7	USA 12, Japan 0
April 8	Canada 2, USA 1 OT (Gold Medal Game)

Team USA Leading Scorers: Karyn Bye, 5 GP, 9-2-11; Cammi Granato, 5 GP, 4-7-11; Stephanie Boyd, 5 GP, 1-10-11

1996 Pacific Women's Hockey Championship
Vancouver, BC
3-2-0 Overall/Silver Medal

April 1	USA 4, China 2
April 2	USA 16, Japan 0
April 3	Canada 3, USA 2
April 5	USA 5, China 0
April 6	Canada 4, USA 1 (Gold Medal Game)

Team USA Leading Scorer: Cammi Granato, 5 GP, 6-3-9

1997 Women's World Championship
(scores listed on page 281)

USA HOCKEY WOMEN'S HOCKEY PLAYER OF THE YEAR AWARD

1994	Erin Whitten	Glens Falls, NY	Goaltender
1995	Karyn Bye	River Falls, WI	Forward
1996	Cammi Granato	Downers Grove, IL	Forward
1997	Laurie Baker	Concord, MA	Forward

ALL-TIME U.S. WOMEN'S NATIONAL TEAM ROSTER

	National Team(s)	Hometown
Goaltenders:		
Mary Jones	1990	Madison, WI
Kelly Dyer	1990, 92, 94, 95	Boston, MA
Jennifer Hanley	1992	Edina, MN
Erin Whitten	1992, 94, 95, 96, 97	Glens Falls, NY
Sara DeCosta	1996	Warwick, RI
Sarah Tueting	1997	Winnetka, IL
Defensemen:		
Sharon Stidsen	1990	Waltham, MA
Yvonne Percy	1990	South Hadley, MA
Judy Parish	1990	Hanover, NH
Kelley Owen	1990	Golden Valley, MN
Lauren Apollo	1990, 92	Scituate, MA
Shawna Davidson	1990, 92, 94, 95	Duluth, MN
Kelly O'Leary	1990, 92, 94, 95, 96	Auburn, MA
Jeanine Sobek	1990, 92, 94, 95, 96	Coon Rapids, MN
Ellen Weinberg	1992	Dallas, TX
Michele DiFronzo	1994	Chelmsford, MA
Stephanie Boyd	1994, 95	Kilworthy, Ont.
Vicki Movsessian	1994, 95, 96, 97	Lexington, MA
Christina Bailey	1994, 95, 96, 97	Marietta, NY
Tara Mounsey	1996, 97	Concord, NH
Angela Ruggiero	1996, 97	Harrison Twp., MI
Kelly O'Leary	1997	Auburn, MA
Forwards:		
Julie S.-Andeberhan	1990	Durham, NH
Heidi Chalupnick	1990	Fairbanks, AK
Maria Dennis	1990	S. Windsor, CT
Kimberly Eisenreid	1990	W. Seneca, NY
Tina Cardinale	1990, 92	Hudson, MA
Cindy Curley	1990, 92, 94, 95	Leominster, MA
Beth Beagan	1990, 92, 94, 96	Falmouth, MA
Sue Mertz	1990, 92, 94, 95, 96	Greenwich, CT
Lisa-Brown Miller	1990, 92, 94, 95, 96, 97	Union Lake, MI

Cammi Granato	1990, 92, 94, 95, 96, 97	Downers Grove, IL
Kathy Issel	1992	Ann Arbor, MI
Kim Haman	1992	Fairbanks, AK
Michele Amidon	1992	Harpswell, ME
Wendy Tatarouns	1992, 95	Billerica, MA
Karyn Bye	1992, 94, 95, 96, 97	River Falls, WI
Colleen Coyne	1992, 94, 95, 96, 97	E. Falmouth, MA
Shelly Looney	1992, 94, 95, 96, 97	Trenton, MI
Sandra Whyte	1992, 94, 95, 96, 97	Saugus, MA
Gretchen Ulion	1994, 95, 97	Marlborough, CT
Stephanie O'Sullivan	1994, 95, 96, 97	Dorchester, MA
A.J. Mleczko	1995, 96, 97	Nantucket, MA
Meaghan Sittler	1996	E. Amherst, NY
Alana Blahoski	1996, 97	St. Paul, MN
Laurie Bake	1997	Concord, MA
Tricia Dunn	1997	Derry, NH
Katie King	1997	Salem, NH

Chapter 16

Roller Hockey

*The In-Line Craze Catches On Out West
and Spreads Into the South*

No longer is it necessary for hockey aficionados in warm weather locales to rent ice to play the game. The advent of the in-line skate has given ice hockey a close cousin called roller hockey/aka in-line hockey. This exciting new sport is allowing many more people a chance to enjoy the speed, grace and intensity of the ice game.

Across America's Sun Belt it's not uncommon to see kids — and adults — skating on tennis courts, parking lots, back alleys and cul-de-sacs while whacking a puck around and imitating their favorite NHL Gods. Federov, Jagr, Amonte, Hull — you too, can be them on asphalt.

Like ice hockey, roller hockey is a "boom" sport of the '90s. In fact, a 1995 National Sporting Goods Association survey reported it to be the fastest growing sport in the U.S. and the world, rising 43 percent from the previous year. The overall number of people playing in-line hockey in the U.S. has grown from approximately 1.5 million in 1993 to nearly four million in 1997. The NSGA also reported an increase in the sales of in-line skates from 21 million in 1989 to 460 million in 1995.

Roller hockey is much like ice hockey with the exception of several basic rule differences. Unlike the ice game, roller hockey is played with no offsides, no icing, no checking and one less skater (four-on-four in front of the goalies) per side. In some cases a ball is used instead of a puck.

Fighting is not tolerated under any circumstances, and two-minute minor penalties are handed out for infractions such as holding, tripping, charging, slashing and interference. The game is divided into two halves instead of three periods and tournament and playoff games still tied at the end of one overtime period of five minutes are decided by a "shoot-out."

With only four on a side and players having the opportunity to pass the puck anywhere on the surface, the floor is opened up. It allows players to create scoring chances not possible in ice hockey. As in women's ice hockey, the absence of body checking lends more finesse to the action.

The in-line hockey craze failed to catch on until the late 1980s in California, but its ancestor, roller skating, has a history in the United States dating back at least to the first half of the 20th century.

In 1937 The United States Amateur Confederation of Roller Skating (USAC/RS) was founded in Detroit, Michigan, as part of the

Steve Babineau

No need to find an ice rink, no expense for ice rental. Just pull the van into an empty parking lot, open the hatch and lace 'em up.

Roller Skating Rink Operators Association. The organization moved to Lincoln, Nebraska, in 1968 and began running some of the first roller hockey tournaments in America.

The highest quality roller hockey during the days of the "quad" (four separate wheels) skate was in New York City's Bay Ridge (Brooklyn) section, where the Fort Hamilton Roller Hockey League was producing such future NHL stars as Nick Fotiu, Jim Pavese and the Mullen brothers, Joey and Brian.

Roller skating became very popular during the 1970s when one of the sport's most notable hot spots was the Venice Beach, California boardwalk, where tube tops, tacky colors and disco music were part of daily scene. Another roller skater's haven was San Francisco's Golden Gate Park, where by the late '70s as many as 20,000 skaters would convene each weekend.

A popular roller skate of the late '70s was the Super Sport Skate, which sold for $29.95 a pair. The skate was developed by former NHL forward Ralph Backstrom and future owner of Roller Hockey International's Anaheim Bull Frogs Maury Silver.

Fueled by a desire to play hockey year-round, in 1981 Minneapolis native Scott Olson developed an in-line skate based on a 1966 Chicago Roller Skate Company patent designed to simulate ice skates. Olson's design led to the birth of Rollerblade, Inc., which in 1985 was bought by Robert Naegele, Jr., current owner Mission Roller Hockey Company of Santa Ana, California.

In 1987 the USAC/RS separated from the Roller Skating Rink Operators Association and became recognized as the official national governing body for all competitive roller sports in the United States. The USAC had been involved with roller hockey since the late '60s, running national championship tournaments on an annual basis. For years the events were held in relatively small buildings, but as the sport grew the USAC expanded the events to larger facilities and added regional qualifying rounds to the competitions.

The catalyst that ignited a booming interest in roller hockey in Southern California during the late 1980s was Wayne Gretzky. Gretzky, who joined the Los Angeles Kings via a trade from Edmonton in June 1988, would lead the Kings to an upset playoff triumph over his former club in 1988-89 and to the Stanley Cup Finals in 1992-93. Gretzky's influence was instrumental in spawning the runaway growth of in-line hockey throughout the Golden State and into other warm climate areas.

In 1992 Koho Equipment Company ran an in-line hockey tournament called the Koho California Cup. The event was a big hit and the following season Koho expanded into other cities nationwide. By 1997 competitions were run in ten other states and three in Canada with a total of well over 6,500 amateur players participating. The Koho California Cup is considered to be the grandaddy of all roller hockey tournaments.

"As a manufacturer and distributor it made the most sense to start putting some time, energy and money into the grassroots programs and the best way to do that was to put on these tournaments," explains Robin Racine, marketing coordinator for Koho. "Our philosophy is to provide a fun, safe environment for amateur players to play the game and to have a certain competitiveness to the tournaments."

In 1993 two professional leagues were organized — the World Roller Hockey league (WRHL) and Roller Hockey International (RHI). The WRHL, which was a TV-only league, was founded by David MacLane, creator of the novelty cable TV show of the late '80s called "GLOW" (Gorgeous Ladies Of Wrestling). RHI, which was founded by Dennis Murphy, Alex Bellehumeur and Larry King began its first season with 12 teams located mostly in warm-

Steve Babineau

Outdoor roller hockey rinks are becoming commonplace from Miami to Seattle.

When Gretzky laced them up for the L.A. Kings in 1988, he had no idea what a beautiful monster he would help create.

weather markets across the U.S.

In 1994 RHI and the WRHL merged under the name RHI. The revised league fielded 24 teams and ESPN, which was part owner of the defunct WRHL, began to telecast its games. But then franchises began to drop like flies. The number dipped to 19 teams in 1995 and to 12 by the beginning of the 1997 season. The struggling league, which no longer had a television contract with ESPN, did manage to secure a deal with Fox to air some of its 1997 championship playoff games.

Apart from its basic league commitments, RHI sponsors an organization called RHI Amateur. The organization, which is based in Long Beach, California, provides programs for coaches and referees as well as for kids who wish to compete at organized roller hockey. Although its priority lies in California, RHI Amateur has also expanded to 12 other states, including such in-line hotbeds as Florida and New York.

One of RHI Amateur's goals is to motivate kids to aspire to be professional roller hockey players. Part of their strategy is to teach kids to play by the same rules as the pro leagues.

"We set out to teach kids to play the same rules as the pro leagues are playing across the world and have them be able to move up through the system so they one day can play the game of roller hockey," says LA Blades star Mike Doers, who also serves as director of referee and coaching programs for RHI Amateur. "There are a lot of kids here in California who aren't playing baseball or ice hockey. They want to play professional roller hockey because that's their main sport growing up."

This poses the question: Will in-line hockey continue to serve as a supplement to ice hockey or will kids someday want to emulate their favorite roller hockey superstars?

Probably both, but what's certain is that the top roller hockey tournament on the continent is the North American Roller Hockey Championships. Although the Koho Cup is considered to be the grandaddy, it is acknowledged by many that NARCH produces the top-level champions of the world.

The inaugural NARCH tournament was held in 1994 in St. Louis with 39 teams from all over the U.S. and Canada vying to become the best on the continent. The following year the competition expanded to a regional qualifying format with 10 regionals. Seventy-nine teams advanced to the finals which were once again held in St. Louis. By 1997 the qualifying format had grown to 24 regions with the top two teams in each age division earning a trip to the finals in Vancouver. Teams that failed to qualify for the finals were given the option of competing in another tournament called the Summer Cup, which took place in Las Vegas in late July.

Other events recently added to the NARCH agenda were the Winter Nationals, held at Coast to Coast Rink in Huntington Beach, California, and a worldwide tournament called "The Silver Cup," played at Wayne Gretzky's Roller Hockey Center in Irvine, California. "Our business is the tournament business," says Paul Chapey, a partner of National Roller Hockey, the corporation that owns NARCH. "We're not an association. We don't compete in the association business. Their business is primarily selling insurance and they do tournaments by virtue of the fact that they have to, but our tournament series is open to all comers. You don't have to be an association member to compete. That's how we keep it extremely high caliber."

The NARCH tournaments are unique not only because they include Canada's best teams but also because their sponsorship commitments exceed all leagues and associations.

In December 1994 USA Hockey created a program called USA Hockey InLine. The program was formed to fill a void within America's in-line hockey movement for structure, stability, organization and administration at the grass-roots level.

In December 1996 USA Hockey InLine acquired the National In-Line Hockey Association (NIHA). Like USA Hockey InLine, NIHA, was an independent organization that developed and promoted amateur roller hockey. Formed in January, 1993, NIHA also staged major tournaments each year. In October 1995 100 teams representing every U.S. state and Canadian province competed in the NIHA National Championship in Las Vegas, Nevada.

By acquiring the NIHA, USA Hockey InLine took what it considers to be a major step in the unification of in-line hockey. "What that did was consolidate the sport and the industry, thereby creating a set of standardized playing rules and a situation that made it easy

Ross F. Dettman

Organized indoor roller hockey is usually played with a puck instead of a ball.

for inter-league play," says Chuck Menke, coordinator of media and public relations for USA Hockey InLine. "Whereas before for insurance reasons or for playing-rules reasons a NIHA league would not compete with a USA Hockey In-Line League. The acquisition made the playing field similar and put everybody on the same page."

In its first full season (1995-96) USA Hockey InLine registered 17,915 players, coaches and referees competing in more than 135 leagues. By 1996-97 the numbers grew to 85,533 and 630 leagues, respectively, making it the world's largest in-line hockey organization. This growth was aided by the fact that an additional 40,000 members came via the acquisition of NIHA. But subtract the 40,000 and the rate at which USA Hockey InLine has increased its membership is still very high.

Ross F. Dettman

The annual NARCH tournament is a showcase for some of roller hockey's finest players.

The top three states in terms of popularity are California, Florida and Texas. And what bodes well for the sport's future is the fact that 63 percent of members are of the age category "17 and under."

"We're projecting that our organization is going to be about 200,000 strong by the year 2000," says Mark Rudolph, the program's director. "USA Hockey really believes that this sport is here to stay and it's not only going to be a great addition to ice hockey, but it is going to be great separate entity from ice hockey.

"There are some significant things that have to occur in order to facilitate this growth," adds Rudolph. "We need to set some standards for in-line hockey. Right now there seems to be so many people doing so many things in so many different ways and we need to begin to standardize the ways in which the in-line hockey program is administrated worldwide."

USA Hockey InLine is currently involved in running two traveling tours — USA Hockey InLine/Triple Crown Sports Showdown and NHL Breakout.

The former, which is a partnership between USA Hockey and Triple Crown Sports, is one of the largest outdoor in-line hockey tournaments. In 1997 the multi-city tour spanned 47 U.S. cities from March to October.

"Triple Crown Sports had been operating its own individual in-line hockey tour which was called the Triple Crown Hockey Series," says Menke. "What we've done is come in and provided our resources and helped improve the series as much as possible. Last year was the first year we joined in. Participation varies from medium towns and cities like Duluth, Minnesota, where there might be 20-25 teams, to places like Chicago where you'll have 75 to 125 teams."

NHL Breakout, which is staged by NHL Enterprises, is a traveling weekend festival of both street and in-line hockey competitions. The event includes skills contests, entertainment and instructional clinics. The clinics are put on by former NHL stars such as Brian Mullen, who learned his hockey both in the streets and on wheels. USA Hockey pitches in by providing registered referees to officiate games and registered coaches to conduct skills contests. In 1997, the third year of the series, the tour visited 20 cities — 16 in America and four in Canada. NHL Breakout also has a European series called NHL Breakout Europe, which travels to such major cities as Stockholm, Munich, Zurich and Barcelona.

"We've been able to take the influence, the authenticity, the excitement and enthusiasm of the National Hockey League and extend it all the way down to the asphalt," claims Ken Yaffe, vice president of fan development for NHL Enterprises. "This has been a very important initiative for me and Brian Mullen and Mark Rudolph as we have put sticks into the hands of thousands of kids. It has been a highly-exposed vehicle for the NHL over the course of the last year."

USA Hockey InLine held its first national championships in August, 1996, in Minneapolis-St. Paul. The tournament, which included both youth (17 and under) and adult teams, saw 36 teams compete in regional and final competitions. In 1997 the format was changed to include only youth teams. A total of 80 teams divided into four divisions of 20 each (17 and under, 14 and under, 12 and under and 10 and under) competed in regional competitions to advance to the finals held in Chicago in early August.

In order to accommodate the adult divisions, the program created another tournament called the USA Hockey InLine Cup. The event, which was held in Las Vegas in September, was divided into five divisions. Included were two men's divisions, a women's division, a street hockey division and a college club division.

USA Hockey InLine and the National Hockey League are both involved in assisting the International Ice Hockey Federation with its world championships. The second annual IIHF World Championships were held in Ana-heim, California in late July, 1997. The field included the United States, Canada, Australia, Finland, Russia, Czech Republic, Germany, Italy, Switzerland, Austria and Japan.

The IIHF reports that 30 countries — most of which are not traditional ice hockey nations — compete at roller hockey. In Italy, Spain, Portugal and Argentina, roller hockey is second only to soccer in popularity. The sport is featured every four years at the Pan American Games and a form of roller hockey called "ball and cane hockey" was featured as a demonstration sport at the Barcelona Summer Olympic Games in 1992.

What began in Southern California in the late 1980s as a brush-fire sport is spreading like wildfire throughout the United States and on a world-wide basis as well. Much work, however, is needed to be done to get the various tournaments, leagues and organizations on the same page.

When unity is finally achieved, roller hockey will not only continue to accelerate the growth of ice hockey, but will also occupy its own prominent niche in both the American and international sports landscapes.

Left: Manhattan native Brian Mullen, whose road to the pros began in the streets, has been an integral part of NHL Breakout. *Right:* In-line still life.

Steve Babineau

Steve Babineau

Chapter 17

The Future

*Hockey's Popularity and Its
Potential in America*

In the past ten years Hockey's growth rate has been amazing.

What about ten years from now?

What effect will the NHL's and the women's participation at the Winter Olympics in Nagano in February, 1998 and Salt Lake City in 2002 have on interest and participation? Will hockey continue to grow in the Sun Belt?

Hockey's leaders can maximize on the game's potential by marketing it effectively to enlarge the growing fan base and talent pool.

NHL senior vice president of hockey operations Brian Burke offers a simple, effective strategy:

"The biggest single thing we have to do is get people to see one game. Our experience has been that that's enough. It's the world's greatest professional sporting event and the reason that it more or less has been a regional game has been under exposure rather than any flaw in the game itself."

What can be done to make that "one" game the thrilling and graceful, yet rugged sporting event it should be? What can be done to prevent a lot of the clutching and grabbing that has robbed the game of some of its beauty?

Rules have been implemented but they have not worked. In late spring of 1995 the NHL's Board of Governors convened to discuss the "clutch and grab" problems and how it was slowing down the game. They were looking to devise a way to limit the interference and return the game to its stars. The result of these meetings was a series of obstruction penalties that zeroed in on forwards who impeded the progress of opposing non-puck-carrying forwards in the neutral zone (between the blue lines). Enforcement was erratic. The experiment failed.

If penalties are not a long-term solution, then what else can be done to open up the ice for the finesse-style players? One of the more popular solutions suggested by some is to remove the red line.

"I'd love to see the red line removed in the NHL," says college and pro hockey TV commentator Dave Shea. "Because the way the game is played now you can really stuff a team in the neutral zone with clutching and grabbing that goes on when you clog up the middle. You're taking away some of the real ballet of the game — the speed and the grace and the skill that some of these players possess. The red line neutralizes their abilities and

Steve Babineau

The old and the young. Gretzky and Kariya.

really brings them down with that of the average NHL player, which still in its own right is an excellent hockey player — one of the best in the world. Those chosen few that have the great skills — if they took the red line out the guys who could skate like the wind would really stand out and it would take the game to another level."

But as Burke points out other problems would be created: "Taking out the red line would generate some more outnumbered attacks," Burke claims, "but it would also require our defensemen to leave (give up) the blue line almost immediately."

Concern about removing the red line is that it would result in too much open ice. Games

Steve Babineau

Michigan-born Derian Hatcher, younger brother of Kevin, is a big part of the Dallas Stars' future plans.

Steve Babineau

Edmonton Oilers ace Doug Weight is another in a long line of Michigan boys to excel at hockey's highest level.

would become too high-scoring.

Former NHL and Olympic coach Herb Brooks claims he has an even better idea:

"One of the things they should do is move the goal line out 15 feet to reduce the neutral zone," says Brooks. "This would open the corners. It would eliminate the scrums and the slow-down in play. And it would give the skilled players a better chance to play. This would do an awful lot to help the flow and the speed of the game in the NHL. The other thing that should be considered is using the red line just for icing and taking away the two-line pass. Then you'd open up the ice more and really showcase the players' abilities; especially those who emphasize the speed and

creativity. Moving the goal line out is a real doable thing and should be done immediately."

There is a supposedly "perfect" solution but the NHL owners would never apply it. That is to enlarge the ice surface. Contemporary players are much bigger and skate much faster than they did 25 years ago, yet they are playing on the same size ice surface (200' x 85') as back then. It only seems logical to enlarge the rink's ice surface — about 10 feet in length and four feet in width.

Unfortunately, no owner will invest in remodeling his arena and, in doing so, sacrifice a few valuable rows of expensive seats. One can only ask the National Hockey League to

Steve Babineau

Left: Craig MacTavish, who retired after the 1996-97 season, was the last NHL player to play helmetless. Above: Philly fans are pinning their hopes on Flyers superstar Eric Lindros to bring the Cup back to Broad Street.

consider elimination of the red line as an experiment, perhaps during an exhibition season. If there's a possibility that The Game would improve as a result, why not give it a trial?

Another issue often discussed is head gear (helmets, face shields and cages). Some argue that with so much protection players have become more careless with raising their sticks. The helmet, which is supposed to prevent injuries, may actually cause more of them.

"The facemask was to take away the remote possibility of someone losing an eye and that probably was a good thought," says Boston University coach Jack Parker. "But now the game is so physical; there are so many more severe injuries and people could end up in wheelchairs."

Use of helmets also is considered necessary because of the ongoing possibility of a law-

suit. No league or association wants to be the first to eliminate the helmet or mask and then be sued the moment somebody gets hurt.

One recommended solution would be the two-referee system. With two sets of eyes instead of one to detect infractions, it would be more difficult for players to get away with such swashbuckling antics.

Other cogent issues that should be addressed are the size of the crease, tie games and preserving traditions:

Many goals were disallowed during the 1996-97 Stanley Cup playoffs because a players' skate was in the crease. In some cases a goal was disallowed even if the player whose skate was in the crease was out of the play and in no way obstructing the goaltender. However, too many goal reviews spoil the game's pace and rob it of its most thrilling moments. The solution is to make the crease smaller. Today's crease makes it hard for attacking forwards to position themselves for rebounds without accidently breaking the rule.

As for the overtime issue, there has been an ongoing debate as to whether a better way than one five-minute period could be employed. A longer period — perhaps 10-minutes — or a shootout have both been suggested alternatives.

Longer periods mean longer games and later nights. The shootout is a radical solution which has been used to decide games in Olympic competition. Many argue that shootouts give an unfair advantage to the team with the most snipers.

Another problem, accelerated by construction of ultra-modern arenas, is the loss of the revered "old-time" ambience. NHL franchises with rich traditions, such as Boston, Chicago and Philadelphia, have lost some of their luster at the expense of progress. New arenas with luxury suites and more seats — but less atmosphere — have replaced the venerable buildings these clubs once occupied.

"We need to find ways to bring interactive kiosks and museums into our arenas to provide value-added and to connect people to the history and the heritage of the great old buildings," says Ken Yaffe of NHL Enterprises. "Those same types of interactive kiosks and attractions provide a very important educational tool and element as we look to bring many new hockey fans into the sport."

Traditional franchises can preserve their history and identity by keeping the same uniforms. For marketing purposes teams have changed their uniform designs, and in some cases their logos.

Another oft-discussed issue is fighting. The NHL has averaged less than a fight per game during the past several regular seasons. During the playoffs fisticuffs are virtually non-existent. Fighting in pro hockey is now

Steve Babineau

Above: Former BU star Mike Grier of Holliston, Mass., became the first African-American to play in the NHL when he stepped onto the ice for the Edmonton Oilers in October, 1996. *Below:* Canadian-born Anson Carter starred at Michigan State before turning pro in 1996.

Steve Babineau

the exception and no longer the rule.

Yet another dilemma — accented by expansion — is the problem of maintaining an adequate talent pool.

The NHL and USA Hockey are to be commended for their efforts in making street and in-line hockey accessible to kids in non-traditional areas. Programs such as NHL Breakout, Nike NHL Street and USA Hockey/Triple Crown Sports Showdown have already done wonders in allowing kids of both genders and all ethnic and economic backgrounds a chance to compete.

"It's our goal to hit every strata of society, economically and racially," says Brian Burke. "and get more kids playing and following hockey."

The NHL is aggressively working to bring the sport into inner city areas: Programs such as Ice Hockey in Harlem, PUCK (Positive Upliftment of Chicago's Kids), Disney Goals (Anaheim), SCORE (Boston, Sportsmanship Character Opportunity Respect and Education), Detroit Hockey Association, Fort Dupont Youth Hockey (Washington D.C.) and Mariucci Inner City Hockey (St. Paul) are all part of the NHL's Diversity Task Force Program, sponsored by USA Hockey and the NHL.

The development of youth and amateur ice hockey players is another area in need of improvement. Some experts believe that USA Hockey must improve the direction of its development programs in order to maximize the potential talent pool available in the United States.

"We need USA Hockey," says Brooks. "We need a real good national governing body, but one that is responsible to its members. Right now we have a top-down approach, an elitist approach and that will not make our country as good as it can become. The base of our pyramid is too narrow, therefore limiting the peak. We have a bunch of one-week 'select' camps.

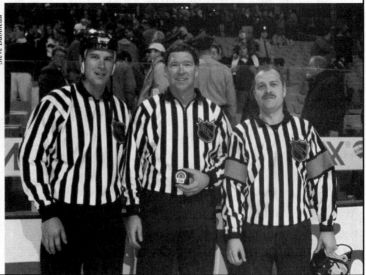

Left: Veteran NHL and IHL defenseman Jim Paek was the first Korean-born player to play pro hockey. *Below:* NHL linesman Kevin Collins (C) after becoming the first American-born on-ice official to work 1500 games.

Steve Babineau

But all they are are 'identification camps' for pros and colleges. You don't get better in one or two weeks, you get better over a longer period of time, year after year. If we start developing kids from ages 11 to 17 in a well thought-out developmental program on the ice and off the ice in various times during the 12-month calendar, we will be better."

The problem with select camps is that too few youngsters are invited to compete. Therefore tens of thousands of kids are falling through the cracks.

Jack Parker concurs: "Recruiting is easy because they're all in the same camps — Lake Placid, Colorado Springs, etc. The sixty best 17-year-olds in the country are right there. That offsets some late bloomers who might not get a chance to play and that's what's wrong with taking them all like that."

The U.S. is just beginning to build a strong hockey talent pool. It is important that we not waste potential talents. An example would be Mark Messier, who at age 17 showed no signs of a future Hart Trophy winner.

Nevertheless, hockey's future in America is bright. NHL and minor league expansion into non-traditional areas, the advent of in-line hockey and the growing interest in hockey among women have each played a part in awakening a sleeping giant.

Hockey may never eclipse the three other major American sports, but it's a good bet that by the spring of 2002 it will have significantly closed the gap.

Appendix

JOHN MARIUCCI AWARD

The former coach at the U of Minnesota was not only an outstanding college coach, but also a driving force behind the growth of hockey in the U.S. In 1987, the American Hockey Coaches created this award to honor a secondary school hockey coach who best exemplifies the spirit, dedication, and enthusiasm of "The Godfather of U.S. Hockey," John Mariucci.

1988 — Larry Ross, International Falls, MN High School

1989 — Ed Burns, Arlington, MA High School

1990 — Willard Ikola, Edina, MN High School

1991 — Henry Hughes, Melrose, MA High School

1992 — George Ankerstrom, Kimball Union Academy

1993 — Bill Belisle, Mt. St. Charles Academy

1994 — Al Clark, Culver Military Academy

1995 — John Chambers, Needham High School

1996 — Stan Moore, Sr., Massena High School

1997 — Harold "Ben" Foote, Lynn English (MA) High School

JOHN MACINNES AWARD

Established by the American Hockey Coaches Association in 1982 to honor former Michigan Tech Coach John MacInnes. This award recognizes the people who have shown great concern for amateur hockey and youth programs. Recipients have had high winning percentages as well as outstanding graduating percentages among their former players. The winners have helped young men to grow not only as hockey players, but more importantly as men.

1983 — Amo Bessone, Michigan State

1984 — Jack Riley, U.S. Military Academy

1985 — Bob Johnson, U of Wisconsin; Calgary Flames

1986 — Murray Armstrong, Denver U

1987 — Ned Harkness, RPI; Cornell; Union

1988 — Vic Heyliger, Michigan; Air Force

1989 — Charlie Holt, UNH

1990 — Murray Murdoch, Yale

1991 — Bill Cleary, Harvard

1992 — Len Ceglarski, Boston College

1993 — Don Roberts, Gustavus Adolphus

1994 — Herb Brooks, U of Minn; '80 Olympic Team

1995 — R.H. "Bob" Peters, Bemidgi State University

1996 — Fern Flaman, Northeastern University

1997 — Bill O'Flaherty, Clarkson University

UNITED STATES HOCKEY HALL OF FAME INDUCTEES

1973
Taffy Abel
Hobey Baker
Frank Brimsek
George Brown
Walter Brown
John Chase
Cully Dahlstrom
John Garrison
Doc Gibson
Moose Goheen
Malcolm Gordon
Eddie Jeremiah
Mike Karakas
Tom Lockhart
Myles Lane
Sam LoPresti
John Mariucci
George Owen
Ding Palmer
Doc Romnes
Cliff Thompson
Thayer Tutt
Ralph Winsor
Coddy Winters
Lyle Wright

1974
Bill Chadwick
Ray Chiasson
Vic Desjardins
Doug Everett
Vic Heylinger
Virgil Johnson
Snooks Kelley
Bill Moe
Fido Purpur

1975
Tony Conroy
Austie Harding
Stewart Iglehart
Joe Linder
Fred Moseley

1976
Bill Cleary
John Mayasich
Bob Ridder

1977
Earl Bartholome
Eddie Olson
Bill Riley

1978
Peter Bessone
Don Clark
Hub Nelson

1979
Bob Dill
Jack Riley

1980
Walter Bush
Nick Kahler

1981
Bob Cleary
Bill Jennings
Tommy Williams

1982
Cal Marvin
Bill Stewart

1983
Oscar Almquist
Jack McCartan

1984
William Christian
William Wirtz

1985
Bob Blake
Dick Rondeau
Hal Trumble

1986
Jack Garrity
Ken Yackel

1987
Jack Kirrane
Hugh "Muzz" Murray, Sr.

1988
Richard J. Desmond
Lawrence Ross

1989
Roger Christian
Robert Paradise

1990
Herb Brooks
Willard Ikola
Connie Pleban

1991
Robbie Ftorek
Robert Johnson
John Matchefts

1992
Amo Bessone
Len Ceglarski
James Fullerton

1993
John H. "Jack" Kelley
David Langevin
Charles M. Schultz

1994
Joe Cavanagh
Wally Grant
Ned Harkness

1995
Henry Boucha
James Claypool
Ken Morrow

1996
Sergio Gambucci
Reed Larson
Craig Patrick

1997
Charles E. Holt, Jr.
William D. Nyrop
Timothy K. Sheehy

About the Photographer

Steve Babineau, who supplied over seventy percent of the photographs for his book, began his professional career in 1973 as team photographer for the New England Whalers. In 1977, Steve became the color photographer for the Boston Bruins, a position he has held ever since. Steve has also done work for hockey and baseball card companies, as well as rock icon Neil Young.